Pr
Co

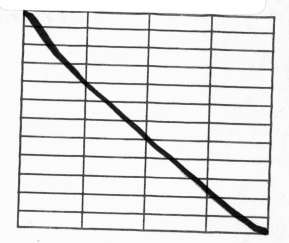

SUNY Series in the Constitution and Economic Rights
Ellen Frankel Paul, Editor

Property Rights and the Constitution

Shaping Society Through Land Use Regulation

Dennis J. Coyle

STATE UNIVERSITY OF NEW YORK PRESS

Published by
State University of New York Press, Albany

For information, address State University of New York
Press, State University Plaza, Albany, N.Y., 12246

Production by E. Moore
Marketing by Bernadette LaManna

Library of Congress Cataloging-in-Publication Data
Coyle, Dennis J. (Dennis John)
    Property rights and the constitution : shaping society through
land use regulation / Dennis J. Coyle
        p. cm. — (SUNY series in the constitution and economic
rights)
    Includes bibliographical references (p.   ) and index.
    ISBN 0-7914-1443-4 (CH : acid-free). — ISBN 0-7914-1444-2 (PB :
acid-free)
    1. Land use—Law and legislation—United States.   2. Right of
property—United States.   3. United States—Constitutional law.
I. Title. II. Series.
KF5698.C674 1993
346.7304'5—dc20   92-16680
[347.30645]   CIP

10 9 8 7 6 5 4 3 2 1

For father and son

Contents

PART IV: APPENDIXES

Tables

UNITED STATES

Acknowledgments

There are two groups of persons in the world: those who read prefaces and those who do not. When I open a book, the preface is one of the first things I read, as it may give insights on the author's perspective, and it is for kindred souls that I offer these acknowledgments.

Everett Ladd did not read this manuscript, discuss the topic with me or even teach any of the courses I attended in graduate school. But when this wayward agriculture student returned to college, he opened my eyes to the possibilities of the intellect through his shining example of inquisitiveness, energy, and rigorous argument. He was forceful and articulate, forgiving of naivety but demanding of effort, and soon I was hooked on political science. He showed me the rewards of a career of teaching and scholarship, and his fine example has stayed with me through the years.

This book began as that most cumbersome of literary forms, the dissertation, and I would like to thank the members of that God Squad of doctoral study, The Committee. The seed for this book was a seminar paper written for Robert Kagan, who later shepherded the dissertation with that tricky balance of warm support and thorough criticism. The gentle spirit of Sandy Muir has touched the lives of many students; he has set a standard for a marriage of intellectual curiosity and personal decency to which I aspire. Martin Shapiro was an ideal outside reader—quick to grasp the essence of an argument, incisive in his criticism and warm in his support. Aaron Wildavsky has the most keen and playful mind I have encountered and boundless intellectual energy, and my debt to him is enormous. I have adopted several of his habits—the messy desk, the illegible scribble, the many simultaneous projects. I hope some of his originality and rigor will rub off as well.

The Institute of Governmental Studies and Survey Research Center were very helpful in making their facilities available.

Graduate study at Berkeley has its special moments, and I fondly remember the Saturday nights spent writing in the basement of the SRC building near Peoples Park, serenaded by police sirens and Hari Krishna chanters. Berkeley was an intellectual feast, albeit a bizarre and bewildering one at times, and I thank those who pushed me to consider new perspectives and encouraged me to develop my own ideas, including Malcolm Feeley, Martin Landau, Todd LaPorte, Philippe Nonet, Michael Rogin, Philip Selznick, Eric Sundquist, Daniel Rubinfeld, Jeremy Waldron and Ray Wolfinger, who is a beacon of common sense in the sometimes ethereal world of academia.

The Institute of Governmental Studies, the Bradley Foundation and the Earhart Foundation helped make ends meet at crucial moments. The Institute for Humane Studies arranged a workshop where some of this material was presented, and Jeremy Shearmur and Walter Grinder provided support and encouragement. For their comments, ideas and suggestions at various stages, I would like to thank Gus Bauman, Walter Berns, Edward Connor, Richard Cowart, Robert Ellickson, Richard Epstein, William Fischel, John Gray, Gideon Kanner, Douglas Kmiec, Harold McDougall, Jeffrey Morris, Dan Polisar, Carol Rose, Joseph Sax, Ed Sullivan, Cass Sunstein and Alan Tarr.

Clay Morgan of the State University of New York Press has guided this manuscript and its bewildered author through the trials of publishing. Ellen Frankel Paul, deputy director of the Social Philosophy and Policy Center and editor of the SUNY Press series, The Constitution and Economic Rights, in which this volume appears, provided constant encouragement and an extensive and perceptive critique of the manuscript, and it is much the better for it. She is remarkably productive and insightful, one of those rare scholars who listens and reads as well as she thinks and writes. The Social Philosophy and Policy Center was generous in its support, and provided a hospitable home in which to work on this manuscript. Little had I known that the center of the intellectual universe might be hidden in the cornfields of Ohio. I especially appreciated the encouragement and stimulating comments of Fred Miller, who as executive director of the center looks after the needs of fellows with humor and dispatch. The staff was unfailingly competent and pleasant, and has continued to provide invaluable assistance with this manuscript. I particularly would like to thank Mary Dilsaver, Dan Greenberg, Tamara Sharp, Kory Tilgner and Kim Kohut, photocopier extraordinaire.

Somehow, my wife and children endured the crazy hours, financial hardships and perverse anxieties of graduate study and assistant professorship, and I am grateful. I owe a special debt to my son, whose rocky arrival on this earth put the more trivial concerns of graduate school in perspective.

My lifelong appreciation for the relations between land, freedom and community began as child growing up on a small hill farm. My father had little education but was a fine philosopher, and conveyed his values, beliefs, and perceptions through his actions and his stories. If I can leave a legacy of decency and dignity half as large to my own children, I will be fulfilled.

I gratefully acknowledge permission to reprint excerpts from the following works:

Victor John Yannacone, Jr., John Rahenkamp & Angelo I. Cerchione, *Impact Zoning: Alternative to Exclusion in the Suburbs*, in *The Land Use Awakening: Zoning Law in the Seventies* (Robert H. Freilich & Eric O. Stuhler eds.), copyright (c) 1989 by the American Bar Association. Reprinted by permission of the publisher.

Melvin Levin, Introduction, reprinted with permission from *The Best of Planning*, copyright 1989 by the American Planning Association, 1313 E. 60th St., Chicago, IL 60637.

Frank Popper, *Land Use and the Environment*, reprinted with permission from *The Best of Planning*, copyright 1989 by the American Planning Association, 1313 E. 60th St., Chicago, IL 60637.

Herman Schwartz, *Property Rights and the Constitution: Will the Ugly Duckling Become a Swan?* copyright (c) 1987 by the American University Law Review. Reprinted by permission of the publisher.

Eric H. Steele, *Community Participation and the Function of Rules: The Case of Urban Zoning Boards*, in Law and Policy, vol. 9. Copyright (c) 1987 by Basil Blackwell Ltd. Reprinted by permission of the publisher.

William Moshofsky, *The Regulatory Trampling of Landowner Rights*, copyright (c) 1980 by Business and Society Review. Reprinted by permission of the publisher.

Roger Pilon, *Property Rights, Takings and a Free Society*, copyright (c) 1983 by the Harvard Journal of Law and Public Policy. Reprinted by permission of the publisher.

John McClaughry, *The New Feudalism—State Land Use Controls* in *No Land Is an Island,* copyright (c) 1975 by the Institute for Contemporary Studies Press. Reprinted by permission of the publisher.

C. S. Holling, *Myths of Ecological Stability: Resilience and the Problems of Failure,* in *Studies on Crisis Management* (C. F. Smart & W. T. Stanbury eds.), copyright (c) 1978 by the Institute for Research on Public Policy. Reprinted by permission of the publisher.

Richard F. Babcock *The Zoning Game: Municipal Practices and Policies.* Reprinted by permission of the Lincoln Institute for Land Policy and Richard F. Babcock.

Michael M. Berger and Gideon Kanner, *Thoughts on the White River Junction Manifesto: A Reply to the "Gang of Five's" Views on Just Compensation for Regulatory Taking of Property,* copyright (c) 1986 Loyola of Los Angeles Law Review. Reprinted by permission of the publisher.

T. O'Riordan, *Environmental Ideologies,* in Environment & Planning A, vol. 9. Copyright (c) 1977 Pion Limited. Reprinted by permission of Pion Limited.

John M. Payne, *Delegation Doctrine in the Reform of Local Government Law: The Case of Exclusionary Zoning,* copyright (c) 1976 Rutgers Law Review. Reprinted by permission of the publisher.

Harold Gilliam, *What is Deep Ecology?* copyright (c) 1988 San Francisco Chronicle. Reprinted by permission.

Alfred A. Porro, Jr. and Lorraine S. Teleky, *Marshland Title Dilemma: A Tidal Phenomenon,* copyright (c) 1972 Seton Hall Law Review. Reprinted by permission of the publisher.

Martin Shapiro, *The Constitution and Economic Rights,* in *Essays on the Constitution of the United States* (M. Judd Harmon ed.), published by Kennikat Press, copyright (c) 1978 by Martin Shapiro. Reprinted by permission of the author.

Edward J. Erler, *The Great Fence to Liberty: The Right to Property in the American Founding* in *Liberty, Property and the Foundations of the American Constitution* (Ellen Frankel Paul & Howard Dickman eds.). Reprinted by permission of the State University of New York Press. Copyright (c) 1989 State University of New York.

Charles F. Hobson, *Republicanism, Commerce, and Private Rights: James Madison's Path to the Constitutional Convention of 1787* in *Liberty, Property and the Foundation of the American Constitution* (Ellen Frankel Paul & Howard Dickman eds.) Reprinted by permission of the State University of New York Press. Copyright (c) 1989 State University of New York.

Norman Williams, Jr. & Thomas Norman, *Exclusionary Land Use Controls: The Case of North-Eastern New Jersey,* copyright (c) by Syracuse Law Review. Reprinted by permission of the publisher.

John P. Frank, Book Review of *Developments in State Constitutional Law* (Bradley D. McGraw ed.) & *State Supreme Courts in State and Nation* (G. Alan Tarr & Mary Cornelia Aldis Porter eds.). Published originally in 63 *Texas Law Review* 1339–1346 (1985). Copyright (c) by the Texas Law Review Association. Reprinted by permission.

Matthew O. Tobriner, *Retrospective: Ten Years on the California Supreme Court,* originally published in 20 *UCLA L. Rev.* 5–12. Copyright 1972, The Regents of the University of California. All rights reserved. Reprinted with permission of the UCLA Law Review and Fred B. Rothman & Co.

Sarah E. Wilson, *Private Property and the Public Trust: A Theory for Preserving the Coastal Zone,* in the UCLA Journal of Environmental Law and Policy, vol. 4. Copyright 1984, The Regents of the University of California. Reprinted by permission of the Regents of the University of California.

Matthew O. Tobriner and Joseph R. Grodin, *The Individual and the Public Service Enterprise in the New Industrial State,* copyright (c) 1967 by California Law Review, Inc. Reprinted from 55 California Law Review 1247–1283 (1967) by permission of the publisher and Joseph R. Grodin.

James Madison, *Property,* in *The Papers of James Madison, Congressional Series, Volume 14: 6 April 1791–16 March 1793* (Robert A. Rutland and Charles F. Hobson, eds.), copyright (c) 1983 the University Press of Virginia. Reprinted by permission of the publisher.

Editorial, April 3, 1975, The Wall Street Journal. Reprinted with permission of The Wall Street Journal. Copyright (c) Dow Jones & Company, Inc. All rights reserved.

Joseph L. Sax, *Some Thoughts on the Decline of Private Property,* copyright (c) 1983 by Washington Law Review. Reprinted by permission of the publisher.

Howard Kurtz, *New Jersey's Ground-Breaking Supreme Court: Rulings on Social Issues Produce National Reputation for Innovation, as Well as Local Backlash.* Copyright (c) 1988 The Washington Post. Reprinted by permission.

Vaclav Havel, speech printed in the Washington Post as *Our Freedom.* Copyright (c) 1990 The Washington Post. Reprinted by permission.

Norman Williams, Jr., *The Background and Significance of Mount Laurel II*, copyright (c) 1984 Washington University Journal of Urban and Contemporary Law. Reprinted by permission of the publisher.

Pennsylvania, New Jersey and California Supreme Court cases published in West's Pacific Reporter 2d and West's Atlantic Reporter 2d, copyright (c) 1965–1989 by West Publishing Co. Reprinted by permission of the publisher. Complete lists of these cases are in the appendixes.

PART I: LANDOWNER RIGHTS AND POLITICAL CULTURE

Chapter 1

Why Land Use Rights?

The instant I enter on my own land, the bright idea of property, of exclusive right, of independence, exalt my mind. . . . This formerly rude soil has established all our rights; on it is founded our rank, our freedom, our power as citizens.

—J. Hector Crevecoeur

This is a book about private property, in particular, land, about government attempts to control it and the constitutional rights that protect it. But it is about more than land and law; it is about freedom and community, values and culture. There is an inescapable tension in liberalism between the individual and the state that is played out in regulatory conflicts over the use of private land. Embedded in debates over constitutional property rights are conflicting visions of the proper polity.

Landowner rights have been orphans of the courts for most of this century. Half a century ago, the U.S. Supreme Court interred property rights in the constitutional graveyard.[1] Henceforth, there would be two classes of constitutional rights: those meriting vigilant protection (such as freedom of expression, voting rights, and equal protection of the laws), and those, including the rights of landowners, that would virtually be abandoned, no longer serious obstacles to government action. For decades, the constitution was essentially irrelevant to the land use regulatory process.

Why, then, do landowner rights merit the attention of an entire book? Are they not the dinosaurs of legal doctrine, extinct symbols of an era forever gone, when strong property rights roamed the country, occasionally stopping to squash legislative attempts at regulation? Twenty years ago, property rights may have appeared to be irrelevant anachronisms. For decades, a profound silence on constitutional property rights echoed across the nation: Between 1928 and 1974, the U.S. Supreme Court did not even hear a zoning case, and most state courts gradually adopted the "see-no-land-rights, hear-no-land-rights" attitude of the Court. But in the past two decades, state and federal justices increasingly have questioned the wisdom of the simple double standard of constitutional rights that has been the foundation of jurisprudence since the New Deal. As a consequence, zoning and the other tools of land use control are no longer sacrosanct. For example, beginning in 1975, the New Jersey Supreme Court, long a leader in deference to legislative control of land use, issued a series of widely hailed decisions condemning the exclusionary effects on the poor of local zoning practices, and ordering radical changes.[2] The U.S. Supreme Court has begun to face the deleterious effects that regulations may have on fundamental rights,[3] and has struck down local land use ordinances or administrative decisions that threatened free expression,[4] entangled church and state,[5] or discriminated against the retarded.[6] And before the Court closed shop in June 1987, it issued two decisions—*First English Evangelical Lutheran Church of Glendale v. Los Angeles County*[7] and *Nollan v. California Coastal Commission*[8]—that together formed the most profound and potentially far-reaching statement on the constitutional rights of landowners the Court had made in fifty years.

We are entering a new constitutional era in which the New Deal double standard of rights has become blurred and property rights are once again the focus of attention in the highest courts of the land. In the future, it will be essential that land use regulators, and scholars who seek to study the process, "know the constitution."[9] Just what sort of rights are emerging from the courts, what their implications are likely to be for government regulation and the autonomy of landowners, and how they reflect the clash of political cultures in the American polity are the subjects of this book.

OF ASPIRATIONS AND RIGHTS

When I was young, a state inspector came around to our family dairy farm. He had two requests. The milkhouse door, which opened inward, as doors often do, would have to be changed so that it swung out. This was because someone had decided that fewer flies would enter a building if the door opened out, and the inspector, vested with the authority of the state, could require that we put that theory into practice. The actual number of flies around our milkhouse (admittedly, farm flies are difficult to count) was not of concern to the inspector, nor was the general level of sanitation in the barn. The door had to open in the prescribed manner, and that was that. The inspector also informed us that the electric cooler, which protected the milk until we whisked the cans down to a rendezvous with a tank truck in town, had to go. In its stead we would have to install a shiny new storage tank so that the milk could be piped directly into the truck at the farm. Again, there was not an issue of the quality of our milk or the care we took. Milk cans were simply passé. Now milk tanks, unlike shoes, do not come in a wide range of sizes. Our small operation did not produce enough milk to take up much room in the typical tank, which also would be prohibitively expensive and larger than the entire milkhouse. My father considered the demands of the state and the bleak outlook for small farmers, and decided it was time to embark on a new career. So the cows were sold, and our small contribution ceased to flow into the great stream of commerce. And to this day the milkhouse door still swings inward.

Many years later, I was a reporter for newspapers in New England. Since I worked part-time, I was paid by the inch, and the surest way to generate a plentiful supply of inches about local controversies was to go to the meetings of the planning and zoning commissions. Readers who have not had the opportunity to witness these grand clashes do not know what they are missing. Of course, the professional life of the local land use regulator does not always match the excitement and glamour of, say, Donald Trump. Officials can drone on in an obscure bureaucratic tongue that will sedate the most energetic observer. But that is part of the fascination of the process: Fundamental issues about how people shall live become encoded in terms of art such as "mitigating circumstances" and "projected maximum load capacity." And just beneath the thin veneer of obfuscation lie the simmering disputes about the freedom, equality, and community of local citizens. When man meets bureaucrat in a local regulatory proceeding, the result is often lively, with owners demanding their rights, neighbors seeking to restrain them, and officials purveying their visions of social sanity. As a laboratory for finding everyday people grappling with the great questions of social life in circumstances with direct impact on the participants, a hearing at the local land use commission is hard to beat.

Let me give you an example. Marlborough, Connecticut, is a suburb on the fringes of the Hartford area. As the population has become dominated by middle-class commuters, land use regulation has become increasingly strict and complex and holds a prominent place on the political agenda. While I was covering the town, the home of a local family burned to the ground. They were not well off and had no other place to keep the family together while they rebuilt their home. They sought to put a mobile home on their land until the new home was ready. But lo, Marlborough had an ordinance forbidding mobile homes. The owners appealed, but town officials would not budge. To the working-class owners of burned rubble, the land use process seemed absurdly unjust, keeping them out of their hometown. To the middle-class officials who devoted their evenings to enforcing the regulations, zoning was a benevolent way to preserve the aesthetics and community order they cherished.

Land use regulation is here to stay. By joining together under the banner of government, individuals can extend their control beyond their private world. Land use regulation cannot help but confront the basic social issues of freedom and community. It can be a potent weapon for stopping nuisances before they start (in economists' terms, controlling the externalities). Or it can be a covert way to rig the socioeconomic makeup of a community, excluding those deemed undesirable. And it can leave an homeowner vulnerable to the whims of local residents. Regulation is sometimes benign, sometimes oppressive, absurd at times, and at least occasionally sensible.

Individual property rights are a key element in keeping regulation reasonable. Rights, when enforced, keep procedural hurdles and substantive outcomes from becoming too abusive. And the language of rights permeates controversies over the uses of land. The fire victim in Marlborough spoke of his "right" to a home. My father thought he had a right to let the milkhouse door swing freely and to use whatever milk storage system was safe and economical. The property owners I observed running the regulatory gauntlet in California, where I labored mightily in graduate school, often spoke of rights as if they were moral trumps that would vindicate their positions. A sense of rights seemed to be an underlying phenomenon that drove regulatory proceedings. I became curious to know just what those rights are, as interpreted by the courts, and how the courts reconcile conflicting visions of the proper relations between land use, personal freedom, and community.

LOOKING FOR LANDOWNER RIGHTS

When landowners speak of their "rights," they do not necessarily restrict their claims to constitutions. Statutes and local ordinances that authorize land uses or provide procedural safeguards may benefit property owners. But rights imply a moral foundation and a permanence that do not characterize the pragmatic legislative compromises of shifting political forces. Compared with constitutional provisions, statutory laws are more likely to be perceived as products of inordinate political power rather than as fundamental statements of the moral ideals of the society. The detail and cumbersome language of laws and ordinances may aid implementation, but they also put the substance of laws beyond the grasp of most citizens and reinforce suspicions that complexity hides loopholes for the powerful. And in the land use field most statutory innovations have expanded state control over private property. The liberties of landowners may then be reduced to what can be read between the lines; that which is not yet forbidden may still be allowed. But then the landowner may be accused of subverting the intent of the law, and action to "close the loophole" may result. Statutes and ordinances also are more easily amended than constitutions[10] and thus provide less secure protections. A constitutional clause, in contrast, has a simplicity that makes interpretation uncertain but serves as a readily perceived rhetorical statement of values. Constitutional rights carry a moral and symbolic power not shared by statutory protections. Rights are emphatic statements in simple language of what is good and important to a free society.

Lest anyone think this work is a celebration of symbol over substance, I would point out that constitutional rights, when enforced, have played a critical role in land use litigation. "The most important part of this field [land use law] has been concerned with constitutional law," Norman Williams has pointed out. "Nevertheless, there has been a striking lack of clearly articulated constitutional doctrine."[11] The impact of constitutional law has largely been through the state courts in disparate decisions of many courts across the land, often in obscure language. Even a comparison of the wording of constitutions provides little guidance to the actual status of rights, as different courts may give widely varying interpretations to nearly identical language.[12] Constitutional clauses do not create effective rights unless the courts are willing to enforce them. To understand what rights landowners have, I will evaluate the reasoning and context of court decisions upholding constitutional protections against government encroachment.

The study of doctrine has fallen out of favor in the social sciences, and that is regrettable. On the book reviewer form for the *American Political Science Review*, for example, there is no category for "law," only for actors and processes such as courts, judges, and judicial process. There is little recognition that the language and logic of legal doctrine is an important factor in the outcome of decisions and more fundamentally in the character and tone of society. This distrust of doctrinal studies stems from an understandable suspicion of backseat judging under the guise of scholarly analysis. But to ignore doctrine is to ignore some of the fundamental rules that affect individual behavior and policy outcomes. The precedental value of the law means that court decisions are not simply solutions to narrow disputes but constraints on the policy process and can be studied as such. And in order to give social legitimacy to decisions rather than simply choose between the conflicting arguments of the litigants in a particular case, the justices must develop some rationale, some vision of the acceptable political and social relations in a polity of democracy and individualism.

In the next chapter I present a framework for analyzing those competing visions, or cultures. I then briefly summarize constitutional land use law prior to the 1980s. Three chapters on different jurisdictions follow. First I look at Pennsylvania where we find a court strong on rhetoric celebrating property rights but as likely to favor municipalities as landowners in its decisions, with outcomes often depending on small factual differences. Exclusionary zoning doctrine, the centerpiece of constitutional land use law in Pennsylvania, vividly shows the cultural conflicts that beset the court, particularly as it struggles to incorporate the more activist approach of its neighbor, the New Jersey Supreme Court, while maintaining a view uniquely its own. Next I turn to California where the Supreme Court has remained steadfast in its deference to government regulation of property, and finally to the U.S. Supreme Court, which has come out of its shell with several significant rulings on behalf of property rights, broadly construed. The Court's rulings may point the way to the future because of their national impact and their resonance with current conflicts of political culture. In the penultimate chapter I discuss the significance of continuing pressures for expansion of the regulatory state. I conclude with a summary of developments in property rights, and recommend doctrinal changes— such as greater procedural protections for landowners, a higher level of substantive scrutiny, and emphasis on the extent of deprivation in a takings clause case rather than on the government's interest— that would strengthen landowner rights while still accomodating the perspectives of conflicting political cultures.

SEARCHING THE THICKETS OF CONSTITUTIONAL LAW

In my quest for the elusive rights of landowners, I have followed two basic strategies: Developments in state supreme courts, which have loomed large in the land use field for decades and are even more important today, have been given major emphasis, and for the jurisdictions given most emphasis, all constitutional decisions from the 1980s on the rights of property owners in the land use regulatory context have been included to provide a fuller and more balanced perspective on the status of rights.

Legal scholarship has tended to focus excessively on the U.S. Supreme Court. This is quite understandable as it is easier than following the doctrinal twists and turns of fifty relatively obscure state tribunals. In land use regulation, however, the court was virtually silent for half a century, leaving the state courts to fashion their own doctrines. The Supreme Court cannot be ignored, of course, since understanding its abstention from the land use field is key to understanding the wide discretion that regulatory bodies have enjoyed and why that autonomy may now be narrowing. And the Court may be returning as a major player in the field of constitutional property rights.

State high courts have had the final say in the bulk of landowner cases, and many are increasingly willing to find rights in state constitutions, sometimes with explicit encouragement from federal justices,[13] that the Supreme Court has been reluctant to read into the U.S. Constitution. The state courts are beginning to receive some overdue attention,[14] but the comprehensive, comparative study of state constitutional doctrine has been a neglected field. While selected cases, such as the *Mount Laurel* decisions attacking exclusionary zoning in New Jersey,[15] that warm the cockles or draw the ire of commentators receive inordinate attention,[16] the great mass of constitutional litigation receives scant notice. "What is most lacking," according to James Kirby, "is close study of cases in which laws are upheld, as well as invalidated."[17] The unusual cases must be placed in a context of cases in which regulations are upheld or struck down for predictable reasons to get a balanced view of the nature and extent of constitutional rights.

A few authors have made serious attempts to canvas the state of land use law.[18] Although they make extensive reference to recent decisions in many different states, their coverage is selective, and thus they do not provide a comprehensive picture of the state of rights even in the jurisdictions they cite. They make impressive attempts to summarize the law but do not provide methodical, comparative analysis. These treatises also do not seek the underlying social visions that help us understand the development of the law and predict its future, and do not consider the implications of the decisions for competing ways of life.

A notable example of an attempt to bridge the gap between social science and legal doctrine is the study of land use cases in California conducted by Joseph DiMento, Donald Hagman, and their associates in the late 1970s.[19] Their work was both broader and more narrow than my project. They studied all state decisions related to land use, including constitutional and other decision bases such as statutes, ordinances, and regulations. Less than 15 percent of their cases were decided at least partly on state constitutional grounds,[20] and thus their findings, while supporting the general perception that the California court is hostile to development, are of limited help in assessing the extent of constitutional rights. Their study also stopped before the 1980s and did not employ a comparative approach. And their attention was focused primarily on the outcomes of cases rather than on the visions of society sketched out by the opinions. Nonetheless, it is encouraging to see such careful work creeping into the law reviews.

Searching through the thicket of state constitutional law can be daunting. Although I have strived to be constitent in the selection of cases, it is occasionally a judgment call whether a case turns on a property rights issue. As Norman Williams has noted, "A literal minded reading of the case law will show that, in perhaps nine out of ten cases involving constitutional questions, there is no indication as to which constitutional doctrine was involved."[21] Indeed, in some opinions, there may be no mention of a constitution at all, even though constitutional analysis is employed. I have concentrated on the decisions of supreme courts. The decisions of lower state and federal courts are important in particular disputes, and may presage the adoption of innovative doctrines by a high court but are not final[22] and may be conflicting, and thus do not give a good picture of the fundamental rights established in a jurisdiction.

Rather than cover every state in detail, which would tax the stamina of the most devoted reader, or every state superficially, which would not convey the depth and nuances of debates and developments in the property rights area, I have concentrated on two—Pennsylvania (with comparisons to New Jersey) and California—that represent quite different trends in state constitutional law. Instead of relying on my own impressions, I asked eight specialists in land use law[23] to suggest states that were the most protective of landowner rights and states that were the least protective. California was a near unanimous choice as the state least likely to protect landowner rights. Californian municipalities are well known as leaders in the development of public controls over private land and are accustomed to meeting little resistance from the state courts.[24]

It may be indicative of the generally low state of property rights that finding a vigilantly protective jurisdiction is no easy task. Pennsylvania and Illinois were most frequently cited by those I consulted.[25] Illinois does have a reputation as a protective state. The state is "strongly developer minded," accordingly to Williams,[26] while Ellickson and Tarlock portray Illinois as an activist court "at the other pole" from California.[27] But when I reviewed Illinois cases in the 1980s, I found the court supported the rights of the landowner in only one-third of the constitutional cases. Either the court has shifted direction, or the extent of its protectionism has been exaggerated, which is easy to do, given the contrast with courts deferent to regulation. Of the courts I reviewed, the Pennsylvania Supreme Court was most likely to rule in favor of constitutional property rights, with about half of its decisions favoring the landowner.[28] The Pennsylvania court is an especially attractive subject because it has been a leader in the development of "exclusionary zoning" doctrine, which has been widely heralded as an innovative approach to land use. Pennsylvania and its neighbor New Jersey dominated the citations on exclusionary zoning.[29] Including Pennsylvania in the study provided an opportunity to assess whether decisions requiring local zoning plans to accommodate low-income residents represent victories for landowner rights or merely a new doctrine of state control.[30] The answer, it turns out, depends in part on which bank of the Delaware one is standing on.

THE LEFTWARD LEAN OF LAND USE COMMENTARY

During the stormy days of the hearings on the nomination of Judge Robert Bork to the Supreme Court, Lawrence Tribe of Harvard Law School warned, in all seriousness, that Bork was out of the "mainstream" of legal scholarship. What he declined to mention was that the legal mainstream has veered well to the left of the American public. In legal scholarship on constitutional law, there is a distinct sense of déjà vu when reading one commentary after another. "Almost all the scholarly treatments of the modern Supreme Court," Martin Shapiro has noted, "have been produced either by active proponents of and participants in the New Deal or by its intellectual and political allies and successors."[31] The land use literature is often more informative of the preferences of the author than the state of the law. The gospel on land use law goes something like this: *Lochner*[32] and its ilk were bad; the double standard created in the *Carolene Products* footnote[33] is good; and the *Mount Laurel* court made a laudatory attempt to correct regulation by making it more egalitarian.[34] Law is ultimately about values, and critical reviews and normative arguments play an important part of thinking about law. What is distributing is how uniform the voices have been and how little candor there has been in acknowledging the pervasiveness of ideology. And what "should be" is not the same as what "is." It often is difficult to distinguish the two in the land use literature. I hope to remedy this by presenting a study that is comprehensive and balanced in the cases selected for study and will critically examine the value premises underlying land use regulation, adding a discordant voice to the harmony of New Deal commentary.

"The reader should know through what spectacles his advisor is viewing the problem," urged William Douglas.[35] Too often, he said, arguments were put forward by "special pleaders who fail to disclose that they are not scholars but rather people with axes to grind."[36] Now, Douglas was never one to walk around with a dull ax, but he was straightforward about his opinions. Too often, opinions in the land use literature are portrayed as the inescapable conclusions of objective experts. Norman Williams, Dan Mandelker, Richard Babcock, and their coauthors wrote a diatribe against the unremarkable position that the constitution requires compensation when governmental restrictions are so severe as to effectively "take" private property, as if their cumulative reputations (which are substantial) should suffice to silence the opposition.[37] In a reply, Berger and Kanner noted that the writers of the "Manifesto," as it was titled, "tend to toil in government vineyards"[38] representing the parties that are seeking to avoid paying for takings (the Manifesto authors had neglected to mention this point). "In *The Manifesto* they are polemicists, not scholars."[39]

To cite another example, Robert Anderson, an accomplished land use scholar, praised "Professor Williams' careful and dispassionate examination" of New Jersey zoning law,[40] although Williams's article reads like a call to arms on behalf of egalitarian regulation. There is a "value judgment rapidly coalescing among thoughtful people," Williams and Norman claimed, that regulatory barriers to equality must be eradicated.[41] The implication was that if you are thoughtful, you agree with the authors; if you disagree, you are thoughtless. Yet the issue of exclusionary zoning is not simple, and reasonable people can disagree on the values to be served and the means to achieve them. Diversity of philosophy and vigorous debate between closely balanced ideological forces have not been hallmarks of the land use literature. "For many decades," Ellen Frankel Paul has noted, "liberals just did not have to confront many free-market advocates during their normal, scholarly routines. They could go about unperturbed, all nodding in acquiescence to the same set of canards inherited from the New Deal."[42]

Some of what I will say may set heads bobbing, but they may not be nodding in agreement. I think abdication by the courts has exposed property owners and users to flagrant abuses of their fundamental rights, rights that are crucial to individual freedom in a democracy. And I am wary of rationales for attacking exclusionary zoning that with their emphasis on putting the coercive power of the state behind preferred visions of where and how people should live, legitimate further governmental intrusions into individual autonomy. In its zeal to justify an expanding regulatory state, the land use establishment—the Mandelkers and Williamses and articulate justices on deferent courts—has undermined the freedom critical to the American polity and has supported the dilution of the Constitution beyond the bounds of credible interpretation. Given the pro-regulation uniformity of much land use commentary, I hope my criticisms will serve to broaden the debate.

Judging from developments in the courts, it is hard not to be encouraged that property rights are on the rebound, although some may consider this cause for worry rather than rejoicing. In the coming years, landowners will likely continue to gain constitutional protections that they have lacked for decades in many jurisdictions. But this recovery of rights has not begun because lawyers and laymen have been dazzled by the forceful arguments of, say, Richard Epstein, a frequent critic of the regulatory state, and reluctantly concluded that indeed the twentieth century is unconstitutional. Rather, it is because regulation has become so pervasive that even

judges, scholars, and average citizens predisposed to support government have begun to fear that things have gotten out of hand, that
the control of land is restricting freedom of expression, perpetuating
inequality, eroding personal privacy, and creating obstacles to economic opportunity. For private property rights do not only protect
the liberty of wealthy developers or large corporations. One need
not be hostile to regulation to be disturbed by some of the abuses
that have been perpetuated by governments ostensibly acting for the
public good. My hope is that a detailed review of constitutional
rights in the land use arena will encourage appreciation of the essential role of private property in liberal democracy and awareness
of the often absurd regulatory gauntlets that property owners and
users may face, and that common ground may be found between differing perspectives to strengthen protection of landowner rights.

A BRIEF INTRODUCTION TO CONSTITUTIONAL
AND LAND USE LAW

Constitutional law largely is a matter of logic (or illogic), so I
hope readers unfamiliar with the arcane mysteries and dubious science of the law will not be deterred by the emphasis on doctrine.
Before moving on, I will review some of the basic legal concepts and
terminology I will be using throughout the book.[43] Hardened veterans of land use litigation may wish to skip ahead to the next chapter.
For others, the following discussion of constitutional law[44] and land
use regulation may be helpful.

Constitutional rights protect the individual from government;
they do not protect individuals from interference with their legal
rights and interests by other private individuals, such as their neighbors. Those disputes are resolved by the common law,[45] supple-
mented by state statutes. If you insist on enjoying the sun in my
backyard without my permission, for example, I could take you to
court for trespass. If the city government has provided a basis for
your intrusion, as by declaring all private backyards open to the
public, then I might also claim the city has infringed my constitutional rights. Constitutional law deals with the classic conflict in
liberalism between the power of the state and the freedom of the
individual.

The greatest jurisprudential legacy of the New Deal has been
the creation of two classes of constitutional rights. Preferred rights,
such as freedom of speech, protection against racial discrimination,
and now privacy, have been elevated to the status of "fundamental"

rights, which generally cannot be infringed unless the state can show its actions are essential to serve a compelling governmental interest. Other constitutional rights have been given an inferior status and can be infringed at will unless the government's action lacks any rational relationship to a legitimate objective. The major clauses in the U.S. Constitution under which property rights have received protection, the takings clause and the due process clause, by and large have been relegated to the second category, although states vary in the degree of seriousness they attach to landowner rights.

The due process clause[46] protects individuals from arbitrary or capricious governmental action and has both a procedural and a substantive element. Literally, the government must follow the "process" that is "due," or its actions may be invalidated by the courts. Procedural protections are intended to ensure that individuals are treated fairly. Requirements in administrative processes, which are most pertinent to the land use field, usually include the right to notice of governmental action, an opportunity for a formal hearing, and a decision based on the record. Actions classified as legislative, which in theory are general statements of policy rather than resolutions of particular disputes, need not meet these requirements.[47] But a regulation or law[48] may be struck down if it is too vague (the "void for vagueness" doctrine), essentially because it fails to give clear notice of impermissible conduct or leaves too much discretion with the enforcing agency.

These procedural protections do not guarantee that the property owner will retain any autonomy in the use of land; they require only that restrictions be imposed properly. But one procedural protection, the *vested right*, may create substantive guarantees of rights to use land. A property owner's right to use land in a specific way may "vest" if the owner has acted in reliance on prior approval by the government. If a building permit is issued and construction subsequently begun, for example, a municipality cannot revoke the permit simply because it changes its mind. Generally, however, property owners are subject to the fluctuations of public policy. A manufacturing company that purchases a tract of land zoned industrial may find the property rezoned to forbid its intended use or may be able to gain permit approval only by agreeing to onerous conditions.

The due process clauses of the Fifth and Fourteenth amendments and their state constitutional kin also have substantive components. A statute approved in the proper fashion or a regulation adopted after notice and hearings may nonetheless be unconstitutional if it lacks a sufficient relationship to an appropriate governmental objective, even if it does not violate any explicit constitutional right. This is a controversial area of constitutional law as it requires that a court evaluate the proper ends and means of government, a task arguably better suited for an elected legislature exercising its "police power," its authority to act on behalf of the public health, safety, and welfare. Since the New Deal, the Supreme Court has required only the most minimal rationality of governmental action except when preferred constitutional rights are at stake. In those cases, judicial evaluation of governmental ends and means is unavoidable, as even the most protected of rights may be overcome if the state's justification is compelling. Justice Holmes's classic example is that shouting "fire" in a crowded theater is not protected by the First Amendment.

Closely related to due process concerns are matters of equal protection. Under the equal protection clause[49] of the Fourteenth Amendment, courts may evaluate the rationality of governmental actions, distinguishing between different groups of persons. Even if a municipality has the power to forbid industrial uses, a court might look closely at a regulation that singles out one or two uses. Equal protection challenges typically are not more successful than due process attacks on land use regulations unless a "suspect class" such as a racial minority is affected. In those cases, judicial scrutiny is much stricter.

The takings clause of the Fifth Amendment states, "Nor shall private property shall be taken for public use, without just compensation."[50] The clause implicitly authorizes the taking of private property, which can be done through *eminent domain* procedures. When a government initiates eminent domain, constitutional questions may arise whether the proposed use of the property constitutes a "public" use and whether "just compensation" is being provided. If the government takes private property without beginning eminent domain proceedings, the owner may file an "inverse condemnation" suit seeking compensation or an injunction to prevent the taking, or both. The hottest area of constitutional law involves "regulatory takings;" a landowner claims his property has been effectively taken through restrictive regulations limiting use of the property even though the government has not asserted title to the property.

For most of this century, the Supreme Court has given little support to property rights under the takings or due process clauses yet has been much more protective of rights it has deemed "fundamental" or "personal," such as freedom of expression or privacy. Government restrictions on private property may be challenged under these doctrines of preferred rights. Most important in the land use context is the First Amendment,[51] which protects freedom of speech and the free exercise of religion and forbids the governmental establishment of religion. Zoning restrictions on billboards and adult bookstores are frequently challenged on First Amendment grounds. As the courts have been especially protective of expressive rights, in some cases these doctrines may provide greater prospects of success than a takings or substantive due process claim.

Both federal and state constitutions protect rights that are not explicitly mentioned. Following the enumeration of individual rights in the first eight amendments to the Constitution, the Ninth Amendment provides an additional, open-ended guarantee: "The enumeration in the Constitution, of certain rights, shall not be construed to deny or disparage others retained by the people." The enumeration of rights in the Declaration of Rights of the Pennsylvania Constitution, typical of state charters, begins with "All men are born equally free and independent, and have certain inherent and indefeasible rights, among which are," implying that the following explicit rights are not meant to be exhaustive.[52] Yet the courts have been reluctant to specify just what those rights might be for fear of intruding on the legislative process. An exception has been the right of privacy, the origin of which has been tied to the Ninth Amendment, the due process clause, and the "penumbra," or peripheral implications, of more specific clauses. In land use, for example, the privacy right has been used to strike down restrictions on who may live in a "single-family" zone.

Prior to the rise of governmental controls, land uses were regulated through suits in common law, especially trespass and nuisance, and private covenants. Covenants, which remain common today, are contracts between buyers and sellers restricting the uses of property. Entire neighborhoods may eliminate uses damaging to adjoining property owners (or "negative externalities," in the language of economics) through private covenants attached to property deeds.[53] A nuisance is the use of one's property in a way that interferes unreasonably with another person's use of her property. If the rock music emanating from your garage shatters my windows, I could file a nuisance suit. Early land use regulation was defended as a more efficient application of nuisance principles. Rather than wait for damage to occur or to require every person facing a nuisance to sue individually, a regulation might constrain or forbid certain uses of property before they could do damage. In *Miller v. Schoene*,[54] for example, the U.S. Supreme Court upheld an act requiring the destruction of red cedar trees to prevent the spread of cedar rust to apple orchards on adjoining private property.

The most common tool for public regulation of land use is zoning, in which different uses of property are relegated to different areas, or zones, in a municipality. Typically, there are zones for residential, commercial, and industrial uses, with several subcategories for each. Although zoning may forbid certain uses entirely in some districts, it also explicitly permits them as a matter of right in other districts.

In order to have more control over uses that ostensibly are permitted in a given zone, municipalities have created additional, discretionary permit procedures. The oldest and most common are subdivision regulations. More recent are aesthetic or "design review" regulations covering signs or architectural styles and special permits for modification of historical structures. "Conditional use permits," which may go under a variety of labels, are required for many uses. These discretionary procedures effectively eliminate land uses as a matter of right and may require landowners to agree to extensive modifications and conditions in exchange for permission to use the property. Especially in times of fiscal restraint, "development exactions" attached as conditions to permits may require developers of office buildings or subdivisions to provide or pay for substantial public services, such as roads, schools, day care, libraries, or museums. The constitutionality of these "voluntary contributions" is frequently challenged in the courts.

So much for the constitutional and land use lingo. Beneath the arcane language and technicalities, disputes about property rights reveal fundamental clashes between opposing perspectives on the proper society, and it is to those visions, or cultures, that I now turn.

Chapter 2

Land Use and Culture

Nature becomes a code for talking about society, a language in which justifications and challenges can be expressed. It is a medium of social interaction.

—*David Bloor*

Land use is not just about dirt and cement anymore; indeed it never was. The question of what uses will be allowed where on the land and who shall decide are inexorably tied up with issues about the nature of society, issues of freedom and responsibility, community and democracy. "All public planning must be considered social planning," Paul Davidoff, an advocate of participatory planning processes, has said.[1] Land use regulation is contentious not because the world is full of aspiring soil and water engineers but because regulation directly affects the social choices of individuals. Ordering the uses of land orders the users.

The arguments for or against land use regulation, arguments that have been heard for decades in legislative chambers and town zoning board hearings, academic conferences, and court opinions, can be categorized according to three basic beliefs. A well-ordered community is desirable and is promoted by land use controls. Or land use regulation violates the basic freedoms of the individual. Or greater equality of conditions is desirable, and land use controls

should be used to redistribute resources and power in society. The language of land use disputes mirrors the debate over the comparative merits of social arrangements, or cultures, based on three fundamental values: liberty, equality, and order.

A culture is composed of shared social practices and the values and beliefs that legitimate them.[2] Two aspects of this definition are particularly relevant to land use disputes. First, culture incorporates both ideas and practice. It is both more and less than ideology— more, in that the more mundane aspects of life such as eating and gardening habits are as much a part of culture as the ideological theories of elites; and perhaps less if anchoring thought in the details of day-to-day living is perceived as less elevating than the rarefied pursuit of pure ideology. Few participants in land use disputes are rigidly or even consistently ideological, but everybody has ideas about how they live. Whom we live with, what we do for work, what style of language or mannerisms we adopt—all have broader connotations for our way of life. Land use disputes raise basic questions of social life, of freedom and responsibility, but they are more accurately characterized as cultural conflicts in which ideas and values are implicit in different physical arrangements of land use than as consciously ideological disputes. That said, little harm will be done if readers prefer to regard my categories as "ideologies," as coherent packages of ideas are a part of each culture. But it would be a mistake to say that these ways of life must be self-consciously advocated by the participants to be valid descriptors or that their arguments must be logically consistent in every detail. An argument characterized as egalitarian, libertarian, or hierarchical is consistent with a social order based on the respective fundamental value, but I do not mean to imply that the speaker is a card-carrying proponent of that culture. Aspects of these cultural types are often blended in response to conflicting personal preferences or political pressures.

Political culture is about both values and beliefs, and that also makes it a convenient tool for land use analysis. Land use debates are rife with both value and belief assertions, and often the two are confused. Arguments about land use inescapably include value premises (e.g., "the pursuit of equality is the end of government") and empirical beliefs ("large-lot zoning restricts equality of housing opportunities"). In political culture, both kinds of ideas are essential. In the following sections, I will describe the approaches to land use regulation of three ideal cultural types, in which the preeminent values are hierarchy (order), liberty, and equality.[3]

LAND USE AND HIERARCHY

Modern land use controls in the United States began with the development and legal vindication of zoning in the early 1900s. Zoning was just one product of the impulse of the Progressives for order and predictability. The early enthusiasts for zoning, which was introduced in New York City in 1916 and encouraged by the U.S. Commerce Department through the publication of a Standard State Zoning Enabling Act in 1922, were fighting a holy war against the libertarian sins of nineteenth-century development. James Metzenbaum praised the "stout champions of zoning" (who included himself) and the "great sacrifice and almost supreme efforts on the part of many noble men who consecrated themselves" to zoning.[4] Control over land use would be removed from the amoral hand of the market and entrusted to expert elites removed from politics and business. Zoning is a "necessary first step to prevent utter chaos in municipal life, coming after years of unregulated development," Newman Baker, an attorney prominent in the creation of zoning, declared. The very basis of social relations in a democracy must be changed: "The laissez faire theory of government is no longer tenable," asserted Baker.[5]

Proponents of planning have had to compromise with a strong individualist tradition in America that makes central control controversial, and regulators must contend with recurring claims of owner rights. Melvin Levin, a planner and scholar, has criticized "those fossils who cherish the notion that planning in practice is somehow alien and un-American. . . . [A]llegations that planning is by its very nature radical and socialistic are seen to be delusions without substance."[6] Yet "planning's essence is to centralize power in order to control allocation,"[7] which is not a bad description of socialism. In part, advocates have sought to downplay the social and political significance of planning by arguing that planning controls land and other natural resources, not people. But the value of resources lies in their social utility, so man and land cannot be so neatly separated. Many modern planners readily admit that planning is social and seek to make it serve their senses of justice.[8] Some, however, following in the steps of the Progressive pioneers, continue to maintain that as Michael Vasu, a planner and academic, writes, "Planning . . . is concerned with the use of physical space. This . . . distinguishes American planning from the ideological implications of a more comprehensive type of social planning practiced in many socialistic countries."[9]

John Dewey understood the suspicion with which Americans greeted proposals for centralized control and urged that advocates of planning adopt the term *liberal*, which would have more political appeal than *socialist*.[10] Centralized planning, according to Dewey, was "the sole method of social action by which liberalism can realize its professed aims."[11] It is a curious irony that central control, against which liberal institutions were designed to protect, should be promoted as a means to achieve liberal ends. The rise of the business establishment, reformers argued, made reliance on individualism obsolete. The only solution was to create a public hierarchy to confront the private power of big business.

The antidote to the excesses of individualism was to be "a system of regulation which established a hierarchy of uses . . . a community whose planned and orderly development provided a place for everything, and kept everything in its place."[12] At the pinnacle of the Progressive planning hierarchy was the single-family home, which Metzenbaum declared to be "the bulwark and stamina of this country. . . . It is generally conceded that the home owner who has the opportunity to have his little garden, to rear his family in a house and to raise his children with a greater freedom of fresh air and abundance of light, is one of the important factors in the sustaining of the American people and American ideals."[13]

Home ownership could be the solution to the corrupting influences of economic and political freedom. Responsibility to home would breed responsibility to society, elevating the character of the public and tempering the volatility of democracy. The unpredictability of democracy is anathema to the hierarchical craving for order, and home and family obligations were seen as a way to bring the unwashed masses up to grade. To accomplish this social mission, special zones would be set aside as sanctuaries in which the homeowner could follow his calling.

The pressure for zoning, particularly in New York, followed decades of rapid growth that were accompanied by the influx of millions of immigrants. Zoning proponents were predominately WASPs, and Constance Perin[14] has argued that zoning was a barely disguised tool of class and ethnic discrimination. In effect, the hierarchists of America were having trouble finding a room in their house for the new groups. Early zoning advocates justified their measures as necessary to avoid the fate that had befallen urban ethnic neighborhoods inhabited by the new arrivals, who "crowded [the city's] hospitals, have taxed its juvenile courts, have greatly impoverished it tax returns, have made greater police and fire departments necessary, have increased its daily accidents and have driven out many of its homes."[15] Serene neighborhoods of single-family homes on large lots segregated from the harshness of industry and the temptations of commerce would not suffer these social ills; nor, perhaps not coincidentally, would they provide the proximity of services and jobs that would encourage ethnic immigration.

In the South, zoning was a tool for preserving racial segregation. Atlanta's zoning law divided residential areas into "three race districts, white, colored, and undetermined."[16] Bruno Lasker warned that "as a precedent it opens up the possibility of new zoning ordinances embodying restrictions against immigrants . . . persons or certain occupations, political or religious affiliations, or modes of life."[17] Robert Whitten, the author of the Atlanta zoning ordinance, also led the development of zoning laws in the North,[18] although they were not explicitly racial.

The contemporary environmental movement, with a reliance on specialized expertise and the anticipation and regulation of all environmental effects of human actions, is rich with the language and the logic of hierarchy.[19] Linowes and Allensworth have advocated creating an environmental hierarchy, a Court of Ecology, composed of elite experts "from various walks of life—including lawyers, architects, engineers, hydrologists, geologists, urbanologists, conservationists, and planners." The purpose of this panel would be to "control the environment in the public interest."[20] With its emphasis on management by elites and limits on social change, environmentalism recalls the motivations behind zoning and is vulnerable to similar criticism that it can limit opportunities for socioeconomic mobility.[21] Hierarchy relies on correct organization to produce essential knowledge, such as what the public interest is and how it can be obtained.[22] Yannacone, Rahenkamp, and Cerchione, for example, advocate "impact zoning," which "is based on the concept that the full impact of any specific proposal for development on the natural, social and economic environment of a community can, and must, be evaluated."[23]

The hierarchical political culture, as is the case for other visions of land use, depends on a set of beliefs about nature that support the need for order and predictability. C. S. Holling, an ecologist who has developed a typology of environmental philosophies similar to the cultural categories,[24] describes this idea of nature as a "mesa with a depression at its top."[25] Life is a ball in the depression; society may alter nature moderately, and the ball will harmlessly roll around in its bowl. But should there be major, uncontrolled changes, the ball will roll out of the depression and go skittering off the edge of the mesa, dooming society. The lessons for social organization are that man may manipulate nature, and society itself, if actions are carefully controlled. As Holling has put it, "The task is to carefully control the variables to keep them well away from the dangerous separatrix (the edge of the matrix) . . . in the highly responsible tradition of engineering for safety, of nuclear safeguards, of environmental and health standards. It demands and presumes knowledge. . . . The goal is to minimize the probability of failure."[26] T. O'Riordan has labeled this emphasis on centralized management of the physical environment as the "technocentric" approach, characterized by "professional and managerial elitism, scientific rationality, and optimism."[27] The early conservationists, according to O'Riordan, were

> quite conceited about their own abilities: they honestly believed that they were competent to allocate resources without political interference. They felt that politics confused matters, created inefficiencies, and thus frustrated rational and efficient decisions. The idea that the 'lay' public should in any way be involved in conservationist principles was an anathema to them: the management of resources was a matter for experts.[28]

The regulatory state in America is hardly the hierarchical ideal. Richard Babcock, a land use scholar and attorney, has described the planning utopia as "a bunch of happy, well-informed people with a social IQ of 150 sit[ting] around making decisions in complete freedom from outside pressure."[29] The early zoning legislation envisioned thorough planning and creation of zones pursuant to those plans; what would go where would be carefully circumscribed and known in advance. As any exasperated planner will tell you, reality does not match the ideal. Politics can play a central role.

In a nation with strong traditions of democracy and localism, land use controls have been more subject to community political control than hierarchical planners think wise. Local governments can be keenly sensitive to shifting political winds in regulating land use. "The institution which has emerged from the initial idea of zoning," Steele has noted, "is far more fluid and participatory than is implied by the explicit text of zoning ordinances and enabling acts."[30] Often an uneasy working alliance exists between the professional staff and the planning and zoning commissioners, who are usually lay citizens of the community. Creating a role for elected or appointed officials who are not planning specialists helps to reconcile planning with democratic control, but it is often criticized for leading to inconsistent or ill-advised land use decisions. "The only group that is rather uniformly certain that the plan commission ought to be abolished," according to Weaver and Babcock, "is composed of the professional planners for whom the plan commission is an insulting interference."[31]

The indignities that advocates of hierarchy must suffer in local land use regulation can be seen in the administration of the variance, which frequently frustrates the designs of planners. If an individual is dissatisfied with the uses he is allowed in a particular zone, he may appeal for a variance, which theoretically is to be granted only in situations of "undue hardship" due to the unique character of the lot, not the circumstances of the owner. For example, if houses are to be thirty feet back from a property line but the shape of a particular lot makes it impossible to meet both the minimum-square-footage requirement and the setback requirement of the zoning regulations, a variance may be granted. Say, however, a family simply needs to add a room because their house is overcrowded by a growing collection of children. They would be out of luck. Requirements must be upheld and order preserved. If they wish to have reasonable room for a large family, they should move. Variances and rezoning (in which a parcel is officially placed in a different zone, creating what critics call "spot zoning") allow discretion to meet individual circumstance but create erratic and unpredictable patterns of exceptions. Although attention to individual needs may take the harsh edge off of hierarchy, the potential for favoritism is great, and variances are frequently condemned by both opponents[32] and proponents[33] of property rights.[34]

In defense of these chinks in the armor of hierarchy, Carol Rose has argued that variances and participatory procedures are tools of community control.[35] "While professionals view zoning as a failure of chaos, arbitrariness and inconsistency," Steele has agreed, "zoning is viewed by many community residents as direct citizen participation and local neighborhood control over vital community matters."[36] The planner must "play politics" if he is to see his plans effected, although this is not a role that fits comfortably in the hierarchical world.[37] Alan Altshuler has described the fate of one Minneapolis planner who began his career in 1929 when acquiescence to the wisdom of the planner was advocated by zoning proponents: "He alienated virtually every participant in the city's governmental system. By the postwar period, he had only one other professional planner under him. He never lost heart, however; he continued to issue reports and proposals right up to his 'encouraged' retirement in 1955."[38]

Planners, befitting a class of hierarchical elites, tend to see themselves as "repositor[ies] of frequently ignored wisdom"[39] who function as "an urban social conscience."[40] Rarely are they as forthright as Melvin Levin, who has written that "planners are bringing bad news to the unheeding; we resemble killjoy adults among frolicking children."[41] Frustrated by the constraints of hierarchy, the "frolicking children," such as an owner seeking to use her property, may look to the low-grid culture of libertarianism for an alternative vision of land and society, and it is to that perspective that we now turn.

LAND AND LIBERTY

Imagine that you are a skilled watch repairer who owns a small shop in a lower-middle-class, ethnically heterogeneous neighborhood in downtown Cincinnati, Ohio. You are far from wealthy, yet your modest business affords you many satisfactions, not the least of which is a long association with your customers, some of whom recall the days when your father, and even your grandfather, fixed their watches and exchanged pleasantries in this very same store. Then one day your hear disturbing rumors. The city council . . . is contemplating a proposal from a group of out-of-state developers to construct several luxury hotels, condominiums, and office buildings. . . . Lamentably, the block upon which your shop now stands lies precisely at the spot where the projected redevelopment will occur. Several months later, you receive a condemnation notice: your property will be taken from you. You are to receive "fair market value" and relocation costs, but no recompense for such psychic detriments as loss of business goodwill, possible loss of income due to the dismemberment of the community from which you drew your customers, and the incalculable losses associated with leaving a business you loved. This is eminent domain.
                                        —Ellen Frankel Paul[42]

The libertarian conception of social good and evil is virtually a mirror image of the hierarchical. For the founders of zoning, central control was a way to replace the nightmare of unregulated development with the serenity of order. The *police power*,[43] under which the government may regulate private property on behalf of the general welfare, and the power of eminent domain,[44] which allows the government to take property, are the chief legal tools by which state control is exercised. For libertarians like Paul, it is these coercive powers that destroy community and individual satisfaction, as in the fable of the watch repairer.[45] Libertarians tend to see themselves as the rightful heirs of the constitutional founders, wary of strong government. Liberty, not democracy, was the preeminent value of the creators of the American Republic, according to Martin Diamond: "For the founding generation it was liberty that was the comprehensive good, the end against which political things had to be measured; a democracy was only a form of government which, like any other form of government, had to prove itself adequately instrumental to the securing of liberty."[46]

From this perspective, the best way to serve the public is to promote the private. "In our society," Bernard Siegan has declared, "there is no greater public interest than the rights of the individual to be secure against the state."[47] Advocates of liberty like Paul[48] and Richard Epstein[49] argue that justice, logic, and the Constitution require a substantial retraction of the government tentacles reaching over private land use. Any diminution of the rights to possess, alienate, or use property is a taking that must be compensated by the government, according to Epstein. And these takings are unconstitutional if they are not strictly for "public use" (the explicit wording of the takings clause of the Fifth Amendment). Among the modern governmental powers that would fail Epstein's standard are wealth redistribution,[50] estate and gift taxes,[51] urban renewal,[52] rent control,[53] most zoning,[54] and minimum wage and maximum hour regulations.[55] "It will be said" Epstein has concluded, "that my position invalidates much of the twentieth century legislation, and so it does."[56]

Critics charge that individualism results in wasteful competition and leaves social needs unmet. The libertarian response is that freedom is not only best for individuals but best for society. The market encourages people to meet the social needs of others without the need to be especially altruistic by making social responsiveness economically rewarding.[57] And the decentralized control of an individualist system allows many avenues of activity to be pursued simultaneously, increasing opportunities for beneficial discoveries.[58] A role for planning remains in the libertarian ideal; the key distinction is that no one has the exclusive power to plan. "Self-governing societies," Vincent Ostrom has written, "depend upon the planning capabilities exercised by everyone—not by a select few."[59] Competitive planning limits the effects of the mistakes of any single person or business. For the libertarian, uncertainty is more an opportunity than a frustration.

In contrast with the free-market approach, "inherent in the push for land use planning and controls is the expectation that government knows best, can and should anticipate all of man's needs, and can see that they are met," according to William Moshofsky.[60] But, James Huffman and Reuben Plantico have argued, it is extremely difficult for government planners to approximate the complexity and speed of response of the market in calculating "social optimality."[61] The further planning is projected into the future, the greater the errors, according to Ostrom, because the constantly expanding knowledge base cannot be taken into account.[62] And central planning "means committing ourselves to only one guess about the future," Eamon Butler has complained.[63] Private users will learn from their experiences, according to the libertarian argument, and refine their plans for land use, while public planners are divorced from the responsibilities of ownership and the detailed feedback it provides. Consequently, Bernard Siegan has asserted, using planners "is akin to asking the blind to lead those who can see."[64]

Free enterprise may not always be serene or aesthetic, but, Siegan has argued, "human existence often requires the ugly as well as the beautiful, particularly when the ugly performs an essential function and leads to economic tranquility. And that is beautiful."[65] The most serious consequences of land use regulation, Moshofsky has written, are "the losses to society from land uses not permitted, from interference with private land stewardship, from resources never used, jobs not created, products never produced, and taxes not generated."[66]

Libertarians argue that public power can be dangerously unchecked as well as error-prone.[67] Public power can be used to fulfill desires without the need to pay, or even consider, social costs. Unlike the discipline of the market, M. Bruce Johnson has written, "no such check exists on the greed of environmentalists," who can use public control over resources to serve their own preferences.[68]

"Environmentalism" is not a part of the libertarian culture if it implies an obligation to consider what is good for nature separate from our preferences. The "free market environmentalism" school argues that there is nothing so unique about the environment that it cannot best be protected through the market pursuit of self-interest.[69] Individuals who are disturbed by effects on the environment can respond through the market, which will force them to pay the full social costs for their preferences.[70] Trees don't have property rights, but their owners do, and people who value trees can pay for them, as by banding together to purchase a nature preserve. Or private covenants restricting the use of private property, which for decades have been the primary means of controlling land use in Houston,[71] may be negotiated. Even for pollution a market solution may be possible: I might pay an industry owner to stop his pollution, or the owner might pay me for permission to pollute my property.

Because transaction costs may make it difficult for parties to negotiate exchanges and property rights may not be fully defined, some policy analysts, such as Milton Friedman, urge the creation of market incentives such as "pollution taxes" calculated to reflect social costs.[72] In a similar vein, Bjork[73] advocates the replacement of zoning with a system of payments for the right to reduce environmental quality. Such mechanisms are not as coercive as "command and control" regulation as they allow the individual or firm to make their own choices. But artificial fees still require complex calculations, leaving the risk of interference with social optimality.

As an alternative to buying out the neighborhood polluter, I might take her to court and seek monetary damages or an injunction to stop the invasion. Most libertarians, such as Murray Rothbard, would recognize a property right protecting against physical invasion of my property by pollution.[74] Such nuisance litigation may not be as dependent on individual bargaining as negotiated contracts, but it can provide more clear protection of property rights. And it is far superior, from the libertarian perspective, to regulation, which can prohibit whole categories of land use based on speculation that some of those land uses might someday cause harm. Court damages, in contrast, are not available until actual harm has been proved. An injunction may prevent the harm but runs a greater risk of forbidding activity that would be legitimate.

Even the housing needs of the poor arguably can be met best without governmental control. The poor, the libertarian argument goes, need housing, but not necessarily new housing. Rather than construct public housing or prevent builders from selling their units at market prices, communities should encourage the unrestrained development of housing in response to market demand. As qualified home buyers move into new homes, they will move out of their old ones, and the housing opportunities will "filter down" to those most in need. A survey (cited by Siegan) conducted at the University of Michigan found that each creation of a new housing unit resulted in 3.5 relocations. Imposition of government coercion, such as rent control, is argued to be not only unjust (depriving property owners of their rights) but also foolish, as it will only discourage the production of new housing and the maintenance of existing housing.[75]

The unpredictable society preferred by the libertarian is not for the risk-averse. Many will be the mistakes, but, it is argued, greater will be the social rewards. Such an experimental approach implies that nature will be as tolerant as our neighbors should be. The "nature benign" myth described by Holling[76] best captures libertarian optimism regarding the environment. From this perspective, we live in a natural valley shaped like a bowl. We can knock about and experiment with the environment without worry of going over the brink and destroying mankind. Nature is presumed to be as adaptable as man.

The claims of the libertarian purist are rather grandiose: "Only we offer technology without technocracy, growth without pollution, liberty without chaos, law without tyranny, the defense of property rights in one's person *and* in one's material possessions," according to Rothbard. "Liberty has never been fully tried in the modern world; libertarians now propose to fulfill the American dream and the world dream of liberty and prosperity for all mankind."[77]

In this shining utopia, there are no transaction costs to impede voluntary bargaining and efficient exchange, no resource deprivations severe enough to subvert personal freedom. But libertarianism is not the only cultural challenger to hierarchy. I will next turn to a cultural approach to land use that seeks to reconcile the libertarian concern for the individual with the hierarchical acceptance of public control.[78] In doing so, it creates an alternative social vision rooted in the pursuit of equality that is fundamentally at odds with both libertarianism and hierarchy.

THE PURSUIT OF SOCIAL AND ENVIRONMENTAL EQUALITY

Respect for liberty implies expansion rather than restriction of collective control over the constitutive rules that govern the allocation or distribution of property.

—C. Edwin Baker[79]

Egalitarianism seeks to reconcile the libertarian concern for the individual with the hierarchical acceptance of public control, to combine, in other words, the low grid of libertarianism with the high group of hierarchy. In doing so, it creates an alternative social vision rooted in the pursuit of equality that is fundamentally at odds with both libertarianism and hierarchy.

Traditional planning and conservation are offensive for three reasons: First, they place control in the hands of specialists, divorcing the common citizen from control over her environment. Second, they can perpetuate, intentionally or not, social inequality. And third, they take a paternalistic attitude toward nature. All three offenses are, in the language of cultural theory, aspects of *grid*, the imposition of constraints (external to the individual) that limit opportunity. These criticisms mirror the complaints of libertarians, with whom egalitarians share a disdain for high-grid cultures.

Yet egalitarians also decry the libertarian indifference to the larger group, to the social consequences of individual actions and the "natural" inequalities that can arise in the absence of centralized control. They seek to combine the social responsibility of hierarchy with freedom of libertarianism, to be both high group and low grid. Jennifer Nedelsky, for example, criticizes private property as an impediment to participatory democracy yet also values individual autonomy.[80]

Egalitarians share a commitment to two fundamental goals: broad participation in decision making, as in regulatory procedures, and greater substantive equality of resources, including those in land. Disagreement over how those goals are to be reached and which goal should take precedence divides egalitarians into two camps: the social idealists, best represented by the "deep ecology" proponents, and the pragmatic egalitarians, who emphasize using the power of the state, in essence a bargain with hierarchy, to restructure society.

Egalitarians share with hierarchists a faith in public control of land use. But reliance on specialized expertise is troubling, as it creates inequalities of power. What is desired is an "ongoing dialogue in a community of equals."[81] Certainly some of the reforms in administrative law, such as the broadening of legal standing to intervene in suits, the public funding of adversarial groups, the expansion of notice and hearing requirements, and the requirement of administrative responses to public comments, have progressed in this direction.[82] The pursuit of equality of participation can be daunting—often making it very difficult for decision making to be binding, as some citizens may change their minds—or delegated to specialists. "The demands for participation," Jerry Mashaw has observed, "begin to look like a demand that the administrative state be dismantled, and that all decisions instead be made by some combination of popular referendum, adversary adjudication, and negotiation to consensus."[83] Regulatory proceedings in recent years have become increasingly drawn out and complex as everyone with a claim to be affected by a decision has their say.

At its best, the process allows an informed deliberation about preferences and produces a decision accurately reflecting community sentiment. In theory, when all citizens have an equal influence over a regulatory outcome, they will choose a solution that benefits all fairly. In what Richard Stewart calls the "interest representation model,"[84] the voice of the property owner can be drowned out by other claimants. "This ideology," according to Patrick McAuslan, a British scholar of land use regulation, "denies the property-owner any special place in participation; such an interest is merely one of a great number to be considered in the democratic process of decision-making and by no means the most important."[85] If there are no rights tied to ownership that merit special protection, this is not troublesome. If land uses should reflect group preferences, there is no reason to vest an owner with privileges just because his name is on the deed.

Environmental protection is to a large degree inescapably hierarchical; the trees and toads cannot speak for themselves,[86] so it is incumbent upon man to look after the inferior creatures of the wild. But an egalitarian rationale for environmentalism emphasizes the injustice of man's domination over nature.[87] Essentially, the group within which equality should be maintained is extended to include the natural world. O'Riordan notes there are two distinct strands of environmentalism: the "technocentrism" of hierarchy and the egalitarian "ecocentrism."[88] Proponents of the latter view "visualize *Homo Sapiens* as part of a 'seamless web of life' from which he cannot extricate himself, so any attempt to stand apart from (and hence dominate) nature is a senseless act of arrogance that is doomed to failure."[89]

Both man and nature can be liberated through the proper intentional community,[90] as advocated by the "deep ecologists."[91] As the journalist David Gancher describes it, deep ecology "reduces a vast amount of philosophical meandering to two basic premises: 1) self-realization by humans will bring us into harmony with Nature, and 2) 'Biocentric Equality,' the belief that all Nature—including worms, germs and rocks—have equal value."[92] Self-realization and

biocentric equality are, according to Arne Naess, a Norwegian philosopher and environmentalist who first used the term *deep
ecology*,"[93] "ultimate norms which are themselves not derivable
from other principles or intuitions."[94] These are the bedrock principles, precisely what we would expect in the low-grid, low-group
box of the cultural model: the belief that humans (and nature) can
and should be both free and equal.

The achievement of social and environmental justice become
inseparable. "It is the theme of social justice which is central to the
environmentalist debate" O'Riordan declared.[95] By freeing nature,
man frees himself, and, conversely, if he frees himself, he will treat
nature properly. "The environmental problems of technocratic-
industrial societies are," according to Devall and Sessions, "coming
to be understood as a crisis of character and of culture."[96] Solutions
that might prove beneficial for the environment are seen as inadequate unless they also promote social equality, autonomy, and community. For example, Devall and Sessions reject the free-market
approach (turning natural resources over to private owners and fully
defining property rights) because it is "human-centered,"[97] even
though they acknowledge it might eliminate the "tragedy of the
commons."[98] Similarly, technological solutions are appropriate
only if they are "compatible with the growth of autonomous, self-
determining individuals in nonhierarchical communities."[99]

Openness to nature is essential for human development, according to O'Riordan. "Contact with open spaces and natural experiences is regarded as an essential part of existence, without which
the individual will never achieve full human potential."[100] This
contact is best achieved in small, self-sufficient communities,
which not coincidentally also best promote social equality.[101] The
ideal of the egalitarian environmentalist is, in O'Riordan's words,
"the 'human-scale' self-reliant community connected to, but not
dependent on, thousands like it scattered across the face of the
land . . . living in harmony with his natural surroundings in a class-
less society."[102]

This marriage of social and natural equality can be seen in the
platform of the Greens, a loose political coalition gaining popularity
in America,[103] which includes "an ecological view of humans as
part of the community of nature, respect for the rights of other species, local responsibility, nonviolence and what they call ecofemin-
ism."[104] The Greens seek to practice what they preach, rooting their
environmentalism in a consensual, egalitarian process. According
to a platform published by a Green group in California, "We conduct

all our meetings according to the principles of consensus democracy, emphasizing unanimous or near-unanimous agreement on all decisions. No representative may make decisions on behalf of the Greens without the approval of the entire membership. We encourage the use of consensus democracy in all social, economic and political institutions."[105] Decision making by consensus can be time-consuming and tedious, as disparate opinions are gradually molded into a common view. Not surprisingly, it works best in small groups that already share certain values, such as the Green party and the "affinity groups" used in antinuclear protests.

The egalitarian idealist, like her libertarian compatriot, sees her culture as a universal panacea. According to Amory Lovins, ecotechnology

> simultaneously offers jobs for the unemployed, capital for business people, environmental protection for conservationists, enhanced national security for the military, opportunities for small business to innovate and for big business to recycle itself, existing technologies for the secular, a rebirth of spiritual values for the religious, traditional values for the old, radical reforms for the young, world order and equity for globalists, energy independence for isolationists, civil rights for liberals, states' rights for conservatives.[106]

In the world of practical politics, the compatibility of social and environmental equality is not always apparent. "There is a powerful almost existential urge," notes O'Riordan, who is sympathetic to egalitarian environmentalism, "to safeguard objects of physical and environmental meaning regardless of the distributive consequences."[107] Environmental protection can raise the costs of economic development, shrinking the pie that feeds the poor as well as the rich. Those who are socioeconomically deprived may put a higher priority on food and housing than communing with nature. As A. Lawrence Chickering asked, "Why are there no poor people in the Sierra Club?"[108]

At an Amherst conference of the Greens, Murray Bookchin assailed the socially exclusive connotations of deep ecology. "Among those who claim to be ecologists, Bookchin said, are 'barely disguised racists, survivalists, macho Daniel Boones and outright social reactionaries.' " Deep ecologists " 'talk about biocentrism, meaning all species are equal. I'm a social ecologist; I put human beings first.' "[109] Bookchin's comments created quite a stir at the conference, offending the consensual ethic of the Greens. "Back-room efforts by some of the participants to persuade Bookchin to be 'less violent,' " reports Harold Gilliam, a journalist supportive of the Greens, "resulted in a hugfest, with all participants smiling broadly and Bookchin vowing in the future to discuss differences of opinion 'without being too sharp.' "[110]

Even if social and environmental equality are ultimately compatible, how the ideal social state is to be reached is a bit mysterious. In the practical world of policy disputes, egalitarians tend to advocate using the power of the state to reduce disparities. The policy preferences of egalitarianism—social equality and environmental protection—have been forcefully pursued by enlisting the courts and legislatures in their cause.

At the community level, which best combines the consensual possibilities of small size with potential control over resources, land use planning can be a weapon against inequalities of resources and power. A British commission on planning, for example, urged that "planning can help towards a more equitable distribution of life-chances and social welfare among different sections of society."[111] Land use controls may be used to increase substantive equality by imposing special burdens on property owners and providing special protections for lower-income land users. For example, the city of San Jose enacted a rent control ordinance, upheld by the U.S. Supreme Court, that could require landlords to charge lower rent for poor tenants.[112]

The leading example of the push for equality in land use is the demand for an end to "exclusionary" zoning and the adoption of inclusionary techniques. Zoning is seen as the linchpin that holds together a system of social inequality. "We cannot solve a single one of our other domestic problems," Linowes and Allensworth assert, "without launching a direct attack on community zoning."[113] Restrictive land use regulations constrain the freedom of all land users, but egalitarians are particularly concerned with the fortunes of those near the bottom of the economic ladder. "Exclusionary zoning," according to Paul and Linda Davidoff, "may be defined as the complex of zoning practices which results in closing suburban housing and land markets to low- and moderate-income families. All regulations are, in a sense, exclusionary. For example, they are exclusive in that they restrict degrees of individual freedom." But such coercion is "not of concern here."[114] Only limits on the rights of the poor should be termed "exclusionary," Norman Williams has argued; other groups may be only "highly restricted."[115]

The first step in breaking down exclusionary barriers is to remove regulations, such as minimum lot size and floor-size requirements, that make it difficult to erect inexpensive housing. But equality can demand more: Municipalities can be required to accommodate their "fair share" of the region's poor by building housing, subsidizing rents, and requiring builders to sell units at designated prices.[116] If housing choices were left to the market, inequalities between communities could still result, as different socioeconomic groups might prefer different packages of amenities. Equality at the community level is important, as it provides more equal educational, economic, and social opportunities and makes remaining inequalities more local and thus visible rather than insulating them in islands of exclusion. Market indicators of where individuals would choose to live, therefore, are not relevant. According to Yannacone, Rahenkamp, and Corchine: "Fairshare calculations (of regional housing needs) are based on the actual capacity of a community to accommodate development rather than pro rata extrapolations of immediate local demand."[117] Communities that already have their "share" of the poor can exclude latecomers, they argued.

Each community should be roughly identical, under what Ellickson and Tarlock in their land use casebook have called, rather irreverently, the "Waring Blender" model.[118] It is important to put new housing for the poor in all communities, Anthony Downs has argued. This would "block the basic middle-class escape pattern [by convincing] middle- and upper-income households that they cannot escape less affluent neighbors by moving somewhere else."[119] Daniel Mandelker has pointed out that the demand for equal communities is fundamentally a moral argument, a statement of how people ought to live. The distribution of jobs makes it questionable whether such an arrangement would actually serve the material interests of the poor, working class.[120]

As democratic control is of great concern to egalitarians, reliance on judicial coercion creates an ethical dilemma: Is it just to force communities to be equal? Some commentators resolve the dilemma by arguing that courts are more democratic than local governments. The dictates by the Supreme Court of New Jersey to the township of Mount Laurel "reassert[ed] . . . democratic values," according to Norman Williams.[121] The argument is that if elected governments are perpetuating inequality, as by zoning out low-income housing, democracy is in such a state of disrepair that the courts must intervene on behalf of excluded groups; true democracies would exclude no one. The author of a note in the *Harvard Law Review* dismissed the argument that state courts should be constrained by fear of excessive judicial activism and urged them to "reconceive their purpose in terms of elaborating and employing a theory of majoritarian, rather than antimajoritarian, review."[122]

In contrast, local governments are portrayed as oligarchic. Zoning is the creation of a self-interested elite, according to Linowes and Allensworth: "Zoning is king—and it is no less ruthless than the monarchs we read about in history books. It serves class ends, it serves an elite, it is used to advance the interests of the few."[123] True, the arguments of the early proponents of zoning have elitist implications, and zoning can have discriminatory effects. But zoning plans must be adopted by popular vote. A majority of voters in the municipalities have voluntarily chosen to live with land use restrictions, and as Linowes and Allensworth note, "a majority of the population in the nation's metropolitan areas now resides in the suburbs."[124] Exclusive land use controls have been adopted by local majorities, and those populations compose a majority of the region.[125] Zoning may perpetuate inequality and deprive fundamental rights of property owners and users, but it is hard to argue that it is not democratic.

Justifying coercion in the name of democracy is important because in other ways the egalitarian movement is fundamentally liberal. That is, the freedom of the individual is the justification for the political order. Coercion is justified when its absence would leave in place a system of private property rights that by legitimating inequality of resources, egalitarians argue, impairs freedom. For example, although he agrees with libertarians that property can play an important role in protecting preferred freedoms, C. Edwin Baker, quoted at the beginning of this section, concludes that freedom requires collective control over distribution of property.[126]

In place of property rights to exclusive control of material resources, egalitarians urge entitlements to basic levels of material support. Instead of rights to the fruits of one's own labors, one may have rights to the fruits of others, with the transfers effected by the central government. This is the "new property" of Charles Reich,[127] which has received at least procedural constitutional protection in the courts—rights to financial support and education, health services, and a clean environment.

While traditional property rights are rejected, personal property remains an important concept in egalitarianism. Egalitarians seek to distinguish rights of property that contribute to individual freedom without depriving others of freedom from those that impede the freedom of others. Property rights that protect free expression, for example, are valued. Margaret Jane Radin would protect those property rights that she perceives as promoting "personhood,"[128] while approving of regulations such as rent control.[129] The double standard of rights that has dominated constitutional doctrine since the New Deal is the epitome of egalitarian jurisprudence: It seeks to do what libertarians claim is impossible—protect personal rights while leaving economic rights vulnerable to legislatures. Separating "economic" and other private property rights is not always easy, however, and the expansion of personal rights is contributing to a renewal of property rights, as I will discuss in Chapter 8.

POLITICAL CULTURES AND LAND USE REGULATION

Social transformations do not inevitably follow from environmental prescriptions; rather, our environmental arguments may be vehicles for promoting our preferred way of life. As Eric Steele has observed, "Zoning provides a forum, frames the issues, and provides a vocabulary for communicating about normative conflict."[130] We are likely to stress the problems with land use and be receptive to solutions that are compatible with our basic cultural orientation. Even when land use disputes are caught up in discussion of peak-traffic loads, energy-efficient construction techniques, and sewer-system capacities, issues of individual freedom and social accountability are at stake.

The three cultures of land use that I have described are ideal types, not likely to be found in unadulterated form in the everyday world of land use regulation. Hierarchies are never entirely controlled or static; libertarians usually endorse some constraints (such as compliance with the discretionary judgments of judicial authorities in contract disputes) or group awareness (e.g., responsibility for family).[131] As an egalitarian group on a large scale is difficult to maintain, arguments for equality are often aligned with a competing culture, such as an alliance of liberty and equality against the constraints of hierarchy or a resort to the coercive power of the state, associated with hierarchical culture, to compel greater equality. This latter course can create a predicament that Steinberger, following Rousseau, calls "forced to be free."[132]

Despite the commonality that may arise through expediency or uneasy accommodation of conflicting values, profound differences remain between the cultural perspectives in the everyday world of land use disputes. The three cultures—libertarian, egalitarian, and hierarchical—have distinctive ideas about the nature of man and the environment, and the proper extent of individual freedom to use land. Libertarians will emphasize the right of the individual to act freely and to respond to land use problems caused by others on an individual basis through private negotiations, covenants, and the law of trespass and nuisance. What they will not accept is the prior prohibition of an entire set of land uses, on the assumption that those uses might at some future time impinge on the rights of others. Advocates of hierarchy will place their faith in centralized expertise rather than direct control by individual owners or the lay public and will seek to anticipate land use problems and establish predictable, orderly land use patterns. Egalitarians will prefer public control of land use decisions as long as that power is used to promote equality. Expressive and privacy rights, which are not seen as creating economic inequality, will be protected.

Now I will turn to how the conflicts between these three cultures are reconciled through constitutional litigation, which structures the regulatory environment that decides the reach of freedom for the property owner. After a brief historical review, I will analyze the doctrines developed in the last decade in the high courts of the United States where property rights are emerging after a long hibernation; of California, widely known for judicial abstention from the regulatory field; and Pennsylvania, considered by many commentators to be especially sympathetic to landowner rights.

Chapter 3

The Demise of
Landowner Rights

If a lawyer defending a restriction [on land use
rights] was struck dumb as he rose before the
court, and could think of nothing to say, the
restriction would be in some real trouble—but
as long as he could manage to keep on making
a noise like a lawyer, all would be well.
                                —Norman Williams

In some mythical past, property and economic rights were facades used by the Supreme Court to subvert the will of the people
by striking down enlightened social legislation that offended its economic ideology. Leading justices of the Court before the New Deal
enlightenment "professed, with little qualification, an economic
creed," according to Walton Hamilton, and "read 'free competition'
into the constitution."[1] Substantive due process[2] has long been regarded as a judicial Frankenstein, a creature with a life of its own
that wreaked havoc in society and imperiled its creator, the Supreme
Court. Mere mention of *Lochner v. New York,*[3] the infamous case
that became the symbol for an era of judicial excess, can draw mur-
murs of disdain from legal scholars. *Lochnerian* is often the most
damning label used by justices.[4]

There is a grain of truth to the reputation of the "old court,"[5]
as it did strike down many legislative initiatives.[6] Yet these decisions stemmed from the upholding of basic rights, particularly "lib-

erty of contract,"[7] not simply a judicial preference for one economic theory over another, just as the modern right of privacy has arisen from judicial concern for individual freedom.[8] And even during the era of liberty of contract, "far more exercises of the police power (some very stringent and costly to business and industry) were sustained than invalidated."[9] The Supreme Court before the New Deal, as Martin Shapiro has shown, "was not a blind, fanatic champion of laissez-faire."[10] Even in *Allgeyer v. Louisiana*, the case that started the substantive due process era, Justice Peckham acknowledged that "individual liberty of action must give way to the greater right of the collective people in the assertion of well-defined policy, designed and intended for the general welfare."[11] The sin of the *Lochner*-era court in the eyes of modern legal scholars may be not that it never sustained legislation but that it deigned to uphold private property rights at all.

Decisions by the Supreme Court upholding regulation prior to the 1930s were by no means trivial. The 1926 decision[12] (authored by none other than Justice Sutherland, one of the "reactionary" Four Horsemen) that upheld zoning is still the Court's most profound decision upholding restrictions on landowner rights. In that case, zoning in Euclid, Ohio, was challenged by an owner of vacant property in a predominantly industrial area. The town had zoned the property residential, destroying 75 percent of its market value. A federal court invalidated the ordinance, and the judge assailed the imposition of what I term social hierarchy: "The purpose . . . is really to regulate the mode of living of persons. . . . The result to be accomplished is to classify population and segregate them according to their income or situation in life."[13] Ambler Realty argued that in cultural terms, liberty trumps hierarchy: "That our cities should be made beautiful and orderly is, of course, in the highest degree desirable, but it is even more important that our people should remain free."[14] But on appeal to the high court, government regulation won the day over the individual liberty advocated by Ambler Realty.

Justice Sutherland reasoned that zoning was in the public interest because it was essentially an extension of the common law that prohibits nuisances: "A nuisance may be merely a right thing in the wrong place,—like a pig in the parlor instead of the barnyard."[15] But it is not clear who owns the pig and who the parlor, and thus whether any public nuisance exists. If I keep my own pig in my parlor, it is not a nuisance. Indeed, a pig in a parlor is a rather fashionable pet these days. If my pig prefers your parlor but you do not prefer my pig in your parlor, then it is a nuisance. But such nuances were ignored by Justice Sutherland; any pig in any parlor is a nuisance, not just those that invade another person's property right (the classical liberal conception of nuisance). Offending the new hierarchy of land use was sufficient to be condemned as a nuisance; pigs, factories, and homes would now be required to stay where they belonged. *Euclid* was important not only because it sustained zoning but also because its rationale signaled the acceptance of hierarchical controls by the highest court of the land.

In an era of frequent court rebukes to regulatory attempts, *Euclid* was "the most incomprehensible decision of this decade," according to Bernard Siegan.[16] But *Euclid* was not an errant decision. Indeed, it was a harbinger of the silence to come: After *Nectow v. Cambridge*[17] (1928), in which court struck down the application of a constitutionally valid zoning ordinance to a particular piece of property,[18] the court refused to even hear another zoning case until 1974. It would be forty-nine years until substantive due process would reappear in federal land use doctrine, this time in the more fashionable form of a right of privacy.[19]

Any doubts that judicial protection of landowner rights was passé were erased during the New Deal. Beginning in 1937,[20] the Court declined to look closely at legislation for abuses of "economic" rights. The following year, in *United States v. Carolene Products*,[21] the court effectively announced that not all constitutional rights were created equal. "Regulatory legislation affecting ordinary commercial transactions [that is, property or economic interests] is not to be pronounced unconstitutional," wrote Justice Stone, "unless . . . it is of such a character as to preclude the assumption that it rests upon some rational basis within the knowledge and experience of the legislators."[22] The basis for legislation need not be evident: "Any state of facts either known or which could reasonably be assumed" would suffice.[23] This is an extraordinarily lenient standard, tantamount to abdication of judicial review, and for forty years no governmental action was invalidated under this standard of minimal rationality.[24] If that was all there was to the story, modern constitutional law would be of little consequence, and many constitutional scholars would be teaching torts or selling cars. But in the famous footnote 4, Stone carved out categories of rights that the court would continue to protect: "when legislation appears on its face to be within a specific prohibition of the Constitution, such as those of the first ten amendments"; when legislation "restricts . . . political processes; and when legislation is "prejudice[d] against discrete and insular minorities," such as "religious, or national, or racial minorities"[25] No specific standard of review for these exceptions was articulated in *Carolene Products*, but in time they would become protected by the "strict scrutiny" standard, which requires a showing that a restriction is necessary to achieve a compelling governmental objective. Under such a high standard, legislation is almost invariably invalidated.[26]

In the decades after *Carolene Products*, property rights were relegated to the constitutional wastebasket of the "any conceivable rational basis test," as the minimal level of scrutiny is often described. All that would be required to win Court approval of restrictions on property rights would be to "make a noise like a lawyer."[27] "After chastisement by President Roosevelt," Martin Shapiro wrote with a healthy dose of sarcasm, "the Supreme Court saw the truth. And the truth was that the Court should never, never interfere in the realm of economic policy making. . . . Instead, it took on the approved New Deal task of protecting the constitutional rights of the underdog, and these rights were civil and personal, not economic. And so the Court lived happily ever after."[28]

Carolene Products marked the emergence of the modern alliance between hierarchy and egalitarianism in support of strong government. The libertarian vision of a unified sphere of rights protecting the individual was torn in two; personal and political rights deemed essential in the egalitarian ideal would be preserved, while property rights were separated from person and left vulnerable to hierarchical control. The double standard of constitutional rights has enjoyed remarkable popularity, stature, and influence since the New Deal. "Rarely has a Supreme Court doctrinal pronouncement been more transparently political," declared Shapiro, who argued that the double standard provided a rationale for the court to reward the friends of the New Deal and punish enemies.[29] The unequal protection of the law has often been defended, either as constitutionally justified[30] or at least as practical policy. Robert McCloskey raised a voice of concern about the double standard, only to conclude that it was just as well to let sleeping rights lie to conserve scarce judicial resources for more important matters: "It seems best that the cause of economic rights be left by the Supreme Court to lie in its uneasy grave."[31] Even when property rights were acknowledged to have constitutional basis, they were considered too trivial for attention.

For nearly a half-century, the Supreme Court ignored the great legal battles over the steady advance of governmental control of land use.[32] Owners, neighbors, and planners fought before zoning boards and city councils in communities across the nation and occasionally resorted to the state courts. But the Court, having learned its New Deal lesson, stayed above the fray, content to let governments regulate without constitutional check, clinging to what Norman Williams called a "mistaken . . . belief that no basic values are involved."[33] Between 1928 and 1974, the Supreme Court did not hear arguments on a single zoning case. Only two cases involving land use disputes were heard, and both resulted in government victories. In *Berman v. Parker*,[34] the Court upheld public condemnation of private commercial property to be conveyed to another private owner for redevelopment, and in *Goldblatt v. Hempstead*, the Court approved a regulation that effectively closed down, without compensation, a gravel operation because it was judged to be a nuisance due to recent residential growth in the area, even though "the ordinance completely prohibits a beneficial use to which the property has previously been devoted."[35] The spirit of *Berman v. Parker* is aptly captured in a dictum by Justice Douglas that is frequently and fondly quoted by governmental planners, attorneys, and deferent judges: "Once the legislature has spoken, the public interest is well-nigh conclusive."[36] Even though the Constitution limits governmental condemnations of private property to "public uses," for the Court any public purpose would do, and the judgment of the legislature would not be questioned. "The concept of the public welfare is broad and inclusive," wrote Justice Douglas in deference to governmental control. "The values it represents are spiritual as well as physical, aesthetic as well as monetary. It is within the power of the legislature to determine that the community should be beautiful as well as healthy, spacious as well as clean, well-balanced as well as carefully patrolled."[37]

As in *Euclid*, the Court used language sweeping in its implications, in its embrace of the norms of the hierarchical culture. It would now be the prerogative of the state to decide what is "aesthetic," what is "well-balanced," and to enforce its preferences by forbidding or seizing the ugly and the profane. *Berman* made clear that private property could be taken for any reason, without the approval of the owner, as long as compensation was paid. In lieu of condemnation, a government could restrict uses of private property severely without any compensation or worry that the Court might invalidate its restrictions. The implicit message of the Court throughout this era of acquiescence was that in land use regulation, the king can do no wrong.

Throughout the decades of Court abstention, one anomaly remained: The 1922 precedent of *Pennsylvania Coal Co. v. Mahon*,[38] a relic of the dark ages of activism, had never been overturned. Occasionally the Court would reverently recite Justice Holmes's famous pronouncement that "when regulation goes too far it will be recognized as a taking."[39] But for sixty-five years after *Mahon* no regulatory restriction on land use was declared a taking by the Court.[40]

The sole exception to the Court's abdication of property rights has come when a government sought physical access to private property without paying for it. The Court has been willing to protect the right of exclusion, that is, the right to sit on one's property without being disturbed by unwanted visitors. Occasionally, the Court has held that physical invasions government constitute compensable takings. Frequent low-level flights were found to constitute a taking, comparable to a physical invasion of land, of the airspace above a chicken farm in *U.S. v. Causby*.[41] The noise and lights of the military aircraft disturbed the Causbys and caused great havoc among their feathered flock, leading 150 chickens to suicide. In *Kaiser Aetna v. United States*,[42] the Court ruled that the federal government must pay compensation if it wished to require public access to a private marina, which the owner had created from a private pond adjoining a bay. The Court's defense of the right of exclusion, while it would permit any restriction on use or compensated seizure, has seemed a bit ludicrous a times. The Court, for example, stood by the right of an apartment building owner to keep television cables intended for tenant use from being placed on the outside walls of the building.[43] But other than keeping the neighbors off your property, there has been no constitutional guarantee that you could use your land.

"Constitutional protections," Douglas Kmiec lamented, "have proven largely illusory for most landowners,"[44] Some scholars have expressed alarm over the collapse of landowner rights,[45] but it has been viewed by most academics as a welcome, perhaps even inevitable development. Joseph Sax gradually weakened his support for landowner rights,[46] finally declaring that private property was disappearing altogether.[47] For Sax, private property has been a "functional failure" resulting in "incorrect" land use decisions that obstruct public values.[48] The decline in property rights may be a natural response to a supposedly increasing resource scarcity, according to David Callies.[49] To Hans Linde, a nationally respected justice on the Oregon Supreme Court, although regulation of property "stirs special atavistic memories of the feudal and pioneering past,"[50] it is now obsolete. Herman Schwartz has argued that property rights should remain in disrepute, despite recent rumblings that property may be important after all:

> In constitutional law, property rights are now like the ugly duckling before it became a swan. They receive very little constitutional protection against legislative or administrative interference. . . . In the fairy tale, the little duckling became a beautiful swan because it really was a swan and had been one all along. Property rights, however, are not and were not intended to be the swan of constitutional law—they really are just ducks, after all, despite all the quacking.[51]

Private ownership of property has been portrayed as a curious, archaic institution advocated only by those who view the world through eighteenth-century glasses. For decades, many state court justices have been accused of wearing such blinders. In states where substantive due process survived the *Carolene Products* purge, "Justice Peckham and other . . . men of the 'old' court . . . still have their disciples," Dick Howard bemoaned.[52] Alas, wrote Monrad Paulsen, "the ideals which these state courts value are those of Nineteenth Century Liberalism."[53] Gradually from the 1940s through the 1960s, the double standard of rights seeped into the jurisprudence of state courts[54] as state after state took "a major (and a necessary) step forward [toward] faith in local autonomy"[55] by refusing to give serious review to violations of property rights. "The principle theme in American planning law for the last thirty years," wrote Norman Williams in 1974, "has been the gradual spread among the state courts of the implications of the constitutional revolution of 1937."[56]

No sooner had state courts adopted the deferential fashion of the New Deal court than they began to be criticized for capitulating to national legal standards.[57] The last major treatise to give significant attention to state constitutional law was published in 1927,[58] and in the intervening decades "we have allowed American constitutional law to become lopsided. . . . The rule of state law is no longer itself taken seriously."[59] John Frank has complained that state constitutional law "has tended to be a sort of pallid metooism."[60] Criticism of the debased stature of state courts has come from justices of the courts as well. The state high courts had become, according to Stanley Mosk of the California court, "mere bus stops on the route from trial courts to the Supreme Court."[61] The state supreme courts had become superfluous to the constitutional process, and Shirley Abrahamson has written that when she joined the Wisconsin Supreme Court, the reaction of friends was "What's a nice person like you, interested in civil rights and civil liberties, doing on a state supreme court?"[62]

Now that state courts had learned to defer to the national court, why were academics and justices calling on the courts to reassert themselves? Because the U.S. high court was no longer held in unqualified esteem by liberals. Under Chief Justice Burger,[63] the Court had extended the liberal initiatives of the Warren Court into new areas, such as affirmative action[64] and busing.[65] But the court did not always move as quickly, and certainly not with as much fervor as its predecessor. In other areas, particularly criminal law, the court began to draw limits around the landmark decisions of the Warren Court.[66] The new appreciation for the state courts went hand in hand with criticism of the federal court. The Court had "abandoned . . . the role of keeper of the nation's conscience," declared Donald Wilkes,[67] and a decade later John Frank's prognosis was grim:

> Criminal suspects will know less about their constitutional rights than they did in the recent past, homes will have less protection against warrantless searches, and the wall of separation between church and state will have only 5–4 support. The female majority of the population will have to wait decades for complete equality under the federal constitution, and racial and ethnic minorities will suffer even more.[68]

With judicial ardor cooling at the national level, critics of the court began turning to state courts "where the rights of free citizens may find refuge,"[69] urging the courts to use their own constitutions to go beyond federal doctrine in protecting preferred rights. "The retreat of the Burger Court," according to Peter and Lawrence Galie, "has caused enlightened state supreme courts to ground their constitutional decisions on their own governing law."[70] Justice Brennan, now frequently in the minority on the Court, joined the chorus of encouragement: "State courts no less than federal are and ought to be the guardians of our liberties."[71] As Dick Howard has noted, there is a certain irony in the enthusiastic embrace of state judicial power by advocates of political and social equality. "In one respect it has taken a curious form—the invocation of a kind of states' rights by people for whom that philosophy might seem alien."[72] For decades state political leaders were the symbols of resistance to the mandates of federal law and doctrine, and state courts were perceived as reactionary backwaters. Now that the egalitarian campaign had weakened at the national level, however, the diversity of federalism began to seem more attractive.[73] By 1985, there had been more than 250 state court decisions that relied on state constitutional provisions to go beyond Supreme Court constitutional standards.[74] By basing their decisions on "independent state grounds," state justices could make their decisions immune from federal reversal.

Given the reluctance of the Court to say a word against land use regulation, there was a large void waiting to be filled by the newly activist state courts. State courts, Edward Sullivan wrote, "are becoming increasingly sensitive to the relationship between zoning practices and a wide range of contemporary problems."[75] For commentators concerned about forging a more egalitarian society, zoning and other hierarchical land use controls were no longer seen as entirely benevolent or irrelevant to the quest.[76] Norman Williams has praised the entry of at least some state courts during the 1960s and 1970s into the era that he calls "sophisticated judicial review . . . wiser, more skeptical and more realistic."[77] The danger, from the perspective of egalitarian commentators, was that the resurgence of state courts, coinciding with their critiques of land use controls, might lend legitimacy to the old economic and property rights they disdained—substantive due process and limits on governmental takings of private property. Marlin Smith complained that "substantive due process is alive, well and living in the state courts. Indeed, in Illinois it is running amuck."[78] New Jersey in particular has won acclaim from Norman Williams for its attempts to change land use regulation without resurrecting property rights.[79]

As the abdication of property rights seeped from the Supreme Court down through the state courts, two countertrends developed: The stature of the state courts rose, and land use regulation came under increasing criticism from an egalitarian perspective. In the next few chapters, we will see what the consequences were for the protection of property rights in the 1980s. We will begin our travels through the dense forests of land use litigation with a stop in Pennsylvania where the older tradition of providing substantive protection for landowner rights has survived. I will compare the exclusionary zoning cases of Pennsylvania with those of the New

Jersey court, which has cut an egalitarian swath through the deferent doctrines of hierarchical land use controls. Developments in California, where judicial deference reigns supreme, will be considered next. Finally, I will examine doctrinal changes in the Supreme Court, which has begun to unearth the property rights it buried sixty years ago.

PART II: LANDOWNER RIGHTS IN STATE AND NATION

Chapter 4

Cultural Conflict in Pennsylvania and New Jersey

*The zoning law of Pennsylvania is definitely
the oddest of any major state.*
                        —Norman Williams

Pennsylvania is a state of contrasts and continuity. The birth-place of the nation, Independence Hall, is surrounded by the high rises, congestion, and gaudiness of modern commercial Philadel-phia. To the west of the dense suburbs of Philadelphia lie the fertile farmland of Lancaster County, home to Old Order Mennonites and Amish, and the state capital of Harrisburg, known to many for its proximity to the Three Mile Island nuclear power plant. Farther still are the dark hollows of the Allegheny Mountains and the suburbs and hamlets of the Pittsburgh area, producer of steel and football quarterbacks. The supreme court is the oldest in the nation, dating back to the Provincial Court established by the colonial legislature in 1684, and court records contain documents signed by leading co-lonial and revolutionary figures, including William Penn, Benjamin Franklin, George Washington, Alexander Hamilton, and Aaron Burr. The size and diversity of the state is reflected in the organization of the court, as the supreme court maintains chambers and holds ses-sions in Pittsburgh to the west and Philadelphia to the east, as well as in Harrisburg. Seated in stately chambers and surrounded by the ghosts of history, the justices must nonetheless heed the vagaries of public opinion, as they run in competitive elections, and face a retention vote every ten years.

Few states have such a split personality between rural and urban, between tradition and innovation, and perhaps that contributes to the varied character of its constitutional law. The Pennsylvania Supreme Court has kept alive the natural law traditions of private property rights yet is as likely to uphold local regulations of land use as to strike them down. The court recognizes that the commonwealth has a long tradition of township autonomy. But the court also has incorporated recent conceptions of "fair shares" of regional burdens for localities. And state environmental measures also impede local control.

To understand how the court views the proper relation between owner and community, I will review constitutional property rights developments in Pennsylvania in each major issue area, paying greatest attention to the jurisprudence of exclusionary zoning, which is the centerpiece of land use doctrine in Pennsylvania. I will begin with a trip back to the 1960s, when the modern era of constitutional land use litigation in Pennsylvania began and will also review developments in New Jersey jurisprudence, which has had a profound effect on the Pennsylvania court. Together, Pennsylvania and New Jersey have led the judicial attack on exclusionary zoning.[1]

OPENING UP THE SUBURBS

Zoning is a tool in the hands of governmental
bodies which enables them to more effectively
meet the demands of evolving and growing
communities. . . . Zoning is a means by which
a governmental body can plan for the future—
it may not be used as a means to deny the
future.
                                        —Justice Roberts[2]

The modern era of attacks on hierarchical zoning as unconstitutionally exclusionary of protected groups or land uses began in *National Land and Investment Co. v. Kohn*[3] when Justice Samuel Roberts led a divided Pennsylvania Supreme Court in invalidating[4] large-lot suburban zoning. Roberts's opinion presaged both the distinct approach the Pennsylvania court would take over the next two decades and the ambiguous reasoning that would divide the court. The Pennsylvania court was the pioneer in exclusionary doctrine and has since struggled to develop its own approach to the rights of property owners and the public needs of the region.

The population of Easttown, a developing suburb only twenty miles from Philadelphia, rose 22 percent in three years, from 6,907 in 1960 to over 8,400 in 1963. National Land bought, contingent on approval of a subdivision plan, a large tract there in 1961. The following year, Easttown rezoned the property and 30 percent of the entire town to require a minimum lot size of four acres for every house to be built. The company claimed the lot size was unconstitutional, and the court agreed.

Through its opinions, the court has struggled to find the proper, or at least constitutional, role for government in a polity based on individual rights. As in *National Land*, the court often invokes libertarian language reminiscent of natural rights theorists such as Locke, who argued that free individuals have consented only to a limited government charged with facilitating and protecting individual achievement.[5] The role of government, from this perspective, is to facilitate, not to control, private action.[6]

The legitimate purpose of zoning, according to Roberts, is to enable government to "meet the demands of evolving and growing communities." Libertarians regard growth as desirable for two reasons: It is a natural outgrowth of individual initiative and creativity, as the pursuit of personal preferences creates social wealth and is thus a sign of a healthy society.[7] Second, growth creates a larger pie to be shared, so there are more opportunities for individuals to achieve what they wish without limiting the opportunities of others.[8] And growth should "evolve naturally" rather than be controlled by government, or it may simply become another tool for preserving or increasing the inequalities of a status society. Roberts repeated the preference for spontaneous development throughout the *National Land* opinion. Local governments must shoulder the responsibilities that "time and natural growth invariably bring" and cannot "stand in the way of the natural forces which send our growing population into hitherto undeveloped areas in search of a comfortable place to live."[9] Regulations that may impede this development, such as limitations on housing density, are to be subjected to close scrutiny.

Roberts did not find any health or safety justification for the zoning ordinance and was critical of the rationale that large-lot zoning would preserve rural character. Roberts argued that preserving character is not a justification for regulation (although it might be from a hierarchical perspective) as it is a matter of personal taste, not public health, safety, or welfare. But even if the objective is assumed to be legitimate, Roberts reasoned, "it could not be seriously contended that the land would retain its rural character. . . . It would simply be dotted with larger homes on larger lots."[10] Although a hierarchical objective might be tolerated, then, it must be substantially served to justify restricting the owner's autonomy.

Large-lot zoning, Roberts argued, simply reflects the desire of some citizens to compel by government fiat that which they have been unable or unwilling to achieve through voluntary agreements. There surely is some minimal lot size that townships could require for health or safety reasons, Roberts wrote, although

> at some point along the spectrum . . . the size of lots ceases to be a concern requiring public regulation and becomes simply a matter of private preference. . . . There is no doubt that many of the residents of this area are highly desirous of keeping it the way it is. . . . These desires, however, do not rise to the level of public welfare. This is purely a matter of private desire which zoning regulations may not be employed to effectuate.[11]

An asserted need for large lots is "purely a matter of private desire" only if we assume libertarian premises. From the group-oriented perspectives of hierarchy or egalitarianism, it might be appropriate to expect individuals to defer to deeply felt preferences of their neighbors.

Although Roberts asserted that large-lot zoning was not a legitimate exercise of governmental power, he noted that citizens desiring seclusion from the suburban hordes could pursue their preferences in the private market: "The general welfare is not fostered or promoted by a zoning ordinance designed to be exclusive or exclusionary. But this does not mean that individual action is foreclosed. 'An owner of land may constitutionally make his property as large and as private or secluded or exclusive as he desires and his purse can afford.' "[12] Without the benefit of government coercion to support their aims, citizens would have to decide if they were willing to pay the price for their exclusionary predilections. From the libertarian perspective, the resulting housing patterns may best reflect the preferences of individual citizens.[13]

So far, Justice Roberts's opinion sounded as if he were in the vanguard of property rights libertarianism. This would be a surprise, given Roberts's paltry support for landowner rights during the 1980s (see Tables 4 and 7), and would no doubt be news to Roberts himself. The ambiguity in Roberts's opinion, which has dogged the court in the years since, is that he supported both a liberal system of property rights and a role for government without articulating a clear rule for discerning the limits to that power.[14]

The courts must protect "a landowner's constitutionally guaranteed right to use his property, unfettered by governmental restrictions," Roberts declared. But he inclined a caveat: "except in very specific circumstances."[15] Roberts listed the "specific circumstances" in a footnote: if a property owner is in violation of the Constitution; if he has created a nuisance; if he has violated a covenant, restriction, or easement on the property; or has violated valid state laws, including zoning regulations.[16] The last exception, however, creates a gaping hole in the wall of property rights. The implication of Roberts's statement is that a property owner is free to do anything he wishes except that which is illegal. The crux comes when the court must decide what laws and regulations are valid. Roberts gave little clue, other than to make clear that large-lot zoning in East-town was illegitimate.

Zoning can be used to "plan for the future—it may not be used . . . to deny the future." This is an appealing simple distinction but like many simple distinctions ultimately false. Planning that does not affect the future is a frivolous and pointless exercise. Governments plan precisely because they *do* want to make the future different than it otherwise would be. If planning has any affect at all, then the future that would have occurred will not and effectively has been "denied." Roberts defended natural growth and limited government but then approved of governmental planning. How can this power be constitutionally exercised? Can it affect the type, location, and speed of growth? Is regulation unconstitutional anytime it significantly limits the liberty of property owners or only when it has broad consequences for large classes of citizens, such as seekers of low- and moderate-income housing? If the latter is true, do governments have an affirmative obligation to promote their interests or simply refrain from erecting additional barriers? Roberts did not answer these difficult questions. The courts of Pennsylvania and New Jersey have struggled with these issues in the years since *National Land*, at times producing contradictory decisions. The opinion of Justice Roberts in *National Land* contained both the seeds for this conflict and a message that has figured prominently in several subsequent decisions by Pennsylvania justices: A regime of private property rights, if not obstructed, may best create social opportunities.

AMBIVALENCE TOWARD PLANNING

The Pennsylvania court continued its dialogue on the appropriate role for government in two 1970 cases, *Appeal of Girsh*[17] and *Appeal of Kit-Mar Builders*.[18] Neither Providence, the township under scrutiny in *Girsh*, was a community of 13,000 in Delaware County. Most of the town was zoned for single-family housing, and there were no provisions in the zoning ordinance for multifamily housing. The court concluded that the omission in the ordinance effectively prohibited multifamily housing and that such a complete ban was unconstitutional.

The township "has in effect decided to zone *out* the people," Justice Roberts declared for the majority, "who would be able to live in the Township if apartments were available."[19] Excluding an entire type of residential land use excluded an entire group of land users, and this was intolerable. For evidence that individuals were being denied opportunities, the court looked to the free market: "The simple fact that someone is anxious to build apartments is strong indications that the location of this township is such that people are desirous of moving in, and we do not believe Nether Providence can close its doors to those people."[20] Roberts's reasoning again reflects the libertarian position, which sees the individual pursuit of preferences as socially valuable and constitutionally protected.[21] Roberts did not ask whether potential residents *should* live in Nether Providence, only whether they wanted to, and market demand was a clear sign that they did.

Girsh could appear to be a resounding rejection of hierarchical land use control. The town leaders cannot effectively deny others the opportunity to live in town, and they cannot use the power of government to keep the rural character of the township: "Protecting the character—really the aesthetic nature—of the municipality is not sufficient justification for an exclusionary zoning technique," declared Roberts.[22] He also asserted, however, that the municipality had an obligation to bear a "rightful share of the burden" for new housing. This qualification raised the possibility that in the future the court might find a community had its "share" of housing and thus could limit the rights of aspiring residents. This ambiguity— whether exclusionary zoning was unconstitutional because it violated the rights of the land users[23] or because a town had not done its "share"[24]—later would trouble the court as it reacted to the exclusionary zoning rulings made by its neighbor the Supreme Court of New Jersey.

In *Kit-Mar Builders,* the court struck down a zoning ordinance that required two- and three-acre minimum housing lots. "Absent some extraordinary justification, a zoning ordinance with minimum lot sizes such as those is completely unreasonable," asserted Justice Roberts, again writing for the majority.[25] Roberts declared that minimum lot sizes must be no larger than is necessary to build a house (he suggested one acre) and rejected the township's reasons as "thinly veiled justifications for exclusionary zoning."[26] Even the lack of an adequate sewer system was irrelevant because the township cannot "keep people out, rather than make community improvements."[27] So far, the opinion is a libertarian delight, demanding the removal of impediments to individuals using the land as they see fit. The obligation of the municipality is to provide the public services essential to growth, not to freeze growth and deny opportunities.

But Roberts had another message to deliver in his dicta: A township "may not refuse to confront the future. It is not for any township to say who may or may not live within its confines, while disregarding the interests of the entire area. . . . We fully realize that the overall solution to these problems lies with greater regional planning; but until the time comes that we have such a system we must confront the situation as it is."[28] Although Roberts had emphasized the property rights of the individual, he now implied that a municipality may "say who may or may not live within its confines" *if* it does not "disregard the interests of the entire area." Perhaps the constitutional offense was not that individual opportunities had been limited but that they had not been limited on a wide enough scale. Roberts threw a dash of hierarchy on the libertarian flame he had lit and made it clear that the desirable solution was not a land use system based on individual control but rather on "greater regional planning." Deference to property rights, then, may be only an expedient until localities cooperate in, or capitulate to, regional regulation.

Doubts and ambiguities about the desirability of private control of land use did not muddy the concurring opinions of Chief Justice Bell in *Girsh* and *Kit-Mar Builders.* He vigorously defended property rights as the foundation of free society, and decried governmental interference:

One of the most important rights, privileges and powers which
(at least until recently) has differentiated our Country from
Communist and Socialist Countries, is the right of ownership
and the concomitant use of property. . . . Then along came
zoning with its desirable objectives. . . . Courts, legislators,
and zoning bodies, and most of the public have forgotten or
rendered meaningless Article 1, Section 1[29] of the Constitution of Pennsylvania.[30]

Chief Justice Bell did not mince words, and his energetic opinions provided emphatic defenses of liberal land rights. But it is the
very ambiguity in the opinions of Justice Roberts that make them
fascinating as he attempted to work out the demands of conflicting
constitutional cultures. Ultimately, his more muddled approach
may best provide judicial protection for property rights, as he acknowledged the validity of differing approaches and attempted to
balance competing claims through reason. For Chief Justice Bell,
property rights were an article of faith.

The early exclusionary cases of the court have been criticized
by legal scholars not for the court's equivocation about local land
use regulation but for its modest protection of property rights.[31] For
many academics, the problem with zoning has been only that it may
not adequately serve what they see as the public welfare, not that it
has limited property rights. The Pennsylvania court was misguided
because it was not doing enough for the poor, wrote Leonard Rubinowitz, and was instead allowing owners to seek unethical
"profits."[32] Norman Williams and Thomas Norman were more emphatic: "Briefly, two very different lines of argument [in attacking
zoning] are emerging, which might be called the Pennsylvania rationale and the sensible rationale. . . . Pennsylvania decisions . . .
mistakenly assume an identity of interest between developers and
those who are excluded from good housing."[33] They painted of picture of owners not as people with legitimate interests meriting protection, but as exploiters: "It would not be difficult . . . to develop a
rationale which in the real world would lead to large capital gains
for landowners, large profits for builders, despoliation of some of
the state's remaining attractive landscapes—and no inexpensive
housing."[34] The rationale of the Pennsylvania court did not conform to their egalitarian standard. Much more comforting to such
critics was the "sensible rationale" being developed across the
Delaware by the New Jersey Supreme Court.

BREAKING DOWN THE BARRIERS IN NEW JERSEY

All persons are by nature free and independent,
and have certain natural and unalienable
rights, among which are enjoying and defend-
ing life and liberty, of acquiring, possessing and
protecting property, and of pursuing and obtain-
ing safety and happiness.
        —New Jersey Constitution, Art. I, Sec. 1

The New Jersey Constitution, like that of Pennsylvania, begins with a declaration of the rights of citizens, an assertion that the freedom of the individual is preeminent and the powers of governmental secondary. And foremost among the rights of the individual, in order to seek and secure happiness, are the rights of property. New Jersey and Pennsylvania have nearly identical constitutional bases for their doctrines on exclusionary zoning but have developed strikingly different rationales and remedies. While Pennsylvania has struggled to balance the rights of the individual and the power of democratic government, the New Jersey Supreme Court has undermined them both and has used the Declaration of Rights in the state constitution as a pretext to impose, by hierarchical means, its egalitarian vision of the correct society. I will consider here the first act in the saga of exclusionary zoning in New Jersey and then evaluate the reaction of the Pennsylvania court in its jurisprudence before returning to the New Jersey fray.

The New Jersey court grabbed the exclusionary zoning spotlight in 1975 when it ruled in *Southern Burlington County NAACP v. Township of Mount Laurel (Mount Laurel I)*[35] that suburbs must accommodate their "fair share" of the region's poor. That decision and its offspring, *Southern Burlington County NAACP v. Mount Laurel (Mount Laurel II)*,[36] have been hailed widely by scholars pleased to see a court willing to use its considerable power to restructure local communities.[37] "The New Jersey Supreme Court is as innovative and creative a tribunal as there is," proclaimed Laurence Tribe.[38] The court is "the most innovative in the country" agreed Yale Kamisar.[39] The *Mount Laurel* cases have generated more conferences, articles, and symposiums than any other area of state constitutional land use doctrine.[40] The *Mount Laurel* cases provoked an explosion of litigation as the zoning regulations of every municipality were called into question. To begin to deal with the onslaught, the court consolidated cases faster than a corporate raider merges companies; the two major cases of the 1980s, *Mount Laurel II* and *The Hills Development Co. v. Township of Bernards*,[41] included twenty eight and thirty six teams of attorneys, respectively. The full title of *Hills Development* takes up more than five pages in the Atlantic Reporter.

The New Jersey justices have gone to great lengths to explain their prescriptions for the good society. While the typical exclusionary case in Pennsylvania is mercifully brief, the New Jersey cases can run scores of pages of small print in the Atlantic Reporter. *Oakwood at Madison, Inc. v. Township of Madison*,[42] perhaps not the most important but certainly the longest of the New Jersey cases, fills eighty pages with doctrine, dicta, declarations, and doubts. Justice Clifford bemoaned the "barrels of ink already lavished upon this case" but felt compelled to add his observations in a concurring opinion.[43] The justices have never been at a loss for words, and their expansive writing creates opinions ripe with cultural connotations. "The court consistently has broken ground," journalist Howard Kurtz has written, "often with sweeping prose that delights its admirers and infuriates critics."[44]

New Jersey took a quite different tack than Pennsylvania, expressing concern not for the rights of the landowners but criticizing local governments for not correctly identifying the "general welfare." The court professed to be driven by a policy concern for the "desperate need for housing."[45] Housing and racial segregation problems are considerable in New Jersey where many older central cities have declined while suburbs have remained islands of exclusion, forming a "tight white noose around black cities," in Constance Perin's pungent phrase.[46] But the court did not simply reject ordinances that it concluded did not promote the public welfare and then allow governments to try again.[47] The court sought to instruct localities in the correct interpretation of the general welfare, specifically by prescribing the amount of low-income housing each community must incorporate. The problem was not that local regulations interfered with individuals but that they did not interfere in the manner considered most desirable by the court. The solution was not to reduce government intervention but to increase it. The court shifted control over policy away from local legislatures and toward the centralized judiciary and, in a later case, the state bureaucracy.[48]

Mount Laurel, the subject of so much unsought attention, is a small suburb about a dozen miles from Philadelphia. Its population had grown steadily, from 2,817 in 1950 to 5,249 in 1960 and 11,221 a decade later. The town is crossed by the New Jersey Turnpike and Interstate 295, and at the time of the *Mount Laurel I* trial, 65 percent of the land was said to be vacant or devoted to agricultural use. Most of the town (70 percent) was zoned residential; there were four zones, all single-family. The town had approved multifamily housing in several planned-unit developments, although the units would not be what the court considered low cost.

Justice Hall framed the question in *Mount Laurel I* to serve the court's policy goal of requiring low-income housing: "The legal question before us is whether a developing municipality like Mount Laurel may validly, by a system of land use regulation, make it physically and economically impossible to provide low and moderate income housing in the municipality for the various categories of persons."[49] The court was concerned with the housing available to groups, or "various categories of persons," and was quite candid that it had no concern for the aspirations of more affluent would-be residents or for the rights of property owners. What "rights" might be protected by the court, if the incidental benefits to individuals from the promotion of preferred social policies can be called rights, depended not only on the "extent of their income and resources" (the more money, the less court concern) but also on the location of the community the individual wished to build in or move to. The court, according to Justice Hall, was concerned only with correcting the values and policies of "developing" communities; towns and cities that were fully developed or that lay beyond the reach of immediate growth pressures were exempt from scrutiny.

Exempting these communities from egalitarian housing demands allowed the court to concentrate on communities where social engineering would be most practical. "Developing" communities would have both sufficient land remaining and enough demand for housing to make substantial change in the socioeconomic makeup of the community feasible. And letting some communities off the hook might weaken political opposition to the court's initiative. As Tarr and Porter have noted, the "court had no significant political allies" in its assault on the suburban citadels.[50] Neither the state legislature nor local governments—and not even the intended beneficiaries, the urban poor—were pressing for a transformation of suburban zoning.[51] But the exemption for developed urban communities where demands for affordable housing can be quite intense would later be harshly criticized by Justice Pashman.[52] It does not seem intuitively obvious that developed communities should escape such an important social imperative, and indeed recently the state agency set up to implement the *Mt. Laurel* principles ordered municipalities to permit demolition if that is necessary to make room for low-income housing.[53]

Even developing municipalities were free to regulate away, Justice Hall asserted in *Mt. Laurel I*, as long as they "zone primarily for the living welfare of the people and not for the benefit of the local tax code."[54] Of course, a majority of voters in Mount Laurel may have thought zoning out low-cost housing projects *did* serve their "living welfare," but by "the people" Hall meant the entire region. The court criticized what Williams and Norman had called the "odd notion that the statutory reference to the 'general welfare' refers to the general welfare of each individual municipality."[55] It seems logical, however, that each layer of government should be responsible and accountable to its citizens. How can, and why should, local democratic governments discern and accommodate the interests of citizens who do not reside or vote in the locality? By placing an unrealistic demand on local government, the court was creating a pretext for the assertion of greater judicial power and regional land use controls.

"It is plain beyond dispute that proper provision for adequate housing of all categories of people is certainly an absolute essential in promotion of the general welfare," Justice Hall declared, vetoing the possibility that citizens might disagree with his position.[56] Each developing community would be required to promote the social balancing the court desired by accommodating "the municipality's fair share of the present and prospective regional need" for low- and moderate-income housing.[57]

Although pursuing an egalitarian goal, the court's approach evokes a hierarchical conception of society in which individuals are classified and rights and responsibilities assigned to each class. To reverse Sir Henry Maine's evocative phrase, the court promoted a return from "contract" back to "status."[58] A libertarian would argue that if individuals could freely contract for their housing preferences, then as the middle-class moved up, their former housing would be available to those less affluent.[59] The court rejected this contractarian approach in favor of centralized control. The housing needs of the region would be determined in advance, not discovered as people pursue their preferences through the market. Each town or city must then include its "fair share" of low- and moderate-income housing in order to reduce socioeconomic differences between municipalities.

It was the disparities between communities, not the lack of housing for the poor, that most offended the egalitarian values of the court. In an analysis of the impact of the *Mount Laurel* cases and subsequent legislation, John M. Selig of the Center for New Jersey Affairs at Princeton concluded that "in fact the court was really more concerned with economic integration than with housing provisions, because if housing had been the concern, there would have been no reason to focus so heavily on construction in the suburbs."[60] Thus the correct share of each type of housing was critical, even though, Alan Mallach has written, "suburban housing opportunities . . . are not a priority issue for the urban poor."[61]

The court made clear it was not limiting the power of government but requiring that it be used for preferred social ends. "Proper planning and cooperation" provided the solution for communities, wrote Justice Hall, "if they use the powers which they have intelligently and in the broad public interest. Under our holdings today, they can be better communities for all than they previously have been."[62] In the eyes of the court, towns should take their medicine and be grateful because they will be "better communities for all." Apparently, municipalities suffered from a "false consciousness" that obscured their real interests and should cease their sinful ways of the past when each town acted "solely in its own selfish and parochial interest."[63]

Although hierarchical land use regulation was discredited by the court, the answer was more control, not less. "We do not intend that developing municipalities shall be overwhelmed by voracious land speculators and developers," Hall cautioned.[64] The court avoided difficult questions about the rights of individuals in a free society by painting a caricature of property owners. Justice Hall declined to speak of homeowners or landowners (or even of property), preferring to portray them all as "voracious land speculators and developers." In cultural terms, he did not consider the libertarian tradition worthy of serious discussion. Although Hall was pursuing an egalitarian goal—leveling of communities—he endorsed a coercive, hierarchical means—greater central planning. Once a court has defined the appropriate region, wrote Hall, "through the expertise of the municipal planning adviser, the county planning boards and the state planning agency, a reasonable [fair share] figure for Mount Laurel can be determined, which can then be translated to the allocation of sufficient land therefor on the zoning map."[65]

Justice Hall was willing to accept the power inequities of the hierarchical approach (that is, the experts have the clout) as the best way to reshape communities and would allow communities to perpetuate status distinctions within each municipality: "They can have industrial sections and sections for every kind of housing from low cost and multifamily to lots of more than an acre with very expensive homes."[66] It is hard to reconcile tolerance of such socioeconomic segregation with egalitarianism as anything more than a step on the road to equality. Indeed, in Yonkers, New York, Judge Leonard Sand found that the relegation of low-income public housing to one part of the city violated civil rights and ordered the city to disperse low-income units throughout the city.[67] Yonkers had proportionately more low-income residents than many neighboring communities, yet this "fair share" did not deter the judge from ordering a more egalitarian housing distribution.[68]

Justice Hall did not fully explain just how "fair shares" were to be accommodated and admitted that "courts do not build housing nor do municipalities."[69] The court did require that selected exclusionary obstacles be removed: Municipalities must permit multifamily housing, including units with several bedrooms; must permit small houses on very small lots; and must zone for high density. Somehow, municipalities must also provide housing "affordable and adequate" to employees of any industry in town. The court declined to order every remedy available. It forbade only a few exclusionary measures. It required affirmative steps but did not specify what they were. The decisions of the New Jersey court would continue to reflect this hesitancy until *Mount Laurel II*, when the court made an even more far-reaching ruling.

In his concurring opinion in *Mount Laurel I*, Justice Pashman argued that the court had not gone far enough. He was willing to carry the egalitarian banner across the entire state by forbidding rural areas from using exclusionary techniques and requiring all metropolitan municipalities, developed or not, to include their "fair-share" of the region's poor. Pashman professed concern with the broad sweep of the court's decree, however, and offered a rather unconvincing disclaimer: "It is not the business of this Court or any member of it to instruct the municipalities of the State of New Jersey on the good life."[70] Yet he then proceeded to educate communities: "As there is no difference between the love of low income mothers and fathers and those of high income for their children, so there is no difference between the desire for a decent community felt by one group and that felt by another."[71] What might seem like difficult sociological questions were transformed into articles of faith by Justice Pashman. His opinion was filled with pungent disdain for the suburban lifestyle; because he was a state justice, he could conclude that what was personally distasteful was unconstitutional. He asserted that suburbs are socioeconomically homogeneous and that similarity in financial status translates into "almost total similarities of taste, habit, custom and behavior."[72] He declared that such communities are "culturally dead and downright boring,"[73] although he did not explain why, then, suburbs are so popular. But in New Jersey perhaps it is unconstitutional to be boring.

While Pashman attacked the alleged homogeneity of the suburbs, he demanded that they be uniform in comparison to each other, each having a proportional share of each socioeconomic class. Somehow, this uniformity was constitutionally required, while homogeneity within a community was constitutionally forbidden. Pashman even asserted that the court's decision was the only outcome acceptable to right-thinking Americans: "The people of New Jersey should welcome the result reached by the court in this case, not merely because it is required by our laws, but more fundamentally, because the result is right and true to the highest American ideals."[74] Rather than acknowledge that there are competing cultural traditions in America with different conceptions of justice and of the role of the individual and the state, Pashman implied that his vision of state-imposed community equality was the only correct one and that doubters were traitors to the "highest American ideals."

The *Mount Laurel I* decision was greeted with acclaim by many academic writers, but there were a few skeptics. John Payne, although supporting state development of affordable housing, argued that the "obvious truths" of the court might not be compatible with sound planning:

> It becomes necessary to ask whether the central premise of *Mount Laurel,* that each community has a proportional responsibility for each component of the region's socio-economic makeup, makes sense. . . . Even in a world of perfect social motivation, and of perfectly equitable distribution of public resources, it seems self-evident that rational planning would require corridors of growth, concentration of housing of various sorts in appropriate locales, preservation of natural amenities on the basis of absolute merit rather than proper share and so forth.[75]

Payne was not offering a defense of property rights but the traditional hierarchical argument of land use regulation—that experts should control land uses and users for the good of everyone. Payne saw distinctions between communities as justified, while for the New Jersey court, they are damaging and unconstitutional.

While Payne emphasized the virtues of central planning, the *Wall Street Journal*, which usually can be counted on to criticize governmental intrusion, defended the tradition of local regulation in market terms, arguing that it creates choices for consumers,[76] and added, "We find a great deal wrong with trying to establish common community denominators by judicial fiat, so that there would be no appreciable difference between Princeton and Paterson, Summit and Somers Point, Ocean Grove and Ocean City. Pushed to its logical conclusion, that is where New Jersey decision would seem to lead."[77]

In a pair of 1977 decisions, the court wavered in its enthusiasm for the "fair share" doctrine. Justice Hall had retired, and Justice Mountain, who had concurred in the *Mt. Laurel* decision on narrower statutory grounds, had been joined by two other cautious voices, Sidney Schreiber and Milton Conford, an appellate judge who was temporarily filling a court vacancy.

In *Oakwood at Madison, Inc. v. Madison,*[78] the New Jersey Supreme Court found the town's zoning ordinance to be unconstitutionally exclusionary, even though more than 27 percent of the town's housing stock was apartments. Madison, which was bisected by the Garden State Parkway, was a rapidly growing community about twenty miles from Elizabeth and Newark. Although its population had grown from 7,366 in 1950 to almost 50,000 in 1970, 40 percent of the land in Madison was still vacant, according to the court. A 1970 zoning ordinance that required one- and two-acre minimum lots for new houses and allocated minuscule acreage for multifamily housing had been invalidated in the courts. The town responded with a ordinance decreasing lot sizes and increasing the allotment of multifamily housing, but the state high court struck it down.

Justice Conford, writing for the court, argued that the township still had not incorporated its share of the poor because various "cost generating" exactions, as for open space and road improvements, imposed on developers would put multifamily housing beyond the financial grasp of the poor and working class. The court cut down the ordinance with the *Mt. Laurel* ax, but shied away from taking another egalitarian swing when it considered the remedy. Conford concluded it was not up to the courts to determine the housing region and "fair share" allocation for the township. Housing markets and policies, he acknowledged, are quite complex, and the factors to be considered are so many "as to preclude judicial dictation or acceptance of any one solution as authoritative."[79] Conford agreed with critics that the state supreme court should not become the housing czar of New Jersey. But then how was the township to meet its fair-share obligation? Conford's solution was simple: The township should remove obstacles to construction of housing and allow the market to determine region and fair share.

Oakwood was, in the words of Jerome Rose, a "blow to the *Mount Laurel I* ideological underframe."[80] For a brief moment, libertarianism flickered on the New Jersey court. The duty of the township was to stop being an obstacle to the achievement of private preferences. It must zone for "least-court housing"[81] by allowing houses on tiny lots and more multifamily housing, relaxing restrictions on the number of bedrooms, and removing exactions that stick private developers with the bill for public services. Conford concluded there was no constitutional obligation to take "affirmative" measures to provide housing: "Municipalities do not themselves have the duty to build or subsidize housing."[82] The court would look at the opportunities for housing seekers, not results. Removing obstacles would increase the freedom of property owners to devote their land to housing if they so chose.[83] But would any housing for the poor result? Judge Conford adopted the libertarian argument that creating housing opportunities for all will create opportunities for the poor: While "least-cost" housing "may not provide *newly constructed* housing for all in the lower-income categories mentioned, it will nevertheless through the 'filtering-down process' . . . tend to augment the total supply of available housing."[84]

Judge Conford's opinion, while supporting a decision quite similar to the one in *Mount Laurel*, contrasted sharply with Justice Hall's.[85] Justice Schreiber concurred with the majority decision and criticized the leveling impulse of *Mount Laurel:* "The general welfare calls for adequate housing of all types," he wrote, "but not necessarily within any particular municipality."[86] The court's endorsement of least-cost housing, according to Jerome Rose, signified a *"major* retreat by the court because of the profound change of ideals it represents."[87] But despite the more libertarian tune being sung by the New Jersey court, *Oakwood* marked a pause, not a reversal, in the court's egalitarian attack on exclusionary zoning.

Justice Pashman remained the keeper of the egalitarian flame in *Oakwood.* He would have gone "farther and faster" than the rest of the court by requiring the lower court to determine the housing region and fair-share allocation and by decreeing that Madison must establish a housing authority, require housing developers to include a designated percentage of low-income housing, grant zoning variances for low-income housing,[88] and freeze other construction until the low-income housing was provided.

The court faced a simple choice between good and evil in Pashman's eyes: "In *Mount Laurel,* this Court began to deal with the sinister side of municipal land use controls. . . . Powerful judicial antidotes may become necessary to eradicate the evils of exclusionary zoning."[89] Aggressive judicial involvement in land use regulation raises serious questions about the rights of property owners, the legislative powers of democratic governments,[90] and the ability of the court to derive and implement sound planning.[91] But Pashman did not address the ambiguous world of conflicting rights and limited powers, in part because his vision of equal communities was a moral trump, right and just and to be pursued whatever the obstacles. One attorney critical of Pashman's inclination to substitute judicial for legislative power commented, "Pashman does not know what legislatures are for except to raise judicial salaries, and, since they do not do that fast enough, he would really like to take that function away from them too."[92]

In *Pascack Association, Ltd., v. Washington,*[93] the second whimper by the New Jersey court after its *Mount Laurel* roar, while the court did little to cheer either libertarians or egalitarians, it did give a momentary respite to the beleaguered defenders of local autonomy in land use regulation.

Washington Township is a small community (three square miles) in Bergen County, near New York City and Newark. At the time of the trial, single-family housing covered nearly 95 percent of the town. There was a small commercial area and no multifamily housing. The trial court declared Washington's zoning scheme unconstitutional, but the high court reversed, repeating that the constitution did not require a fully developed municipality to open its gates. "There is no per se principle," Judge Conford declared, "in this state mandating zoning for multifamily housing by every municipality regardless of its circumstances with respect to degree or nature of development."[94] *Pascack* strengthened the exception made in *Mt. Laurel* for built up communities. The decision was a blow to the community leveling advocated by egalitarians,[95] as the court was rewarding municipalities that had excluded so successfully that they were now fully developed. The very communities that most offended the egalitarian ideal were immune from retribution. "Maintaining the character of a fully developed, predominantly single-family residential community," declared Conford, "constitutes an appropriate desideratum of zoning."[96]

Conford was ready to cede back to the towns the control over land use the court had claimed in *Mount Laurel*. "It would be a mistake," he wrote, "to interpret *Mount Laurel* as a comprehensive displacement of sound and long established principles concerning judicial respect for local policy decisions in the zoning field."[97] Yet *Mount Laurel* had been heralded precisely because it *was* an aggressive challenge to local autonomy in land use regulation. True, the *Mt. Laurel* court would tolerate governmental regulation of private land as long as the ordinances did not offend fair-share principles. But Conford went further, denying the fundamental message of *Mount Laurel*—that municipalities must promote the court's conception of the general welfare:

> The overwhelming point we make is that it is not for the courts to substitute their conception of what the public welfare requires . . . for the views of those in whom the Legislature and the local electorate have vested that responsibility. . . . The judicial role . . . is limited to the assessment of a claim that the restrictions of the ordinance are patently arbitrary or unreasonable . . . , not that they do not match the plaintiff's or the court's concept of the general welfare.[98]

Conford's argument was a reasonable criticism of judicial activism, but its pronouncement in the name of a court which had set new standards for judicial involvement in zoning policy was incongruous. Conford rejected the soul of *Mount Laurel* while ostensibly honoring the precedent. Either his colleagues (two of whom joined both Conford's opinion in *Oakwood* and Hall's majority opinion in *Mount Laurel*) were momentarily wary of what they had wrought, or they were willing to tolerate Conford's rhetoric in the narrow factual context of a tiny, fully developed municipality.

Justice Pashman did not go along with the crowd. In a long and vigorous dissent, he accused the court of disregarding the "intent and spirit" of *Mount Laurel*.[99] Indeed, it is hard to come to any other conclusion about the court's ruling. Pashman criticized the majority for rewarding "municipalities which have already attained 'exclusionary bliss.' "[100] Mature communities should be subject to fair-share demands, according to Pashman, and should be required to take affirmative steps to open their kingdoms to the poor. The majority, Pashman wrote, ignored the "depth and the magnitude of the measures needed to correct decades of exclusionary zoning."[101] The demands of equality should take precedence over democracy: "We live daily with the failure of our democratic institutions to eradicate class distinctions."[102] Much to the frustration of Justice Pashman, the New Jersey Supreme Court had paused in its egalitarian assault on zoning.

THE RIPPLE EFFECT IN PENNSYLVANIA

*[Mount Laurel] went far beyond anything this
court has ever decided or suggested.*
                    —*Justice Roberts*[103]

How would the Pennsylvania court, whose *National Land* decision had been cited by New Jersey as one of the precedents for *Mount Laurel*, respond to the rumblings from the court across the Delaware? The New Jersey court had taken the libertarian premise of *National Land*—that land use regulations may deny constitutional rights by effectively excluding individuals from desired locales—and turned it into an egalitarian decree. Would the Pennsylvania court adopt the religion of the New Jersey court or write its own jurisprudence gospel based on competing cultural principles? The Pennsylvania justices would do both. After *Mount Laurel I*, the Pennsylvania court blended the egalitarian rhetoric emanating from the New Jersey court with its more libertarian approach.

Justice O'Brien, writing for the court in *Willistown v. Chesterdale Farms, Inc.*,[104] endorsed the New Jersey perspective, which classified individuals and saw the obligation of the court as ensuring protection of the lower classes, when he quoted extensively from *Mount Laurel* on a township's obligation to accommodate its "fair share" of the regional need for low- and moderate-income housing.[105] Willistown's rezoning of less than 1 percent of the township for apartments was rejected by the court as "tokenism." Was the Pennsylvania court getting into the housing business, ready to dictate a low-income housing quota for each town and specify what measures it must take to entice its "fair share"? Not exactly. While espousing the "fair share" gospel, Justice O'Brien also quoted approvingly from Pennsylvania's precedents, arguing that government must respond to housing preferences expressed through the market rather than artificially control settlement: "It is not for any township to say who may or may not live within its confines."[106] Towns must respond to natural growth, O'Brien added,

not forbid it: "Suburban municipalities within the area of urban outpour must meet the problems of population expansion into its borders by increasing municipal services, and not by the practice of exclusionary zoning."[107]

O'Brien did not acknowledge the conflicts between the egalitarian approach (redirecting the police power) and the libertarian approach (limiting the police power) but simply placed them side by side. Either he was reluctant to admit a conflict, or he assumed the two goals, liberty and equality, to be mutually supportive. O'Brien could make the argument, which has a rich history in American thought, that lowering barriers to individual freedom (in this case, the opportunity for landowners to devote their property to apartments) will further equality (by increasing housing opportunities).[108] But he leaves the reader to wonder whether the contradiction was left unresolved by design or accident.

The court provided a builder's remedy, ordering the lower court to see that the plaintiff would get permission to build the apartments. But was this because the owner had a basic right or because the apartments would serve low-income home seekers? "In *Willistown*," lamented Stephen Kopelman, "there was no discussion of whether the plaintiff-developer's apartment complex would benefit low- or moderate-income families."[109] For Kopelman, this was distressing. But if the objective of the court was to protect the rights of the owner rather than promote equality, the immediate effect on housing for the poor was not important. And if the court believed lowering the barriers to construction would help the poor, both goals would be served simultaneously, and a separate discussion of housing effects would not be necessary.

Willistown must accommodate its "fair share" of the poor, but the court, as Justice Pomeroy pointed out in his dissent, provided no criteria to determine what was fair. By quoting *Mount Laurel*, O'Brien appeared to endorse the New Jersey preference for judicial or bureaucratic determination of shares. But "fair share" might also be grafted onto the Pennsylvania court's preference for letting individuals register their demands through the housing market. "Fair share" might then be another phrase for the natural growth a community would experience if it did not erect artificial obstacles. By adopting the language of *Mount Laurel* while adhering to Pennsylvania precedents, Justice O'Brien added to the ambiguities of the court's doctrine.

The township of Upper Providence was the scene of the next major skirmish over exclusionary zoning in Pennsylvania. Upper Providence lies about twelve miles west of Philadelphia and had about 9,200 residents at the time of the case. The township was overwhelmingly single-family housing: Only 1 percent of the land area was zoned for commercial uses and multifamily housing, and even this land was already developed. In *Surrick v. Zoning Hearing Board of Upper Providence*,[110] the supreme court agreed with the plaintiff, who sought to build apartments in another part of town, that such a small allocation for multifamily housing was unconstitutional.

For the first time, the Pennsylvania court in *Surrick* sought to distinguish the conflicting lines of analysis it had been developing since *National Land.* Justice Nix, writing the majority opinion (in which O'Brien, the *Willistown* author, joined), developed two distinct rationales for triggering close judicial scrutiny of local land regulations. Citing the *Girsh* precedent,[111] Nix concluded that a total ban of a legitimate land use was unconstitutional absent extraordinary circumstances. Even the most fully developed suburb or the most isolated hamlet could not completely ban a legitimate land use. In effect, the court was saying it would probably tolerate hierarchical land use controls; municipalities might determine which parts of town could best accommodate different land uses. But a total ban would be exclusion, not accommodation. Nix distinguished such a case from a situation, as in *Willistown*, in which a town restricts, but does not ban, multifamily housing. In this case, fair share principles would determine constitutionality. Yet it could be argued, following the more libertarian reasoning of *National Land*, that there is no need to create a two-tier analysis or to invoke fair share principles, as any significant restrictions on multifamily housing would interfere with property rights and the natural expansion of population and thus should not be tolerated.

Pennsylvania followed the lead of New Jersey, limiting its fair share requirements to developing municipalities in growth areas. The rights and remedies available to plaintiffs would depend in part on where they happened to reside or wished to reside. But once Justice Nix determined that Surrick was subject to fair share requirements, he asked only whether the township intended to[112] or effectively "zone[d] out the natural growth of population."[113] He was still looking to the private market for evidence of exclusion and saw the accommodation of those pressures as the constitutional solution. Nix did not require that the courts designate a housing region and determine a "correct" share. Nix did not prescribe any affirmative measures (such as mandatory set-asides of 20 percent of all new housing for the poor), and he did not require that every community include the same proportion of the poor. While speaking the language of fair share, Nix was promoting opportunities, not requiring equality. "Fair share" was to be enabled through the removal of barriers, not imposed through greater controls. In *Mount Laurel*, the New Jersey court "went far beyond anything this court has ever decided or suggested,"[114] wrote Justice Roberts, the chief architect of the *National Land* doctrine, in his *Surrick* concurrence. He rejected the fair share approach and decried the tendency to "convert courts into regional planning commissions,"[115] noting the more chastened attitude displayed by the New Jersey court in *Oakwood*.

Justice Nix had turned the ambiguities of *National Land* and its offspring into two distinct tests. Unlike New Jersey's, the Pennsylvania court would reject complete prohibitions of legitimate land uses in any municipality, thus showing a willingness to protect the rights of landowners, regardless of their location. Nix borrowed a second test from New Jersey, subjecting a restrictive ordinance in a developing municipality to close scrutiny. But even in these cases Nix sought to remove impediments to natural growth, not promote egalitarian policy. Remedies in Pennsylvania would focus on removing restrictions and requiring municipalities to issue permits to plaintiffs.

NEW JERSEY REJOINS THE CRUSADE

The basis for the constitutional obligation is simple: the State controls the use of land, all of the land. In exercising that control it cannot favor rich over poor.
　　　　　　　—Chief Justice Wilentz[116]

While the Pennsylvania Supreme Court was struggling to integrate the innovations from the New Jersey court into its more libertarian tradition, the New Jersey justices were rejecting the cautionary note they had entertained in *Oakwood* and *Pascack*. The court emerged from its crucible of doubt with renewed zeal, and Mount Laurel again became the reluctant target of the New Jersey court's ambitious assault on local control of land use. Justice Pashman was finally vindicated in *Mount Laurel II*[117] as the court unanimously embraced the more intrusive remedies he had advocated years earlier. *Mount Laurel I* had created the "right" to be protected (the requirement that each community accommodate a specific allocation of low- and moderate-income housing), and *Mount Laurel*

II was the definitive statement on the remedies available to enforce the court's will.

Mount Laurel I had been remanded to the lower court for enforcement, and the township had added to its zoning ordinance three new zones for multifamily housing and detached homes on small lots. The trial court, following the more timid precedents of *Pascack* and *Oakwood*, ruled in 1978 that Mount Laurel, having made a bona fide attempt to accommodate its share of affordable housing, was at last off the judicial hook. But Mount Laurel's victory was short-lived. In 1983, the state high court struck down the revised ordinance, finding the twenty acres set aside for lower-income housing inappropriate and insufficient. "Papered over with studies, rationalized by hired experts, the ordinance at its core is true to nothing but Mount Laurel's determination to exclude the poor," declared Chief Justice Wilentz.[118] The court declared that even good faith efforts to facilitate "least cost" housing would no longer suffice. "Fair share" was to be determined by the courts, and townships could be required to do whatever was necessary to meet their quotas. Results, not effort or intent, would be the measure of constitutionality.

"We may not build houses, but we do enforce the constitution," declared Justice Wilentz,[119] and apparently the state constitution was quite precise in its requirements. It would be up to the judge to determine just what the fair share was and what steps the township must take to meet the judicial goal. The judge could demand that towns require that builders reserve a set proportion of their new housing (usually 20 percent) for low-income housing, provide subsidies for low-income residents, and build low-income units first. Resale of low-income homes could be controlled indefinitely, and the lower court could require towns to permit mobile homes (as long as the mobile home developments met low-income quotas). If necessary, courts could require "over-zoning, i.e., zoning to allow for *more* than fair share," to ensure that there would be equal results.[120]

As in *Mount Laurel I*, the court made reduction of distinctions between communities its primary goal. The court did not explicitly overturn *Oakwood*, but Wilentz made it clear that the case was no longer good law. In *Mount Laurel II*, Wilentz rejected reliance on the free market to create least-cost housing. He admitted that relaxed regulation probably would allow affordable housing to "filter down" to the poor but rejected this solution because it would "exacerbate the economic segregation of our cities and suburbs."[121]

Once again, the rights of landowners did not concern the court, which portrayed owners as unethical developers and speculators. "Builders may not be able to build just where they want—our parks, farms, and conservation areas are not a land bank for housing speculators," declared Wilentz. "The specific location of such [affordable] housing will of course continue to depend on sound municipal land use planning."[122] The court railed against the barriers to individual opportunity raised by local regulation but then put its faith in hierarchical regulation. Wilentz assailed what he saw as the inevitable consequences of liberty in land use:

> The lessons of history are clear, even if rarely learned.[123]. . . .
> Unplanned growth has a price: natural resources are destroyed, open spaces are despoiled, agricultural land is rendered forever unproductive, and people settle without regard to the enormous cost of the public facilities needed to support them. Cities decay; established infrastructures deteriorate for lack of funds; and taxpayers shudder under a financial burden of public expenditures resulting in part from uncontrolled migration to anywhere anyone wants to settle, roads leading to places they should never be—a pattern of total neglect of sensible conservation of resources, funds, prior public investment, and just plain common sense.[124]

The fluctuating fate of mobile home owners in the New Jersey court illustrates the priority of policy over rights. In *Mount Laurel II*, Chief Justice Wilentz overturned a 1958 precedent, *Vickers v. Gloucester Township*,[125] which had upheld local prohibitions of mobile homes. But Wilentz justified the change not by arguing that liberty was essential but by explaining that mobile homes had changed. In short, they were not as tacky, so respectable communities must let them in.[126] Perhaps the homes had not changed as much as the attitude of the court. As with the other inclusionary measures, allowing mobile homes now was necessary for the "general welfare." Mobile home owners would benefit only if they were serving the social crusade of the court; mobile homes would be allowed in developing municipalities as long as a sufficient proportion was set aside for low-income housing.

Similarly, for the fortunate owners in "developing" communities, the courts could intervene to ensure approval of housing projects over the objections of local governments. But once a municipality had met its "fair share," nothing more would be required by the courts, and restrictions on landowner rights would be subject only to the empty ritual of "any conceivable rational basis" review.

In *Mount Laurel II*, Wilentz latched onto the State Development Guide Plan, an obscure report issued by a state bureau, as a simple guide to which municipalities must shoulder their "fair share" and which could exclude with virtual impunity. All communities in "growth" areas, as decreed by the state, would be subject to *Mount Laurel* requirements; communities in areas where the state wished to limit growth could continue their exclusionary ways. Opportunities for mobility would depend on central government, not on individual preferences, and Wilentz saw this as cause for celebration: "The obligation to encourage lower income housing will hereafter depend on rational long-range land use planning rather than upon the sheer economic forces that have dictated whether a municipality is 'developing.' "[127]

Mount Laurel II, cautioned Wilentz, was not "an indiscriminate broom designed to sweep away all distinctions in the use of land."[128] As in *Mount Laurel I*, vestiges of hierarchy acceptable to the court could be maintained. Communities in official growth areas could still relegate the poor to certain parts of town; rural areas, such as those designated as agricultural or conservation districts by the state, could maintain their barriers. Perhaps even socially conscious jurists desire a quiet refuge where they may escape the rigors of the battle to restructure erring cities and suburbs.

Ironically, the New Jersey court was using article I, section 1[129] of the state constitution, which explicitly protects the "liberty" and "property" of citizens, as a pretext for greater central control of land use. "The basis for the constitutional obligation is simple: the State controls the use of land, all of the land," declared Wilentz in *Mount Laurel II*.[130] The court implied that as in the feudal tradition, all land rights belonged to the state and could be meted out to individual citizens in return for what the state considered socially desirable (such as the inclusion of appropriate low-income housing). Deducing such a mandate from a constitution ostensibly intended to limit government was not only defensible, according to Wilentz, but "simple." Once land rights have been given to the state, the egalitarian imperative follows; surely the state "cannot favor rich over poor."[131]

If the court's mandate was "simple," then it could openly pursue social engineering. "It is nonsense to single out inclusionary zoning," Wilentz declared, "and label it 'socioeconomic' if that is meant to imply that other aspects of zoning are not."[132] Indeed, land use regulation is fundamentally about people, and zoning has been a primary tool for shaping social relations in communities.[133] The New Jersey court had no qualms about direct social engineering, "rather than through a mass of detailed regulations governing the 'physical use of land,' "[134] because it was untroubled by constitutional limits on governmental fiddling with private concerns. Explicit requirements of low-income housing might be necessary, wrote Wilentz, "if the municipality's social goals are to prevail over neutral market forces."[135] Yet the court created the *Mount Laurel* tempest because municipalities *were* pursuing their social goals (but not the correct goals) so effectively.

Mount Laurel II was decided shortly after a presidential commission on housing, led by property rights advocate Bernard Siegan, had recommended that all land use regulations be invalidated unless shown to promote a "vital and pressing" public purpose.[136] The hope behind the recommendations was that property rights would be strengthened and housing needs better served through a freer market. "*Mount Laurel II* confirms the soundness of the Commission's recommendations," concluded Douglas Kmiec, a Notre Dame land use scholar who served in the Justice Department.[137] Land use should depend on the market, he wrote, not the "misguided opinions of a central planner."[138] He was viewing the opinion through rose-colored glasses, however. For while the New Jersey court was willing to say no to Mount Laurel, it was calling for greater centralization, not an unrestricted market.

Wilentz admitted that the regulatory imposition of costs on a property owner might raise "legal issues."[139] But he rejected any legal problem in a brief footnote where he argued that "the builder who undertakes a project that includes a mandatory set-aside voluntarily assumes the financial burden."[140] There could be no taking because the right to control use was freely given away. But the "builder"[141] may have little choice: Either accept the conditions or drop the project.

Implicitly acknowledging the questionable constitutional roots for its decree, the court asserted that "the doctrine does not arise from some theoretical analysis of our Constitution, but rather from underlying concepts of fundamental fairness."[142] Constitutional niceties were not to stand in the way of enlightened social policy. As Jerome Rose has put it, "The court found it necessary to *fabricate* a principle of state constitutional law that would put their policy beyond repeal by the state legislature and not subject to review by the United States Supreme Court."[143] Wilentz himself noted after *Mount Laurel II* that the court followed "a tradition of reform . . . not so bound by prior decisions that you don't achieve sensible, reasonable results."[144] Whether or not the results have been sensible or reasonable, he is quite right that legal precedents— or for that matter constitutional clauses—have had little effect on the court's land use jurisprudence.

In the name of justice, the court took control from both the property owners and the elected local governments. "It is the function of judges to vindicate the basic values of our civilization," applauded Norman Williams.[145] Fundamental values are crucial to the polity, but the court did not reveal why it alone can discern those values and how it does so. One might think the constitution is just the place to look for fundamental values adopted by the polity, but the court threw off the shackles of its own constitution. Howard Kurtz, a journalist, has noted that most of the New Jersey justices have come from political backgrounds.[146] Chief Justice Wilentz formerly was a Democratic assemblyman, and it appears that for the New Jersey court, judicial review has been a way to carry on politics by other means.

If *Mount Laurel* analysis were applied to free speech, the right of Nazis to speak in Skokie (a large group seeking entry to an exclusive and culturally different community) might be protected, while the city of Berkeley could legally restrict the speech of Socialists (as Berkeley has more than its "fair share" of boisterous radicals) and Stowe, Vermont, could forbid all public rallies (which might disrupt the rural serenity). Individuals who cannot live where they choose or use their property as they wish due to restrictive land regulations suffer the same infringement on their rights whether the community is Trenton, Mount Laurel, or the Pinelands.

The unequal protection of rights provided to landowners and users is understandable in light of the New Jersey court's fundamental concern with correct policy. *Mount Laurel II* was an attempt to impose greater equality in housing through hierarchical means, and the constitution was a weapon in this crusade.[147] The case, planner Ernest Erber has written approvingly, was "the New Jersey Supreme Court's way of giving the state comprehensive planning, as dreamed of by planners, despite the cowardly, essentially anti-planning, stance of the state's governors and legislators."[148] As Tarr and Porter have written, the New Jersey Supreme Court "has eagerly embraced opportunities to promulgate policy for the state and doctrine for the nation, confident of its own abilities and of the legitimacy of the activist posture it has adopted."[149] But the court was promoting public policy without democracy. A court that is conscientious about protecting rights and respecting democratic government may tell governments what policies they *cannot* pursue but will be loath to tell governments what policies they *must* pursue.[150] Even the New Jersey court had equivocated for eight years following *Mount Laurel I* before issuing the affirmative mandates of *Mount Laurel II.*

The detailed controls favored by the court clearly lacked democratic support or there would have been no need to go to court. Yet to judge from the laudatory reactions of some scholars, one might think the court had responded to the voice of the people. Wrote Norman Williams: "The New Jersey Supreme Court has dared to assume that basic democratic values can be vindicated now, over powerful political and institutional opposition."[151] This is a remarkable statement. The New Jersey court was acting to remedy what it saw as a *failure* of democracy. The danger in deluding ourselves that control by the court, however just, is somehow democratic is that we will choose the valium of euphemism rather than confront the very real conflicts between rights, democracy, and judicial power. If democracy is redefined to mean equality of condition on the assumption that there can be no true democracy without equality, then it becomes possible to grasp how a court might impose "democratic values" (that is, the preconditions for eventual democracy) over "political opposition" (products of false consciousness perhaps). "The court has taken a brave and necessary step," applauded Kayden and Zax,[152] and perhaps in time reeducated communities would legislate correctly without court supervision. As in Marxist orthodoxy, the dictatorship of the proletariat may wither away, but in New Jersey the dictatorship is robed.

MOUNT LAUREL II: THE MORNING AFTER

The floodgates had been opened by the court in *Mount Laurel I,* and in *Mount Laurel II* the court struggled with the deluge. *Mount Laurel II* consolidated several cases pending before the court; involved twenty eight teams of attorneys representing municipalities, owners, builders, housing advocates, and civil rights groups; and covered 120 pages of small print in the Atlantic Reporter. Fears that the court would become a self-appointed state land use commission appeared to be well founded as the justices struggled to contain the workload. To shift the burden, Wilentz decreed that future exclusionary cases would be handled by a special three-judge panel.

Each member would be principally responsible for a different region of the state and would become a sort of court-appointed land use czar for that region.

 Mount Laurel I and *II* provided the definitive statements of the New Jersey judicial approach to exclusionary zoning. Two subsequent cases, *In the Matter of Egg Harbor Associates (Bayshore Center)*[153] and *The Hills Development Co. v. Bernards,*[154] illustrate the obstacles and allies the court has found in its quest for the correct community.

 The New Jersey Department of Environmental Protection (DEP) was accepted by the court as a volunteer in the fair share crusade in *Egg Harbor Associates.* Under the state Coastal Area Facility Review Act, the state DEP was charged with overseeing coastal development to safeguard natural resources. The department approved the Bayshore Center plans, which included a marina, hotel, offices, and housing, on the condition that a specific number of units be set aside for low- and moderate-income housing. With only Justice Schreiber dissenting, [155] the court approved the imposition of fair share requirements by the DEP. "Powers delegated to DEP," wrote Justice Pollock, "extend well beyond protection of the natural environment."[156] Pollock had no qualms about extending broad social regulatory powers to a specialized agency charged with protecting the environment. "It would make no sense at all," he asserted, "to hold that the general welfare encompasses the provision of low and moderate income housing at the behest of municipalities, but not of state agencies."[157]

 The court effectively dissolved the boundaries between the social and natural environment, implying that any government entity with responsibility to protect or enhance quality of life should promote the egalitarian ideal preferred by the court. But as Justice Schreiber pointed out in dissent, "It would be a strained construction of 'environmentalism' that would find 'fair-share housing' among its concerns."[158] Even Schreiber was not concerned with the possible infringement of property rights by the DEP's expansive use of its regulatory powers.[159] He was concerned only that the court had distorted the intent of the Coastal Act and taken away rightful powers of municipal governments. The Coastal Act, which predated *Mount Laurel,* was intended to protect the environment *from* residential development, according to Schreiber, and did not grant a general zoning power, which remained with municipalities. But the court majority appeared willing to grant broad powers to any land use regulatory agency that would adopt the fair share perspective.

The courts were being overwhelmed by the avalanche of litigation in the wake of *Mount Laurel II*, and in *Hills Development Co.* the court took the opportunity to transfer primary responsibility for the enforcement of fair share principles to state government. It may be an exaggeration to write, as journalist Anthony DePalma did, that the court "essentially washed its hands of the whole mess,"[160] but it was certainly a "strategic retreat."[161] After years of resistance, the state legislature had approved a plan for policing local governments, the Fair Housing Act,[162] that satisfied the court. Finally, the branch of government with the legal power to legislate for the general welfare was falling into line. Under the act, a Council on Affordable Housing, using the state development plans, would determine regional housing needs and certify compliance by localities. State suits that claimed local regulations were unconstitutionally exclusionary would be transferred to the council. Although the court cautioned that it would take active control if the council faltered in its mission, the justices accepted the invitation to transfer some of the political heat to a new body.[163]

In the *Mount Laurel* cases, the court had awarded a builder's remedy intended to allow the property owner to proceed with his project. A few owners and developers might profit, but the court was using them only as a convenient means to an egalitarian end. The builder's remedy was "not for the benefit of any builder," Chief Justice Wilentz declared for a unanimous court in *Hills Development Co.*, but "simply a method for achieving the 'constitutionally mandated goal' " of equitable distribution of low-income housing,[164] so the justices approved a moratorium on builder's remedies imposed by the Fair Housing Act.[165] The collaborationist builders were no longer needed in the battle and could be dismissed. Owners whose cases had been pending for years under the *Mount Laurel* doctrine were now without a remedy; the court explicitly gave local governments the green light to rezone or even develop a disputed tract. Wilentz saw no legal objections to pulling the constitutional rug out from under the owners, explaining that "builders generally are experienced in the unpredictability of litigation."[166] Wilentz acknowledged the capricious regulatory and judicial maze that landowners must run but saw no cause for concern: "If there is any class of litigants that knows the uncertainties of litigation, it is the builders. They, more than any other group, have walked the rough, uneven, unpredictable path through planning boards, boards of adjustment, permits, approvals, conditions, lawsuits, appeals, affirmances, reversals, and in between all of these, changes in both statutory and decisional law that can turn a case upside down."[167]

Property owners have been subject to such procedural abuses precisely because courts have been reluctant to step in and protect their rights. Yet the reward for owners who have endured is to lose an effective remedy; the court gave owners a dubious compliment by implying they were tough enough to endure. The New Jersey court never actually referred to property rights or owners, however, preferring to speak of "builders" and "developers," as if only crass economic interests, not fundamental rights, were at stake. Rights, after all, would merit protection, while mere interests can be left to the shifting winds of political fortune.

The exclusionary attack in New Jersey, in contrast to that in Pennsylvania, was never motivated by protection of property rights. The New Jersey court sought to redirect the regulatory power to serve egalitarian ends; along the way, an individual owner or builder might benefit. Across the Delaware, the Pennsylvania court had continued to develop a doctrine of constitutional property rights while also expressing concern for "fair shares" and local autonomy. How the court sought to achieve this balancing act in the 1980s is my next subject.

BACK IN PENNSYLVANIA: A DOCTRINE IN SEARCH OF A RATIONALE

During the 1980s, the Pennsylvania Supreme Court continued to justify the invalidation of regulations as a protection of individual liberty while still incorporating the "fair share" principles of the New Jersey court. The standard of review employed by the court varied, depending on the fact patterns and on which justices reached agreement on an opinion, and occasionally it varied even within a single opinion. Even when the court did not employ heightened scrutiny, approval of regulations was not a foregone conclusion. Indeed, the court's weakest scrutiny could be quite searching at times. The hypothetical flights of fancy undertaken by the U.S. and California high courts in search of imaginative justifications for regulation, which I will discuss in subsequent chapters, have been virtually unknown in Pennsylvania. As in the other constitutional land use areas, the court split its exclusionary and related cases evenly between victories for localities and for plaintiffs (Table 6). No particular circumstances ensured certain victory for property rights, but on the other hand, none spelled certain defeat. In part, the uncertainty indicates a court in flux, groping for a consistent, acceptable doctrine.

Down on the Farm

In *Hopewell Township Board of Supervisors v. Golla*,[168] the court considered the constitutionality of an ordinance restricting development on agricultural land. This was just one of many restrictions on farmland enacted by communities throughout the state and beyond to "save the family farm."[169] The only problem was that not all farm owners wished to be saved. Andrew Kinzler and George Ritter noted in regard to farm restrictions in New Jersey that "the interest group . . . most conspicuously absent from the side of farmland preservation, was the local farmers themselves."[170] "Right to farm" laws,[171] to the extent that they reduce the options of farm owners, might be termed "obligation to farm" laws. Farmers wishing to sell to housing developers have often found the restrictions substantially reduced the value of their property.[172] In *Golla*, the owners of a farm wanted to subdivide the property into as many as fourteen lots for single-family homes, but Hopewell Township allowed a maximum of only five lots on farmland, regardless of the size of the original tract. The court rejected this ordinance as unreasonable, although the path by which it reached this conclusion is slippery and provides a good example of the adventure involved in studying state constitutional law.

Justice Flaherty, writing for the court, included a long quote from *Kit-Mar Builders* vigorously defending the role of property rights as a bulwark against communism, and castigated the regulation because it did not meet a stiff standard:

> The restrictions on landowner rights imposed by the ordinance are too severe to be regarded as "clearly necessary" when their burdens are balanced against the public interest sought to be protected. The zoning scheme of Hopewell Township unquestionably has *some* relationship to the goal of preserving farmland; . . . the deficiency is the failure of the municipality to use *less restrictive* means of furthering the goal of agricultural preservation.[173]

Flaherty's language reflects the "strict scrutiny" standard used by the U.S. Supreme Court to protect preferred rights such as freedom of speech. Only if a regulation is clearly necessary will it be upheld, a very difficult burden to carry. It is not surprising that Justice Flaherty found the Hopewell ordinance lacking, but it is remarkable is that Flaherty used three standards in his opinion. The ordinance failed under all three, and Flaherty apparently considered the tests interchangeable.

In *Surrick*,[174] the court had indicated it would formally raise the level of scrutiny when a municipality was in the path of likely population growth or totally banned a legitimate land use. In these cases, the burden would shift to the municipality to prove there was a "more substantial" relationship between the regulation and the public purpose. But neither of those conditions applied in the Hopewell case. The township was not forbidding single-family homes, merely restricting them. And the court gave no consideration of the growth potential of the community, possibly because it considered the issue irrelevant when no multifamily projects were at stake. Why Flaherty used heightened scrutiny in *Hopewell Township* is not clear.

The mystery deepens because Flaherty asserted that the court's opinion was compatible with a state law requiring the court to find that there is no "reasonable" relationship prior to striking down an agricultural preservation regulation. The statute's weak level of review appeared to present a serious roadblock, as even Flaherty admitted there was some relationship between the ordinance and agricultural preservation.[175] The court could either lower its standard of scrutiny or declare the statute an unconstitutional infringement of the court's power of judicial review, as the lower court had done. But Flaherty took neither course; instead, he read a stricter standard into the statute. A "reasonable relationship," he argued, implies that an ordinance must be "substantially related" to a proper governmental objective and must not "unreasonably restrict" a landowner's right. The court raised the hurdle from "reasonable" to "substantial" and added a second obstacle, the effect on property rights, all under the aegis of a statute clearly intended to restrain the court. Under this interpretation, the impact on the owner's rights doomed the Hopewell ordinance. Although the regulation promoted agricultural preservation, "the public interest in preventing irretrievable loss of agricultural land does not presently warrant overriding appellees' interest in using the land in a less restricted manner, including their right to use property in less than the most efficient manner."[176]

Flaherty's argument reveals recurring themes in the court's opinions. Unlike more deferential courts like the U.S. and California supreme courts, the Pennsylvania court takes landowner rights very seriously. And the justices have been very wary of the sort of social engineering embraced by their New Jersey brethren. But it would be wrong to characterize the Pennsylvania court as an activist developer's court. The court has not promoted a particular vision of social efficiency, a society growing by leaps and bounds while developers grow rich, but rather has been concerned with the rights of owners to do as they please, whether that be to build housing, farm, or just enjoy the view. And if a group of suburbanites collectively wished to preserve the view of farmland, the court implied, they (or the town) could buy the property. Unfortunately, Flaherty's opinion also illustrates the inconsistent reasoning common in Pennsylvania decisions. The justice used different levels of scrutiny with no hesitation or acknowledgment. In his concurring opinion, Justice Hutchinson asserted simply that the ordinance lacked a "reasonable relationship," which was the standard specified in the statute and quite distant from Justice Flaherty's rhetorical flourishes.

The court had recklessly crossed the line into policy activism, complained Justice McDermott in his dissenting opinion: "The majority has determined to set its own standards for what is good in Hopewell Township."[177] Using a low level of scrutiny, McDermott would have deferred to the judgment of the township. The disproportionate impact of the ordinance on large landowners was not constitutionally fatal, in his view. Since large owners held more of the agricultural land, they could reasonably be expected to give up more for its preservation. Unlike the plurality opinion, which did not consider the exclusionary impact of the ordinance at all, McDermott argued that the closer scrutiny applied to exclusionary regulations was inappropriate in Hopewell, although he did not explain whether that was because the township lay outside the path of growth or because the exclusionary impact of the ordinance was inconsequential: "This is not an ordinance designed to save one's happy valley from unwanted strangers; it is a salutary and essential consideration, for the welfare of all, that unique land be preserved to maintain the very stuff of life."[178] McDermott gave no consideration to the impact of the ordinance, however, "salutary," on the rights of the owner, while for Flaherty, this impact justified overturning the ordinance. Flaherty collapsed three standards into one, while Hutchinson and McDermott ostensibly used similar standards but reached quite different conclusions. Such are the joys and surprises of reading Pennsylvania opinions.

Hopewell Township shows that even when there are not *Surrick*-type circumstances shifting the burden of proof and raising the standard of review, the Pennsylvania court looks closely at land use regulations. But the court does not always side with the property owner, as *Boundary Drive Associates v. Shrewsbury Board of Supervisors*[179] shows. In a case quite similar to *Hopewell Township*, the court rejected a property owner's challenge to an agricultural preservation ordinance. As Thomas Buchanan noted, the court downplayed the impact of the ordinance on the individual owner, emphasizing instead the comprehensive purpose of the preservation plan.[180] *Boundary Drive* stands out as the only constitutional case of the decade in Pennsylvania since 1982 in which the landowner interest lost by more than a single vote.

In *Hopewell Township*, a regulation that prevented a property owner from creating more than five lots on 140 acres was struck down by a 6-1 vote. In *Boundary Drive*, an ordinance forbidding more than four lots on 60 acres was upheld unanimously. How could the court reach such different conclusions with such strong agreement? For the court, the line was clear: The Hopewell ordinance made no provision for different-size tracts (five homes was the maximum, no matter how large the agricultural plot), while Shrewsbury allowed a nominal increase in homesites for large agricultural tracts. Had Golla sought to subdivide in Shrewsbury instead of Hopewell, he could have created seven lots on his 140 acres.

The court seized on a minor factual difference to distinguish the two cases, creating the appearance of moderation in its decisions, but provided little guidance to landowners and local officials. *Boundary Drive* reads more like a decision of the California Supreme Court than the Pennsylvania court. Rather than explain persuasively *why* the modest difference between the two ordinances should be so crucial, the court switched from being vigilant to being deferential. Had the levels of scrutiny been reversed in the two cases, I suspect the outcomes also would have been reversed. Whereas the *Hopewell* court read a tough standard into a weak statute, the *Boundary Drive* court relied on speculative language such as "could rationally conclude that" and "conclusion could be based on the knowledge that." Curiously, the *Boundary Drive* opinion was written by Justice Hutchinson, one of the most vigorous defenders of property rights on the Pennsylvania court. And Justice Flaherty, who authorized the opinion in *Hopewell*, changed his tune in his *Boundary Drive* concurring opinion. The opinions leave the reader to wonder whether the court applied a logical test to the facts or agreed on the results first and then selected the most compatible arguments. Buchanan cast the contradiction between the opinions in a charitable light when he wrote of *Boundary Drive*, "The decision should be read as an attempt by the court to avoid any formulation of a mechanical test, which would lead to greater predictability, but would remove the court from a case-by-case analysis."[181] Predictability has not been the Pennsylvania court's problem.

The agricultural preservation decisions illustrate the promises and pitfalls of a court that treads a middle path. The court has not resorted to a simple rule that mechanically spells defeat or victory for certain parties. It has given serious consideration to arguments on each side, showing some deference to the legislative judgments of governments while also requiring respect for individual rights. By seeking a road between judicial abdication and imperialism, the court has taken on a demanding task, a task it has not always fulfilled in a clear and consistent manner.

The Pennsylvania court did not fully consider the exclusionary impact in these cases of agricultural preservation. Yet the result might be that many families who would like to move into the townships would be denied the opportunity. This lack of attention may show the influence of the New Jersey "fair share" doctrine, which emphasizes exclusion in metropolitan but not rural areas. In the future, the court may be more critical of the exclusionary effects of agricultural ordinances and other environmental measures. Or it may discard the exclusionary banner, preferring to weigh the public purpose of the township against the rights of the owners without attention to the harm to those waiting at the gates of the community.

Keeping Out Multifamily Housing

The Pennsylvania court decided three cases during the 1980s in which a majority of the justices addressed issues of exclusionary zoning. Comparing the rationales of the cases shows the conflicts the court has experienced over how to develop a distinctive jurisprudence of constitutional property rights. In *Surrick* in 1978, the court had announced two quite different threshold questions, either of which would shift the burden to the municipality to show a "more substantial" relationship between the public purpose and the means employed. The first question is whether the locality has completely banned a legitimate land use. The second is whether the community is a logical area for significant growth. In the latter case, fair share principles would apply. But two 1983 cases, *In re Appeal of M. A. Kravitz*[182] and *In re Appeal of Elocin*,[183] show the court has been reluctant to require townships to share what some think is fair.

In theory, there are three circumstances that could cause the standard to shift (boxes I, II, and III in Table 1): a total ban in a

Table 1
Exclusionary Analysis in Pennsylvania:
Threshold Questions

	Logical Area for Growth?*		Question Not Considered*
	Yes	No	
Total ban of legitimate land use	I	III	FERNLEY
Partial ban	II	IV *Kravitz* *Elocin*	
Extent of ban not considered			GEIGER *Boundary Drive* HOPEWELL

*Cases are categorized by their majority or plurality opinions.
UPPERCASE case names indicate landowner victories.
I   Precedents suggest strictest scrutiny.
II, III   Precedents suggest strict scrutiny.
IV   Precedents suggest lower scrutiny.

growth community, a total ban not in a growth community, or a partial ban in a growth community. But the three boxes are empty. In practice, the justices have rarely gone through a two-step threshold analysis. Rather the justices have ignored one or the other of the questions and chosen the sort of scrutiny they preferred. *Elocin* and *Kravitz* were the only cases in which a plurality opinion employed the two-step analysis, and in both cases the court dismissed the complaints after finding that the conditions that would raise the level of scrutiny were not present (box IV in Table 4). In contrast with New Jersey, the fair share doctrine in Pennsylvania has functioned largely to get communities off the judicial hook. When the court has placed an emphasis on evaluating the growth potential of a community and the adequacy of the community's efforts to accommodate that growth, it has rejected the constitutional challenge.

   In *Kravitz*, a property owner claimed that the township was exclusionary because it made no provision for townhouses and allocated only 40 of 6,491 acres for multifamily housing. But the court, in an opinion by Justice Zappala, rejected both claims. Zappala argued that a total exclusion was not sufficient to raise the level of scrutiny. His opinion came closest to the New Jersey approach as he considered potential for growth, not interference with the landowner's rights, the crucial issue. Zappala read the *Girsch*[184] case to permit a total ban if a community was not developing, an interpretation that other justices rejected. By considering the extent of the prohibition first, the lower court "short circuited the analysis," according to Zappala.[185] But he covered all bases by also arguing that even if a total ban on townhouses was unconstitutional, a township need not "provide for" all uses. That is, since the township did not explicitly ban townhouses but simply had no zone that formally permitted them, it passed constitutional muster. And he argued that no use had been entirely excluded because townhouses were not a distinct use but a "particular design type."[186] Zappala's preferred threshold inquiry was whether the township had adequately provided for growth. He found that it had because he considered it to be removed from growth pressures. Thus the only issue remaining was whether a partial restriction on multifamily housing in a community not subject to fair share requirements was constitutional, and Zappala easily found that it was.

Zappala applied his *Kravitz* reasoning again in *Elocin*. The township rejected a plan, after subjecting it to thirty eight public hearings,[187] to construct 872 apartments in a district allowing only single-family homes. The township permitted a limited number of two-story, four-unit apartments but made no allowances for mid- or high-rise buildings or townhouses. The exclusion of particular types of multifamily housing was not seen as a serious issue by Zappala:[188] "We do not agree that a municipality must necessarily provide for every conceivable use."[189] Again he asked if the township was a logical area for growth and whether it had reasonably accommodated regional needs. Zappala declared that the township was fully developed and had sufficient multifamily housing. The restriction on the owner's rights was inconsequential as the town was not in a position substantially to affect housing distribution.

The *Kravitz* and *Elocin* decisions underscore the limited impact of the fair share doctrine in Pennsylvania. As Victor Delle Donne wrote of New Jersey and Pennsylvania, "These sister jurisdictions have parted ways" on the fair share test.[190] Indeed, several members of the court declined to apply fair share principles, and when they were applied, as in Zappala's opinions, the effect was to absolve the community from constitutional obligations toward either the landowners or potential residents. If in the New Jersey fashion egalitarian housing policy and not property rights is the central concern of the court, then the fair share test is the standard by which local regulations shall be judged. Zappala went further than the other justices in adapting this position, indicating in *Kravitz* that even a total ban of a legitimate land use would not provoke heightened scrutiny if the community was exempt from fair-share requirements. The rights of the property owners would then vary depending on the type of community in which they were located. But in both cases Zappala went on to consider the extent of the prohibition, a question that would appear unnecessary to his analysis. He conveniently found that the restricted uses were not land uses in their own right but merely minor categories of more general land uses. He thus avoided the difficult issue of how closely the court would review an ordinance that prohibited a legitimate land use in a community that was not developing.

Both *Kravitz* and *Elocin* were decided by one-vote margins and provoked heated dissents, Justice Hutchinson taking the most libertarian view. He did not ask whether the community was developing, as the infringement of property rights would be the same whether the community was growing or not. For Hutchinson, no township should be immune from scrutiny: "Living communities are at least dynamic things and cannot cease developing."[191] The first question for Hutchinson was whether the restriction on land use constituted a total prohibition of a legitimate land use. In both cases, Hutchinson argued that townhouses are a distinct land use and that the townships failed to justify the bans. Forbidding townhouses not only offended the rights of the owners but also resulted in "practical exclusion of a large class of people from home ownership."[192] The goal of ensuring equitable housing opportunities for low- and moderate-income families was for Hutchinson compatible with an emphasis on property rights. "The simple fact that someone is anxious to build townhouses in this Township," Hutchinson reasoned, "is a strong indication that people desire them. We do not believe Wrightstown Township can close its doors to these people."[193] Hutchinson implied that leaving decisions in private hands would promote housing opportunities while also preserving rights.

Justice Nix took a position between Zappala and Hutchinson, although he did not clearly explain his reasoning in either case. He agreed that the exclusion of townhouses was an unconstitutional total prohibition, yet he also considered whether the communities were developing. Unlike *Zappala*, Nix found that they were, and thus the ordinances were unconstitutional under either test for heightened scrutiny. Nix criticized *Zappala* on two counts: dismissing the significance of the restriction on townhouses and underestimating the potential for development. "The relaxed judicial review of suburban zoning decisions," he wrote in *Kravitz*, "permits virtually unlimited freedom to developing municipalities to erect exclusionary walls on their boundaries, according to local whim, and to use the zoning power for aims far beyond its legitimate purposes."[194]

The *Kravitz* and *Elocin* decisions left questions whether the Pennsylvania Supreme Court was retreating from its leading role in exclusionary zoning cases. No single doctrine for subjecting land regulations to close scrutiny had commanded a majority of the court, and plaintiffs were losing their cases. This trend continued with the *Boundary Drive* case in 1985, in which the court unanimously upheld an agricultural ordinance only marginally different from one it had overturned three years earlier, and without any consideration of the exclusionary implications. But the court returned to the fray in *Fernley v. Board of Supervisors of Schuykill*,[195] when it unanimously struck down a local ordinance as exclusionary.

Schuykill Township had banned all multifamily housing, except that two-family houses were allowed in one zone on lots larger than ten acres, an exception that could hardly be expected to tap a large potential market. But the commonwealth court (the intermediate appellate court in Pennsylvania) rejected the plaintiffs' claim, concluding that the community was not a logical area for growth and that therefore no one had been excluded.[196] This ruling forced the high court to decide whether it would consider fair share policy analysis as the only valid test of constitutionality or would protect property rights in communities deemed not to be developing.

In his majority opinion, Hutchinson acknowledged that the fair share test was "intended to foster regional growth." But as in his earlier dissenting opinion, he argued that "considerations underpinning the fair share principle are irrelevant when . . . a basic form of housing" is excluded.[197] Since the ban was complete, families might be excluded even though the community as a whole expected little growth. In *Fernley*, a majority of the court was finally willing to agree that such a restrictive ordinance was unconstitutional, independent of growth considerations. Justice Papadakos, new to the court, joined with Flaherty and Larsen to forge agreement on the reasoning. The opinion was a promising sign that a majority of the court would move toward agreement on a consistent approach to exclusionary land use regulation.

Justice Nix's concurring opinion again contained something to please both camps of Pennsylvania justices. He found the ordinance unconstitutional under *either* the fair share or total ban approaches and once again gave little clue about which question if either he considered preeminent. McDermott was concurred with the majority but only under the fair share test. The complete prohibition of multifamily housing was too much, even for Zappala. To remedy the abridgment of the landowner's rights, the court awarded a builder's remedy, approving the plaintiff's plan for development over a town's objection. Municipalities see this as a severe price to pay for a little unconstitutional indiscretion, but Nix argued that it was necessary to deter zealous regulators and guard against retaliation directed at the plaintiff. "Obviously, if judicial review of local zoning action is to result in anything more than a farce, the courts must be prepared to go beyond mere invalidation and grant definitive relief."[198]

If the court was willing to strike down only unconstitutional regulations, a town dedicated to keeping out homes with common walls could simply reenact the legislation in slightly different form and force the plaintiff to sue again. Or a town might zone other land for multifamily housing while designating the plaintiff's property as open space, singling him out for punishment. The U.S. Supreme Court has been slow to see the danger in this merry-go-round of regulation,[199] while the California court gave a green light to municipalities.[200] Justice Brennan had urged that because invalidation was not an effective remedy, the Supreme Court should require compensation for regulatory takings,[201] a position finally adopted by the Court in *Nollan v. California Coastal Commission*.[202] Interestingly, the Pennsylvania court "has not been receptive to such an award of damages in the zoning context."[203]

McDermott and Zappala, the justices most reluctant to protect property rights, sharply objected to the builder's remedy in *Fernley*. Zappala asserted that while the township may have exceeded its police power, there was "no substantive right to develop."[204] McDermott argued that municipalities should have an opportunity to mend their ways without being forced to capitulate to the victor's plan. "Communities should be permitted to make a good faith attempt to amend their ordinances," he wrote, "without having a possible white elephant foisted upon them to forever remind them of their past errors."[205] The majority was willing to approve the builder's plan, however, and such strong remedies are a telling indication of the seriousness with which the court regards infringement of property rights.[206]

Mobile Homes

In *Geiger v. Zoning Hearing Board of North Whitehall*,[207] a commonwealth court had struck down an ordinance banning mobile homes from individual lots as unconstitutional on the grounds that it was a total ban on a legitimate use.[208] The supreme court affirmed the decision, but for different reasons,[209] and the opinions provided little assurance that the court was following a consistent analysis. Had the court agreed that the total ban constituted exclusion, as Justice Larsen did in a concurring opinion, it would have affirmed that the extent of the ban was now the line of analysis accepted by a majority of the court. But Justice McDermott, reluctant as usual to find clear limits to local regulation (absent sufficient growth pressures), chose to frame the issue differently in his majority opinion.

Even though he did not ask either question that might result in stricter scrutiny,[210] McDermott found the ordinance unconstitutional. The ordinance allowed manufactured homes to be assembled on-site, and McDermott used this provision to argue that the North Whitehall ordinance was deficient not because it limited a legitimate use but because it did so in an "arbitrary and capricious" fashion,[211] allowing two-section homes but not single-section homes, and thus was "beyond the Township's legitimate exercise of the police power."[212] This is the logic of an equal protection argument, but McDermott did not specify what the constitutional basis was for his ruling. This reasoning left the municipality free to regulate if it changed the wording of its ordinance, possibly to ban both types of houses. McDermott thus checked the power of local governments while providing little substantive protection for property owners. By rejecting the reasoning of the intermediate court, McDermott contradicted the emerging Pennsylvania doctrine that the extent to the prohibition was the important threshold question and avoided all consideration of exclusionary consequences. His opinion muddied the doctrinal waters that were beginning to clear in Pennsylvania.

Justice Hutchinson added to the muddle in a brief concurring opinion in which he asserted that the majority "implicitly recognizes" a distinction in exclusionary zoning doctrine between equal protection analysis, used when people are excluded, and due process analysis, appropriate when the rights of landowners are affected.[213] This is an appealing but deceptive distinction. The court does entertain two distinct approaches to exclusionary zoning litigation, and the libertarian concern with property rights finds more support on the court than the egalitarian emphasis on equality in housing. But McDermott's majority opinion made no direct mention of either constitutional clause, and his criticism of the distinction between housing types could be based on either equal protection or due process.

Searching for Patterns

Although the Pennsylvania justices are not always consistent, some patterns emerge from the 1980s. In exclusionary zoning cases, the justices most protective of property rights, especially Larsen and Hutchinson, tended to employ the total prohibition test. While they were concerned with the dangers of exclusionary zoning, they were reluctant to pursue the lead of the New Jersey court in directing where housing development should take place. These justices tended to translate exclusionary arguments into property rights issues and to emphasize the exclusionary consequences of any significant limit on the owner's right to build. The reasoning of Justice Nix, also a consistent advocate of the rights of landowners, was closer to the moderates on the court. Nix agreed that significant restrictions on property rights merit special scrutiny, but he emphasized that the growth potential of a community was equally important. He was likely to find a constitutional violation but was not so particular about the reasoning. Justice McDermott was less inclined to safeguard property rights and preferred to consider the effect of land restrictions on the housing needs of the region rather than on the rights of individual owners. Justice Zappala, the current justice least likely to rule in favor of landowners, shared Justice McDermott's preference for fair share analysis. But he was most reluctant to find that a community had failed to meet its inclusionary obligations.

VOICE AND VOTE ON THE PENNSYLVANIA COURT

The advocacy of landowner liberty expressed in many of the court's exclusionary zoning opinions builds on a long tradition

Table 2
Pennsylvania Supreme Court Decisions
on Constitutional Rights of Landowners

	Landowner Won	Landowner Lost	Vote
1987	*Hughes v. DOT*		7–0
	Ridley Arms		4–1
1986	*Social Workers*		5–1
	Appeal of Geiger		7–0
1985	*Fernley*		7–0
		Boundary Drive	7–0
1983		*Appeal of Elocin*	4–3
		Layne v. Zoning Board	4–3
		Appeal of Kravitz	4–3
1982	*Hopewell Township*		6–1
		Miller & Son Paving	7–0
	Oil City v. Woodring		7–0
1981	*Hardee's v. DOT*		4–1
		Pennsylvania v. Tate	4–1
1980		*National Wood*	5–0

Landowner wins: 8
Landowner defeats: 7
Percentage won: 53

of property rights protection in Pennsylvania. The state constitution[214] embraces the natural law tradition that rights are inherent in the individual rather than granted by the government. Property rights are given explicit protection in the very first section of the constitution.[215] The rights are "inherent and indefeasible"; they precede and will succeed the state; they cannot be given away. "All men are born equally free and independent," the state constitution proclaims. The language mirrors the Declaration of Independence and is more explicit in one important respect. Men are not created equal but are equally free. It is equality of liberty, not equality itself, that is the ideal on which the commonwealth is founded. The constitutional tradition in Pennsylvania is one of suspicion of strong central government and elevation of liberty to the transcendental value of the polity.[216]

While the words of the Pennsylvania justices often defend property rights, the decisions of the court are more ambivalent. Analysis of the land use cases raising constitutional issues decided by the Pennsylvania Supreme Court in the 1980s shows that the court has hardly been an impregnable fortress of landowner rights.

Table 3
Lopsided and Close Decisions
in Pennsylvania Landowner Cases

	Unanimous Decisions	One Vote in Dissent	Decided by One Vote
Landowner victories:	*Hughes* (1987) *Geiger* (1986) *Fernley* (1985) *Oil City* (1982)	*Ridley* (1987) W. *Penn* (1986) *Hopewell* (1982) *Hardee's* (1981)	
Landowner losses:	*Boundary Drive* (1985) *Miller* (1982) *National Wood* (1980)	*Tate* (1981)	*Kravitz* (1983) *Elocin* (1983) *Layne* (1982)

The court was as likely to reject the claims of landowners as substantiate them during the decade. Of the sixteen constitutional land use cases, property interests won 53 percent (Table 2). Even the unanimous decisions were closely divided (four favoring landowners, three against), indicating the court is not heavily tilted in a particular direction (Table 3).

Although the court divided its constitutional decisions evenly between the opposing interests, victories for government tended to be narrow. All the cases that were decided by a single vote during the 1980s resulted in victories for governments (Table 3). In contrast, every case (with one exception, *Pennsylvania v. Tate*)[217] in which there was only one dissenter was won by the landowner party. Outcomes were balanced, but margins were not. Table 4 shows this tilt toward property rights clearly: Although the court was split in its decisions, the sum of the votes by individual justices leaned toward property rights (60.6 percent of votes favored owners). Only Justices Roberts, McDermott, and Zappala had voting records showing tendencies to support government parties, and only Roberts showed strong opposition to property rights (22.2 percent support). At the other extreme, justices Larsen and Hutchinson have strong records of voting in support of property rights (78.6 and 75 percent, respectively), joined more recently by Justice Papadakos (80 percent voting support for landowner parties).

The Pennsylvania justices supported property rights with their voices as well as their votes. There was a striking contrast between the sometimes strident language and the divided record of the court. "While the rhetoric [of the Pennsylvania justices] is fre-

Table 4
Vote Support for Landowner Rights,
by Pennsylvania Supreme Court Justices

Justice	+	−	Pct.	(+−)	Justice	+	−	Pct.	(+−)
Papadakos	4	1	80.0	+ 3	Kauffman	1	1	50.0	0
Larsen	11	1	78.6	+10	McDermott	5	6	45.5	−1
Hutchinson	9	3	75.0	+ 6	Zappala	4	5	44.4	−1
Nix	10	4	71.4	+ 6	Roberts	2	7	22.2	−5
Flaherty	9	6	60.0	+ 3	Eagen	0	1	00.0	−1
O'Brien	2	2	50.0						
					Total	57	37	.606	

+: votes in favor of landowner party
−: votes against landowner party
+−: favorable votes minus unfavorable votes

quently strongly pro-developer," Norman Williams concluded in 1974, "the pattern of decisions has run definitely in favor of the towns."[218] Although the court in the 1980s did not show the tilt toward government Williams reported, advocates of governmental intervention in land use affairs can still agree with Williams that "the bark is far worse than the bite."[219] More than two-thirds of the opinions (including concurrences and dissents) were in support of property rights (Table 5), while the decisions of the court were evenly split. The justices who most strongly supported property rights were most inclined to put their opinions in print. Three justices, Larsen, Nix, and Hutchinson, wrote more than 75 percent of their land use opinions in support of landowners. Among the justices tending to support government interests, only Justice Roberts approached this consistency. The Pennsylvania court has lacked a forcefully voiced alternative to libertarianism that might unite its scattered pro-government decisions.

THE POLITICAL CULTURES OF THE PENNSYLVANIA JUSTICES

The willingness of the Pennsylvania court to enforce property rights has not created a docket burdened with constitutional land use cases. The court did not accept an unusually high number of land use cases, when compared to California or the U.S. Supreme Court.[220] The court's interest in landowner rights was reflected, however, in the character of the court's caseload. It was more likely

Table 5
Opinions by Pennsylvania Justices
Supporting Landowner Rights

Justice	+	−	Pct.	Freq.	Justice	+	−	Pct.	Freq.
Larsen	6	0	100.0	.43	McDermott	4	2	66.7	.55
Papadakos	1	0	100.0	.20	Flaherty	3	2	60.0	.33
Nix	6	1	85.7	.50	Zappala	2	4	33.3	.67
Hutchinson	7	2	77.8	.75	Roberts	1	3	25.0	.44
					Total	30	14	.682	

+: supporting landowners
−: against landowners
Freq: number of cases in which a justice wrote an opinion, divided by the number of cases in which the justice voted.

to hear traditional land use issues, particularly substantive due process claims, than the California or U.S. supreme courts. More than half the cases heard involved due process (Table 6), and these tended to be the cases most likely to have wide ramifications for local regulation. Unlike the California and U.S. courts, the Pennsylvania court did not during the 1980s hear any claim involving equal protection for preferred groups or free speech claims in which landowners attempt to win under more preferred doctrines.[221] These cases are probably lacking because of two factors: The court has not been quick to latch on to these new doctrines, and since the court has been willing to protect property rights, attorneys for landowners have not had to resort to imaginative schemes such as explaining that a housing development is actually an exercise of free expression.

The cultural conflicts and ambiguity that characterize exclusionary zoning opinions are found throughout the court's doctrines. The contrasting rationales preferred by different members of the court reflect different views of the world, different beliefs about what makes effective policy, and different value preferences for the just society. In choosing a particular line of analysis, the justices reveal their cultural preferences, the lenses through which they view rights, remedies, and responsibilities. The cultural perspectives of the individual Pennsylvania justices are the essential pieces that together create the puzzles of the court, and I will consider the position of each justice as I look at different land use issue areas.

Table 6
Landowner Cases in Pennsylvania, by Constitutional Issue

Issue	Landowner Victories	Landowner Losses
Due Process		
Exclusionary	Geiger (1986)	Boundary Drive (1985)
	Fernley (1985)	Elocin (1983)
	Hopewell Twp. (1982)	Kravitz (1983)
Free Speech	Western Penn. (1986)	Penn. v. Tate (1981)
Other	Ridley Arms (1987)	Nat. Wood (1980)
Eminent Domain	Hughes v. DOT (1987)	
	Oil City (1982)	
Equal Protection		Ridley Arms (1987)
		Layne (1983)
Vested Rights		Miller & Son (1982)

FREE SPEECH AND RIGHTS OF EXCLUSION

In Pennsylvania, the free speech cases did not involve (in contrast to California) property owners who sought constitutional protection under the generous cloak of freedom of speech[222] but property owners seeking to prevent others from exercising speech rights on the owners' property. The court was faced with conflicts, not alliances, between a right preferred under New Deal jurisprudence (freedom of speech) and a right discarded (control of property use). As in so many land use cases, the court split its decisions, ruling for the owner in *Western Pennsylvania Socialist Workers 1982 Campaign v. Connecticut General Life Insurance Co.*[223] but rejecting the property rights claim in *Pennsylvania v. Tate.*[224]

In *Tate*, several off-campus activists were arrested when they tried to pass out leaflets protesting the appearance of the director of the Federal Bureau of Investigation at Muhlenberg College. The college advertised the speech as open to the public by advance registration but refused to allow a protest group to demonstrate on campus. On the day of the speech, members of the group were escorted to a public sidewalk fifty yards from the site of the speech and were arrested on their third attempt to leaflet closer to the building. Writing for the majority in the 4–1 decision, Justice Roberts (one of the more egalitarian of the Pennsylvania justices) argued that private property rights must be subordinated to the rights of free speech. The college had opened its facilities for the speech and invited the public; it could not now choose to exclude incidents of expression related to the speech that it considered undesirable. Roberts acknowledged the college could require permits for political groups but concluded that the permit procedure lacked adequate standards. He relied on the recent ruling of the U.S. Supreme Court, *Robins v. Pruneyard Shopping Center,*[225] which upheld a California Supreme Court ruling[226] that a shopping center was a public forum obligated to provide a platform for the expression of others.[227] But the U.S. Supreme Court had not found such an obligation in the U.S. Constitution; it had found only that both parties lacked federal constitutional protections, leaving the issue to be settled by the states.

The *Tate* decision "chills the exercise of property rights," wrote Justice Larsen in his vigorous dissent.[228] The college should be able to enforce its right of exclusion, he argued, particularly since there was suitable public property so nearby. For Larsen, the chill that caused the most concern was not to free expression but to free use of property. The reputation of the Pennsylvania court as defender of property rights may be due in part to the frequency of opinions, often in dissent, full of rhetorical flourishes in support of property rights. *Tate* is one of many cases in which the heat of the rhetoric did not match the outcome of the vote.

When the rhetoric and the votes do coincide, as in *Western Pennsylvania Socialist Workers,* the result can be an energetic defense of liberal property rights. The court had to confront the *Pruneyard* issue head-on: Do political groups have a constitutional right to petition at private shopping centers and malls? But unlike the California Supreme Court, the Pennsylvania court declined to find such a right, even though the court acknowledged that the commonwealth's constitutional clause was "substantially the same" as California's.[229] Justice Hutchinson's opinion in the 5–1[230] case provides a stark contrast to the approach of the California court. The California court had emphasized that rights are created and regulated by government, and Hutchinson delivered a libertarian reply: "The Pennsylvania Constitution did not create these rights. The Declaration of Rights[231] assumes their existence as inherent in man's nature. It prohibits the government from interfering with them and leaves adjustment of the inevitable conflicts among them to private interaction."[232] State intervention in the name of rights is akin to legislating for the general welfare and is beyond the constitutional power of the courts, he suggested. If it were up to the state to adjust rights, wrote Hutchinson, "significant governmental intrusion into private individuals' affairs and relations would be likely to routinely occur. This intrusion itself would deprive individuals of important rights of freedom."[233]

Hutchinson presented a libertarian alternative to the egalitarian prescription of state intervention. The refusal of the court to require access to shopping malls need not mean political groups would be denied access, he argued. Individuals can best resolve conflicts between their rights when government involvement is kept to a minimum: "We believe that in the area of individual rights the forces of competition are more likely than government interference and regulation to open up our malls to peaceful political activity by all groups. . . . [This] avoids the invocation of increased government intrusion in the name of individual liberty."[234]

The free speech cases illustrate the common pattern: Pennsylvania decisions are split between the protection of landowner rights and deference to state power or other rights, while the opinions, both in number and passion of the arguments, give more vigorous support to property rights. Both speech cases involved public access to private property. When the private property was a college devoted to the exchange of ideas and the event was a speech open to the public, access was required. The *Tate* decision indicates that the Pennsylvania court will restrict property rights when a majority of the justices believe speech must take precedence. But the shopping mall was not required to open its doors to political groups. Hutchinson emphasized that the shopping center, unlike Muhlenberg College, had not opened its property for political activity and so retained a right of exclusion, regardless of the possible restriction of the avenues of expression for the Socialist workers. In these speech cases, the court established two divergent precedents. As in other areas where decisions do not consistently favor one side, outcomes turn on factual distinctions that may not be clearly predictable. If justice requires clarity, the Pennsylvania approach is disappointing, but if justice requires independent consideration of unique circumstances and conflicting claims, Pennsylvania doctrine looks more respectable.

Justice Hutchinson was the most forceful advocate of landowner rights, often devoting several paragraphs to explaining the broader implications of particular affronts to property rights.[235] In most of his opinions,[236] Hutchinson promoted a libertarian ideal in which owners control the use of their land and economic growth is seen as a benevolent force that creates opportunities for individuals. "Living communities are at least dynamic things," he wrote in his *Elocin* dissent, "and cannot cease developing."[237] Development is seen as a spontaneous process triggered by individuals exercising their "substantive right to use their land."[238] The obligation of government is to accommodate, not decree, the direction of development. Justice Hutchinson adopted the libertarian argument that the sin of exclusionary land use regulation is that it denies opportunities to individuals. Fair share allocations of development by central government would seem incompatible with an emphasis on freedom, and Hutchinson showed little enthusiasm for the doctrine.

Most of the other justices showed more appreciation of governmental regulation and were more willing to vote against property interests. It is interesting to compare Justice Hutchinson with Justice Nix, who also was critical of regulation, but from a different perspective. On the Pennsylvania court in the 1980s, only Nix showed much concern for issues of equality in his land use opinions. He was the only justice who consistently expressed his willingness to strike down local regulations under the fair share test.

Nix's dissenting opinion in *Western Pennsylvania Socialist Workers* showed that when expressive rights of some individuals conflicted with property rights of others, he was willing to use the power of the state to coerce private owners. The "mere fact that the area is privately owned," Nix argued, should not permit the mall owners to exclude political groups.[239] Nix did not share Justice Hutchinson's faith that private competition would safeguard speech rights. While both Hutchinson and Nix were critical of governmental regulation in their opinions and their votes, Nix showed more concern with egalitarian values and greater willingness to restrict the freedom of property owners.

TAKINGS AND EMINENT DOMAIN

During the 1980s, the Pennsylvania court did not award compensation for regulations that violated property rights.[240] But when a state or local agency with the power of eminent domain was involved, the court often was willing to go the extra mile to protect the landowner,[241] by broadly construing what actions could arguably be considered takings.[242] Compensation is due "whenever an entity clothed with the power of eminent domain substantially deprives the owner of the use and enjoyment of his property," the court declared in *Redevelopment Authority of Oil City v. Woodring*.[243] In that case, the agency had placed public utility lines underground, requiring homeowners to change their connections to the lines at their own expense. The Pennsylvania court declared this to be a taking requiring compensation because the cost and imposition interfered with the owner's free use of the property.

If the burden imposed on the owners by the redevelopment agency was needed to prohibit a nuisance, there would be "no compensation to the property owner even if there is an actual taking or destruction of property," Justice Larsen wrote for the majority.[244] A broad definition of nuisance could free governments from the constraints of eminent domain and compensation. The Pennsylvania court has limited the potential for abuse by narrowing the legitimate bases for governmental action. Aesthetic concerns alone (i.e., power lines are ugly) do not justify the regulatory police power, according to Larsen. Thus, Oil City still had to pay up, even though it had no intention of condemning the property.[245]

A Pennsylvania state agency was ordered to pay delay damages in *Hughes v. Pennsylvania Department of Transportation*[246] for not telling a farmer waiting to plant his crops just how soon the state would take land for a highway. Unless he could be sure he would still have the land at harvest time, the farmer argued, he could not plant, so the land already had been effectively taken. The farmer's argument faced one awkward legal problem: A state eminent domain statue precluded payment of delay damages if the owner was still in possession of the property. The court's creative solution was to read its constitutional doctrine into the statute, avoiding the need either to enforce a more restrictive statute or strike it down: "Where a declaration of taking deprives a landowner of the full and normal use of his property," wrote Justice McDermott, the owner has effectively lost "possession" and must be compensated.[247] The court was concerned not just with protecting any "reasonably beneficial use" but with protecting efficient use. "If the land cannot be put to its ordinary use because of the condemnation, such a result, without adequate compensation, would be an unjust taking and a waste of the uses of land."[248]

DUE PROCESS AND RIGHTS INCIDENTAL TO LAND USE

Most constitutional land use cases in Pennsylvania have been considered as due process claims rather than takings. But unlike the situation in more deferent jurisdictions, substantive due process never died in Pennsylvania, and the court can be quite specific at times about what rights are protected. Denying a hamburger joint direct access to a state road[249] raised the ire of the court in *Hardee's Food Systems, Inc. v. Pennsylvania Department of Transportation.*[250] "A landowner's right of ingress to and egress from an abutting public highway," asserted Justice Kauffman, "is a constitutionality protected property right."[251] Since highway access was a constitutional right, the court required the agency to conduct a full hearing on the denial.

The due process doctrine of the Pennsylvania court is rather amorphous and can turn up in unusual places. A remarkable example is *Ridley Arms, Inc. v. Ridley Township.*[252] The township required residents to pay for garbage collection even if they did not take advantage of the service. The Ridley Arms apartment complex used a private contractor who picked up garbage more frequently and at lower cost, and the apartment owners challenged the legality of the township fees. A state statute that authorized "reasonable fees and charges" appeared to doom the owners' case, as "reasonable" is usually a very low, elastic standard. Certainly the township could argue that the fees were necessary to provide effective service, even if occasionally an anomaly resulted. But the court, using due process language, transformed the statute into a requirement of economic efficiency. If a government, wrote Justice Flaherty, "cannot provide services at least of a quality and at a cost commensurate with similar services provided by private enterprise, it is, by definition, unreasonable to utilize tax dollars for that purpose. That many have lost sight of that patently obvious idea is an unfortunate as it is surprising."[253] The court implied that free enterprise and private property rights are the natural order and that government must make a strong justification for interference. If the service can be provided more effectively by the private market, the government program is unnecessary, and if it is unnecessary, it is illegal. This is a substantive due process rationale, yet the court never cited the constitution, choosing instead to inflate the statute to incorporate a constitutional standard for rationality more demanding than simple reasonableness. As in *Hughes*, the court's expansive interpretation allowed it to reach its desired conclusion without formally overturning a statute.

Justice Zappala, in dissent, asserted that the majority had "unnecessarily decided a constitutional question"[254] and warned that the court's rationale could enable residents to avoid taxes for basic public services such as schools.[255] Flaherty's indirect use of constitutional principles was not unusual for the Pennsylvania court, however, as particularly exclusionary zoning the court never explicitly cities the state constitution. Such covert constitutionalizing makes the study of Pennsylvania doctrine a particularly inexact science, as relevant cases may be camouflaged by the foliage of statutory interpretation.

Flaherty tempered his zeal for property rights in *National Wood Preservers, Inc. v. Pennsylvania Department of Environmental Resources.*[256] In *National Wood Preservers,* an industrial property owner failed to convince the court that a state order that he clean up groundwater pollution exceeded the state's police power even though the pollution was caused by a previous user and was unknown to the new owner. The forseeability of the potential pollution on the site was sufficient to uphold the abatement order. The owner must accept his responsibility, the court reasoned. "It has always been recognized," concurred Justice Flaherty, "that the 'right' of property ownership carries with it a concurrent 'obligation' which is inherent in the basic relationship of an 'owner' of property to society."[257] Read broadly, his declaration might imply that the use of land in liberal society is not unencumbered after all but tied to feudallike obligations. "Despotic dominion" over one's property, however, does not create a right to damage the property of others. If "obligations" is read narrowly to include traditional notions of nuisance, it is reasonable that a court relatively supportive of property rights would nonetheless rule unanimously against an owner whose property was polluting that of others.

ECONOMIC EQUAL PROTECTION AND VESTED RIGHTS

Landowners had no success before the Pennsylvania Supreme Court in the 1980s with traditional equal protection or vested rights arguments (Table 6). Studying state constitutional law can be a linguistic thicket, and just finding and deciphering vested rights cases is a challenge. I have included these cases as constitutional when they involved rights to use land and were not explicitly based on statutory vesting provisions. A vested right is essentially a procedural protection that creates a substantive right.[258] In vested rights cases, the dispute is not so much over the ultimate legality of the land use (which may not conform to local ordinances and lack substantive constitutional protection) but the process by which it was restricted. If a property owner wins approval for a land use project he may gain a vested right to proceed despite subsequent governmental objections.

In *Highland Park Community Club of Pittsburgh v. Zoning Board of Adjustment of Pittsburgh*,[259] a zoning administrator erroneously granted a certificate of occupancy (which was subsequently revoked) to a small apartment house in a two-family district. The owner argued that he had relied on the permit and thus had a vested right to rent out the units even though the zoning ordinance prohibited them. The court held that there was no vested right because the owner had not made a good faith effort to comply with the zoning code. If the land had been changed after the owner had made a substantial commitment to the project, the outcome might have been different. But even under the *Highland Park* facts, a more assertive court could have ruled that once granted, even in error, a permit could not be revoked or that the city had no right to exclude apartment buildings from the district.

The Pennsylvania court showed little sympathy for equal protection arguments that a regulation discriminated unfairly against certain land uses. For example, an ordinance that permitted rooming but not boardinghouses[260] in a particular zone was upheld in *Layne v. Zoning Board of Adjustment of Pittsburgh*.[261] It may be surprising that a court sympathetic to property rights would reject economic equal protection claims. Indeed, the court's grasping for a rationale to justify the distinction between rooming and boardinghouses[262] was reminiscent of the flights of judicial fancy the U.S. Supreme Court had taken under the "any conceivable rational basis test."

There are not enough equal protection cases to draw any firm conclusions, but when considered along with the court's substantive due process cases, including the exclusionary cases I have discussed in detail, it seems that the court is less concerned about infringement of rights when a particular use is prohibited in a particular zone rather than in an entire community. The lack of attention to equal protection would be more detrimental for landowners if they did not have other, more promising constitutional grounds on which to sue. Inattention to distinctions drawn in legislation and regulation is inconsequential when those measures already have been struck down under substantive due process.[263] Even so, the *Layne* case was closely decided, 4–3, indicating that equal protection arguments may be more successful with a different fact pattern or court personnel.

CULTURAL DIALOGUE AND SUPPORT FOR LANDOWNERS ON THE PENNSYLVANIA COURT

As eclectic as the decisions and opinions of the Pennsylvania court have been, there are nonetheless some common threads. When the court perceived a litigant to be seeking protection for an abusive aspect of land use, it had little sympathy. Thus, an apartment owner who had not made a good faith attempt to comply with fire or zoning codes did not have a vested right to a permit erroneously received (*Highland Park*). An industrial plant owner could be held liable for past pollution (*National Wood*). In *Layne*, the court agreed a municipality could reasonably conclude that boarding-houses, which serve meals, pose a greater health concern than rooming houses. The court resolved these cases by accepting the traditional purposes of the regulatory police power—the protection of public health and safety. Within this narrow sphere, the court was willing to give some latitude to local governments.

Regulation received a much chillier reception from the court when it did not easily fit the health and safety categories. Although the court accepted that local governments have the power to regulate on behalf of the "general welfare," the court was reluctant to interpret the term loosely, cognizant of the danger that the vague term *general welfare* can become so flexible as to justify any governmental rationale for control. The court rejected the notion, in *Oil City*, that aesthetic preferences alone can justify regulation. Even when the government had a substantial reason to impose on the rights of a property owner, as when condemning property for highway improvements, the court required that the government not unreasonably interfere with legitimate land uses. And so the commonwealth Department of Transportation must pay because it interfered with a farmer's spring planting by refusing to commit to a condemnation date. Given a land use that is not creating a public nuisance, the court will be much stricter in its review of regulation. The court has been most critical when a land use such as multi-family housing that is not a health or safety threat is entirely banned from a community.

The tilt of the individual justices toward property rights remains when their votes and opinions are considered together (Table 7).[264] The overall indexes of support do not show the emphatic slant seen in the opinions, but they still show that most of the justices have given moderate or strong support to landowner rights. Justices

Table 7
Index of Support for Landowner Rights

Larsen*	.879	O'Brien	.600	Kauffman	.333
Papadakos*	.833	Flaherty*	.567	Roberts	.289
Hutchinson	.755	McDermott*	.514	Eagen	.000
Nix*	.707	Zappala*	.422		

*Current justices
Index: (weighted vote percent × 2 + weighted opinion percent)/3

Larsen and Hutchinson have anchored the libertarian wing of the court and given consistent support to private property rights. (.879 and .755 respectively), and Justice Papadakos appears to be following in their footsteps (.833). Justice Nix often joined with the these justices to create a pro-landowner majority (he had a .707 support index) and has been attentive to both libertarian and egalitarian arguments. Of the current members of the court, Justices Flaherty, McDermott, and Zappala have formed the moderate wing, voicing varying degrees of support for the arguments that local governments ought to be free to prescribe the rights and duties of local property owners, arguments consistent with the hierarchical culture.

The balance on the Pennsylvania court between strong supporters of property rights and moderate supporters of governmental regulation is likely to continue. Of the current justices, only Zappala has tended to oppose the landowner interest (.422 support index). Roberts, the most vigorous opponent of landowner rights, is no longer on the court. At the libertarian end, Justice Hutchinson, who has written more opinions in landowner cases than any other justice in this decade, recently retired. Overall, the membership of the court has been relatively stable, especially compared to the flux on the California Supreme Court, as we will see shortly.

There are two ways to view the contrast between the balanced outcomes in the Pennsylvania court and the vigorous support for property rights expressed in many opinions. "Police power hawks," who advocate strong regulation of private property, may paint the Pennsylvania court as extremist by pointing to the libertarian rhetoric, and the opinions may bring some cheer to property owners. Certainly the vigorous assertion of libertarian values by some members of the court keeps those values on the political agenda. Rhetoric can become reality, as the arguments of the court lend legitimacy to efforts at the local level to protect property rights. Rights can provide a powerful legal and symbolic base for the pursuit of favorable policies in legislative arenas as well as in the courts. In this way, the rhetoric of the Pennsylvania justices is more than the steam released by a moderate court.

But symbolic support does not always translate into actual victories; stirring rhetoric is a Pyrrhic victory if property owners lose the crucial decisions. A careful attorney or legal scholar must look at the actual decisions, not just at the fireworks in the opinions, when assessing whether a local regulation can withstand judicial scrutiny. And in its decisions the Pennsylvania court has been scrupulous in its pursuit of balance. Although the rationales of the court have not always been consistent, it has attempted to weave a moderate course.

Partisans of strong central control or of unfettered freedom will be frustrated by a middle path, but at least the court has recognized the legitimacy of competing perspectives. I think the Pennsylvania court is a richer court because of the presence of advocates of competing political cultures. It serves to remind the court that there is more than one viable way to organize society. By debating with each other and within themselves, the justices must consider the consistency and persuasiveness of their positions. For example, the moderate justices, such as Flaherty and McDermott, have revealed that they were grappling with the merits of hierarchy and libertarianism and thus were most likely to fluctuate in their votes. The Pennsylvania court is not a model of clarity and consistency, so the predictability of law suffers, but it is struggling with essential cultural conflicts that other courts ignore and attempting to articulate a rationale for finding consensus within the conflict.

Chapter 5

California: Where Deference Reigns Supreme

Today's decision effectively pronounces that henceforth in California title to real property will no longer be held in fee simple but rather in trust for whatever purposes and uses a governmental agency exercising legislative power elects, without compensation.
—*Justice Clark, dissenting in* Agins v. Tiburon

The California soil has proved fertile ground for sprouting land use controversies. Two great forces clash in California—pressure for change and desire for stability. California offers a vigorous economy, top universities, spectacular natural beauty, and an intoxicating climate, and lures newcomers from around the country and the world. Nearly every community within potential commuting distance of an urban center is under growth pressures.[1] With constant pressures for growth and current residents of desirable communities seeking to preserve their pieces of paradise, regulatory proceedings are often packed with pressure and intrigue.

California has a reputation for innovation, whether in lifestyles or industries, and local governments are no exception. They have been in the forefront of developing new techniques to regulate growth and charging land users for benefits such as open space, parks, schools, day care, and art desired by the general public.[2] In part this has been a response to Proposition 13, which cut property taxes to 1975 levels and made general tax increases difficult, forcing municipalities to find alternatives. Proposition 13 was rather like a homeowner's version of rent control—benefiting those fortunate enough to have homes in their preferred communities while increasing the burden on those wishing to move into the state or to a different home. New homeowners must pay property taxes based on current values, substantially higher than the taxes paid by their older neighbors in identical homes. And they also must absorb the "impact" fees imposed on developers by revenue-starved municipalities. "Insofar as Prop. 13 did benefit homeowners," Edmund Andrews, a journalist, has concluded, "it did so by picking the pockets of people buying houses."[3] What many communities view as a problem—pressure for growth—is also a blessing. The desirability of many communities in California emboldens local officials and residents, confident that seekers of growth will always be waiting at the gates, to make greater demands on owners who wish to build houses, construct office buildings, or simply keep the public from trekking across their property.

Land use regulation, when it is allowed to flourish in a sympathetic judicial climate, as in California, can be a powerful weapon for preserving the status quo.[4] Regulations and complex administrative procedures can make attempts to change or intensify the use of land costly or even impossible. Those who pay the price for barriers to change, frequently in the form of housing prices that are inflated or beyond their reach,[5] often cannot even vote in the communities making the rules, as they are just moving in from out of state or have been shut out of their desired communities by the economics of the housing and job markets. Great deference toward regulation by the state supreme court combined with the competitive pressures of growth has given local regulators a strong hand to play.

If local property owners knew they were almost certain to lose their court cases in the 1980s sooner or later, why did they persist in suing local governments? Norman Williams, a leading land use scholar, has argued that when state courts are sympathetic, suits by property owners multiply, but when the courts are hostile, suits dry up.[6] Why has this not happened in California? Are property owners and builders gluttons for punishment? Perhaps they are, as it takes a special personality to endure the twists and turns and intrigues of land use administration and litigation in California. Richard Babcock and Charles Siemon have put it more pungently: "Practitioners in other states have joked about why a developer would sue a California community when it would cost a lot less and save much

time if he simply slit his throat."[7] Many land controls in California
go unchallenged by owners and developers, who may not wish to
alienate the officials upon whose good graces they depend. But there
are rational reasons for litigation. Governments in California are often pushing the frontiers of land use regulation, devising schemes
that have not been previously tested in court. Novel legal questions
are continually being raised, and there is always the hope that the
courts will draw the line and say, "This time, the government has
gone too far." And property owners may be assisted in these suits by
public interest law firms, most prominently the Pacific Legal Foundation, that urge the courts to establish precedents protecting landowner rights. Legal suits can also keep the pressure on local
regulators to be more accommodating. While confident officials
may often place heavy demands on owners who wish to use their
property, forcing owners to endure the time, trauma, and expense of
a protracted court battle to defend their rights, an owner or developer with sufficient resources can also make life more difficult for
recalcitrant local officials by forcing them into court. Even though
the government is likely to prevail in the end, it must weigh the
costs of a protracted battle.

Going to court is also a way for the owner to register her rights
claim. She may strike out before the state supreme court, but running that gauntlet may win her a chance to be heard before the U.S.
Supreme Court. The 1980s saw a renewed interest in land use cases
by the U.S. Supreme Court, and nearly all the major cases considered by the Court originated in California. Some of the cases heard
by the Supreme Court originated in federal courts (such as *MacDonald, Sommer and Frates v. Yolo County*);[8] some came through the
state court system and made the ritual stop at the state supreme
court before proceeding to Washington (*Pennell v. San Jose*);[9] and
others were declined review by the state supreme court (*Nollan v.
California Coastal Commission*).[10] All these cases raised new legal
questions through the application of unusual land regulations to
private property.

Certainly the California high court in the 1980s was not a hospitable environment for landowner rights. "The striking feature of
California zoning law," Norman Williams wrote in 1974, "is that
the courts in that state have quite consistently been far rougher on
the property rights of developers[11] than those in any other state,"[12]
and that remained true in the 1980s. Michael Berger and Gideon
Kanner, an attorney and a scholar who advocate greater protection
of property rights, have written that "California would appear to

represent the closest thing to nirvana for planners, regulators, and their legal apologists."[13] Many supporters of regulation would happily agree. A judicial earthquake recently rocked the California Supreme Court with the purge by voters of three justices.[14] The constitutional landscape may look quite different in coming years. But the new court has not yet shown that it will cancel the blank check issued to local regulatory bodies.

In *Agins v. Tiburon* (1979), the court set the tone for the coming decade when it held that the compensation provisions of the state and federal constitutions did not apply to regulatory takings, a ruling that was not repudiated by the U.S. Supreme Court until 1987. With the exception of William Clark, who would leave the court two years later, the *Agins* decision was supported by every justice, including Rose Bird and Stanley Mosk, who would lead the court through most of the 1980s. The author of the *Agins* opinion was none other than Frank Richardson, one of the stronger supporters of property rights on the court, who would leave the bench in 1984.

The Aginses bought five acres of land on which to build housing in Tiburon. Subsequently, the property was designated for open space by the city and rezoned to allow, contingent on additional regulatory approvals, construction of one to five houses. Eminent domain proceedings to purchase the property for parkland were instituted by the city but later abandoned. The Aginses took the city to court, claiming that the zoning restriction in the context of the city's other actions to preserve the property as open space constituted a taking. Rather than pay for the open space, the city could accomplish the same end through restrictive regulation, and the Aginses claimed the city did not intend to allow development. They argued that the regulation effected an "inverse condemnation" of their land requiring compensation under the takings clauses of the state and federal constitutions.

The California Supreme Court, however, ruled that the Aginses could not even sue for compensation. "We are persuaded by various policy considerations to the view that inverse condemnation is an inappropriate and undesirable remedy," wrote Richardson. "Community planners must be permitted the flexibility which their work requires."[15] Richardson argued that the threat of compensation would "chill" desirable regulation. He did not consider that the risk of discouraging well-intentioned regulation may be the price to be paid for enforcing rights. Richardson reasoned that if compensation is not appropriate for regulatory takings, owners such as the Aginses have no cause of action. The plaintiff "may not elect to sue in inverse condemnation and thereby transmute an excessive use of the police power into a lawful taking for which compensation in eminent domain must be paid."[16] The irony in Richardson's argument is that he would allow compensation for lawful takings through eminent domain but not for unlawful ones through inverse condemnation. Thus, the more arbitrary the government, the less the penalty. Seeking compensation for a regulatory taking, I would argue, does not "transmute an excessive use of the police power into a lawful taking"; it simply asks payment for a taking, lawful or not. To make an inverse condemnation claim that property was taken is not to claim it was lawful; indeed, the allegation is precisely the opposite—by declining to initiate eminent domain proceedings, the government acted unlawfully.[17]

Richardson noted that an aggrieved owner might seek invalidation of an ordinance, but as Clark argued in dissent, this may be "really a nonremedy" for the taking.[18] A municipality can reenact the ordinance in slightly revised form, continuing to deprive the owner of his property.[19] In the end, claimed Clark, owners could be "compelled to walk away from their properties."[20] Clark's assessment that property in California would no longer be held in fee simple[21] may sound a bit extreme, but it captures the central theme of the California court's landowner rights jurisprudence in the 1980s: Land may be privately held, but it is implicitly in public trust,[22] and the privilege to use one's land rests with the judgment of the government. In the land use area, the court has adopted the hierarchical notion that individuals are subservient to the greater good of the state. The court's attitude is almost feudal in character, as I discuss in the conclusion of this chapter and the penultimate chapter. The California court did not show during the 1980s any strong concern for the inegalitarian consequences of land use regulation or its limits on personal freedom.

During the 1980s, landowners won only 21 percent of the constitutional cases heard by the California Supreme Court (See Table 8). Even this rate is deceptively high. Property owners lost all but one of the thirteen cases that involved regulatory limits on property rights to use land. Victories for landowners came only when the government had formally acknowledged the rights of the plaintiff in some way, as in vested rights cases, or when a preferred right, such as free expression or privacy, was implicated (See Table 9). Even the sole takings victory, *Baker v. Burbank-Glendale-Pasadena Airport Authority*,[23] protected the privacy rather than the use of property.

Table 8
California Supreme Court Decisions
on Constitutional Rights of Landowners

	Landowner Wins	Vote	Landowner Losses	Vote
1989	*Lucero*	7–0		
1988			*Russ Building*	6–1
1986			*Pennell*	4–3
	Halaco	4–2		
1985			*Candid Enterprises*	7–0
	Baker	7–0		
			Griffin Development	5–1
	Gilmore	5–0		
1984			*Fisher v. Berkeley*	5–1
			Pardee Construction	5–2
			Nash v. Santa Monica	5–1
			Santa Monica Pines	5–2
1983			*Carson Mobilehome*	6–0
1982			*Pacific Foundation*	7–0
			Venice Properties	4–2
1981			*Fogerty*	4–2
			Lyon	4–2
1980			*Arnel Development Co.*	5–2
			Perez v. San Bruno	4–3
	Adamson	4–3		
			Metromedia, Inc.	6–1
			White	5–2
			Santa Fe	4–3
			L.A. County v. Berk	6–1

Landowner wins: 5
Landowner defeats: 19
Percentage won: 21

I will first discuss the cases in which a property owner objected to a regulatory restriction on his freedom to use his property, including the related group of public trust cases. Next I will discuss a grayer group of cases in which the dispute centered not so much on the use proposed by the owner as whether the government was playing by its own rules. Included here are issues of procedural due process, calculating just compensation, and vested rights in which some action by the government is alleged to constitute authorization for an owner to proceed with her plans. Cases in which the court sees a more "fundamental" right at stake make up the third

Table 9
California Supreme Court Support
for Landowner Rights, by Issue Area

Issue	+	−	Pct	Ratio[1]
Takings[2]	1	8	11.1	1:3
Public Trust	0	4	00.0	1:2
Procedural[3]	2	6	25.0	3:4
Expression/Privacy	2	1	66.7	4:3
Court Total:	5	19	20.8	

[1]The ratio measures the average proportion of support in each issue area. For example, a 3:4 ratio means that, on average, three justices voted to support the landowner party while four justices were opposed.
[2]Cases categorized as takings cases include cases in which a land use regulation, permit denial, or alleged physical invasion prevented the owner from using the land as he or she wished. The court challenges frequently also included equal protection and due process.
[3]"Procedural" cases include procedural due process disputes, vested rights claims, and just compensation cases.

group. I will then discuss briefly what has become of exclusionary zoning litigation in the California court and evaluate the philosophies of the individual justices and where the court might head in the future.

THE PRIVILEGE TO USE PROPERTY

In California the property owner has virtually no fundamental rights to use land under the state constitution, at least as interpreted by the state supreme court. The court in the 1980s supported the view that use of one's land is a privilege, not a right, and that private use may be conditioned on favors toward the state. The California court is the home of hierarchy in which rights are tied to roles and experts or those claiming to speak for the group prescribe the autonomy of individuals. The attachment of public service conditions to land is evocative of the feudal emphasis on status and obligation, and the heavily decentralized regulatory process can make California communities akin to feudal fiefdoms.[24] In the state of California, the supreme court implied that the king could do no wrong, although in a democracy the king is more likely to be a planning and zoning commission than a monarch in robes. During the 1980s, the California Supreme Court heard nine appeals from property owners claiming that regulatory controls on land use unconstitutionally restricted their constitutional rights.[25] Other than *Baker*, which had privacy implications that I will discuss below, the court rejected them all. Only one of the losses[26] was even close. Three decision were unanimous, and the average vote was 3–1 in favor of the government, 6–1 when *Baker* is excluded. In four other cases, the court accepted the argument that the public trust doctrine gives the state control over the use of certain private lands. These cases affected broad claims of state power over thousands of acres. When the public trust cases are added to the regulatory takings cases, there are twelve cases in which private owners objected to government control over the use of their property, and the landowners lost every appeal. These defeats came in a wide variety of contexts, from rent control and condominium conversion to easements and exactions and billboard bans, as we will see in the following sections.

MAKING LANDLORDS SERVE THE STATE

As demand for housing of all types escalates and communities resist new construction, prices for houses and rental rates rise rapidly, and those fortunate enough to have the housing they desire often seek legal advantages. Through rent control, tenants are able to insulate their rental rates from market pressures. In *Birkenfeld v. Berkeley* (1976),[27] the California Supreme Court declared that rent regulation would be upheld unless there was a "complete absence of even a debatable rational basis for the legislative determination."[28] In effect, the court abdicated any substantive review of rent control, very much as the U.S. Supreme Court had done in regard to all "economic" regulation in *U.S. v. Carolene Products Co.* (1938).[29] Any ordinance has at least a debatable rational basis, particularly in the minds of contentious and creative lawyers; indeed, an ordinance would never be passed unless someone saw some merit in it.[30] The California court approved every rent control and condominium conversion ordinance it reviewed in the 1980s despite policy arguments (quite apart from concerns for property rights)[31] that such ordinances exacerbate rental housing shortages, disadvantage poorer would-be renters, and discourage adequate maintenance.[32]

Three cases involved unsuccessful challenges to local procedures for setting rental rates. Chief Justice Rose Bird led a unanimous court in upholding rent control of mobile home sites in *Carson Mobilehome Park Owners' Association v. Carson*.[34] The ordinance had been struck down by a state court of appeals, which reasoned that the delays built into the process for approving increases and the lack of a mechanism for a general increase constituted an unconstitutional confiscation under *Birkenfeld.* The Carson ordinance, which limited rental rates and evictions, required park owners to file a petition each time they sought a rent increase, and gave the rent board up to 105 days to act on a petition. There was no routine procedure to give a general increase (for example, an increase equal to the rate of inflation) to all park owners. But the California Supreme Court, upholding the law, emphasized that the ordinance was more reasonable than the one struck down in *Birkenfeld:*[34] Owners could consolidate all the units in a park for a single application rather than the unit-by-unit procedure in Berkeley; there were only thirty-two parks, so the city could be expected to act in a timely fashion; and the 105-day waiting period at least imposed a deadline for city action. As for the constitutionality of rent control itself, the court had no doubt, declaring it was a "rational curative measure."[35]

Berkeley, undaunted by its setback in *Birkenfeld,* responded with a new measure that allowed the rent board to set a general base increase. Maximum rents would be based in part on the financial investment made by the owner but not on the current value of the property. Owners challenged the rent rules on constitutional and antitrust grounds and lost on all fronts. Writing for the majority in *Fisher v. Berkeley,*[36] Justice Mosk concluded that the ordinance was "facially constitutional under both the federal and state due process clauses: a rent control ordinance is valid if it guarantees each landlord a fair return on his investment; it need not guarantee a fair return on the value of the property."[37]

Mosk, as justices frequently do, confused the due process and takings issues, as if deprivation of value and rationality of governmental action were the same question. More accurately, Mosk rejected the takings claim when he talked of the "fair return." If an ordinance greatly reduces the value of property, it is logical that it may be unconstitutional unless the just compensation required by the takings clause is paid, even if the ordinance is rational. Conversely, an utterly irrational ordinance may nonetheless not be a taking if it does not significantly affect property rights.[38] The due process test of rationality, however confused with takings it may be, was met in *Fisher* without any expression of reasons. Indeed, none was needed, as the spineless standard of *Birkenfeld* and *Carolene Products* may be satisfied by any "conceivable" rational basis, that is, one imagined by the justices, even without a shred of evidence that it played any role in adoption of the ordinance. Mosk also rejected an equal protection challenge to the Berkeley ordinance, arguing that voters could have rationally concluded (again, actual evidence of voter rationality or intention rather than hypothetical speculation was not required) that the investment standard would provide for reasonable rents, even though some landlords would be hurt more than others.

Justice Lucas, the lone dissenter, made his stand on antitrust grounds and did not discuss the constitutional issues. His opinion is interesting, however, because it presents a contrasting cultural perspective:

> If the city fathers (and mothers) believe that rents are too high in Berkeley, several solutions come to mind which would be more consistent with the operation of the free market system. Rent subsidies may be provided to needy tenants. Public housing projects may afford additional rental units. Property may be municipally acquired through negotiated purchase or condemnation. In short, given the foregoing alternatives, why should competition between Berkeley's landlords be stifled in order to provide for the social welfare of Berkeley's tenants?[39]

Lucas was saying the city should pay for what it takes, so that the city would have a more accurate gauge of the social costs involved and would be forced to decide if its investments were efficient. Lucas questioned the rationality of the ordinance in the light of market efficiency rather than emphasizing the fundamental rights of the owners to control their own property. His libertarian prescriptions, then, were based more on utilitarian concerns than on the preeminence of individual rights.

A unique system of regulating rents was challenged in *Pennell v. San Jose*. In many respects, the ordinance was comparatively generous, guaranteeing landlords an 8 percent yearly rent increase and allowing them to petition for a larger increase. A hearing officer would consider seven factors, mostly related to costs and market conditions, in evaluating any request. But the officials could also consider the "economic hardship" for the tenant in deciding on a reasonable increase. Poor tenants could be protected from paying more rent than the city thought they could afford even though more affluent tenants might be required to pay more for an identical apartment from the same landlord. The rate plan thus would extend the subsidies required of landlords under rent control one step further. As usual in rent control, the landlords would be expected to provide the equivalent of a subsidy to their tenants by reducing rents below market rates. In San Jose, owners of units with low-income tenants could be required to pay an additional subsidy, in effect a need-based welfare payment. By requiring private owners to subsidize poor tenants, the city could provide the benefit without paying for it.

The California court upheld the San Jose ordinance by a single vote. Of the eight unsuccessful challenges to regulatory restrictions of land use on takings, equal protection, or substantive due process grounds, only *Pennell* found more than a single justice supporting the plaintiff's claim. Although Justices Mosk, Lucas, and Alex Saldamando, a temporary justice, supported rent control in principle, they were troubled that landlords with hardship tenants[40] were singled out to bear an additional burden. Mosk, blending constitutional clauses once again, wrote for the three dissenters that "such uneven treatment amounts to a forced subsidy imposed on the landlords in violation of the due process clauses of the United States and California Constitutions, which prohibit the taking of property without just compensation."[41] Mosk used the same reasoning, the unfair burden, to argue that the hardship provision violated equal protection principles: "A small class of persons, here landlords of hardship tenants, are required to shoulder what is essentially a public burden, in this case the social necessity of easing the plight of economically depressed citizens."[42] By suggesting there are limits to what may be imposed on property owners, Mosk limited the feudal notion that property owners function to serve the state.

The majority, in an opinion by Justice Grodin, upheld the discrimination under a weak rational basis standard. Since landlords with low- and middle-income tenants had the tenants that the city wished to help, it was rational, Grodin reasoned, to expect those landlords to carry more of the burden even though they might be "similarly situated" to other landlords not saddled with hardship tenants.[43] He added that in effect, the unequal protection of the law was insubstantial because all landlords could get 8 percent increases and the impact of the hardship provision was uncertain.

Mosk replied in dissent that there was no rational distinction between the landlords (although there was a difference between the tenants) to justify the discriminatory treatment. "There is no rational link," he wrote, "either in the benefit gained or the burden created, which would justify imposing that welfare obligation as a one-on-one subsidy, rather than spreading the imposition fairly through the class of landlords generally or taxpayers as a whole."[44] Penalizing landlords who have hardship tenants is not only unjust, according to Mosk, but foolish. Although Mosk has hardly been in the vanguard of libertarian thought, he criticized the city for hurting its intended beneficiaries by fiddling with the free market in language that libertarian advocates of market solutions would find comforting:

> The tragic aspect of the provision is that it will likely prove detrimental to the very interests it seeks to protect. Landlords, who will have a great deal to lose by renting to economically marginal tenants, hereafter will carefully screen potential tenants to assure themselves of remaining entitled to a fair return on their properties. It is ironic that in upholding this unconstitutional ordinance the majority accede to a counterproductive result.[45]

The ordinance also failed, according to Mosk's dissent, on takings grounds (although he did not distinguish this from due process analysis) because it was incapable of nonconfiscatory application. A hearing officer was authorized to decide upon a "fair and reasonable" rent, and the purpose of the ordinance was to avoid excessive rents. The official therefore could not authorize a rent that would be higher than the "fair and reasonable" rent. "If a proposed rent is truly in excess of his due," wrote Mosk, "it will be unreasonable by definition."[46] For the hardship provision to have any effect,[47] the rental reduction must come from what would otherwise be a "fair and reasonable" rent. The ordinance therefore could require that landlords with hardship tenants receive less than a fair rent, and that would be confiscatory. In other words, what is affordable for the tenant may not be fair for the landlord.

Justice Grodin, for the majority, adopted a wait-and-see attitude, arguing that the court could not be certain application of the San Jose rent ordinance would be confiscatory until the city actually set the rent in a specific case.[48] The court's reluctance to sustain a facial challenge to the ordinance and its willingness to speculate on possible circumstances that would avoid confiscatory application indicate the lowly status of property rights in California. In other areas, such as free speech, the court may reject a governmental measure before it is even applied for fear of chilling the legitimate exercise of rights or may strike down an "overbroad" ordinance even if it is applied constitutionally because the court can imagine circumstances under which the same ordinance might someday be used to suppress constitutional rights. But the court has shown little concern for the "chilling" of property rights, and the climate for landowners in California can be quite frigid.

NO WAY OUT

Given the willingness of the California Supreme Court to tolerate increasingly restrictive rent control, it would not be surprising that some landlords might decide it was time to change careers. Some communities have sought to limit the opportunities for building owners to escape the obligations the government would like to impose on them.[49] Conversion of rental units to condominiums may be very attractive to a landlord hemmed in by rent control, but the city of Santa Monica required that units occupied by or affordable to low- and moderate-income renters be maintained as rental housing.[50] The court upheld the ordinance in *Nash v. Santa Monica*.[51] Justice Grodin, writing for the majority, was not troubled by the limits on the freedom of the property owner, taking as an article of faith the assertion that the ordinance "clearly serves important public objectives."[52]

Grodin found that the ordinance did not violate due process or takings principles and even considered (and rejected) the argument that requiring landlords to keep units in rental stock was a form of involuntary servitude in violation of the Thirteenth Amendment of the U.S. Constitution.[53] Nash argued he had a fundamental right to go out of business, but Grodin denied that any fundamental right was at stake. If Nash did not wish to meet his responsibility, he could sell out: "If the owner wishes to pursue his preference, he may be constrained to sell his property and move elsewhere, [even if] the value of his property has decreased as a result of the regulation [and] he may . . . feel economically constrained to continue in his present field of endeavor."[54] Control of the property had been effectively divorced from ownership; the city had decided rental housing was the appropriate role for the property, and the owner was expected to shoulder his responsibilities in the land use hierarchy or sell to someone who would. Grodin noted that "the strict scrutiny standard which Nash invokes would call into question a variety of land use regulations which have thus far withstood constitutional attack."[55] Indeed it would, but that is not a sufficient reason to discard meaningful scrutiny. When rights are considered important, the expediency of not enforcing them does not sway the court. The

California court has followed the lead of the U.S. Supreme Court in invoking a double standard of constitutional rights that permits strict scrutiny to protect egalitarian rights, such as expression and equal protection for minorities, but uses minimal scrutiny to abandon rights of property.

The Santa Monica limits on personal freedom were more troubling for Chief Justice Bird, who nonetheless concurred in the court's decision. Bird agreed with Nash that strict scrutiny was merited but found the restraints on freedom to change businesses minimal and the purported purpose of the ordinance, the promotion of affordable housing, essential. Normally, strict scrutiny would insure victory for the individual, but in property rights cases victory is never certain.

Justice Mosk, in dissent, assailed the majority for allowing a government effectively to forbid an individual from going out of business. He saw the Santa Monica restriction as an intolerable affront to a basic freedom. The court majority, according to Mosk, was in effect saying "Persons who do not choose to abjectly submit to the city violating their fundamental rights should get out of town."[56] While the majority emphasized the general acceptability of rent control and saw the unique restrictions in Santa Monica as insignificant, Mosk argued that the added limits on owner autonomy comprised the central issue: "If the question is whether a municipality may exercise its police power to reasonably regulate the rental business, the answer is: generally it may do so. But if the question is whether a city may compel a landlord to remain in business against his will, and give him only the alternative of a forced sale, the answer is: not in a democratic society."[57] Not only is the freedom of the owner being curtailed, Moss noted, but he is also forced to accept legal liability as a landlord that he does not wish to accept. For the majority, it was enough that the restrictions arguably served a public purpose of preserving rental housing. Why landlords should not be forced to stay in business in a "democratic society" is not self-evident. If that is what the public wants, would it not be democratic? The protection, if any, to be provided to the owners must be rooted in the security of individual rights that limit democracy in a liberal polity.

EXACTIONS: THE PRICE OF USING LAND

Perhaps the largest set of land use cases in California involve instances in which a municipality is willing to accommodate the wishes of the owner partially, but only at a price. In return for the privilege to use his property as he wishes, the owner must provide certain services to the government. These exactions are usually over and above basic zoning restrictions and health and safety standards imposed on property. Under a zoning system, many uses are forbidden, but others are allowed as a matter of right. Often municipalities will not allow some uses in *any* district as a matter of right but require "conditional use permits" so that exactions may be required in every case. In other situations, entire districts are discretionary, such as "planned unit districts," which allows officials to condition all uses. Also, subdivisions usually require separate approval, creating an additional point at which conditions may be attached. In sum, nearly every private land use may be subject to conditions at some point. The additional costs to be imposed upon the owner are largely discretionary and may vary with the preferences, negotiating skills, and determination of city officials. Often an owner must make a specific, well-documented proposal for land use before the owner's obligations to the city are determined, adding to the uncertainty landowners face when they seek to use their property.

Exactions have proven quite popular in California as a way for municipalities to obtain public benefits without paying for them. Raising taxes is politically risky and since the passage of Proposition 13, often legally difficult. Owners wishing to use their property, given little protection by the state high court, are a tempting target.[58] The state supreme court heard and rejected three constitutional challenges to exactions during the 1980s, and in only one case was there a single justice in dissent.

The California Coastal Commission (CCC) had been created subsequent to the approval by California voters of Proposition 20, the Coastal Zone Conservation Act, in 1972.[59] The commission was charged with developing regulatory procedures and guidelines for limiting growth and increasing public access along the Pacific coast. The state and regional coastal commissions routinely demanded easements for public beach access from property owners seeking to build on their land, and by 1987 more than 1,800 easements had been required.[60]

In *Pacific Legal Foundation v. California Coastal Commission*,[61] a shoreline owner, Mr. Jackson, sought to improve the seawall that protected his property. In exchange for permission, the commission sought an easement to the entire beach area, even though there was no relation between the work on the seawall and the availability of public access. State regulations allowed exemptions from the easement requirements for seawalls that would protect existing buildings and improvements that would not reduce public access. Jackson won a court injunction, on takings grounds, requiring the commission to issue a permit. Only then did the CCC acknowledge that it had erred by requiring an easement, and the commission dropped its appeal to the state supreme court. By settling with Jackson, the commission had avoided a potentially damaging appellate precedent had the state high court agreed with the lower courts that the commission's guidelines were unconstitutional as applied. When the case reached the supreme court, only the facial challenge to the law, brought by the Pacific Legal Foundation, remained. The lower courts had refused to issue a declaratory injunction, which would have struck down the commission's regular practice of demanding easements.

The California court unanimously rejected the argument by PLF that the commission's guidelines, which were quite aggressive in seeking easements, were unconstitutional on their face. Justice Mosk, in the majority opinion,[62] relied on the hypothetical possibility that the commission could use its discretion to allow applicants to use their property without demanding easements, despite the commission's history of seeking hundreds of easements even when exemptions were specified by statute.[63] "It is sheer guesswork," asserted Mosk, "to conclude that the Commission will abuse its authority by imposing impermissible conditions on any permit required."[64] Until the court had a case of a blatant misuse of power by the commission against a specific applicant, constitutional challenges would lack "urgency and definiteness." By settling before reaching the high court, the CCC had avoided a showdown.

Despite evidence that the commission had in the past demanded questionable easements and might continue to do so, the court declined to consider the basic merits of the facial case. In other areas, such as free speech, the court often chooses to act on a facial challenge lest the presence of a censorship ordinance that might be unconstitutionally applied in the future deter the exercise of constitutional rights. Justice Mosk ridiculed the free-speech analogy. "Plaintiffs speciously contend," wrote Mosk,

> that facial review of the guidelines is appropriate because the mere presence of the guidelines chills the exercise of constitutionally protected property rights. The cited cases are entirely inapposite; they rest on the traditional preferred place of the First Amendment in our system of government and the fragile

nature of First Amendment rights. It would require truly contorted logic to extend them to the land use context.[65]

The logic that would put landowner rights on a par with expressive rights might or might not be contorted, but it would be libertarian. Mosk is again indicating the court's unwillingness to
embrace an expansive libertarian view of rights while nonetheless
protecting selective "preferred" rights. Because of the subordinate
status the California court has assigned to property rights, the court
is not concerned that they might be chilled. Consider also the
court's attitude toward awarding attorney fees to plaintiffs. Even
though the lower court had ruled that the California Coastal Commission had violated the Jacksons' constitutional rights, the state
high court refused, in *Pacific Legal Foundation,* to award attorney
fees to Jackson. Contrast this with the awarding of attorney fees, in
Press v. Lucky Stores,[66] to individuals who were prevented from
gathering signatures for a petition outside a store. Chief Justice Bird
rejected the argument that the plaintiffs in *Press,* as in *Pacific Legal
Foundation,* were only protecting their own interests and did not
win a broadly applicable ruling that would merit attorney fees.
Chief Justice Bird saw a clear difference in the importance of the
rights protected in the two cases. According to Bird:

> *Pacific Legal Foundation. . .* enforced plaintiffs' right to be free
> from an unconstitutional taking of their private property.
> While that right was certainly important, the economic inter-
> ests protected in that case can hardly be considered as funda-
> mental as . . . the freedom of speech and petition rights
> enforced in the present case. . . . Only plaintiffs' personal eco-
> nomic interests were advanced [in *Pacific Legal Founda-
> tion*]. . . . In this case, by contrast, plaintiffs had no personal
> pecuniary interest in the subject of the litigation. Instead, they
> sought to enforce their fundamental rights to speak freely and
> to petition the government. Litigation enforcing these rights
> necessarily confers a significant benefit on society as a
> whole.[67]

Reading Bird's opinion, you might think the Jacksons sought to
profit from their land use. But the Jacksons were simply a couple
who sought to rebuild a seawall so that their home would not float
out to Tahiti and did not relish the thought of strangers trooping

across their beach. True, a home protected by a seawall is worth more than one ruined by the relentless Pacific, but Bird does not explain why the preservation of value should discredit the exercise of basic rights. The Jacksons had vindicated a right that was, in Bird's words, "certainly important," and their victory could well benefit a larger class of homeowners. Yet their rights are not valued as highly by the court as the rights of potential leafleters, rights more in tune with an egalitarian culture.

The grocery store petitioners deserved attorney fees, according to Bird, because they "had no personal pecuniary interest." But the *Press* plaintiffs may well have had a significant self-interest in their avocation either because they would benefit from the policy they were advocating or because of the self-satisfaction they gained from the effort. And distributors of leaflets might be paid, although it is not clear why this should or would undermine their speech rights. Even if we grant the arguable premise that economic interests are inherently less deserving of protection, the question of which party has more to gain, the homeowners seeking privacy or the citizens seeking signatures, does not have a self-evident answer.

The California court has not been troubled about the constitutionality of fee exactions. In *Candid Enterprises, Inc. V. Grossmont Union High School District*,[68] the court unanimously upheld the imposition of a school funding fee on housing developers against an equal protection challenge. Grossmont singled out certain developments proposed in 1978 and 1979 when the school district needed money to expand facilities; the district did not demand the exactions from subsequent developers.[69] Candid Enterprises, one of the developers in the wrong place at the wrong time, argued unsuccessfully that singling out a few developers violated equal protection.

"Developers do not constitute a 'suspect class,'" Mosk declared, "and development is not a 'fundamental interest,'"[70] so only minimal scrutiny and not the strict scrutiny that protects preferred rights would apply. Mosk argued that the relevant "class of similarly situated persons," the members of which (in equal protection analysis) should be treated the same, was the group of developers who entered into agreements with the district to pay the fee. Since the plaintiffs are only compared to other developers who have been similarly imposed upon, they have all been treated the same, and no rights have been violated. Yet it seems that only comparing a plaintiff to others who likewise have been singled out renders it difficult if not impossible to find that equal protection has been denied.[71]

The fees, which must be absorbed by home buyers, would in effect impede the mobility of aspiring residents by forcing on them a cost not faced by earlier or later immigrants. Perhaps that is justifiable, but it at least raises an equal protection issue that the court did not face. By asserting that property rights are only "economic," the court has been slow to see the human implications of land use controls that have pushed egalitarian courts in other states, notably New Jersey, to look more closely at regulations.[72]

THE EROSION OF TRUST ALONG PRIVATE SHORES

The clash between public needs and private rights has made clear the need to reevaluate traditional notions of private property. . . . We as a society must change our entire way of thinking if we are to continue to enjoy the resources now available.
                              —*Sarah E. Wilson*[73]

The public trust, a common law creation dating back centuries,[74] has emerged as a potent rationale for extending unprecedented public control over private property. Until recent years, the public trust has been a sort of asterisk attached to liberalism, prescribing a legitimate area for limited government intervention. But in a series of California cases, the doctrine has been reinterpreted from an environmentalist perspective and could, if the trend continues, be applied to all private land.

Traditionally, the purpose of the public trust has been to keep the waterways open so that the fruits of private enterprise would not wither and die at the whim of an obstructionist owner. Public rights to navigate and exploit the fisheries of tidelands have been protected by the public trust doctrine under which navigable tidelands cannot be sold to private owners except to promote the purposes of the trust. Where title goes, obligations to the trust follow. For example, a vengeful downstream owner could not attempt to put Albany out of business by impeding trade on the Hudson River. But an owner who built docks or dredged and filled might be serving the trust.

Beginning with *Marks v. Whitney* in 1971,[75] the California Supreme Court has extended the public trust doctrine to cover vast areas hundreds of miles from tidelands and has demoted the traditional function of the trust—to facilitate private commerce and development—in favor of a new ethic discouraging private exploitation. Less and less a tool to complement a liberal regime of private rights, the public trust in California is becoming a rationale for the state to exercise hierarchical control over potentially all land. Justice McComb decreed the new ethic of preservation in *Marks*. "One of the most important public uses of the tidelands," he wrote, "is a preservation of those lands in their natural state, so that they may serve as ecological units for scientific study, as open space, and as environments which provide food and habitat for birds and marine life, and which favorably affect the scenery and climate of the area."[76]

In the years since *Marks* the court has used the trust to support the claims of governments to control over greater and greater areas.[77] Analyzing the environmental decisions of the California court of the 1970s, Joseph DiMento and his coauthors concluded that the court was moving from an era of deference to local governments toward a more activist preservationist stance.[78] The public trust doctrine has allowed the court to fill both roles at once. In four cases during the early 1980s the court rejected the claims of landowners that the government was unconstitutionally taking their land under the guise of the public trust. The cases provoked unusual controversy among the justices, and in no case did more than four justices support the steady extensions of trust jurisdiction. But the dissents were usually limited to Justices Richardson and Clark, who had both left the court by mid-decade.

Justice Mosk led the court in expanding the public trust. In *Berkeley v. Superior Court (Santa Fe)*,[79] he wrote an opinion affirming that the state retains a public trust in tidelands even when title to the lands has been officially conveyed to private owners. In this case waterfront land in Berkeley had been conveyed to the Santa Fe company by the state legislature following an 1870 act authorizing sales of trust lands to further purposes of the trust. Santa Fe was developing plans for construction along the waterfront, and the city claimed it controlled use of the property under the public trust. Santa Fe sued to quiet title to the property but lost. The Santa Fe case signaled that no owners of tidelands could be confident they were exempt from the trust no matter how much reliance had been placed on official government documentation of their claims. But the court stopped short of requiring that Santa Fe erase the effects of a century of land use; the trust would be applied retroactively only to lands that had not been filled. This concession reduced the immediate impact of the decision on the Berkeley waterfront, but the case was an important legal precedent.

In *Los Angeles v. Venice Peninsula Properties,*[80] the city wanted control over a privately owned lagoon so that the city could dig it out for use by boaters. The owner's title traced back to a Mexican grant, which had later been confirmed in a federal patent proceeding. The property had never been owned by the government. In ruling for the city, the California court rejected the argument that the property had been properly conveyed free of the trust and extended the trust to tidelands characterized as "nonnavigable" in Justice Richardson's dissent and referred to euphemistically as "seminavigable" by the majority.

Santa Fe and *Venice Peninsula* established that tidelands were subject to the public trust whether they were navigable or not and regardless of evidence that property had been expressly conveyed free of the trust. Two other cases sandwiched between these decisions extended the trust doctrine far from the salty shore to embrace any navigable waters in the state. In *California v. Superior Court (Lyon),*[81] the Lyons sought to repair a levee and reclaim land by Clear Lake. The state Fish and Game Commission, concerned about the potential loss of wildlife habitat, sued, claiming that title on all lands to the high-water mark belonged to the state. Mosk, for the court majority, concluded that Lyon owned the property but subject to the public trust and reiterated that the preservation of the natural environment was an important trust purpose. The public trust was extended to the entire shoreline of Lake Tahoe in a companion case, *California v. Superior Court (Fogerty).*[82] As in *Santa Fe,* Mosk sought to soften the immediate blow to property owners on the lake by ruling that they could not be required to dismantle "previously constructed docks, piers and other structures in the shorezone" unless the owners were compensated.

Although Mosk diluted the direct impact of *Lyon* and *Fogerty* by limiting retroactive application, the basic doctrine enunciated by the court was sweeping. Lands bordering all navigable waters in the state could henceforth be subject to the trust obligations of preservation. In *Fogerty,* Mosk made extensive reference to studies documenting the environmental importance of shorelands. He approvingly quoted from a U.S. Forest Service symposium: "If nature bats last, wetlands may be the natural team's designated hitter."[83] There is no doubt which team is in the court's favor. In the land use hierarchy, the court has taken on the role of seeing that the official representatives of the state have the legal tools they need to decide what use of private property is best for society. And in doing so, the obligation of man to protect the environment must be foremost.[84]

After *Lyon* and *Fogerty,* a doctrine developed for the tidelands could reach to the mountains and beyond. Perhaps the impact of the decisions seems very limited, as only the lands between high and low water along waters with no discernible tide are at stake. But in a state of environmental extremes like California where parched months of broiling heat may precede a winter of record snowfalls in the mountains, the seasonal variations between high and low water can be great. *Lyon* and *Fogerty* would have an impact on four thousand miles of shoreline along thirty-four navigable lakes and thirty-one navigable rivers, the court acknowledged. Both the reach of the public trust and its justification had been dramatically changed. The trust was becoming another tool by which government could make private owners promote its policy preferences without compensation. It was no longer a modest means by which to limit private obstruction of transportation.

The loyal opposition in the public trust cases, Richardson and Clark,[85] objected to the court's rulings on both policy and rights grounds. In *Venice Peninsula,* Richardson expressed a concern for the future of property rights. "I confess," he wrote, "to a growing unease about what I view as an accelerating erosion of private property rights of California citizens. . . . Preserving the sanctity of a citizen's private property is a singular responsibility of government and its courts."[86] Many Californians and legal specialists, troubled by what they see as abuses of the natural environment by private landowners, may say it's about time property rights were eroded. But even critics might agree that an expanding public trust doctrine is a major challenge to property rights. An owner cannot claim that the actions of the state have "taken" her property if the court rules that in effect she never owned it. That which is not possessed cannot be taken.

A 1983 case, although not involving a private landowner, illustrates where the court has been heading. For decades the city of Los Angeles has quenched the thirst of its booming population through an elaborate water delivery system stretching from Lake Mono, east of the distant Sierras. Environmentalists have been concerned that depleting the water in the lake was changing the ecosystem. The California Supreme Court handed them an important victory in *National Audobon Society v. Superior Court (Los Angeles Department of Water and Power)*[87] when it ruled that all tributaries, no matter how tiny, of navigable waters were subject to the public trust. Los Angeles could not continue to draw water from the Mono basin without attention to the environmental imperative of the trust. Subsequently, the state courts in further suits by environmental groups have actively reviewed the diversion of water by the city to determine whether environmental needs, such as the preservation of fisheries, have been sufficiently considered.[88]

In nearly all land use cases, the California court has deferred to the policy preferences of the government. Usually this has not been a difficult decision for a majority of the justices, as judicial deference coincides with the promotion of environmental preservation, thus serving both of the court's preferences identified by Di-Mento and his coauthors.[89] When a private owner's rights are at stake, the government is usually in court because it is seeking to block a use by the owner. *National Audobon* showed that when a municipality is the party accused of abusing the natural environment, the court may place its preservationist policy preference above judicial self-restraint.[90] When government is the exploiter, deference may stop.

The California court has been working its way upstream on the waterways in the state, steadily extending the reach of government control. Including the shorelines of all navigable waterways under the trust doctrine was a major step, and including tributaries was a veritable legal leap. Nearly all the waterways in the state are tributaries to navigable rivers or directly to tidelands along the ocean. One river alone, the Sacramento, drains the huge Central Valley, which stretches from south of Bakersfield to north of Redding, a span of several hundred miles. If the court is serious about protecting the environment of every tributary, the trust would logically implicate entire watersheds. Should the court take that step, it would have used a doctrine that was once part of the legal framework supporting property rights potentially to remove private control over the use of all land in the state.

Even if the public trust applied to the entire state, that might not seem exceptional. The state supreme court, we have seen, indulges a wide variety of local land use regulation. Why is the public trust doctrine unique and not just another drop in the regulatory bucket? The answer is vividly described by Sarah Wilson, a Florida attorney who advocates basing coastal preservation on the public trust:

> Since the state has an affirmative duty to protect these rights [of environmental preservation], it does not need [as public "trustee" of the land and water] to resort to the police power, let alone its power of eminent domain, to prevent a private

owner from interfering with them. . . . Thus, a law passed to protect land held in the public trust does not run the risk of "going so far" that it becomes a taking. The owner cannot reasonably expect to infringe upon public rights. This does not mean he cannot exploit his property; it only means that he must pay for that exploitation. . . . Where the public trust is utilized, there is no need for the courts to resort to any of the theories customarily relied upon in taking jurisprudence.[91]

Under the police power, the traditional basis for regulation, the government must justify that it has sufficient reason to make specific intrusions upon the affairs of private individuals. For property rights, the courts may not look too closely into the dark corners of government rationality, but at least they go through the ritual. Each time a regulation is challenged, the justices must consider whether it exceeds the proper reach of government. When the courts are protecting rights they prefer, such as free speech, they may be quite demanding. The public trust is a radical departure from the liberal tradition because it provides a blank check for government control of private land since the reasoning behind constitutional scrutiny of police power regulation does not apply. The trust removes the private right to use property, and thus when the government takes specific actions, there is nothing to intrude upon. The government is performing a managerial function, looking after its own resources. The owner no longer has rights tied to the land but must seek permission from the government and perhaps even provide payment for the privilege to use the property. That is what excites advocates, such as Sarah Wilson, of an expansive police power for environmental protection—the legal roles are reversed. It is the owner who must justify his actions while the government is unfettered. Property owners and their attorneys may understandably fear the public trust license to government is akin to letting the regulatory fox into the landowner henhouse.

Interestingly, Wilson used the language of rights, such as a right to environmental purity, while rationalizing unlimited governmental control. But rights in the liberal tradition do not create affirmative duties for government; rather, they provide safeguards against government. The rhetoric of rights obscures the advocacy of a transcendent public policy, environmentalism, over private rights. Perhaps such priorities are essential, but it is disingenuous to characterize policies as rights rather than face the difficult questions about limits on government.

DIVESTING THE PROPERTY OWNER

In direct clashes before the California Supreme Court between
the power of government and the rights of owners to control land
use, the government was undefeated in the 1980s. But there is a
middle group of cases, partially procedural in character, in which
governments have acknowledged that specific property owners do
have some rights yet seek to limit their reach. In these cases, victories for the state have not been quite as certain. In many respects,
the vested rights cases are quite similar to the disputes over regulation I discussed earlier. *Santa Monica Pines, Ltd. v. Rent Control
Board of Santa Monica*[92] was a challenge to limits on conversion to
condominiums, just like *Nash* and *Griffin*. The owners in *Russ
Building Partnership v. San Francisco*[93] attacked the exaction of
special fees, as in *Candid Enterprises*. *Halaco Engineering Co. v.
South Central Coast Regional Commission*[94] was another challenge
to state control of coastal property. But the vested rights cases have
an additional legal wrinkle: In all of these cases, the government
had at some point given the owners specific assurance that they
could use their property.

The owners would likely lose on constitutional grounds, but
their chief argument is that previous assurances from the government have caused their rights to "vest."[95] Once having said yes, the
government cannot say no.[96] Vested rights are fundamentally procedural, not substantive rights. Even when regulating land use,
which the courts usually tolerate, the government must adhere to
basic norms of due process and not treat owners arbitrarily or ca-
priciously. The key issue in the vested rights cases usually turns not
on an abstract constitutional right but on whether the government
has violated some previous agreement or promise. The state or federal Constitution may not even be explicitly mentioned, but the
cases are included here because the constitutional requirements of
due process are the foundation of vested rights, as the court occasionally acknowledges.

The Pardee Construction Company had been engaged in a
fourteen-year struggle to build housing when its turn to lose before
the California Supreme Court came in 1984.[97] The city of Camarillo had approved a master plan for housing in the disputed area in
1970 and had annexed and zoned land for housing. Two years later,
the subdivision maps for Pardee were approved. But in 1973 the city
passed ordinances to reduce the density of new housing. Pardee won
a judgment in which the city agreed that the company had a vested

right to proceed with housing construction. The company was not out of the legal woods yet. City voters approved a growth control initiative in 1981 that set strict quotas for new housing. Builders would have to compete for housing allotments on a subjective point system. Pardee sued again, asserting that the growth cap violated its vested rights under the earlier judgment, which specified that the city "shall issue permits on request." Otto Kaus, in the majority opinion, sided with the city, explaining that the growth ordinance limited only the "timing" of construction. Sooner or later, if Pardee waited enough years, the company might eventually get all its permits, so the court could not be certain the city ultimately would not comply with the agreement.

"One wonders," complained Mosk in dissent, "whatever happened to vested property rights."[98] What more could the company be expected to do to protect its rights, as it had already won a court judgment allowing construction? The growth control ordinance required substantive review of building projects, which violated the letter and intent of the agreement, Mosk argued. He accused the majority of bending over backward to make a "strained interpretation by picking and choosing among the provisions" of the agreement in order to support the city. Although Mosk strongly supported government regulation of land use and rental units, he was willing to object to what he saw as fundamentally unfair restrictions by the government.

Restrictions on use of property along the coast were again litigated before the court in *Halaco Engineering.* Halaco had an extra card that had not been available to the Pacific Legal Foundation in its unsuccessful challenge of the coastal commission—a vested right supported by statutory law. The California Coastal Act of 1976 gave the state great control over land uses near the coast, but it also provided that owners had a vested right to continue existing land uses as long as they had obtained their building permits and engaged in substantial construction prior to passage of the act.

Even this statutory protection was not sufficient to protect owners from subsequent governmental attempts to limit or condition their continued land uses. In 1977 the high court ruled in *South Coast Regional Commission v. Gordon*[99] that owners could not assert their vested rights against regulatory actions by the coastal commissions unless they had previously submitted their claims to the commission. Owners would be forced to prove their rights before a commission with a self-interest in limiting those rights. Neither the constitutional basis of vested rights nor the explicit assurances in the statute would be sufficient to protect the owners. They would be subject to regulation unless they could prove themselves immune. If the owners did nothing, their rights would evaporate.

A scrap metal recycling plant had been operated by the Halaco company for several years near the coast. Permits had been granted by local authorities, who assured the company that a separate permit for the settling pond was not necessary. Halaco submitted its vesting claim to the regional commission in 1978. A year later, the commission agreed Halaco had a vested right to continue the plant but not the pond or a propane tank that had been installed on the property. Halaco appealed, claiming vested rights under both the statute and the state and federal constitutions. A state trial court declared the commission's ruling had been arbitrary and capricious and concluded that Halaco had a vested right to both pond and plant. On appeal, the supreme court upheld the trial court decision.

Halaco was at least a partial victory for the owner, but the circumstances were unique. The court reviewed only the standard of judgment and the reasonableness of the trial court's findings and did not take a substantive stand on Halaco's claim. The court based its decision on deference to the interpretation of vested rights incorporated into the statute by the state legislature. Thus it did not have to reject the position of government; it was favoring one governmental unit (the legislature) over another (the regional commission). The victory by Halaco is noteworthy nonetheless because the majority at least rejected the dissenting argument by Cruz Reynoso that no vested right could be "free of reasonable regulatory conditions."[100] Had Reynoso's argument won the day, a vested right could be meaningless since the owner would still be subject to the vagaries of regulation.

Fee exactions were challenged in *Russ Building Partnership* after San Francisco assessed transit fees against recently approved and future buildings, not the entire downtown. Amounts to be collected under the $5-per-square-foot fee were not limited to transit costs generated by the new buildings and totaled several million dollars for each building. As in *Candid Enterprises*, the developer claimed it had been unconstitutionally singled out for the fees, and again as in *Candid Enterprises*, the company was trounced in court. The Russ company did not use the equal protection argument that had failed in *Candid Enterprises*; instead, it claimed that the conditions of its building permits gave it a vested right and that imposition of the fees violated due process. But the court held that the fee plan was "fair" because it had been democratically enacted and applied to all new buildings. As in *Candid Enterprises,* the court was allowing the city to determine the class of owners relevant for comparative purposes, assuring court approval. Justice Broussard, writing for the majority, did not explain how democracy ensures fairness. If voting majorities were always "fair," there would be no need for minority rights.

Although few California justices were willing during the 1980s to defend the substantive rights of landowners, the procedural issues implicated in vested rights cases raised some concern on the court. In *Halaco,* the property owner was even able to win a limited victory. But the majority opinion in *Halaco* and the dissents in *Santa Monica Pines, Pardee,* and *Russ* were not based on the basic liberty of the owner to use land but on the inconsistency of the government's actions. If prior assurances had not been made, the owners would have had precious little constitutional ground to stand on. Even with the apparent prior vesting of their rights, the landowners lost three out of the four cases.

DECIDING WHAT PROCESS IS DUE

When the issues faced by the California court have been procedural, the court often has been troubled, even when there was no specific vested right. As we will see again in *Arnel Development Co. v. Costa Mesa,*[101] however, the disputed procedures were usually approved.

The Arnel Development Co. owned fifty acres zoned primarily for moderate-density housing in Costa Mesa. In 1977, the city approved plans by the company to build 127 single-family homes and 539 apartment units on the property. A local homeowners' association, which objected to the construction of apartment buildings, began a successful petition drive to put an initiative on the ballot to rezone the entire property and two smaller adjoining pieces for single-family housing only. City voters approved the initiative ordinance, and Costa Mesa officials subsequently refused to process applications for building permits by Arnel. The company took its case to court, arguing that a rezoning aimed at a specific project and restricting only three property owners required formal notice and a hearing to comply with due process and thus could not be accomplished through the initiative process.

But Justice Tobriner, writing for the majority, disagreed, reasoning that rezoning ordinances, like the original zoning ordinances, were legislative acts immune from administrative due process requirements. In contrast, subdivision approvals, variances, and conditional use permits had been designated as adjudicatory by the court. Such a simple dichotomy, without regard to the size of the tract or number of owners affected, had "the obvious advantage of economy," wrote Tobriner.[102] The label on the proceeding would determine the process due; the court need not engage in delicate line drawing. But, Richardson argued in dissent, "I find it wholly anomalous that, had appellants voluntarily sought a zoning variance or use permit for their own property, a due process hearing would have been required. . . . Yet . . . when third parties, by an initiative, effect for the owner an involuntary change of use against the owner's will such notice and hearing is denied the owners, the very parties most directly affected."[103]

In the everyday world of land use administration, rezoning is more similar to subdivision approval or conditional use permits, processes for which the California court requires notice and a hearing. Developers frequently require rezonings for their plans, and thus rezoning is commonly just one part of the administrative approval process.[104] The area to be rezoned may be much smaller than the entire tract of a proposed subdivision. Zoning paints with a broad brush, delegating large areas of a city for different uses and classifying individual properties accordingly. But rezoning, by contrast, is usually site-specific and, more relevant to a discussion of rights, owner-specific. Given Tobriner's general lack of regard for property rights, it is not surprising that the potential for unfairness to individual owners did not concern him. But legislative rezonings may also grant special favors to owners. Other state courts have been critical of legislative and initiative rezonings because, particularly when enacted without the safeguard of supporting reasons necessary in administrative proceedings, rezonings can result in a crazy patchwork of "spot" zoning without rhyme or reason.[105]

Rezoning initiatives threaten the rights of the property owner because voters may in effect gang up on the owner. However, according to Tobriner, because a development proposal may generate wide interest and the majority of those voting will prevail, "the specter of a few voters imposing their selfish interests upon an objecting city and region has no basis in reality."[106] Yet the traditional constitutional concern is not that the few may impose on the many, rather that the many may violate the rights of the few. Tobriner may be correct when he concludes that the voters are not likely to reach a decision contrary to the wishes of the city,[107] but the focus in considering the constitutionality of a procedure should not be on who may be *benefited* by an ordinance (the neighbors, the community "character") but who may be *harmed*. The greatest danger is not that the selfish few will impose their preferences on the community (although this may happen if voter turnout is low and dominated by the offended neighbors) but that the many will shift their burdens to the vulnerable property owner. When zoning decisions are made by the voters, Gregory Hile has written, "the property owner becomes simply a voice in the wilderness left to compete with the some-times selfish desires of society in general. He may be left saddled with the burdens of ownership while the initiative action takes away the benefits of ownership."[108]

When costs are concentrated and benefits spread widely, the rights of the few are most likely to be abused.[109] It is interesting that Tobriner could "see no basis to distinguish a downzoning case" from cases in which a referendum or initiative decides whether to rezone to intensify use; a zoning change is a zoning change. But in the latter case, defeat of the rezoning proposal leaves the property owner with the same development rights that he had before. Since voter-approved downzoning can actually take away prior legal rights, the potential for abuse of individuals is much greater.

Justice Richardson, in his dissent, attacked the majority opinion in *Arnel* on both constitutional and administrative procedure grounds. He assailed Tobriner for justifying the lack of notice and hearing as reasonable in light of the "administrative cost" of a more rigorous process:

> We have been traditionally hesitant as a court to place a price tag on a constitutional right. . . . One need go no further than the very first section of the very first article [of the California Constitution] before learning that the sovereign people of this state have identified "acquiring, possessing, and protecting property" as rights which they have described as "inalienable." . . . In determining priorities, appellant's constitutional protection comes first, and any administrative convenience, efficiency or economy comes a distant second.[110]

But rights outweigh costs only when those rights are given some value. Few justices would share the high regard in which Richardson and Clark, who joined the dissent, held property rights.

COMPENSATION AND JUSTICE

The California court has been reluctant to find that any land use regulation constitutes a taking and for years maintained that an owner could never be awarded compensation for such a taking. Consequently, municipalities could often accomplish by regulation what they would find costly to achieve through eminent domain. But when local governments have chosen formally to condemn and take possession of private property, the court has looked more closely at whether just compensation has been provided.

San Diego County condemned private land to widen a road and calculated compensation for each of the affected owners. But to finance the improvements, the county levied special assessments against each of the owners, reasoning that they would benefit from the improved road and could thus be expected to pay more than taxpayers at large. Remarkably, the assessments for benefits to be received by each property owner were precisely equal to the amounts the city was willing to pay for the appropriated property. In effect, the assessments canceled the compensation, and the county gained title to the property free. A majority of the supreme court in *White v. County of San Diego*[111] approved the county's creative economizing. Justice Newman concluded that assessments need be only loosely related to the benefits received and that the equivalency of assessment and compensation was not inherently unfair.

"The county's scheme," Justice Mosk, joined by Clark, argued in his dissent, "is a cynical method of automatically shifting the cost of an improvement benefiting the public onto the backs of a few landowners because of the fortuity of their location. . . . I strongly disapprove of this acquisitive device by which a public entity, in order to obtain private property, puts funds therefor in a landowner's pocket—and then proceeds to pick the pocket."[112] Mosk showed, as in some of the rent and condominium regulation cases, that he was wary of plans that do little more than shift the cost of public benefits to private shoulders.

The state and federal constitutions specify that private property may be taken only for public use, and California has followed the lead of the U.S. Supreme Court in taking a very elastic view of what constitutes "public use." In *Redevelopment Agency of Burbank v. Gilmore*,[113] for example, although the court objected to the way Burbank calculated compensation, there was no question that a city may condemn private land for redevelopment, even when the property ends up in other private hands.[114] A vivid example of the court's indulgence of the acquisitiveness of local governments is provided by *Oakland v. Oakland Raiders*[115] in which the court gave Oakland the green light to proceed with its attempt to condemn a football team whose owners wished to relocate to Los Angeles. Although the case did not involve a landowner and is not included in the vote summaries of this study, it nonetheless shows the court's deference to government declarations of public need. It is up to the government to decide the limits of its eminent domain power, Justice Richardson wrote for the majority. Past precedent need not restrain governments combatting modern concerns:

> While it is readily apparent that the power of eminent domain formerly may have been exercised only to serve traditional purposes, such as the construction and maintenance of streets, highways and parks, these limitations seem merely to have corresponded to the accepted, but narrower view of appropriate governmental functions then prevailing. The established limits were not imposed by either constitutional or statutory fiat. Times change.[116]

Times may change, but it is less obvious that constitutional rights should fluctuate with legislative whim. The malleable reading of the takings clause by the majority raises the question whether the court would be willing to impose any limits on eminent domain. This troubled Chief Justice Bird: "May a city condemn *any* business that decides to seek greener pastures elsewhere under the unlimited interpretation of eminent domain law that the majority appear to approve? . . . Can the City acquire personal employment contracts as simply as it can acquire a tract of land? . . . In my view, this court should proceed most cautiously before placing a constitutional imprimatur upon this aspect of creeping statism."[117] Despite the searching questions she raised about the abuse of the rights of both owners and business employees, Bird concluded that she could find no grounds to rule against the city. She concurred, albeit reluctantly, and followed the majority to the new frontier of eminent domain. None of the justices dissented.

Oakland Raiders shows again the great reluctance of the court to protect property rights. The justices have voted overwhelmingly to reject constitutional challenges to regulation, siding with the culture of hierarchy over libertarianism. The public trust cases tended to raise more voices in dissent, but all of the decisions still favored the government. There are two limitations to the court's deference that made the procedural and related cases much closer. You may take or regulate what you will, the court has told governments, but pay fairly for that which you condemn, and stand by past assurances to owners that they may use their property (if reliance has been sufficient to "vest" the owners rights). Although the procedural cases, including compensation disputes, have tended to be close decisions, landowners still lost six out of eight cases. But privacy and expression, preferred constitutional rights compatible with an egalitarian conception of property rights, triggered far more vigilant protection by the court.

PROPERTY AND FREE EXPRESSION

When James Madison spoke of property, he included the expressive and creative products of the individual.[118] Security of property was argued to be essential to the dignity and development of each citizen. Under the modern double standard of rights, Madison's conception of property was split in half. Expressive and privacy rights have been given vigilant protection, while real property rights have been virtually discarded, and never the twain shall meet. But the real world is not so neat, and legal disputes often intertwine claims of various rights. What happens when land use disputes implicate First Amendment values of free expression? To be consistent with the double standard, should justices treat the cases as disputes over economic interests and defer to government officials, or should they vindicate expressive values by striking down government infringements? They cannot do both at once, and either solution may produce precedents that obscure the double standard.

When San Diego banned billboards, the California court was confronted with just such a puzzle. The billboard owners claimed the ordinance did not meet minimal due process and equal protection standards because some owners were required by law to be compensated[119] while others were not. These were standard claims in property rights cases, and defeat for the plaintiffs could be expected. But the Metromedia billboard company also claimed the ordinance violated the free speech rights guaranteed by the First Amendment of the U.S. Constitution and article 1, section 2, of the state constitution. The restrictions were argued to be invalid because they infringed the right of the company to advertise and were overbroad, threatening the expression of noncommercial speech traditionally favored by the court. On a 6–1 vote, Justice Tobriner led the court in upholding the billboard ban in *Metromedia, Inc. v. San Diego.*[120] Justice Clark, the lone dissenter, based his opinion not on the property rights of the owners or even the suppression of commercial expression but solely on the grounds that the ordinance un-constitutionally restricted noncommercial speech. According to the facts agreed to by the parties, "valuable commercial, political, and social information is communicated" on the billboards, Clark noted.[121] The ordinance was thus overbroad. A more narrowly drawn billboard restriction limited to commercial messages might have passed without dissent.

Tobriner admitted that the ordinance affected speech but em-phasized that commercial speech was the main loser. Had the sup-pression of political or social speech been the central issue, the city would have been required to show the ordinance was necessary to promote a compelling governmental interest, a much higher hurdle to surmount. The impact of the ban on preferred speech was only "incidental," according to Tobriner, and he relied on the inclusion of twelve exceptions[122] in the ordinance to safeguard at least some ex-pressions of noncommercial speech. The regulation of commercial property, not speech, was the main purpose and effect of the bill-board ban, according to Tobriner, and as such it need meet only the rational basis due process standard. He found the ordinance justified both because of traffic and aesthetic concerns. Indeed, aesthetics alone justify regulation,[123] Tobriner stated, and the government could thus reasonably impose public tastes on individual owners.[124] Metromedia argued that San Diego could not effectively prohibit a business that had not been found a public nuisance,[125] but Tobriner asserted that the government could do whatever it pleased when it came to commercial uses of property as long as there was an argu-able relation to the public welfare.

To protect the rights of the billboard owners, Tobriner de-clared, would be to succumb to a "bleak materialism." A libertarian he was not. Because of the federal Outdoor Advertising Act, owners of billboards within 660 feet of highways must receive some compensation, but, Tobriner wrote, "we reach that conclusion reluctantly."[126] That some owners would be compensated while others would not did not raise any serious equal protection con-cerns, according to Tobriner, because it was entirely up to the leg-islatures to decide payment. Without great deference to legislative regulations, Tobriner argued, "present day city planning would be virtually impossible."[127] Yet if the interference with property rights has become so severe that the enforcement of rights would upset the regulatory applecart, that is a reason to act sooner, not later, with more vigor, not less. Political popularity or convenience do not substitute for constitutional justification and are the epitome of what a constitution is designed to guard against.

The court was much more exercised when a dancer at the Hip-hugger bar in San Jose was charged with violating a city ordinance by baring her buttocks during a performance. The property owner was not a party to the case, which I do not include in the compilations of court decisions, but the case provides a revealing (no pun intended) comparison with *Metromedia* and other cases in which land use restrictions have been upheld. Before the U.S. Supreme Court, property owners engaged in so-called adult entertainment have successfully claimed some First Amendment protection,[128] and *Morris v. Municipal Court*[129] showed that the California court is more sympathetic to property or "economic" cases that implicate free expression. The San Jose ordinance prohibited nude entertainment except in a concert hall, theater, or similar establishment "primarily devoted to theatrical performances." Although commercial activities receive less protection from the court than "noneconomic" rights, "it is immaterial whether an activity which enjoys First Amendment protection is carried on for profit," the court concluded in an unsigned opinion.[130] The expressive rights overshadowed the economic concerns in this case, in the eyes of the court, and so Ms. Morris would not be penalized even though her means of expression was also her employment.

The display by Morris may well have "involved a good deal more than the mere baring of her buttocks," admitted the court, and thus may have been obscene and subject to legitimate limitation.[131] But because the ordinance could be applied to nonobscene nude entertainment as well, it was unconstitutional. In contrast, when a property right is at stake, the court is reluctant to consider possible future constitutional violations.

How could the court so heavily favor regulation of billboards in *Metromedia*, which implicated rights of expression, yet come to the aid of the gyrating bar dancer in *Morris?* Because in *Metromedia* the justices saw primarily a property rights case while *Morris* was a matter of free expression, and the court chose to draw the dividing line of the double standard between the differing factual circumstances. Each aspect of a case that indicates an issue of property or business is central predisposes the court against protecting rights. But as long as property owners wish to pursue a use that arguably is protected by the First Amendment, such as an "adult" bookstore or theater, they may persuade the court to apply stricter scrutiny or strike down restrictions because they are overbroad.

PRIVATE PROPERTY AS A PROTECTOR
OF PERSONAL PRIVACY

Although the court often gives the impression that landowner rights may be obsolete in the modern regulatory world, a majority of the California justices still support the classically liberal notion, compatible with both libertarian and egalitarian conceptions of rights, that property is a guarantor of privacy. The court has detached many traditional functions of property, such as to provide a secure means for an individual to reap the rewards of her creativity and industry, from the privacy role of property. Although autonomy in land use is largely unprotected, privacy often prevails. Justice Douglas of the U.S. Supreme Court was justly famous (or infamous) for finding a federal right of privacy in the blank spaces between the lines, or the penumbrae, of several clauses of the constitution.[132] Privacy is explicitly listed in the first article of the first section[133] of the California constitution, giving the right an arguably firmer basis in the state constitution than in its federal counterpart.

Adamson owned a large house (twenty-four rooms no less) in which twelve unrelated adults lived communally. Santa Barbara did not look fondly upon this little utopia and sought an injunction against the inhabitants pursuant to a city ordinance that prohibited more than five unrelated adults from living together in single-family zones.[134] But in *Santa Barbara v. Adamson*,[135] Justice Newman, writing for the majority, admonished the city that "in general, zoning ordinances are much less suspect when they focus on the use than when they command inquiry into who are the users."[136] The ordinance infringed on the family privacy rights of the residents, Newman declared, and could be sustained only if shown to be essential for a compelling public purpose. Had the court viewed the case as hinging on the property rights of the owner rather than the privacy of the inhabitants, minimal scrutiny would have been applied,[137] and the ordinance would almost certainly have passed, given the court's ability to imagine a "conceivable " rational basis. But for the majority, a preferred personal right was at stake, and this distinguished the case from other zoning challenges. Santa Barbara could properly seek to limit noise, traffic, and other disturbances in family neighborhoods, Newman declared, but those problems did not necessarily follow from nontraditional living arrangements. Santa Barbara could combat those problems with means that would be less intrusive on privacy.

Curiously, the justices most inclined to honor traditional property rights, Richardson and Clark, joined the dissenting opinion of Justice Manuel. Because the issue had been framed as one of privacy, not property, the case had crossed the great divide of the double standard, breaking up the usual alliances in landowner cases. The constitutional right of privacy, Manuel argued, was intended to limit snooping and gathering information about people's personal lives, not to defeat zoning. Manuel rejected the majority's conclusion that there is a privacy right "to live with whomever one wishes or, at least, to live in an alternative family with persons not related by blood, marriage, or adoption."[138]

The priority given by the court to the privacy aspects of property can be seen again in *Baker v. Burbank-Glendale-Pasadena Airport Authority*.[139] *Baker* was a takings case with a twist: The owner was not seeking the freedom to put his property to whatever use he wished but to limit the use of other property (in this case a public airport) that intruded upon his serenity. The court took the opportunity to sustain a takings claim without promoting autonomy in land use. As in *National Audobon*, the Mono Lake case, *Baker* pitted environmental preservation against the government, and the court sided with preservation.

Baker claimed that by invading his property with its noise and vibrations, a nearby airport had effectively taken his property.[140] "Leave me alone or pay up," he was telling the airport authority.[141] The airport countered that Baker could not sue for inverse condemnation since the airport had no authority to condemn and take property and that in any event *Agins*, the regulatory takings case from Tiburon, foreclosed the possibility of collecting compensation for inverse condemnations. But to protect the privacy aspects of property, the court was willing to create an exception to its usually weak enforcement of the state and federal takings clauses. Baker should be allowed to sue, Reynoso wrote for the majority, because "a landowner whose property has been invaded by a public entity that lacks eminent domain power suffers no less a taking merely because the defendant was not authorized to take."[142] The willingness of the court to allow that inverse condemnation action contrasts with the position taken in *Agins* where a property owner who alleged his property had been taken through excessive regulation could not even sue for inverse condemnation because the court would never allow the awarding of compensation. Reynoso sought to isolate *Baker* from regulatory takings cases: "The instant case does not involve allegations of unreasonable zoning or regulatory permit activity . . .

the remedy for which, of course, is not an inverse condemnation suit for damages, but declaratory relief or mandamus."[143]

In allowing inverse condemnation in *Baker*, the court did not make clear why regulatory takings should still be immune from the compensation remedy. But the decision to allow Baker to sue makes sense if we view the court as protecting the privacy of individuals rather than their freedom to use their property. Baker just wanted to be left alone and was not creating any harm to the public, in the eyes of the court, while land development creates problems that governments should be left free to control. Both privacy and preservation could be served by the court's decision.[144]

OF POT, PLANES, AND PROPERTY

Two fascinating and puzzling cases centered on the limits of aerial surveillance of suspected marijuana crops. These cases, concerning criminal conduct, are not included in the case tabulations, but they show the court's ambivalence toward privacy and property. *People v. Cook*[145] and *People v. Mayoff*[146] turned on very similar fact patterns and were announced exactly one year apart. Both opinions were written by Justice Grodin, and there was only one dissenter in each case. Yet the two opinions reached opposite conclusions.

Local narcotics officers had received a tip that marijuana was being grown behind Larry Cook's house in a "semirural area" of San Diego County. The officers went to investigate but could not see over a high wooden fence surrounding the property. Not to be deterred, the officers flew over the property in an airplane, and took photographs from 1,600 feet of "lush green" foliage growing in an enclosure behind the house. A warrant was issued on the basis of the photographs, and the police discovered that the plants were indeed marijuana. Cook was charged with unlawful cultivation but moved to suppress the evidence, asserting that it was gathered pursuant to a warrant based on an illegal aerial search. The trial court judge refused to bar the evidence, and Cook turned to the supreme court. The state argued that Cook's expectation of privacy was unreasonable because the backyard could be routinely observed by any aircraft flying overhead. Justice Grodin, writing for the majority in *Cook*, emphasized that the legal question was primarily one of privacy, not property: "Constitutional limitations on police searches and seizures protect 'people, not places.' "[147] Individuals should not be "required to erect opaque cocoons" to have privacy, Grodin argued.[148]

"The 'reasonableness' of an individual's expectation of privacy is not defined solely by technological progress," Grodin asserted. "We reject the Orwellian notion that precious liberties derived from the Framers simply shrink as the government acquires new means of infringing them."[149] The court's stand for the intent of the founders contrasts sharply with its willingness to weaken property protections as "times change," as the court said in the *Oakland Raiders* takings case. The state constitution gives rights to citizens, but some constitutional clauses are more rightful than others, the court implies. In deciding a case in which both privacy and property are implicated, the court must choose between its traditionally lenient attitude toward regulation of property and its more vigorous defense of privacy. Grodin solved this dilemma by describing, as the U.S. Supreme Court had done,[150] a hierarchy of protection for property: "We guard with particular zeal an individual's right to carry on private activities within the interior of a home or office, free from unreasonable governmental intrusion. We also recognize a high privacy interest in the 'curtilage' of a residence—that zone immediately surrounding the home where its private interior life can be expected to extend."[151] In contrast to these areas of sanctuary is property more distant from the home, such as open fields, that can be searched without a warrant. The court cited past state precedents that allowed "surveillance conducted at substantial heights over rural land" that involved "no intensive scrutiny of private yards."[152] The owner does not have a privacy right in property, according to the court, but in his person, and that includes the immediate surroundings of the home. The farther property extends from the home, the less protection it merits.

For the majority, pot and property were worth protecting as the price to be paid for a broad privacy right. But one year later the court rejected a privacy claim in similar circumstances. Like Cook, Allan Mayoff was arrested and charged with cultivating marijuana after plants were found growing on his property. In both cases, a search warrant had been issued based on photographs taken during aerial surveillance. But Mayoff was growing his crop deep in the woods of the "Emerald Triangle" near Garberville rather than in San Diego County. Therein lies the difference that apparently persuaded a majority of the justices to step off the privacy pedestal and defer to state power.

Two factors may explain the different outcomes in the two cases: the extent of the criminal activity being investigated and the type of property targeted for surveillance. The social costs of protecting privacy for criminal activities were more apparent to the court in *Mayoff* where it saw a threat to innocent passersby. Most marijuana growers in the Emerald Triangle, according to the Court, "guard their plots with firearms. . . . A number of deaths and serious injuries have resulted. . . . The transformation of rural tracts formerly open to recreational use into illegal armed camps posing a danger to innocent wanderers is a major social and environmental problem which itself implicates precious personal freedoms."[153] And the commercial character of the enterprise was clear—these growers were out for big bucks.[154] The noneconomic interests of recreation seekers were threatened by the violent commercial activities on the property of the growers, so the court did not so clearly see the "personal" rights as being on the side of the growers.

In addition to the pressing social need to combat armed drug camps, the court emphasized the remote, uninhabited character of much of the property observed. In the hierarchy of property, open fields and mountainous areas far from the typical centers of personal life are less deserving of "privacy" protection. Grodin emphasized that the marijuana was seen in a "secluded, mountainous area." But if one cannot expect privacy in a remote, secluded location, where can one? Even if we wish to protect privacy, not property, tolerance toward invasions of remote property may not be appropriate. In seeking to separate privacy from property and create a hierarchy of protection for property, the court has underestimated the instrumental value of land.

Privacy, a right valued by both egalitarians and libertarians, motivated the justices to grapple with a fundamental role played by private property in a liberal society. The court was willing to hang a "do not disturb" sign on some property. This could weaken the double standard that has banished property rights to the doghouse of constitutional law without requiring the court to abandon completely its preference for expressive and personal rights.

EXCLUSIONARY ZONING AND THE CALIFORNIA COURT

We touch in this area deep social antagonisms.
We allude to the conflict between the environ-
mental protectionists and the egalitarian

humanists, a collision between the forces that
would save the benefits of nature and those
that would preserve the opportunity of people
in general.
                              —Justice Tobriner[155]

In reviewing the constitutional land use cases of the California Surpeme Court in the 1980s, I have said nothing about exclusionary zoning, which has been a central constitutional issue in Pennsylvania and New Jersey. To understand the silence of the California court on this subject, we need to go back to 1976 when the court refused to apply anything more than minimal scrutiny to an exclusionary ordinance. At issue in *Associated Home Builders of the Greater Eastbay, Inc. v. Livermore*[156] was an initiative approved by city voters that prohibited the issuance of any new residential building permits until local services were greatly expanded but did not provide for any expansion of those services. The builders' group attacked the ordinance as an attempt to exclude new residents that exceeded the police power of the government. But with Justices Mosk and Clark writing dissents, the California court upheld the growth control. Tobriner characterized the ordinance as just another land use regulation subject to minimal scrutiny. Striking down the ordinance, he warned, "would result in wholesale invalidation of land use controls and endanger the validity of city and regional planning."[157] Rather than rock the boat of the regulatory state, it would be better to defer to the city government, Tobriner implied. But if upholding rights would require the "wholesale invalidation of land use controls," perhaps that is all the more reason for the courts to step in and say enough is enough.

Tobriner did consider the argument that land use controls may unconstitutionally exclude the poor. Just one year before *Associated Home Builders*, the New Jersey Supreme Court had announced its landmark *Mount Laurel* case[158] in which it ruled that large-lot zoning was unconstitutional when it did not allow housing affordable by poor and working-class citizens. Tobriner also noted the precedents set by the Pennsylvania state court in exclusionary litigation,[159] but the New Jersey case was particularly important because of the widespread laudatory attention it had received among legal scholars and the liberal reputation of the New Jersey court.

California and New Jersey often have been considered the leading (and most egalitarian) state high courts, but here was an issue where Tobriner was not willing to follow the New Jersey path. While the New Jersey justices pressed on into the brave new world of egalitarian remedies for the inequities of zoning, the California court was adhering to its preference for hierarchical land use controls, preferably enacted by legislative bodies. "For a time," Donald Hagman wrote, "the California Supreme Court and the New Jersey Supreme Court ran a neck-and-neck race to be liberal in sustaining any regulation attempted by a city in a zoning ordinance."[160] When the New Jersey court began striking down exclusionary zoning, "the California Supreme Court continued upholding restrictive ordinances in its 'see no evil,' aesthetic, preserve-the-environment way."[161] In the years since *Associated Home Builders*, the California and New Jersey courts have represented two contrasting "liberal" approaches to land use regulation—deference to local hierarchy or redirection of regulation toward egalitarian goals.

The universality of the exclusion in Livermore saved the ordinance from the *Mount Laurel* attack, according to Tobriner. In Mount Laurel, large-lot zoning discouraged the construction of affordable housing but did not prevent the building of residences for the wealthy. But in Livermore, no building permits meant no new housing, period. The initiative "impartially bans all residential construction, expensive or inexpensive;"[162] rich and poor must suffer together. Remarkably, the Livermore ordinance escaped the burden of more exacting scrutiny because it did Mount Laurel one better—it excluded everyone. But the moratorium on new housing would inflate prices in Livermore and nearby communities, and thus would still hit the poor hardest.

Although Tobriner did not follow the New Jersey lead, he did acknowledge the "competing interests" served by the divergent strands of modern liberal jurisprudence. In one of the most telling excerpts from a California Supreme Court opinion, quoted at the beginning of this section, Tobriner described the two cultural groups that had legitimate conceptions of the public interest: "the environmental protectionists and the egalitarian humanists."[163] Thus there are two great forces of justice in the world: the hierarchical, which accommodates the orientation of mainstream environmentalism, and the egalitarian. The force of the state should be used to constrain individuals and preserve the natural and social order for the good of all or to reduce inequality. In land use regulation, the two cultures collide, as techniques that relegate different uses to their socially proper places and frustrate change may place housing beyond the reach of the poor.

Missing from Tobriner's dichotomy was any mention of another basic perspective on the public interest—libertarianism, in which individuals seek out their own preferences and it is not society's function to "save," or impose on, anyone. This absence is not surprising, as the California court has been loath to protect libertarian, or classical liberal property rights. Otherwise, the Livermore ordinance would have been in trouble, as it limited the freedom of property owners in the city and of all those, rich or poor, who would like to move into the city.

Stanley Mosk dissented vigorously in *Associated Home Builders*. He solved the conflict between hierarchical environmentalism and egalitarianism by relegating each to its own place (much as the New Jersey court had created an exception for rural communities in *Mount Laurel*):

> Limitations on growth may be justified in resort communities, beach and lake and mountain sites, and other rural and recreational areas; such restrictions are generally designed to preserve nature's environment for the benefit of all mankind. . . . But there is a vast qualitative difference when a suburban community invokes an elitist concept to construct a mythical moat around its perimeter, not for the benefit of mankind but to exclude all but its fortunate current residents.[164]

Mosk did not explain why resort communities should be allowed to be exclusive and why suburbs should not put the protection of their social and natural environment first. But Mosk's bicultural compromise does focus the attack on elitism in the growing communities where housing pressures are likely to be greatest. Mosk employed the minimal rationality test, but there were teeth in his test. He was not satisfied with the superficial explanations that the ordinance was concerned only with the deleterious effects of swamped services. Although sympathetic to preservationism, Mosk showed an awareness of the ways "environmental" requirements and procedures may be a guise for accomplishing impermissible purposes. He also expressed greater concern than Tobriner for the market effects of Livermore's "Chinese Wall":

> If Livermore may do so, why not every municipality in . . . Northern California? With a patchwork of enclaves the inevitable result will be creation of an aristocracy housed in exclusive suburbs while modest wage earners will be confined to declining neighborhoods, crowded into sterile, monotonous, multifamily projects, or assigned to pockets of marginal hous-

ing on the urban fringe. The overriding objective should be to minimize rather than exacerbate social and economic disparities, to lower barriers rather than raise them, to emphasize heterogeneity rather than homogeneity, to increase choice rather than to limit it.[165]

Mosk argued that by opening up housing opportunities in communities like Livermore to all (the libertarian approach), the poor and working class would have the most to gain (an egalitarian preference). Liberty can enhance equality. But Mosk's voice remained a minority one, and subsequently the court showed little interest in attacking exclusionary practices on constitutional grounds. Exclusionary concerns have not been entirely neglected by the California court, but they have usually been addressed as statutory, not constitutional issues.

The question of the standard of review of exclusionary local initiatives came up again in *Building Industry Association of Southern California, Inc. v. Camarillo.*[166] Justice Lucas, in the majority opinion, ruled that the burden of proof must be on the city to prove that its growth control initiative is "necessary for the protection of the public health, safety, or welfare of the population." Had the court abandoned the leniency of *Associated Home Builders* by shifting the burden of proof and demanding a higher standard? Actually not. Since the Livermore case, the legislature had revised the state evidence code to require proof of necessity for growth controls. The legislature, not the court, had taken the lead in attacking exclusionary land use controls,[167] and the court was content to support these efforts by ruling that the evidence code applied to voter initiatives. Mosk concurred, repeating a "low-grid" (libertarian and egalitarian) critique of growth controls: "An impermissible elitist concept is invoked when a community constructs a legal moat around its perimeter to exclude all or most outsiders."[168]

The California court has been reluctant to make the leap from deference to hierarchy to the aggressive egalitarianism of the New Jersey court. But there are geographic factors, as well as philosophical, that reduce the importance of constitutional attacks on exclusionary land use regulation in California. The development of municipal government in the state has tended to follow the expansion of suburban population, not vice versa. The undeveloped areas of the state are predominantly controlled by county governments, while growth controls and exclusionary zoning are practiced most religiously by the cities and towns. If a city such as Livermore has clamped down on new development, a builder may be able to find an unincorporated area of the county where there is less organized resistance. The concentrations of homogeneous populations most conducive to exclusion tend to be scattered as the fringes of the metropolitan areas are reached. In New Jersey and Pennsylvania, by contrast, the entire states are divided into small cities and towns with strong traditions of local control. As the urban wave reaches rural shores, the towns may be already mobilized to resist. There are no blank spaces on the maps of Pennsylvania or New Jersey where growth may be diverted, so the cumulative effects of exclusion by each town may be greater.

DEFERENCE TO HIERARCHY IN CALIFORNIA

California land use opinions tended to have a rather dry tone in the 1980s. Discussions of rights were usually brief and prosaic, in contrast with New Jersey where the justices often have left no gem of rhetoric untouched in their zeal to defend their values.[169] In most land use cases, the California court just did not have much to say. In the overwhelming majority of cases (nineteen out of twenty-four), the court simply sustained the policy initiatives of elected officials or administrative agencies, and the basic message of the court was "Do what you want." The "any conceivable rational basis" test created in *Carolene Products* and favored by the California court cheapens the cultural dialogue by excusing the court from having to persuasively justify its substantive conclusions. There is little serious consideration of deprivations of personal freedom. It is only a slight exaggeration to say the court's reasoning often could be reduced to "The legislature did it, so they must have had their reasons. Sustained."

In a 1967 article,[170] Justice Tobriner and future justice Grodin laid out the rationale that best explains the court's deference during the 1980s to hierarchical regulation. Society was now "complex, interdependent," and individuals served "exceedingly specialized" roles while "economic and political power [were] highly centralized."[171] Autonomy for the individual was anachronistic, and the social changes "imply increased regulation of his behavior." The role of the law would now be "to impose duties and obligations on the basis of status or relationship." Tobriner and Grodin even expressed their admiration of feudalism, that classic form of social hierarchy that was supplanted by the rise of liberalism.[172] In the land use arena, their perspective helps explain the court's apathy toward liberal property rights, those vestiges of individualism, and deference toward the hierarchy of land use regulation, which would impose appropriate duties.

In the view of the California court, primary responsibility for decreeing the proper use of land lies with government. Although only a few cases technically fall under the public trust doctrine, the court extended its assumptions of private subservience to public authority to nearly all its land use cases. Occasionally, the court showed its preference for hierarchical order by being actively preservationist rather than deferential,[173] as in *National Audobon*. More commonly, the court upheld limits placed on owner autonomy by the state. As the government party typically was telling an owner he could not do as he wished, supporting the government also furthered preservationist goals. When the government was the party actively exploiting the land, as in *Baker* (the airport noise case), the court was more likely to side with the owner.

While the court may have been preoccupied with equality in other areas such as education and access to justice, it largely declined to consider the detrimental effects that land use regulation can have for social and economic equality. In *Associated Home Builders* the court acknowledged the cultural conflict when Tobriner wrote of the "collision between the forces that would save the benefits of nature" and the "egalitarian humanists" yet still deferred to government. Unlike the New Jersey Supreme Court, the California court declined to use the tools of hierarchy to forge a more egalitarian distribution of land use opportunities. But there is no indication that the court would object if local governments and agencies did so.

In two broad areas, "personal" rights and administrative procedure, the court did not automatically favor the government. The procedural cases, including vested rights and just compensation decisions, reflect the court's interest in ensuring that government fulfill its obligations in the hierarchy by avoiding arbitrary and capricious actions. In none of these cases, such as *Halaco Engineering* or *Gilmore*, was the court endorsing the substantive preferences of the property owners. The emphasis on procedure does not in itself establish a regime of individualism, but it does help prevent hierarchy from degenerating into despotism.[174]

By protecting privacy and expression, the court departed from a hierarchical model of land use control. There may indeed be an island of autonomy within which the state may not tread, the court

suggested. Because property may provide seclusion, the privacy doctrine has given landowners some basic protections in California.
They may be free in certain circumstances from intrusion by warrantless flying photographers (*Cook*) and airplane noise (*Baker*) and can
define their "families" in untraditional ways (*Adamson*). But the
court rejected other aspects of ownership, especially autonomy in
use, essential in libertarianism. The court was hostile to libertarianism while respecting conditions that complement egalitarianism.

JUSTICES AND CULTURE ON THE CALIFORNIA COURT

The tilt of individual justices against property rights in the
1980s can be seen in Table 10. The right-hand column gives the percentage of voting support from each justice for the landowner parties. The average support figure is 34.9 and would be much lower
were not Clark out in left (or perhaps right) field. Justice Clark was
the most consistent supporter of property rights, with a support figure of 77.8. While Clark voted for the landowner party in all but two
of his cases, no other justice until Malcolm Lucas joined the
court[175] did so in more than half the cases.

Justice Tobriner ranked as the strongest supporter of government in constitutional land use cases (see Tables 10 and 12); only in
Adamson, a privacy case, did Tobriner support the property-owning
party. Four other justices (Newman, Bird, Reynoso, and Manuel) had
vote measures at or below 20, with two more (Broussard and Grodin)
below 30. This wing of the court determined the outcomes of most
of the land use cases and defined the court's culture during the decade. When these justices departed from their pro-government
stance, they (with the exception of Manuel) supported procedural
rights and most of all privacy and expression rights (see Table 10). In
contrast, support by Justices Clark and Richardson tended in the opposite direction; they were least likely to support egalitarian rights.

After Tobriner left the court in 1981, his legacy lived on in the
votes and opinions of Bird, Broussard, Grodin, and Reynoso, who
formed a majority bloc on the court. Broussard, Grodin, and Reynoso agreed in nine of the ten constitutional land use cases in which
they all voted, and Rose Bird joined them in eight of those cases.
Broussard wrote only a single opinion in the land use cases (Table
11), while Grodin was the most frequent author of the group, writing opinions in more than half of his cases (frequencies of opinion
writing are given in Table 11, right-hand column). This production

Table 10
Voting Support for Landowner Rights,
by California Supreme Court Justices*

	Issue Area						
	Takings/ Property		Procedure		Expression/ Privacy		Total
	Pct.[1]	Rank	Pct.	Rank	Pct.	Rank[2]	Pct.
Clark	100.0	(1)	66.7	(2)	50.0	(2)	77.8
Lucas	75.0	(2)	66.7	(2)	100.0		75.0
Mosk	33.3	(5)	71.4	(1)	66.7	(1)	50.0
Richardson	57.1	(3)	50.0	(4)	00.0	(6)	46.2
Kaus	28.6	(6)	50.0	(4)	—		33.3
Broussard	14.3	(7)	40.0	(7)	100.0		28.6
Grodin	14.3	(7)	50.0	(4)	—		27.3
Newman	00.0	(11)	33.3	(8)	50.0	(2)	20.0
Bird	11.1	(10)	33.3	(8)	50.0	(2)	19.0
Reynoso	12.5	(9)	25.0	(10)	—		16.7
Manuel	50.0	(4)	00.0	(11)	00.0	(6)	14.3
Tobriner	00.0	(11)	00.0	(11)	50.0	(2)	11.1

*All of the justices for whom voting percentages are recorded voted in at least seven landowner cases. Five recent appointees—Justices Panelli, Arguelles, Eagleson, Kauffman and Kennard—voted in two or fewer landowner cases. Of these, only Panelli and Kennard are still on the court.

[1]For each issue area, the pecentage of cases in which each justice voted for the landowner party is listed. The rank is the relative standing of each justice compared to the other justices.

[2]Ranks are given only for justices who voted in at least two privacy cases.

set Grodin apart from the other deferent justices. Although he voted for the landowner in only three cases, Grodin wrote the majority opinion in two of those cases. Indeed, there was only one landowner victory[176] during Grodin's tenure on the court in which Grodin did *not* write the opinion for the court.[177] His opinions made Grodin the major voice explaining the court's willingness to protect privacy[178] and procedure. Although Grodin backed the power of government in every land regulation case, he was more critical when governments condemned land but then deprived the landowner of complete compensation, as in *Gilmore. Cook* and *Mayoff*, the aerial search opinions by Grodin show how the court, with

Table 11
Opinions by California Justices
Supporting Landowner Rights

	+	−	Pct.	Freq.	Justice	+	−	Pct.	Freq.
Clark	5	0	100.0	.56	Reynoso	1	2	33.3	.25
Lucas	3	0	100.0	.50	Bird	1	3	25.0	.24
Richardson	2	1	66.7	.23	Newman	1	3	25.0	.40
Mosk	10	7	58.8	.73	Broussard	0	1	00.0	.07
Grodin	2	2	50.0	.55	Tobriner	0	2	00.0	.22
Kaus	1	2	33.3	.33	Manuel	0	3	00.0	.43

+: opinons supporting the landowner party
−: opinons opposing the landowner party
Freq = number of cases in which a justice wrote an opinion, divided by the
number of cases in which the justice voted.

some difficulty, sought to protect property only when preferred values were threatened and only in narrowly prescribed circumstances.

Although Chief Justice Bird voted in more land use cases during the 1980s than any other justice except Mosk, her influence on the court's property rights doctrines was not as great as it could have been because she rarely wrote opinions. Bird authored opinions in just 24 percent of the cases in which she voted (Table 11) and wrote only one majority opinion (*Carson*, a rent control case in which her opinion consisted largely of quotes from the *Birkenfeld* precedent and narrow factual distinctions). But Bird was usually a reliable vote for the majority bloc in opposition to property rights, especially when no privacy or procedural issues were involved (Table 10).

Clark's support of landowner rights was unmatched. Until he left the court in 1981, William Clark was a one-man wing opposing the deferential majority. His voting record was almost a mirror image of Tobriner, and he was a frequent opinion writer (56 percent of the cases in which he voted), always in dissent. While Tobriner approvingly described the feudal flavor of the court's property rights jurisprudence, Clark was alarmed, as when he warned in *Agins* that "henceforth . . . property will . . . be held . . . in trust for whatever purposes and uses a governmental ageny . . . elects, without compensation."[179] Clark dissented in three public trust cases and saw expansion of the trust as thematic of the court's broad attack on property rights.

Justice Richardson was Clark's most reliable ally. Richardson supported the property owners in all four public trust cases and wrote the dissenting opinion in *Venice Peninsula Properties* after Clark had left the court as well as in *Arnel*, the decision that left landowners vulnerable to initiative rezonings. Richardson was tolerant of most specific land regulations, however, even writing the majority opinion in *Agins*, which denied owners the remedy of compensation for regulatory takings. Based on vote totals (Table 10), Richardson tilted slightly toward supporting the government. Even this moderate level of support put Richardson in sharp contrast to the pro-government majority. But Richardson wrote opinions far less frequently (23 percent of cases in which he voted) than Clark, so his dissenting voice was not only less consistent but also more muted.

In many ways, Stanley Mosk towers over the California Supreme Court. He has served on the court since 1964, decades longer than any other current member. During the 1980s, Mosk voted in twenty-two constitutional land use cases, more than any other justice.[180] Mosk has been a prolific opinion writer, writing opinions in 73 percent of the land use cases in which he voted during the 1980s (Table 11). His seventeen opinions surpassed the output of the next most prolific justice, Clark, by twelve. And the Mosk opinions were singular in tone as well as quantity, written with intellectual vigor and wit.

Mosk wrote seven majority opinions, the most by far of any justice, supporting the government in land use disputes, including all four in the public trust cases. Through his opinions, Mosk has been perhaps the most ardent preservationist on the court, endorsing the extension of state control into unprecedented areas. But when procedural and preferred rights issues were at stake, Mosk supported the rights claims roughly 70 percent of the time (see Table 10). Mosk appears to fit well the dominant California mold of the double standard justice yet is more independent-minded than most. Writing in 1980, DiMento and his coauthors described a decade-long "metamorphosis" of a justice who was "tiring of championing preservationism."[181] Mosk continued to show occasional unpredictability during the 1980s, and his opinions indicate a justice who appreciates the arguments of conflicting cultures.

Mosk dissented in seven cases that upheld governmental actions and wrote an opinion each time. Remarkably, Mosk was the most prolific author of both majority opinions supporting government and dissenting opinions criticizing judicial deference. Reading the land use cases of the California court at times is like listening to Stanley Mosk carry on a debate with himself. Although Mosk often endorsed the hierarchical underpinnings of preservationism, at times he sounded ardently egalitarian or even libertarian. Stephen Barnett has described Mosk's dissents as "eclectic."[182] Mosk certainly has been something of a cultural gypsy and appeared to relish rather than fear the contradictions of each culture.[183]

More than any other justice, Mosk voiced concern for the inegalitarian impact of land use regulation. When the court in *Associated Home Builders* sustained Livermore's moratorium on new construction, Mosk warned in dissent that a "comforting environmental declaration" may have exclusionary effects that keep out the poor and working class from desirable communities.[184] Yet Mosk has been a leader of the court's advocacy of preservationism, and his recommendation in *Associated Home Builders* was a Solomon-like solution: Preservationism shall reign in rural and recreational areas, and metropolitan governments shall not be allowed to obstruct equality.

Equality as a way of life is quite difficult to maintain, and its advocates tend to look to other cultures for assistance. Traditionally in America liberty was seen as conducive to reducing social and economic inequality, but increasingly in the twentieth century egalitarians have looked to the coercive power of government for solutions. The New Jersey court has followed this path in trying to make housing patterns more egalitarian without strengthening individual property rights.[185] Mosk took the alternate tack in *Associated Home Builders* (and he affirmed his continued support for that approach a decade later in the *Camarillo* case), arguing that equality could be furthered by promoting rather than restraining individual choice.

Mosk supported rent control and major expansions of the public trust, but at times he sounded like an ardent libertarian. He seemed to draw a line between a government that tells a property owner he may not do everything he wishes and one that tells an owner what he must do. For example, Mosk was very critical of ordinances designed to block apartment owners from selling their units as condominiums. "If the question is whether a city may compel a landlord to remain in business against his will, and give him only the alternative of a forced sale," he asserted, "the answer is: not in a democratic society."[186] The expectation that a small group of private owners should shoulder public burdens occasionally drew objections from Mosk, as in the *Pennell* case in which San Jose looked to landlords to subsidize low-income tenants rather than using the city's funds. Mosk especially was concerned about procedural abuses, supporting the property owner in 71 percent of those cases (Table 10), more often than any other justice. In *White*, he assailed a scheme by which San Diego County paid owners for land taken for roads improvements and then assessed the owners the same amount in special fees. As Mosk put it, the city put the compensation in the owner's pocket, "and then proceed[ed] to pick the pocket."[187] Mosk was not always protective of the rights of property owners, but he saw the free market as a benevolent (or at least neutral) force, was skeptical of governmental motives, and emphasized that safeguards of individual freedom are essential in a democracy.

The direction of the California court will depend in large part on Malcolm Lucas. The first of the current justices appointed by a Republican governor, Lucas was elevated to chief justice following the downfall of Rose Bird. From his position of leadership and with a proclivity to write opinions (in 50 percent of land use cases in the 1980s), he could be a major factor in constitutional land use cases. In the 1980s Lucas supported the landowner party in 75 percent of the cases in which he voted (Table 10). Lucas's measure of voting support was exceeded only by that of Clark, who left the court well before his arrival. Lucas has supported the rights of landowners in all issue areas.[188] In *Fisher*, Lucas dissented and criticized Berkeley for putting the burden of subsidizing tenants on landlords rather than pursuing policies such as rent subsidies and public housing "more consistent with the operation of the free market system."[189] The jurisprudence of the California court in the coming years may depend in part on whether Lucas expands the kind of policy argument he made in *Fisher* into a libertarian constitutional philosophy.

"The continuing intellectual contest" through informal discussions and written opinions between the opposing philosophical perspectives of different justices on the California court "disciplines its decisions and enriches its product," Stephen Barnett has written.[190] In the landowner rights cases of the 1980s, that dialogue was decidedly lopsided and sometimes entirely absent. The majority of the court adhered to a hierarchical rationale of respect for public authority in most cases. When private owners sought to use their land, the court typically deferred to whatever decision had been made by regulatory authorities. Government actions were subjected to only the most minimal test of rationality: If the justices could imagine any rational justification, the restrictions on property

Table 12
Index of Support for Landowner Rights,
by California Supreme Court Justices

Clark	.858	Grodin	.354	Bird	.202
Lucas*	.833	Kaus	.333	Reynoso	.200
Mosk*	.537	Broussard*	.267	Manuel	.100
Richardson	.500	Newman	.214	Tobriner	.091

Index = (vote percentage + opinon percentage × opinion frequency) / 1 +
       opinion frequency
*Current justices

rights would be upheld. The scrutiny by the court often became a caricature, and the defense of hierarchical controls of land use was reduced to platitudes. This is hardly the product of a court seriously grappling with the basic cultural conflicts that are unavoidable in a diverse society. The lack of consistent advocates of opposing cultures made it easier for the justices to avoid thoughtful arguments. With the departure of Justice Clark, the libertarian perspective on land rights was little heard on the court, and at no time during the decade was there a justice who regularly challenged the court on the inegalitarian implications of land use controls. At times, Stanley Mosk's mind seemed to house more diverse viewpoints and complexity of argument than the court as a whole.

The California court is undergoing a remarkable transformation,[191] although where it will end up is uncertain. The long-dominant "liberal" wing of the court has been depleted (see Table 12, which ranks the California justices by support for landowner rights, taking into account both voting patterns and written opinions). Bird, Grodin, and Reynoso were relieved of their positions by the voters. Their replacements, Justices Arguelles, Eagleson, and Kauffman,[192] have already retired from the court.[193] The newest justices, Joyce Kennard, Marvin Baxter, and Armand Arabian, were named by Governor George Deukmejian, a Republican. Broussard, a fourth justice from the Tobriner wing, has announced he will retire in 1991, and his replacement will be named by the current Republican governor, Pete Wilson. The future of the court will depend on the perspectives developed by the newer members of the court, Panelli, Kennard, Arabian, and Baxter, who are virtually certain to vote more conservatively than Bird, Grodin, and Reynoso.[194] But there is no guarantee that the new justices will be inclined to protect rights in land use cases. Justices who may be less vigilant than their predecessors about protecting criminal or expressive rights may be even less concerned with landowner rights. If one or two of them become outspoken advocates of property rights, the court could be in for some lively debates and close votes in land use cases. But if they are reluctant to overturn the actions of elected and appointed officials (or court precedent), the California trend of deference toward hierarchical regulation will continue, animated now by a conservative disdain for judicial activism or respect for precedent rather than "liberal" hostility to private property. The court is changing, but it may be another case of "the more things change, the more they stay the same."

Chapter 6

The United States Supreme Court: Hesitant Steps toward the Protection of Landowner Rights

When I began studying Supreme Court protection of the constitutional rights of property owners to use their land, the question was whether the modest crumbs the courts had thrown in the direction of landowners were anomalies or the beginning of a modest revival, a revival based on more than wishful thinking or our worst fears, depending on philosophical bent. But in June 1987 the Court issued two decisions—*First English Evangelical Lutheran Church of Glendale v. Los Angeles County*[1] and *Nollan v. California Coastal Commission*[2]—that returned the takings clause to the front burner after six decades of exile.[3] Those decisions left many planners in a tizzy, fearing the end of civilized society,[4] and property owners with visions of victories dancing in their heads. It could hardly be argued that the idea of constitutional rights for landowners had not been revived. It appeared, at least for a few months, that the Court had forsaken its deference to hierarchical regulation and had become a vigorous defender of property rights.

But the gloom and euphoria triggered by *First English* and *Nollan* were exaggerated reactions based more on the outcomes of the decisions than their reasoning or context.[5] The restoration of property rights by the Supreme Court has been neither as pervasive as its proponents wish nor as radical as its opponents fear. Before libertarians declare victory and leave the field, they should realize that while *First English* and *Nollan* have made constitutional rights more important factors in the land use regulatory process, the decisions are limited exceptions to the high court's traditional apathy toward landowner rights. In some circumstances, the decisions will be significant, but most regulation likely will continue to be sustained. While there has indeed been a revival of landowner rights at the federal level, it is a hesitant, reluctant revival.

SEEDS OF A REVIVAL

The dichotomy between personal liberties and property rights is a false one. Property does not have rights. People have rights. . . . A fundamental interdependence exists between the personal right to liberty and the right in property. Neither could have meaning without the other. That rights in property are basic civil liberties has long been recognized.
—*Justice Potter Stewart*[6]

Modern Supreme Court jurisprudence largely has been a pursuit of an egalitarian vision, first by denigrating property rights and more recently by seeking to protect those aspects of property use that ostensibly facilitate personal development without increasing material inequality. "The judicial pursuit of equality," Justice Brennan has said, "is, in my view, properly regarded to be the noblest mission of judges; it has been the primary task of judges since the repudiation of economic substantive due process as our central constitutional concern."[7] The double standard of rights articulated in *United States v. Carolene Products Co.*[8] has been the judicial tool for promoting equality. While New Deal jurisprudence relegated landowner rights to the constitutional dungeon of economic interests, the preferred rights of expression and equality have been steadily expanded until the two categories have begun to overlap.

Rights to use property may in some circumstances protect free expression and equality, so the line between property and person may not be so clear.

The groundwork for renewed attention to land use issues was laid in the 1970s as the Court increasingly recognized property rights, although with a decidedly egalitarian bent. The "new property" of Charles Reich[9] gained Court acceptance in cases such as *Goldberg v. Kelly*,[10] concerning welfare benefits; *Cleveland Board of Education v. LaFleur*,[11] which struck down a school district's pregnancy leave rules; and *Goss v. Lopez*,[12] which required due process for school suspensions. Public employment, education, and welfare services were becoming subject to constitutionally protected claims of entitlement.[13] And the remarkable rise of substantive due process from the graveyard of discarded Court doctrines also helped open the door to property rights. The Court created privacy rights to contraception[14] and abortion[15] from the blank spaces between the lines of the Bill of Rights in the best spirit of the turn-of-the-century Court. In *Griswold v. Connecticut*, Justice Douglas disclaimed any relationship between the new right of privacy and the old substantive due process that protected liberty of contract,[16] but most members of the Court were more candid in recognizing that it was once again reading into the Constitution a right not explicitly protected.[17] And the doctrine that there are a few very specific substantive rights, such as the right of travel,[18] protected by the equal protection clause also restored substantive due process under a more contemporary label.

Once the Court acknowledged that some rights not explicitly spelled out in the Constitution merit protection, it was increasingly difficult to justify why rights of property, which are in the Constitution, should not be protected. The infatuation with "new" property and the restoration of substantive due process were important precursors of the modest revival of landowner rights. The Court could no longer argue that it was protecting only specific constitutional rights or that those rights had no implications for private property. Both the formal distinction of the double standard— explicit rights versus substantive rights deemed implicit to due process—and its practical interpretation (separation of personal from property rights) were being eroded. During the 1970s, the Court acknowledged that unrestricted interference with "economic" rights might unduly impinge on personal freedom after all. Most striking was the statement in *Lynch v. Household Finance* that the double standard is false, that property rights are personal rights. A few more shock waves rippled through the legal and academic communities when the Court dusted off the contract clause and actually used it to strike down state actions in *United States Trust Co. v. New Jersey*[19] and *Allied Structural Steel v. Spannaus*.[20] And ever so cautiously the Court was venturing back into the forgotten wilderness of landowner rights.

THE RELUCTANT REVIVAL OF LANDOWNER RIGHTS

*I would like to believe that among the justices
of our highest court, conservative or liberal,
Democrat or Republican, Southerner or Yankee,
corporate lawyer or ex-professor, there has been
consensus on only one point: if we cherish our
equilibrium, never agree to review a zoning
case.*
　　　　　　　　　—Richard F. Babcock[21]

The Supreme Court awoke from its constitutional slumber in 1974. For the first time, the Court applied the recently unearthed right of privacy in the context of land use regulation. The village of Belle Terre, located near a university, apparently considered the living habits of young college students among the less noble attributes of higher education. The village zoned solely for single-family housing, explicitly excluding fraternities and any household of three or more unrelated persons. The Court was in a bind: A victory for the privacy claims of the students in *Belle Terre v. Boraas*[22] would implicitly provide landowners with a degree of constitutional protection unknown in forty-six years. But a summary rejection of the owners' claim would give local governments a green light to regulate a most personal decision—whom to live with. The Court could reject the double standard of rights or preserve it at a steep price to privacy interests; it chose the latter. The Belle Terre ordinance, according to Justice Douglas, was just another example of "economic and social legislation," and thus the village was free to keep out the college kids in order to protect "a quiet place where yards are wide, people few, and motor vehicles restricted."[23]

The regulation was sustained, but the maxim that the Supreme Court shall hear, see, and speak no land use had been broken, and to this day the Court still has not restored the "equilibrium" of silence.[24] During the 1970s, the Court heard several more land use cases, rejecting nearly every constitutional claim.[25] But in *Moore v.*

East Cleveland,[26] privacy and property finally won a round. East Cleveland, in the spirit of Belle Terre, sought to exclude households of unrelated persons. But the city defined *family* to prevent a child from living with his grandmother.[27] This was a bit much for the Court, which ruled that the city had violated the privacy rights of the Moores protected by the due process clause.[28] In a deft demonstration of line drawing, the Court announced that its decision was entirely consistent with *Belle Terre,* which would still permit regulation of individuals unrelated by blood or marriage. But more significantly, the Court had taken its first tentative step back toward substantive protection of landowner rights. As the 1980s began, with substantive due process creeping back toward respectability and a popular conservative president ready to replace aging justices, the Court was poised for a potential renewal of property rights.

In the 1979–1980 term, the Court had two major land use cases on its docket, both, not surprisingly, from California where restrictive land use controls have flourished with the encouragement of a preservationist court. In *Agins v. Tiburon,*[29] the California Supreme Court held that regulations severe enough to be found as takings were exempt from the just compensation requirements of the state and federal constitutions. The court reasoned that land use regulations were an exercise of the police power, not the eminent domain power, and thus it would be inappropriate to provide compensation for regulatory takings. In *Pruneyard Shopping Center v. Robins,*[30] the California court decreed that the free speech provisions of the state constitution required a private shopping center to accommodate political groups that wished to solicit signatures. Merely agreeing to hear arguments in *Pruneyard* was "Lockeian and Lochnerian," wrote William Van Astyne,[31] invoking the ghosts of natural rights and liberty of contract. Unlike *Belle Terre* and *Moore,* *Pruneyard*[32] and *Agins* did not involve land use rights aligned with more privileged rights. Victories for the owners would be clear victories for property rights. The Court would have to decide whether to perpetuate the denigration of property rights of the prior half century.

A group seeking signatures for a petition opposing a UN resolution attempted to solicit passersby from the central courtyard of the privately owned Pruneyard Shopping Center. The company denied access to the group, which then sought a court injunction that would allow it to solicit on private commercial property. The state supreme court agreed, reasoning that the state constitution created a free speech right incorporating the petitioner's actions and that the owners had no constitutional property right to deny access. The U.S. high court upheld the ruling,[33] although its reasoning was more equivocal. Justice Rehnquist for the majority argued that neither the owners nor the signature seekers had controlling constitutional rights. Shopping center access was not required by the U.S. Constitution, but neither was it forbidden. Thus there was no federal basis from which to overturn the decision of the state court. If the California court wished to create a private speech right of access to private property in those circumstances, it was free to do so.

Interestingly, Rehnquist reasoned that the state could "exercise its police power" by regulating the private commercial property, or it could adopt its own constitutional standard. But it was a court, not a legislature, that was applying a restriction to a private owner in *Pruneyard*. Justice Marshall implied the exceptional nature of the state court's action when he argued in a concurring opinion that to protect the owner's right to exclude would amount "to no less than a suggestion that the common law of trespass is not subject to revision by the State."[34] Indeed, the California court was creating private law, but under the guise of enforcing a constitutional right (to access for free speech) ostensibly applicable only to governments. And the individual right limited by the California court was not simply an aspect of common trespass law but a constitutional right of exclusion. Justice Powell was not so quick to dismiss the significance of the state ruling, noting that "in many situations, a right of access is no less intrusive than speech compelled by the state"[35] and cautioning in his concurrence that the access right should not apply to all speech in all shopping centers.

"One of the essential sticks in the bundle of property rights is the right to exclude others," Rehnquist proclaimed in *Pruneyard*. "And here there has literally been a 'taking' of that right."[36] Yet it did not follow that there had been an unconstitutional taking. For the owners had "failed to demonstrate that the right to exclude others is so essential to the use or economic value of the property that the state-authorized limitation of it amounted to a 'taking.' "[37] Somehow the "essential stick" was not so essential after all. How can there be degrees of "essentialness"? Either something is essential or it is not. Denigrating the right to exclude is surprising because this is the only constitutional property right that the Court has regularly protected, as we shall see in *Loretto v. Teleprompter Manhattan CATV Corp.*[38] and *Nollan*. A pivotal distinction in *Pruneyard* seems to be that the state court had created a constitutional speech right opposed to the right of exclusion. If the right of exclusion was challenged by a legislative regulation and not a constitutional right, the Court might not have been unanimously deferent. Also, shopping centers may merit less protection, in the eyes of the Court, on two grounds: (1) A commercial center open to the general public may have aspects of a "public forum" and thus be subject to constitutional restrictions (such as the protection of free speech) to which private actions generally are immune. (2) The commercial character of the property may taint it as an "economic interest," less worthy of constitutional protection that more "personal" real property. For Justice White in his concurrence, it was important that there were no "property or privacy rights of a homeowner involved." Even within property cases, the double standard of rights lives on, with individuals having greater claims to the privacy of property than commercial firms.[39]

Agins bought five acres of land on which to build housing in Tiburon. Subsequently the property was designated for open space by the city and rezoned to allow, contingent upon additional regulatory approvals, the construction of from one to five houses. Eminent domain proceedings to condemn and purchase the property for open space were instituted by the city but later abandoned. Agins took the city to court, claiming that the zoning restriction in the context of the city's other actions to preserve the property as open space constituted a taking. Rather than pay for the open space, the city could accomplish the same end through restrictive regulation, and Agins claimed the city had no intent to allow development.

Agins v. Tiburon[40] provided the Supreme Court with its first opportunity to grapple with the central constitutional issue[41] of the decade: When regulations go "too far,"[42] do they require compensation for the property rights that have been taken? But the Court unanimously adopted a wait-and-see attitude because, Justice Powell wrote for the majority, "there is as yet no concrete controversy."[43] Until the city rejected a specific development plan, Powell reasoned, the Court could not decide whether there had been a taking. The Court refused to consider whether compensation would be required *if* there was a taking. The Court would use similar reasoning to duck the compensation issue throughout the decade, arguing at one point[44] that the rejection of one development plan does not mean that every alternative plan would also be rejected. Such reasoning conceivably could sentence property owners to an endless cycle of regulatory hurdles immune from judicial remedies. The Court evaded the issue in four cases over seven years[45] before finally facing the compensation question in *First English*.

The opinion in *Agins*, with its muddling of constitutional issues and ducking of crucial questions, unfortunately typifies the
regulatory jurisprudence of the Court. A zoning ordinance could be
a taking, according to Powell, if it "does not substantially advance
legitimate state interests."[46] But this is a due process test, not a takings test, and one does not follow from the other. A regulation might
effectively deny an owner the complete use of his property while
still advancing a state interest. To preserve open space, a city might
rule that all owners of undeveloped scenic property could do nothing more than gaze fondly at their lands. Even the most deferent
court would be hard pressed to decree that such a severe deprivation
could not be a taking, yet that is precisely what would be required
by Powell's reasoning. If preserving open space is a legitimate state
interest, as Powell declares, it does not lose its legitimacy simply
because a measure pursuant to that interest is severe. Conversely, if
a regulation was found to be utterly devoid of a legitimate basis, it
would not follow that any owner could claim compensation if none
of his land use rights had been significantly affected. Legitimacy and
harm are different questions.

Agins and *Pruneyard* typify the decade. Although the Court
was willing to hear landowner claims throughout the 1980s, which
was noteworthy in comparison to its prior lack of involvement, it
usually rejected them. The Court has not imposed duties on property owners under the pretext of protecting constitutional rights,
but neither has it chastised state courts that have chosen to do so.
For example, the Court did not impose an obligation to provide
speech access on the shopping center owner in *Pruneyard*, but neither did it protect a right of the owner to be free from such an imposition. Consequently, the California court was able to require
speech access at private shopping centers with the effective abstention of the Supreme Court. The New Jersey Supreme Court, under
its state constitution, ordered that municipalities impose on developers an obligation to provide a specific proportion of low- and
moderate-income housing, and the Supreme Court has refused to
become involved.[47] And the court has blurred the major doctrines
protecting property rights—due process and takings—so that gaining definitive relief has been difficult. As evident in *Agins* and subsequent takings cases, the Court has been reluctant to find that
regulatory authorities have issued final judgments that might be
evaluated as possible takings, and until 1987 it did not require compensation for regulatory takings.[48] Consequently, an owner could
wait years or even decades for an effective judicial remedy if a

municipality repeatedly rejected land use permit applications or subsequent to a court ruling that a regulation was a taking, enacted a series of similarly restrictive measures.[49]

THE DOUBLE STANDARD OF PROPERTY RIGHTS IN THE 1980s

The Supreme Court did not shake off its New Deal shackles in the 1980s. True, the Court gave more attention to landowner cases than at any other time in the prior five decades. But rights must be enforced to be viable, and repeated defeats may only serve to emphasize the inferior status of landowner rights. A glance at the constitutional land use cases heard by the Supreme Court in the 1980s (Table 13) shows a dominance of white space in the column for landowner victories; claimants of rights may be called, but few are chosen. Landowner interests, even when liberally construed to include operators of pornographic theaters and billboard owners, lost 70 percent of their cases[50] before the Supreme Court in the 1980s. In half of these losses, the decisions were unanimous. And all of the unanimous defeats involved classic land use issues: takings and due process. The only unanimous decision that struck down a governmental restriction on land use was *Cleburne v. Cleburne Living Center*,[51] which was primarily concerned with the equal protection rights of the mentally retarded.

The distinction between issue areas points to the basic patterns of the Court's jurisprudence of landowner rights in the 1980s: When property interests were aligned with more favored rights, those of equality and expression, they stood a fair chance of winning Court protection, but when landowner rights stood on their own, they were likely to fail. This contradicts the conclusion of writers who, emphasizing the trend toward "new property" and the occasional victories the Court has given landowners, have declared that property was the central value of the Burger Court.[52] "Those without personal rights in property have only the weakest and most tenuous claim to personal liberty," according to Van Astyne, "whether of speech, of privacy, or of due process of law."[53] This aptly captures the libertarian notion that private property rights are the essential protector of personal liberties, but it exaggerates the Supreme Court's regard for property. The notion that property is the transcendent constitutional value would come as a surprise to many landowners who have tangled with local officials and to many land use attorneys who have made futile appeals to the

Table 13
U.S. Supreme Court Decisions
on Constitutional Rights of Landowners

Year	Landowner Wins	Vote	Landowner Losses	Vote
1988			Phillips Petro.	5–3
			Pennell	6–2
1987	Nollan v. CCC	5–4		
	First English	6–3		
			Cherokee Nation	9–0
			Keystone Coal	5–4
1986			Cloud Books	6–3
			MacDonald	5–4
			Playtime Theatres	7–2
1985			Riverside Homes	9–0
	Cleburne Center	9–0		
			Hamilton Bank	7–1
1984			HHA v. Midkiff	8–0
			Kirby Industries	9–0
1982	Grendel's Den	8–1		
	Loretto	6–3		
1981	Metromedia	6–3		
			Hodel v. Indiana	9–0
			Hodel v. Va. Assn.	9–0
	Schad	7–2		
			San Diego Gas	5–4
1980			Agins v. Tiburon	9–0
			Pruneyard Center	9–0

Landowner wins: 7
Landowner defeats: 16
Percentage won: 30

Supreme Court. Indeed, from the perspective of the landowner, the opposite is more true. To paraphrase Van Astyne, "Those without personal equality or expressive rights—whether speech, privacy, or due process of law—have only the weakest and most tenuous claim to liberty of property."

During the 1980s, property interests were victorious in two-thirds of the cases in which rights of equality and expression, which survived the Carolene Products purge, were invoked (Table 14). The possible interference with noncommercial speech saved the bill-board owners in Metromedia, Inc. v. San Diego;[54] the expressive connotations of nude dancing clothed the Schad v Mt. Ephraim[55]

owners with constitutional protection; banning a restaurant from
serving liquor because of the wishes of a nearby church was found to
offend the establishment clause in *Larkin v. Grendel's Den, Inc.*;[56]
and protection of the mentally retarded, who might be considered a
"discrete, insular minority" meriting greater protection under the
Carolene Products dichotomy of rights, saved the Cleburne Living
Center. If the landowner happens to be a church, it will also be on
firmer constitutional ground.[57] Since *Moore,* the Court often has
been willing to protect expressive and equality rights, even when
they coincide with rights to use property. As John Costonis has concluded, "The Court has shifted its ground, suggesting that under
some circumstances, property may advance noneconomic values
that are entitled . . . to protection."[58] The Supreme Court in the
1980s did not embrace a libertarian emphasis on the importance
of property rights, but neither did it defer without question to
hierarchical regulation in every case. Although landowners usually
lost their cases, review tended to be more searching than has been
typical since the New Deal, and the Court was sympathetic to
defenses of property uses that protected rights important from an
egalitarian perspective—rights of free expression, privacy, and equal
protection.

FREE EXPRESSION AND PRIVATE PROPERTY

Victories for property owners on expressive grounds are significant for landowner rights, for two reasons. First, they allow property interests at least some protection, albeit only by their
association with preferred rights. Second, the more the courts give
attention to the links between property and other personal rights,
the greater the appreciation of property rights is likely to be. To the
egalitarian supporter of New Deal Supreme Court jurisprudence,
rights that protect expression cannot be all bad. Although a First
Amendment victory may do less for the cause of property rights
than a takings decision, it is nonetheless an encouraging step for
landowners.

But a court may by narrowly defining the grounds for a victory
seek to limit the incidental protection of property. Such was the
case in *Metromedia.* The Supreme Court found that a billboard ban
enacted by San Diego violated the Constitution because it restricted
noncommercial speech, such as some political advertising. The
consequence of striking down the ban would be that all property
owners could put whatever message, commercial, personal, or po-

litical, they pleased on a sign whether it was on a billboard or at a home or business site. Both the property and expressive interests would be fully vindicated. But wait a minute. In an opinion by Justice White, the Court made clear that the property interests related to speech interests in the billboard context could be greatly restricted as long as noncommercial speech was protected. The Court offered a double dose of the double standard, emphasizing that governments can control the "noncommunicative aspects" of billboards and that they may discriminate between different categories of commercial speech, but not noncommercial. The ban thus created two constitutional problems: It regulated communication, and most critically, it particularly restricted "noneconomic" speech. The city had not only ignored the double standard of rights in its billboard regulation; it had inverted it: On-site commercial signs, but not noncommercial, were exempted from the ban. Rather than take the opportunity generally to renounce billboard bans, the Court sent a message, although largely through dicta, that bans would be tolerated as long as they remained true to the double standard, giving less protection to speech that like property rights could be considered an economic as distinguished from personal interest.

Had *Metromedia* been litigated exclusively on the grounds of property rights, the Court likely would have refused to reach the substantive issues or would not have found a constitutional violation. The Court is generally sympathetic to facial challenges to laws that threaten expressive rights out of fear that waiting for a concrete dispute will chill free speech. In property cases, however, such as the series of cases over payment for regulatory takings,[59] the Court has been reluctant to rule on the rights issue until it is certain harm has occurred. In another case, when a rent control law that would require landlords to lower rents for low-income tenants was challenged on its face as an unconstitutional taking, the Court rejected the argument, concluding that until the law was applied, the Court could not be certain that it would be unconstitutional.[60]

The reliance on the First Amendment in *Metromedia* contrasts with how billboard cases were argued prior to the New Deal judicial revolution. Beginning with *Thomas Cusack Co. v. Chicago*[61] in 1917, the Court rejected a series of challenges to billboard regulations. In *Metromedia*, Justice White sought to distinguish these precedents by asserting that the prior cases "did not involve First Amendment considerations."[62] But it was the Court, not the interests involved in billboard regulation, that had changed. True, the earlier billboard cases involved "due process and equal protection challenges."[63] But that was because prior to the New Deal, the Court was sympathetic to substantive due process attacks on commercial regulation and lacked a history of strong protection of free speech, whereas the modern Court has given only ritualistic due process review but takes First Amendment claims very seriously. *Cusack* upheld a requirement that block residents give their consent before erection of a billboard. In *St. Louis Poster Advertising Co. v. St. Louis,*[64] the Court sustained limits on the size of billboards and permit and fee requirements. And *Packer Corp. v. Utah*[65] upheld a state prohibition of the advertisement of tobacco products on billboards. If any of these cases was brought before the Court today, the justices certainly would be most concerned about the restrictions imposed by the laws and ordinances on the manner, cost, and content of expression. Commercial speech receives an lesser degree of constitutional protection today,[66] but were it not for the speech component, there likely would be no protection. Prior to the New Deal, plaintiffs sought to protect the speech aspects of outdoor advertising by claiming rights in property. Today, the reverse is true: Property may be protected by aligning with free expression.

Cases involving purveyors of the "near obscene," as the Court refers to "adult" expression that does not meet the strict Court test of obscenity, also show the heightened protection that can flow from association with preferred rights. Municipalities may concentrate adult uses such as bookstores and movie theatres specializing in sexually oriented material or disperse them[67] but not forbid them entirely. In *Renton*, a zoning ordinance effectively excluded adult theaters from most of the city, but the Court upheld it, concluding that the few sites remaining nontheless provided adequate opportunities to locate the businesses in the city. Adult businesses do not gain as much constitutional protection as expression considered at the core of the First Amendment or free from commercial associations, but they do have more protection than any business use of property unrelated to a preferred right. Daniel Mandelker has noted that except for the heightened protection for adult businesses, "no doctrine in zoning law requires ample opportunity for particular commercial uses. The courts have not adopted an 'adequate number of sites' doctrine for bakeries, for example."[68]

In *Schad*, a local zoning ordinance banned live entertainment in commercial zones, and the borough of Mt. Ephraim, New Jersey, used the ban to prevent nude dancing in an adult bookstore. Although the defendant claimed a violation of property rights based on substantive due process and equal protection (X-rated theaters were not similarly forbidden), the Court avoided those claims and concentrated on the First Amendment issue. In addressing the claim of free expression, Justice White preferred to concentrate on the broader implications of the restrictive ordinance as a ban on all live entertainment rather than consider whether its application was justified in the particular circumstances of the case. The defendants were "entitled to rely on the impact of the ordinance on the expressive activities of others as well as their own."[69] The attention to "overbreadth" is common in expressive rights cases (in contrast to traditional property rights cases) where, as with the consideration of facial challenges, the Court is concerned about the possible chilling effect on lawful expression. The effect of *Schad* was to strengthen the right of the owner to do what he wishes with his bookstore as long as it encompasses expressive activity.[70] The case could be seen as a victory for a libertarian concern with property rights over hierarchical regulation, but it was possible only because of the implication of speech. Mt. Ephraim sought to justify its ban by citing the burdens of additional parking, trash, and police services that it asserted were associated with live entertainment. But the Court, looking critically at the slim evidence presented by the municipality, found these justifications insufficient. If these were indeed problems, the Court reasoned, Mt. Ephraim should use alternative means that would not restrict expression. This willingness to scrutinize the justifications for regulation contrasts starkly with the creative indulgence the Court prefers to show when traditional property rights are at stake. The woes of congestion and additional public services are standard justifications for regulation of property and are usually accepted at face value by the Court, granting to most zoning regulations what Justice Blackmun called, in his *Schad* concurrence, "talismanic immunity from constitutional challenge."[71] When governments fail in "economic" rights cases to provide rational justifications for their actions, the obliging Court has even been known to make up its own.[72] Fortunately for the proprietors of the *Schad* store, the Court saw a preferred right at stake and looked for actual evidence of why the regulation was necessary.

Cloaking nude dancing in a bookstore with the protections of the First Amendment troubled some of the justices in *Schad*. Even though "the foliage of the First Amendment may cast protective shadows over some forms of nude dancing," Justice Stevens cautioned in his concurring opinion, "its roots were germinated by more serious concerns."[73] Chief Justice Burger dissented, arguing that concerns about overbreath should not excuse the extension of constitutional protection to nude dancing: "To invoke the First Amendment to protect the activity involved in this case trivializes and demeans that great Amendment."[74] Burger often objected to the rigid double standard of the liberal Court majority, but his opinions gave little cheer to landowners as he was inclined to narrow the protection of egalitarian rights rather than expand protection of property rights.

Grendel's Den, a bar in Massachusetts, was able to satiate the thirst of its customers thanks to the Court's interpretation of the establishment of religion clause of the First Amendment. A statute that allowed churches to veto the granting of liquor licenses to establishments within five hundred feet of a church was struck down by the court in *Grendel's Den* as an unconstitutional state establishment of religion. As Burger did in *Schad*, Rehnquist dissented in *Grendel's Den*, criticizing the deployment of "heavy First Amendment artillery" to destroy a "sensible and unobjectionable Massachusetts statute."[75] His objection to the double standard of rights was that it protected too much, not too little. A flat ban, Rehnquist observed, would actually be "more protective of churches and more restrictive of liquor sales," and he argued that allowing more discretion "seems to me to be the sort of legislative refinement that we should encourage, not forbid."[76]

In none of the expression or religion cases were the property rights of the owner of paramount concern. The pub owner won in *Grendel's Den*, but his property rights were far from the minds of the justices. The Court's concern to limit the public power of the church, and Chief Justice Burger, writing for the majority, suggested that the government could even impose a flat ban on bars in certain neighborhoods. As in *Schad*, the owner's interests were protected because they raised First Amendment issues. Attorneys and scholars might scoff at considering these cases property cases. But when there has long been a constitutional void, cases such as these form the seeds from which broader appreciation and protection of property may grow. When uses of property implicate preferred values, courts must consider how extensive protection ought to be. Ultimately, any use of property, be it a style of construction or a means of livelihood, is in a sense an aspect of personal expression. Almost two hundred years ago, James Madison declared that all expression was property, thus meriting protection; today it may be more compelling to consider that property use can be expression.

PROPERTY AND EQUALITY BEFORE THE LAW

The only major landowner case focused on equal protection, *Cleburne,* may prove to be one of the most significant decisions of the decade. The city of Cleburne required a special use permit the granting of which depended in part on neighborhood opinion, for group homes for the mentally retarded. The Cleburne Living Center was denied a permit and sued, pointing out that special permits were not required for other groups such as fraternities and boardinghouses. The Supreme Court unanimously agreed with the center. *Cleburne* was a victory for property rights because it affirmed the rights of the owners as well as the prospective tenants, even though the land use setting may have been "incidental" to the Court's rationale.[77]

The most remarkable aspect of the Court's opinion was its rejection of the "strict scrutiny" standard that since the New Deal had been the preferred approach for protected minorities. The mentally retarded did not even qualify for midlevel protection as a "quasi-suspect class," Justice White reasoned, because they formed too large and amorphous a group and had not been shut out of the political process.[78] White cited several laws that served the interests of the retarded and argued that how "this large and diversified group is to be treated under the law is a difficult and often a technical matter, very much a task for legislators guided by qualified professionals and not by the perhaps ill-informed opinions of the judiciary."[79] The language is strikingly similar to the rationale offered by the Court for refusing to criticize legislation affecting rights deemed "economic." Better that the legislatures should be unrestrained than have the courts apply their clumsy hands.

But even under the rational basis test, Justice White struck down the group home restriction. White looked for rationality anchored in sound reasoning, not flights of fancy, and found it lacking. "Requiring the permit in this case," he concluded, "appears to us to rest on an irrational prejudice against the mentally retarded."[80] Although the professed standard was that of minimal rationality, White was far more skeptical than that standard usually connotes. Justice Stevens supported his critical approach in his concurrence, suggesting that the double standard in "equal" protection was a misnomer and that the Court actually used an intermediate standard consistently. Six justices joined the majority opinion, indicating that a majority of the Court was willing to put teeth in rational basis analysis under the equal protection clause, even in a land use case.

Although he concurred in the judgment, Justice Marshall, joined by Brennan and Blackmun, objected to making minimal rationality a serious test. The majority opinion, Marshall noted, conducted "precisely the sort of probing inquiry associated with heightened scrutiny. . . . The rational basis test invoked today is most assuredly not the rational basis test of *Williamson v. Lee Optical*."[81] Indeed, it was not, or the government could not have lost. "Under the traditional and most minimal version of the rational basis test, 'reform may take one step at a time.' "[82] Thus, the very basis of the unconstitutional discrimination, singling out the retarded from other similarly situated groups, would be irrelevant. Just because a special permit was required for some does not mean it must be required for all. The municipality would have the freedom to extend the requirement to other housing groups in due time if it so desired. It may be objected that such an excusing standard provides a blank check for blatantly discriminatory regulation, but Marshall was quite right to suggest that was the essence of minimal rationality in equal protection review. Rather than add substance to the ritualistic review of minimal rationality, Marshall preferred to grant special status to the retarded, triggering heightened scrutiny.

Future cases will reveal whether *Cleburne* heralds a break from the Court's usually automatic rejection of property interests under the equal protection clause.[83] But while the rationale may have been remarkable, the context was not. The mentally retarded share many characteristics of minorities that have won the protection of "strict scrutiny," and White's application of the rational basis reads much like the exacting review of strict scrutiny. There is no assurance that this heightened rational scrutiny would be applied in a land use case absent a group that might be deemed a "suspect class" meriting protection under the double standard of *Carolene Products*. Indeed, he declared in no uncertain terms that the incidental protection of "economic" rights is a serious danger to be scrupulously avoided. He invoked the favorite red herring of the New Deal Court when he warned that the *Cleburne* majority opinion is a "small and regrettable step back toward the days of *Lochner v. New York*."[84]

If the *Cleburne* test becomes the standard whenever minimal scrutiny is applied, no land use rights claim will be cavalierly rejected. The Court could restrict application of this more thoughtful version of the rational basis test to equal protection cases, reasoning that legislatures may do what they wish to "economic interests" as long as they do so in an evenhanded manner. Even that could provide greater hope to property owners, as most land use regulations do raise issues of classification. And the equal protection analysis applied in *Cleburne* could be extended to substantive due process cases as well, as the rational basis standard is identical under the two clauses. Landowners might continue to lose most of their cases, but at least the Court would feel compelled to seek "reasonable reasons" rather than accept the superficial declarations of governments at face value. It seems at least as likely, however, that the *Cleburne* test will either become absorbed into midlevel scrutiny or be a new test of rationality applied only to a few "semi-suspect" classes that are deemed something less than "quasi-suspect." The poor record for landowner rights when they cannot stand on the crutch of preferred rights suggests that Justice Marshall may not have cause to worry. *Cleburne* was a defeat for hierarchical regulation but only because, it appears, rights to use property were aligned with egalitarian concerns.

PROTECTING PRIVACY OF PROPERTY AGAINST SEARCHES

While scouring the decisions of the California Supreme Court for signs of support for landowner rights, I found that the justices tended to be more concerned when the privacy aspects of property were at issue. Although beyond the realm of land use regulation, cases concerning rights to be free from excessive governmental snooping, specifically aerial surveillance of open fields and backyards for criminal conduct, also illustrate the priority given by the California court to privacy aspects of property. Similarly, property surveillance cases decided by the U.S. Supreme Court show how the double standard of rights is reflected in a hierarchy of privacy rights in property. In cases in which Fourth Amendment limits on warrantless searches of open land of criminal suspects were at issue, the U.S. Supreme Court has consistently sided with the government. This is not surprising, as the Burger and Rehnquist courts have tended to be more conservative than their predecessor, the Warren Court, in criminal procedure. It is not that a majority of the Court dismissed the privacy aspects of property in these cases. As we have seen in *Moore*, the Court is quite willing to protect property in the name of personal and family privacy. Rather, the justices have created a hierarchy of private property, emphasizing that some categories of property are more essential for privacy than others. These cases are not included in the tables of landowner cases, as to do so would be to subsume criminal law under the larger category of land use regulation.[85] But a couple of examples are illustrative.

The leading land surveillance case of the decade was *Oliver v. United States*[86] where the Court gave the green light to warrantless police searches of what it termed "open fields." The police had received a tip that marijuana was being grown by Oliver. When they went to investigate, they found a locked gate and a sign forbidding access. Next to the gate was a path, and they followed it until they found a marijuana field about a mile from Oliver's home. Surrounded by woods, fences, and embankments, the field was not visible from any point of public access. Writing for the majority, Justice Powell acknowledged that property may safeguard privacy but argued that "open fields do not provide the setting for those intimate activities that the [Fourth] Amendment is intended to shelter from government interference or surveillance."[87] It is not property per se that merits protection from the perspective of the Court but "intimate activities" that take place in the "sanctity of the home." Property is to be protected only when essential to private activities, and according to Powell, "an individual may not legitimately demand privacy for activities conducted out of doors in fields."[88] Rather than engage in difficult line drawing, Powell concluded that there should be a blanket rule allowing police access to open fields, regardless of fences, warning signs, or the type of activity taking place. Powell extended the double standard of rights into search and seizure, distinguishing land, which would be fair game for searches, from homes, where searches would be more difficult to justify. As the "personal" aspect of property grows stronger in the eyes of the Court, so does its protection.

Marshall, joined by Brennan and Stevens, dissented in *Oliver*, emphasizing that all personal property is important to privacy. "Many of the uses to which such [open] land may be put deserve privacy," he argued, citing the enjoyment of solitude and nature or private meetings.[89] Out of "our respect for the freedom of landowners," the Court ought to uphold the privacy right, Marshall asserted.[90] It might surprise landowners that Marshall professes great concern for the substantive rights of owners, but of course he is not supporting property for its own sake. His commitment to the right of privacy is broad and deep, and he implies that even property owners should be protected when their privacy is at stake. He could advocate a hierarchy of property, such as Powell created, to maintain the elevated status of privacy and the lowly position of property. But that would weaken the right of privacy as well as property by limiting its application, and Marshall chose to provide too much (from the perspective of the double standard) protection for property rather than too little for privacy.

Between the home and open fields lies the "curtilage," the area immediately surrounding a home "to which extends the intimate activity associated with the 'sanctity of a man's home.' "[91] It seems the line between fields and home suggested by Powell in *Oliver* is not so clear after all, as privacy expectations extend out the door to encompass the curtilage.[92]

The lack of constitutional protection for open fields may jeopardize the privacy of protected property, as was the case in *U.S. v. Dunn.*[93] Police placed a beeper on Dunn's truck, which was loaded with chemicals and equipment commonly used for drug production, and traced it back to a barn behind his home. Officers then crossed three fences to reach the outside of the barn, which was locked, and shone a flashlight inside, revealing a drug lab. The Supreme Court upheld the police action. Brennan dissented, arguing that the majority decision "reflects a fundamental misunderstanding of the typical role of a barn in domestic rural life."[94] Barns are an "integral part" of a "farm home," he argued. Writing for the Court, White ducked the issue of the barn, emphasizing instead that the barn was observed from an "open field" (albeit one enclosed by three fences). Even if the barn was a protected area, the police could observe it from the open field, just as they could observe a home from the street. The fact that the field was private property gave no greater constitutional protection to the owner. As long as the Court defends a rigid distinction between curtilage and open fields, privacy interests will lose some of their normally strong protection.

The rights of nude dancers, the mentally retarded, and marijuana growers may seem far afield from traditional constitutional property rights, but these cases are critical to the protection of property interests by the Supreme Court. In the void created by the abandonment of traditional property rights, cases raising issues of equality, expression, and privacy provide opportunities for the Court to reconstruct a jurisprudence of property by considering the relation of property to preferred rights.

THE WEAK LIMITS OF TAKINGS DOCTRINE

In principle, the takings clause would appear to offer the greatest promise for landowner rights as it meets the "specific constitutional limitation" loophole created in *Carolene Products.* In that opinion, the Court advocated judicial deference to legislative judgments but added that "there may be narrower scope for operation of

Table 14
U.S. Supreme Court Support
for Landowner Rights, by Issue Area

Issue	+	−	*Pct.*	*Ratio*[1]
Takings	3	14	17.6	2:7
Equality/Expression	4	2	66.7	2:1
Court Total:	7	16	30.4	
Weighted Total[2]:	10	30	25.0	

[1]The ratio measures the average proportion of support in each issue area. For example, a 2:1 ratio means that on average two justices voted to support the landowner party for every justice who was opposed.
[2]Takings cases are counted twice in the weighted total.

the presumption of constitutionality when legislation appears on its face to be within a specific prohibition of the Constitution"[95] such as the free expression guarantees of the First Amendment. In other words, there must be an additional constitutional source beyond the words *due process* to create a substantive right meriting careful protection. The takings clause satisfies this criterion and indeed was the first specific provision in the Bill of Rights to be applied against the states through the due process clause of the Fourteenth Amendment.[96]

In the 1980s, protection of traditional property rights (substantive due process, "economic" equal protection, and limits on takings of property) was meager. All the landowner rights cases during the 1980s except those in which owners clung to the coattails of preferred freedoms raised takings questions either as the central issue (as in the compensation for regulation cases) or as part of a shotgun approach to property rights (as in the *Hodel* cases in which substantive due process and equal protection claims also were made). Although the takings clause is a "specific prohibition" in the Constitution, however, there has been precious little for proponents of property to cheer about. Only 18 percent of the cases raising takings claims in the 1980s were won by owners (see Table 14).

The *only* takings victory of the decade prior to or after June 1987 was *Loretto*, which protected the fundamental right of landowners to keep television cables from creeping across their walls. A New York statute required owners of apartment buildings to allow the installation of cable television for tenants, which involved the attachment of cables to the roofs and outside walls of the buildings.

Loretto was unique in two respects: First, it involved a physical invasion by the wires and their installers. The right of exclusion is the only property right that the Court has regularly enforced throughout the long drought since *Nectow v. Cambridge*.[97] Second, perhaps as important, the invasion was rather trivial. In *Loretto*, the Court could support the property owner without fear of limiting the power of local land use regulators. "Nonphysical government intrusions on private property, such as zoning ordinances and other land-use restrictions," Blackmun noted in his dissenting opinion, "have become the rule rather than the exception."[98] Yet it is just that sort of regulation that the Court has been most reluctant to limit. *Loretto* was an atypical case with an atypical outcome—the owner won. And the opinion was authored by Justice Marshall, not known as a staunch defender of traditional property rights.

Even when there is a physical invasion and thus a taking of private property, there appears to be no limit to what the state can do as long as the eminent domain power is employed and compensation is paid. The Constitution specifies that private property may be taken only for public use, but his limitation has been virtually read out of the Fifth Amendment by making it synonymous with the ritualistic due process test of minimal rationality.[99] "Public use" no longer requires public *use*; any conceivable public *purpose* will suffice. When considering whether condemnation of property for redevelopment was a legitimate "public use," Douglas wrote for the Court in the 1954 case *Berman v. Parker*,[100] "We deal, in other words, with what traditionally has been known as the police power."[101] Douglas erased the distinction between the police power to regulate for the public welfare and the eminent domain power to appropriate property for public use. By merging the doctrines, Douglas effectively abandoned the public use limitation. "When the legislature has spoken, the public interest has been declared in terms well-nigh conclusive," he proclaimed.[102] What the state wants it takes; the reasons are up to the legislature.

The spirit of *Berman* returned in the 1980s in *Hawaii Housing Authority v. Midkiff*.[103] The Hawaii legislature had used the eminent domain power to force sales of homesites by a small group of landowners who controlled most of the residential property in the islands. The housing authority was empowered to order the major landholders to negotiate the transfer of title to the tenants. If owners refused or negotiations broke down, the authority invoke eminent domain. Trustees for the land estates sued, claiming that the taking was unconstitutional because it was not for public use. Relying on

Berman, the Court upheld the act. The "mere fact" that the land expropriated from large landowners was distributed to private users was no constitutional obstacle, Justice O'Connor reasoned, because the Constitution did not literally require public use. It is fitting perhaps that this Orwellian twisting of plain language, which made it possible to excuse coerced private transfers as "public use," was authored in 1984. O'Connor argued that any legitimate public purpose would suffice; in this case, she found, the need to break up a landed oligopoly and create a viable land market. The Court was not even divided; nary a voice was raised in dissent.[104] *Midkiff* was widely seen as a clear indication that no limits other than the deterrent of having to pay compensation remain on the exercise of eminent domain powers.[105]

TAKING PROPERTY THROUGH REGULATION

The great gray area in takings doctrine is what to do when although the eminent domain power has not been exercised and compensation has not been paid, the landowner claims her property has been virtually taken through regulatory restrictions. Beginning with *Agins,* the Court made a habit in the 1980s of hearing regulatory takings cases only to duck the issue of compensation. Criticizing the lack of clear leadership from the Court became a popular pastime,[106] although the critics differed sharply over the cure.[107] To say the Court has been deferent to legislatures does not begin to describe the extent or impact of the Court's refusal to become involved. The Court has not, with the arguable exception of *Nollan* in 1987, struck down a single land use regulation as a taking since *Pennsylvania Coal* in 1922. As if it were performing an ancient ritual whose purpose has long been forgotten, the Court in every takings case dutifully recites the Holmes mantra[108] that "if regulation goes too far it will be recognized as a taking."[109] Yet, unlike the Allies' advancing bridge over the Rhine, apparently a regulation can never go "too far." The consequences of the Court's aversion to issues of regulatory takings have been enormous. If the police power of the state and the eminent domain power are interchangeable, as the Court has suggested, then the state can require by regulation what it would have to pay for with eminent domain. This leaves the owner without compensation and the public without a bill. It is not hard to guess which, eminent domain or regulation, has been the more popular method of land use control.[110] Why should a municipality make major investments in land in order to preserve open space or "rural character" when the same end can be accomplished by forbidding most development?

The Supreme Court has warily danced around the regulatory compensation issue since the California court decided that the constitutional requirements of compensation would not apply, for "policy reasons," to regulatory takings. The Supreme Court ducked the big question in *Agins* by ruling that there had not been a definitive taking, as it was conceivable that Tiburon might yet permit some development. This not only dashed the hopes of property owners but also raised a new obstacle: If a municipality was sufficiently vague in its restrictions, its actions might be immune from a takings challenge.

This new hurdle was faced again by the property owner in *San Diego Gas & Electric*. The utility bought property zoned for industrial and agricultural use in 1966, planning to build a nuclear plant. In 1973, the city down-zoned the property to limit industrial uses, and the land was included in an open-space plan. A city referendum on a proposal to purchase the property for a public park failed that same year. San Diego Gas sued, and a state court of appeals affirmed the trial court decision that the city, through restrictive regulation, effectively had taken the property. But the Supreme Court, in an opinion by Justice Blackmun, rejected that argument. No decision could be made on whether there had been a taking, Blackmun wrote, until the city made a final judgment on the property. Even though San Diego had attempted to purchase the property, had the property designated as open space, and had a history of enforcing zoning ordinances consistent with the open-space plan, Blackmun held forth the possibility that San Diego might someday allow the utility to use its property.

Brennan argued in dissent that there *had* been a final judgment—the ruling by the California court that a regulatory taking could never be compensated. San Diego Gas would thus be denied relief as a matter of law, even if a taking eventually was found. Two questions must be asked, Brennan wrote: Can regulation ever equal a taking? And would a regulatory taking require compensation? He answered both questions in the affirmative. "From the government's point of view," wrote Brennan, "the benefits flowing to the public from preservation of open space through regulation may be equally great as from creating a wildlife refuge through formal condemnation,"[111] and regulations can "destroy the use and enjoyment of property . . . just as effectively as formal condemnation."[112]

The California Supreme Court decreed in *Agins* that invalidation of the confiscatory regulation was the only remedy, but Brennan argued that this was inadequate. "Invalidation hardly prevents enactment of subsequent unconstitutional regulations by the government," he noted. Unless a city was forced to pay, it could deny an owner the use of her property by an endless series of regulations. A city attorney at a conference in California even advised his peers to pursue that strategy:

> IF ALL ELSE FAILS, MERELY AMEND THE REGULATION AND START OVER AGAIN. If legal preventive maintenance does not work, and you still receive a claim attacking the land use regulation, or if you try the case and lose, don't worry about it. All is not lost. . . . Change the regulation in question, even after trial and judgment, . . . and everybody starts over again. See how easy it is to be a City Attorney. Sometimes you can lose the battle and still win the war. Good luck.[113]

If regulations and condemnation can be equivalent in their public benefits and private burdens, it is essential that they both be treated as potential takings, lest municipalities avoid payment by regulating. Once a regulatory taking is found, the Constitution requires compensation, just as it would for any other taking, Brennan argued. Even if a city chooses to rescind the unconstitutional regulation and the taking is thereby temporary, payment is required: "Nothing in the Just Compensation Clause," wrote Brennan, "suggests that 'takings' must be permanent and irrevocable."[114]

The California court had reasoned that requiring payment would discourage municipalities from enacting beneficial regulation. But Brennan argued this would not necessarily be the case; being accountable for their actions might encourage governments to have more thoughtful regulations and regulatory processes. Even if good policy were discouraged, this would not be germane, Brennan argued: "The applicability of express constitutional guarantees is not a matter to be determined on the basis of policy judgments . . . nor can the vindication of those rights depend on the expense in doing so."[115] Despite the value of regulation, planning officials simply cannot be immune from the Constitution, Brennan concluded: "If a policeman must know the Constitution, then why not a planner?"[116]

Brennan's dissent in *San Diego Gas* was the most vigorous, thorough argument on behalf of property rights of the decade.

Although Brennan lost the battle, he was beginning to win the doctrinal war. Three justices joined Brennan's dissent, and Justice Rehnquist wrote a concurrence indicating that if there had been a clear taking, he would be inclined to agree with Brennan. Court watchers knew that it was only a matter of time until a majority formally endorsed Brennan's argument. Surprisingly, it was written by the leading egalitarian on the Court, not known as a vigorous defender of property rights. Brennan's opinion indicates that unlike many other egalitarians on the Court and in academia, he was willing to acknowledge that the takings clause is a specific prohibition in the Constitution and merits some consideration, even under the double standard of *Carolene Products*.

Had Rehnquist joined Brennan in *San Diego Gas* in 1981, the leading landowner issue of the decade—compensation for regulatory takings—would have been decided. But Brennan's opinion fell one vote shy of a majority. The pattern of *Agins* and *San Diego Gas* was continued in *Williamson County Regional Planning Commission v. Hamilton Bank of Johnson City*[117] and *MacDonald, Sommer, & Frates v. Yolo County*.[118] In each case the Court heard a regulatory takings claim only to announce yet again that there had been no final judgment, either by a planning agency or another court. The constitutional void left planning and zoning commissions free to restrict land use with impunity as long as their requirements were sufficiently ambiguous to conceivably permit some use at some future time. As legions of supplicants before local commissions have learned, planning and zoning bodies excel at finding novel ways to say "not this time, maybe later." Owners who wished to use their property were reduced to submitting costly revised proposals to local boards, waiting, often for years, for an elusive yes, hoping it would come before they went bankrupt or expired. In the eyes of the Court majority, this presented no clear constitutional issue. "A feeling of unreality," Gus Bauman has observed, pervades these opinions of the Court.[119]

Until June 1987, then, the Supreme Court's record of support for landowner rights was rather dismal. At least the Court occasionally would hear arguments. And there had been several landowner victories when their interests were aligned with rights more in favor with the Court. Compared with the silence of earlier decades, there had indeed been a revival of landowner rights. Yet when the expressive and equality cases, in which property rights were not the primary issues considered by the Court, are not counted, there had not been a single significant landowner victory in the 1980s.

A JUNE REVOLUTION?

The policy implications of today's decision are
obvious and, I fear, far reaching. . . . The loose
cannon the Court fires today is unattached to
the Constitution.
                                    —Justice Stevens[120]

The Court imposes a standard of precision for
the exercise of a State's police power that has
been discredited for the better part of this cen-
tury.
                                    —Justice Brennan[121]

In the final days of the 1987 term, the Supreme Court announced two land use decisions and then skipped out of town.
These opinions were not simply more of the same; the justices had
given landowners the two most significant constitutional victories
in a half century. *Nollan* and *First English* might appear to signal a
new regime of vigilant protection of landowner rights. The cases
were not the first shots of a revolution, however, but products of the
modest evolution that has occurred in the Court's doctrine. The
timing of the cases allowed property owners and their attorneys a
few months to celebrate before the Court came back to town and
spoiled the fun.

In *First English*, a church retreat center had been destroyed by
a flood in 1978. The following year, Los Angeles County adopted an
interim ordinance explicitly forbidding all rebuilding in the flood
zone. The church filed an inverse condemnation suit asserting that
the county had denied all use of the property and therefore should
be required to pay compensation for a taking. The trial court struck
the claim, reasoning that the state supreme court ruling in *Agins*
prevented owners from suing for compensation for regulatory takings. The U.S. Supreme Court ruled that if there was a regulatory
taking, it would require compensation, and the Court remanded the
case so that the lower court could consider the church's claim. *First
English* was by any standard a major victory for landowners. For the
first time, a majority of the Court held that the takings clause requirement of just compensation would apply even if the taking was
through a regulatory restriction. Brennan's crusade reached its goal
in *First English* in an opinion, ironically, by Rehnquist, who could
have saved years of uncertainty by joining Brennan six years earlier.
Quoting extensively from the *San Diego Gas* dissent and earlier

cases, Rehnquist's opinion lacked some of the fire of Brennan's argument, but at least the doctrine was now law.

Before compensation must be paid, however, a taking must be found. And the Court has made that none too easy. The Court in *First English* deftly ducked the issue of whether there had been a taking, reasoning that the state courts had foreclosed the possibility of collecting compensation, and thus there was an important federal question that demanded an answer, even though no court had yet found that there was indeed a taking. Rehnquist announced that the Court would simply "treat as true for purposes of our decision" the allegation of a taking. The Court managed to hand landowners an important doctrinal victory while simultaneously keeping its sixty-five-year-old tradition of never finding a regulatory taking untarnished. After the dust settled, the First English Evangelical Lutheran Church of Glendale still found its coffers empty. On remand, a California court of appeal found the ban on rebuilding was not a taking because it was an interim measure, did not deprive the church of all use of its camp, and substantially advanced the government's interest in public safety.[122] Even after *Nollan,* a regulation is likely to be upheld by the Court unless it results in a physical invasion or prevents all economically viable use.[123] Even destroying an existing business may not require compensation as long as there is some public justification.[124]

First English, the case of "God versus the State,"[125] was unusual. Although the county's ordinance forbidding rebuilding in a fire-scarred area was "interim," it was still a complete ban on construction. Such an absolute ban is virtually unheard of in land use restrictions. More typically, development will be limited to a fraction of its potential. Even the most severe ordinances and regulations will leave open some theoretical possibility for development; the municipality can then require that elaborate plans be submitted, conduct extensive hearings and staff review, and after several months or years, announce that the proposal is not satisfactory. The applicant is then free to leap from a tall building, join a monastic order, or submit another plan and begin the punishing process again. If the facts of *First English* are an indication of the circumstances under which the Supreme Court might find a taking, it will be small comfort for landowners. Rehnquist expressly limited *First English* to the facts, writing that it does not apply to the "quite different questions that would arise in the case of normal delays in obtaining building permits, changes in zoning ordinances, variances, and the like."[126] But these so-called normal delays, as

Stevens pointed out in dissent, can create "precisely the same interference with a real estate developer's plan."[127] The Court did not
strike down *MacDonald, Hamilton Bank, San Diego Gas,* or *Agins,*
indicating it may continue to tolerate the merry-go-round of administrative and judicial proceedings.

It is tempting to view *Nollan,* coming on the heels of *First English,* as the dropping of the other shoe. First the Court announced
regulatory takings would require compensation, and then it actually
found a taking that required payment.[128] But *Nollan* was atypical,
and Scalia's opinion emphasized its uniqueness and limited its application. Most regulations restrict the uses to which land may be
put while implicitly allowing the owner to exclude the public. In
Nollan, the California Coastal Commission required the owners to
allow the public to walk across a portion of their property.

In 1982, the Nollans purchased a seaside bungalow, contingent
on the Nollans' promise to demolish the bungalow and replace it
with a three-bedroom house in keeping with the style of the neighborhood. The Nollans applied to the coastal commission for a development permit, which was granted subject to the condition that
the Nollans grant an easement to the state allowing the public to
walk along the beach. The Nollans sued, claiming that the easement was a taking of property without compensation. A state trial
court agreed and issued a writ ordering the commission to strike the
condition. A state appeal court reversed, however, and the Nollans'
appeal reached the U.S. Supreme Court, which found that the easement was indeed a taking.

Scalia developed two alternative rationales in *Nollan.* On one
hand, he argued that the condition placed on the use of the Nollan's
property—the granting of an easement for public access—was not
related to the impact of the Nollans' intended property use of building a larger home. The commission had asserted that the larger
home would affect visual access from the road, and Scalia indicated
that the commission could simply forbid the construction. But the
commission could not condition permission to build on the granting of the easement because, as Scalia put it, there was no nexus between the easement and the reasons that would justify a denial of a
permit. Physical access on the beach was unrelated to visual access
from the road. Thus the easement would not mitigate a harm created by the owners but simply provide a public benefit at their expense. If the state wanted beach access, it could purchase it rather
than expect the Nollans to absorb the cost.

By suggesting that a permit denial would be justified, Scalia indicated the Court remains willing to tolerate even severe deprivations of property use without requiring compensation. Prior to *Nollan*, almost any reason offered by a government would excuse a restriction on property use rights. After *Nollan*, the government's reason must have some connection to the owner's proposed use of property. The clearest consequence of *Nollan* is to encourage officials to use more care when proffering reasons for restrictions on property rights. As William Fulton has put it, "Although the *Nollan* case at first appeared to deal a big blow to public agencies, in fact the rules the Supreme Court laid down are not very different from the rules many municipalities—particularly those outside California— are now following."[129]

Still, the unfair burden is a promising argument for landowners, as it could apply to a wide range of conditions that are attached to permits. Charges for services such as schools, fire protection, and road improvements are now often assessed on developers on the theory that the developer "caused" the growth.[130] Child care, housing for the poor, libraries, parks, and even the provision of space for struggling artists are sometimes demanded as the price for approving a project.[131] And homeowners may be required to provide for a public need they did not cause, such as maintaining open space or a "scenic viewshed,"[132] to receive approval for an expansion. The effective limit on conditions has been not what is just or constitutionally permissible but what the political market will bear. Given strong pressures to provide public amenities at minimal cost, the price tag for land use approval may be substantial. Prior to *Nollan*, there was little need for planners to pay attention to issues of constitutionality in these exactions. The American Planning Association even offered a conference session on exactions entitled "Extortion in the Public Interest."[133] Applying Scalia's unfair burden argument to these conditions could provide significant protection.

The second factor critical in *Nollan* was that the easement permitted a physical invasion by the public. Quoting directly from *Loretto*[134] and *Kaiser Aetna v. United States*,[135] Scalia called "the right to exclude one of the most essential sticks in the bundle of rights that are commonly characterized as property."[136] Judging from the Court's holdings, it may be the *only* stick in the bundle. Viewed as another physical invasion case, *Nollan* is more an heir to *Loretto* (the television cable case) than *Pennsylvania Coal*, and its impact on regulatory takings doctrine is more modest, as the California Coastal Commission is atypical in its insistence on public access. In this sense, *Nollan* simply restated the Court doctrine that physical access by the public may not be required without compensation. The right of exclusion, not autonomy or use, remains the central concern of the Court in land use disputes.

Justice Brennan's stand in *San Diego Gas* as a proponent of individual property rights was tempered by his dissent in *Nollan*. Brennan was reluctant to find a taking that might require the compensation he supported so forcefully in *San Diego Gas*. Because the California Coastal Commission had a well-known history of demanding that owners sign easements as the price for using their lands, the Nollans had "no reasonable claim to any expectation of being able to exclude members of the public."[137] If so, then land rights do not depend on the Constitution but on the practices of regulators. This makes use of one's property less a guaranteed right and more a privilege bestowed by the government at its discretion. The constitutional limit would apparently apply only if a regulatory body singled out an owner for treatment more draconian than its usual demands. A commission that consistently made severe demands would remain unfettered. Brennan's argument echoes the claim of Joseph Sax that "we are already so far along in diminishing developmental rights that owners are viewed, in important respects, as already on notice."[138] This wholesale elimination of constitutional protection is based, Scalia argued in *Nollan*, on "the peculiar proposition that a unilateral claim of entitlement by the government can alter property rights."[139] In Brennan's view, an owner is reduced to just one of many "competing . . . public and private interests" whose fate is up to the "expert opinion of the Coastal Commission."[140] In theory, Brennan showed an acute concern for just compensation, but he was not willing to require such a payment. His takings jurisprudence was an enticing balloon floating above reality with no clue whether it would ever come down to earth.

Despite the *First English* requirement that regulatory takings be compensated and the *Nollan* nexus test, the limits imposed by the takings clause remain weak. After *Midkiff* (the Hawaiian land redistribution case), a government apparently may take private property for any use as long as it pays for it. As Rehnquist emphasized in *First English*, the takings clause "is deemed not to limit the governmental interference with property rights per se, but rather to secure compensation."[141] And a landowner may still be restricted without compensation if there is no physical invasion by the public and the owner is not deprived of all beneficial use. Scalia implied in *Nollan* that even a physical invasion would not require payment if it was related to the impact of the land use. And total denials of use are common in fact, even as they are unconstitutional in theory. As long as the Court clings to the position that "normal" delays raise no constitutional concerns, local officials can effectively impose total bans through repetitive, ritualistic procedures, and foot dragging.

A telling indication of the limits of *Nollan* and *First English* may be *Keystone Bituminous Coal Association v. Debenedictis*,[142] announced three months before *First English* and *Nollan*. This was a classic regulatory takings case: There was no physical invasion or easement to muddy the doctrinal waters. In fact, it was *the* classic regulatory takings case, the second coming of *Pennsylvania Coal*. As in the 1922 case, the state of Pennsylvania was attempting greatly to restrict coal mining that might cause the ground to subside underneath buildings. Just as in 1922, the mining company owned the "support estates"; essentially it had the right to let the surface sag if that was the consequences of mining coal that might otherwise provide support. Once again, the consequence of the regulation, which required that 50 percent of the coal under houses and other structures be left in place, was to deprive the company of a valuable resource embedded in its property. Once again the support estates were separate property entities, and their restriction could constitute a taking in itself without regard to the other mineral holdings of the company. The case was nearly identical to *Pennsylvania Coal*. After decades of dutifully citing the 1922 case, the Court had to decide if it meant what it had repeatedly said—that *Pennsylvania Coal* was still good law.

Justice Stevens began the majority opinion in the usual fashion, explaining that under *Pennsylvania Coal* a regulation that goes "too far" violates the takings clause. But a funny thing happened on the way to the holding: Stevens distinguished *Keystone* from *Pennsylvania Coal* and thereby effectively "distinguished" *Pennsylvania Coal* from its own facts. The law challenged in *Keystone*, Stevens explained, was not a taking because it served the public interest, prevented a nuisance, and still allowed the company some opportunity to profit. Yet precisely the same arguments had been rejected in *Pennsylvania Coal*. Stevens essentially recast *Pennsylvania Coal* to produce a more convenient precedent. As James Burling has put it, *Keystone* was "the Mr. Hyde to the Dr. Jekyll of *Pennsylvania Coal v. Mahon*."[143] In effect, *Keystone* became the precedent by which to recast *Pennsylvania Coal*. This exercise in creative interpretation of

precedent was assailed in the dissenting opinion of Justice Rehnquist, who noted that "the differences between [the facts] and those
in *Pennsylvania Coal* verge on the trivial."[144]

    Keystone provides a cautionary counterpoint to *First English*
and *Nollan* and has given courts predisposed to support regulation a
modern precedent with which to deflate the impact of the latter
cases. The New Jersey Supreme Court, for example, has emphasized
Keystone and downplayed *Nollan* as a narrow exception applying
only to physical invasions.[145] Indeed, the U.S. Supreme Court has
shown no willingness to compensate a taking absent such an invasion. Although the declaration in *Pennsylvania Coal* that a regulation that goes "too far" is a taking may still be honored by the
Court, just what constitutes going "too far" remains a mystery. The
Court even called up *Keystone*—Son of *Pennsylvania Coal*—for review, only to deny the precedental value of the central regulatory
takings case. The Court may be thunderous in its proclamation that
it will tolerate no violations of the constitutional imperative of just
compensation, but given the pains to which to Court will go to
avoid finding a taking, it may be only a mouse that roared.

RETURN TO BUSINESS AS USUAL

    The Supreme Court returned to its deferential ways following
the surprises of *First English* and *Nollan*. In two 1988 cases, *Phillips
Petroleum Co. v. Mississippi*[146] and *Pennell v. San Jose*,[147] the Court
declined opportunities to find takings that might require
compensation.[148] In *Phillips Petroleum*, the Supreme Court extended the public trust doctrine, which traditionally has given
states power to protect navigation and fishbeds by controlling navigable tidal lands, to include nonnavigable tidal bayous. Mississippi
had issued oil and gas leases for the land underlying the bayous and
streams to other companies, but Phillips and another firm objected,
as they held title to that land and had paid taxes on it. They went to
state court to enforce their title and lost, and the Supreme Court
upheld the state ruling that the public trust vested title with the
state regardless of the paper title and purchase by the oil companies.
It did not matter that the waters were not navigable, Justice White
argued for the majority, because the state interest in tidal lands
went beyond navigation. White did not reach the takings issue
since, there being no valid private title, there could be no taking of
private land—there were no property rights to be taken.

Mississippi was pressing "for a radical expansion of the historical limits of the public trust," Justice O'Connor declared in dissent.[149] The leasing of land for mineral exploitation by private parties did not promote traditional purposes of the trust, such as facilitating commerce or protecting fishing, she argued. Interestingly, the decision of the Court mirrors the path taken by the California Supreme Court in extending both the reach of the public trust doctrine and the purposes it may serve. But while the California court has used that doctrine to protect preservationist interests to which it is sympathetic, the effect of the U.S. Supreme Court ruling is the opposite, allowing the state to exploit the resources. But by supporting a broad interpretation of the public trust, the Supreme Court created a precedent that would allow states to use the trust as they wished, whether for preservation or exploitation, without compensating property owners. Although the purposes promoted by the California and U.S. rulings differ, the broader legal consequences are the same: the expansion of state control, the shrinkage of private property rights. "The Court's decision today," Justice O'Connor warned, "could dispossess thousands of blameless record owners and leaseholders of land that they and their predecessors in interest reasonably believed was theirs," noting that nine million acres are classified as coastal wetlands.[150] According to an article quoted by O'Connor, in New Jersey, where a similar rule had been adopted;

> hundreds of properties . . . have been taken and used for state purposes without compensating the record owners . . . prior homeowners of many years are being threatened with loss of title . . . properties are being arbitrarily claimed and conveyed by the State to persons other than the record owners; and hundreds of cases remain pending and untried before the state courts awaiting processing. . . . [151]

The Court's ruling may seem like a modest extension of a centuries-old doctrine. From the perspective of landowner rights, however, the decision is disturbing. Once public title under the trust is established, the state gains a broad power to do as it pleases. It need not follow the tedious regulatory process to control the property, as no one owns it. The impact of *Phillips Petroleum* will depend on whether states have previously relinquished public trust rights and how the decision is incorporated into often complex state rules governing coastal property rights. In states such as California and New Jersey where the governments and courts have used the trust to extend control over private lands, the Court's endorsement is a green light.

In *Pennell*, the Court upheld a provision in San Jose's residential rent control ordinance that required a hearing officer to consider the economic hardship of the tenant when deciding whether a rent increase was fair and reasonable. Rehnquist emphasized that the case was a facial challenge to the regulation; there was no proof that the city would in fact use the hardship provision to reduce an otherwise fair and reasonable rent increase. Rather, the inclusion of both objective factors regarding the state of the rental market, and the condition of the unit, and information on the tenant, "represents a rational attempt to accommodate the conflicting interests of protecting tenants from burdensome rent increases while at the same time ensuring that landlords are guaranteed a fair return."[152] Rehnquist stooped to the low standard of minimal rationality in upholding the ordinance, inventing reasons for the law that were not included in the ordinance. Considering tenant hardship in setting rents, he speculated, might reduce the dislocation of poor tenants. "Particularly during a housing shortage, the social costs of the dislocation of low-income tenants can be severe."[153] The conceivable public purpose led Rehnquist to conclude that the ordinance was neither a taking nor a violation of equal protection on its face, even though it could require a landlord to provide a subsidy to a tenant that might otherwise be provided by the government. If it is reasonable to consider the hardship of tenants, he argued, then it makes sense to single out the landlords of those tenants.

San Jose had no choice but to deny a reasonable rent increase to landlords with hardship tenants, Scalia asserted in dissent, and thus the rent control measure was confiscatory. He relentlessly pursued the logic of the language of the ordinance to reach his conclusion: The hearing officer is charged with preventing excessive rent increases. Thus the most a landlord could legally charge for any unit would be a fair and reasonable rent increase. Any less, and San Jose would be denying a fair return to the owner; any more would be excessive. The hearing officer must, however, further consider the financial straits of the tenant. The ordinance does not make this discretionary. But reducing the rent increase further takes away part of the landlord's otherwise fair and reasonable rent. There is no slack in the system: either the increase is reasonable, or it is not: either the hardship tenant is denied the mandated relief, or the owner is forced to transfer his fair increase to the tenant. There is no choice, then, but to take the owner's property by requiring that he charge low-income tenants rents that are below the reasonable return.

The *Pennell* case could well end up back before the Court with a challenge to the specific application of the ordinance. If Scalia is correct, a taking is inevitable. But his interpretation assumes that the city will act in an utterly rational and predictable manner, feeding in factors about the rental market and unit to produce a precise, fair rental increase. In this case, the deferent indulgence of regulatory procedures by the Court majority may be more realistic. City politics are unpredictable, and administration of laws is rarely precise. If the hearing officers find that a reasonable rent covers a range, not a precise dollar amount, they might seek to allow modest variations within that range, depending on the hardship of the tenants. And while implementation of the hardship provision may be uncertain, other provisions of the ordinance attest to its reasonableness. Landlords are automatically entitled to rent increases of 8 percent, which in many years might easily cover the inflation of costs for the landlords. If a landlord has unusual costs, such as substantial improvements in a unit, he may petition for a greater increase, and consideration of these cost factors is required. Given that procedures have been included to allow for reasonable increases, it is hard to argue that implementation even of the hardship provision will result in certain deprivation.

The unusual aspects of the regulation (such as its automatic approval of 8 percent rent increases) in *Pennell* also reduce its significance as precedent. Although property attorneys may have hoped the Court would take the opportunity to extend the activist trend begun in *First English* and *Nollan, Pennell* did not come as a surprise.[154] The Court has long supported rent control,[155] and it gave no indication in *Pennell* that it would tolerate rent ordinances more blatantly confiscatory than that of San Jose, such as a measure that required landlords to subsidize tenants without allowing reasonable rent increases. With its atypical regulation and lack of a broadly applicable doctrinal rule, *Pennell* is not a major setback for landowner rights. At most, it may encourage cities to enact copy-cat rental regulations.

From the perspective of landowners rights, there are some discouraging signs in *Pennell* apart from the outcome. Rehnquist's excursion into the imaginary world of the "any conceivable rational basis" test, as the minimal level of scrutiny under *Carolene Products* is known, is an indication that the evidence of rationality sought in *Cleburne,* the group home case, was an exception. In most land use cases, at least absent a physical invasion, the Court will likely continue to grant wide latitude to governments in hypothesizing reasons for regulation and add its own when needed.

Scalia continued to blend takings doctrine with due process in his *Pennell* dissent. He emphasized that an ordinance with a sufficient relation to a state interest could not effect a taking (without regard to the severity of the deprivation), although the rent measure lacked this because the landlords did not "cause" the poverty of the tenant. By emphasizing the police power test of rationality rather than the severity of the deprivation, Scalia again, as in *Nollan,* implied that rational regulations that substantially deprive property could escape compensation requirements. Could not a city, for example, reasonably argue that a builder "caused" a loss of open space by developing an open field? If that connection of the owner's actions with a restrictive regulation sufficed, then the city could deprive the owner of the use of his property, preserve the open space for the public, and never pay a cent. The Scalia opinions show that the reasoning of opinions and not just the votes is important to understanding the extent of landowner rights.

THE CURIOUS COALITIONS ON LANDOWNER RIGHTS

Despite the losses in *Pennell* and *Phillips Petroleum,* prospects for landowners rights are better than they have been in decades. Although the Supreme Court is likely to continue supporting most property regulation, the votes have been getting closer. For decades, the Court rarely even considered a land use issue. In the early 1980s, the Court called up several cases but usually sided overwhelmingly with the government. Of the eight unanimous decisions during the decade rejecting the takings claims of owners, four were decided before 1982 and only one after 1985. As Table 15 shows, recent takings cases have been more likely to be decided in favor of the owner and have been more closely contested. Although victories in *First English* and *Nollan* skew the vote ratio toward the landowner parties, defeats also have been close. The property party gained at least two votes of support in every takings case, with one exception, after 1985, while *San Diego Gas* was the only significant takings case prior to 1986 to produce more than a single vote for the owner. Landowners have reason to be cautiously optimistic, or at least less profoundly pessimistic.

Table 15
Voting Margins in U.S. Supreme Court Takings Decisions

Landowner Wins		Landowner Losses				
6-3	5-4	4-5	3-5	2-6	1-7	0-9
English*	Nollan*	Keystone*	Phillips*	Pennell*	Hamilton	Cherokee*
Loretto		MacDonald*			Riverside	
		S.D. Gas				Midkiff (0–8)
						Kirby
						Hodel I
						Hodel II
						Agins
						Pruneyard

*Cases decided after 1985.

The justices of the Court vary widely in their approaches to constitutional interpretation. The future of landowner rights in the Court will depend as much on who is on the Court and how they align as on past doctrinal pronouncements, especially since the Court is a relative newcomer to the land use field. Since several justices have retired or are likely to do so in the next few years, it is helpful to consider the roles of individual justices in the protection of property rights.

When Justice Brennan, the liberal beacon from the Warren era, lays the groundwork for the most important landowner rights victory of the decade, it is apparent that land use cases can make for strange soulmates indeed. The constitutional battles over land use in some ways can be characterized not as the Warren liberals against the Reaganites but as both wings against the so-called moderate justices. In cultural terms, egalitarianism on the Court occasionally combines with libertarian attention to property rights in opposition to hierarchical deference to regulation. The most prominent egalitarians on the Court, Brennan and Marshall, were as supportive (or slightly more so in the case of Marshall) of constitutional rights for landowners as the Court as a whole. This is true even when the takings cases are weighted more heavily than the egalitarian and expressive rights cases (see Table 16, column 3).[156] The justices most hostile to landowner rights have been Stevens and Blackmun, often considered a relatively moderate pair, who apparently combine hierarchical deference to local authority with egalitarian disdain for "economic" rights. The retirements of Brennan and Marshall suggest that the divisions on the Court may shift, with Blackmun and

Table 16
Vote Support for Landowner Rights,
by U.S. Supreme Court Justices

	Issue Area					
	Takings		Equality/ Expression		Weighted total[1]	
Justice	Pct.	Rank	Pct.	Rank	Pct.	Rank
Scalia	83.3	(1)	(no case)		83.3	(1)
Powell	42.9	(2)	66.7	(5)	47.1	(2)
O'Connor	41.7	(3)	50.0	(7)	42.9	(3)
Rehnquist	29.4	(4)	16.6	(10)	27.5	(6)
Stewart	20.0	(5)	100.0	(1)	33.3	(4)
Marshall	18.7	(6)	100.0	(1)	31.6	(5)
Burger	18.2	(7)	33.3	(9)	21.4	(9)
White	17.6	(8)	66.7	(5)	23.3	(8)
Brennan	11.8	(9)	100.0	(1)	25.0	(7)
Stevens	11.8	(9)	50.0	(7)	17.5	(10)
Blackmun	00.0	(11)	83.3	(4)	12.5	(11)
Court	17.6		66.7		25.0	

[1]Takings cases are counted twice in weighted totals.

Stevens anchoring the deferential wing and the "conservatives" fluctuating between hierarchical support for authority and libertarian attention to property rights.

Justice Scalia has not been a constitutional wallflower during his Court tenure. He is the only justice who has clearly favored landowner interests, supporting them in *First English, Keystone* and *Phillips Petroleum* and penning the dissent in *Pennell* and the ground-breaking majority opinion in *Nollan.* He comes closest to being the Court libertarian, consistently defending landowner rights. But he has often counseled caution in the protection of property rights,[157] and his opinions send contradictory signals. Although he has usually found a reason to support an owner's claim of a takings violation, he has conceded extensive regulatory powers to the state as long as there is a logical link between the effects of a landowner's actions and the restrictive measures. Scalia leaves open the possibility that he would tolerate confiscatory land use regulation if only governments would state their reasons more clearly. In sum,

Scalia's votes have been consistent with a libertarian defense of property rights, but his opinions at times have sounded deferential to the local hierarchy of land use control. It will be interesting to see whether his opinions in the 1990s will root more firmly in libertarian thought, emphasizing the need to limit government, or whether he will vote to uphold most land use regulation. He may well continue to be a reliable vote for landowner rights, albeit often with ambivalent opinions.

Perhaps the genial Justice Scalia found willing listeners in the moderate-conservative wing of the Court, pushing other justices from hierarchy toward libertarianism. Or it may be that Scalia's appointment simply coincided with shifting perspectives on the Court. Whatever the catalyst, beginning with *MacDonald* in 1986 and continuing through all the cases Justice Scalia has participated in, several justices have been far more likely to vote in favor of the landowner in takings cases than previously (see Table 17). Justice White did not support the property owners in a single takings case prior to 1986; after that, he supported them in almost half the takings cases. Justice Powell's support rose from 22 percent of cases before 1986 to 80 percent thereafter. Justices O'Connor and Rehnquist shifted from almost always siding with the government in takings cases to voting for the property owner over half the time. It may be a coincidence that the issues these justices could support were heard after Scalia was appointed and Burger departed. Certainly Rehnquist served notice that he was sympathetic to compensation for regulatory takings as early as 1981. Then again, perhaps these justices are shifting from the conservative, or hierarchical, deference of Warren Burger to the more activist, libertarian stance of Antonin Scalia.

Scalia and Rehnquist have been the most active opinion writers in land use cases (see Table 18, column 4), each writing in nearly half the cases in which they voted. If Scalia continues on his libertarian voting path and Rehnquist retains his newfound sympathy for property rights, the two justices may author the bulk of pro-owner opinions in the next few years. O'Connor has been the justice least likely to author land use opinions, and the pattern of her pen is difficult to detect. Although she wrote a strongly worded dissent to the extension of the public trust in *Phillips Petroleum*, O'Connor also authored the unanimous[158] opinion in *Midkiff*, which effectively gave governments unlimited discretion to decide for what purposes private land may be condemned. If her opinions follow the recent

Table 17
Increases in Landowner Support,[1]
by Selected Justices

	1980–85	1986–89	Total
Scalia	—	83.3	83.3
Powell	22.2	80.0	42.9
O'Connor	20.0	57.1	38.7
Rehnquist	10.0	57.1	29.4
White	00.0	42.9	23.3
Court	10.0	40.0	17.6

[1]In takings cases.

Table 18
Weighted Opinions by U.S. Justices
Supporting Landowner Rights

	+	−	Pct.	Freq.		+	−	Pct.	Freq.
Scalia	4	0	100.0	.33	Marshall	3	8	27.3	.27
Brennan	4	2	66.7	.17	Burger	1	5	16.7	.26
White	5	6	45.5	.30	Stevens	2	11	15.4	.35
O'Connor	2	3	40.0	.19	Blackmun	2	11	15.4	.35
Rehnquist	6	13	31.6	.50	Powell	1	6	14.3	.20

+: Weighted opinions supporting the landowner.
−: Weighted opinions opposing the landowner.
Freq: number of cases in which a justice wrote an opinion, divided by the
number of cases in which the justice voted.

trend in her voting, Justice O'Connor may emerge as a firmer vote
on behalf of landowner rights.

Blackmun is the most striking example of a justice attuned
solely to the expressive and egalitarian aspects of land use rights.
With the exception of *Renton v. Playtime Theatres*, he supported
the landowner interest in every case that raised First Amendment
issues. In *Cleburne*, he joined Marshall's concurring opinion, which
was a vigorous attempt to preserve the unequal standard of rights
created by the New Deal Court. The opposition of Stevens to landowner rights has been nearly as dramatic but more consistent across
all areas of rights. Stevens supported the property interest only in
Loretto and *Phillips* (takings), *Cleburne* (equal protection), *Schad*
(free expression), and *Grendel's Den* (establishment of religion). The
votes of Stevens show a greater deference to the hierarchical notion

that properly designated officials may appropriately regulate the behavior of private individuals, while Blackmun is a stronger supporter of the egalitarian double standard, which is suspicious of governmental power over the individual but even more wary of libertarian private property rights.

Brennan and Marshall were the strongest supporters of landowner rights when egalitarian interests, including free expression, equal protection, and criminal rights, were involved, voting against the government in every one of those cases. But unlike Blackmun, they occasionally lent support to a takings claim as well. Their support of the temporary takings doctrine was crucial to its ultimate success in *First English*. Brennan and Marshall combined strong support for the egalitarian double standard with some sensitivity for what could be considered procedural abuses, as in the compensation-for-takings cases, even when property owners are the beneficiaries.

Justice Brennan's primary service on behalf of landowner rights was as an opinion writer, as can be seen in Table 18. His scathing dissent in *San Diego Gas* was the outstanding opinion on land use rights of the decade. Brennan's opinion shocked egalitarians accustomed to tolerating constitutional excesses in property areas and gave tremendous momentum to the quest for compensation for regulatory takings, although it would be six long years before a Court majority would join Brennan in decreeing that a city planner "must know the Constitution."[159] Although his voting record in land use cases was nearly identical to Brennan's, Marshall was more likely to unleash his eloquence in the service of government, emphasizing in his *Cleburne* concurrence and other opinions that landowners are virtually without rights to fend off "economic" regulation. Marshall's concern with procedural fairness conflicted with his disdain for property rights, and his *Cleburne* opinion was a striking attempt to protect the rights of the retarded without taking "a small but regrettable step"[160] toward substantive protection of private property rights.

When votes and opinions in favor of landowner rights are weighed together (Table 19), the performance of the Supreme Court in the 1980s does not suggest that a major shift toward more vigilance on behalf of property rights is about to take place. The justices still on the Court include the most and least supportive of landowner rights. And for property owners, the Supreme Court in the 1980s was not a moderate court. Justice Powell was indeed a moderate in constitutional land use cases; his support index of .416

Table 19
Index of Support for Landowner Rights

Scalia*	.874	Brennan	.311	Burger	.204
O'Connor*	.424	Marshall	.307	Stevens*	.170
Powell	.416	Rehnquist*	.289	Blackmun*	.133
Stewart	.333	White*	.284		

*Current justices.
Index: (weighted vote percent + weighted opinion percent × opinion frequency) / 1 + opinion frequency

indicates that he divided his support almost evenly between landowners and the government. Although he was not a prolific opinion writer, his votes provided crucial support in several areas, most prominently in the series of takings cases culminating in *First English* and *Nollan*. Although it is still too early to tell, the appointment of Anthony Kennedy to replace Powell is not likely to trigger a major shift toward landowner rights, as Kennedy would have to have a strong orientation toward property rights to mark a major change from Powell. It is just as likely that Kennedy might prove to be another Warren Burger indulging the regulatory impulses of state and local governments. Similarly, Brennan's replacement, David Souter, whose state court track record shows no strong tendencies to go out on judicial limbs in pursuit of rights, may prove more hierarchical than libertarian.

Barring unanticipated reversals of doctrine, landowner victories in the Supreme Court still will be difficult to come by. Nevertheless, the splits between the justices and the gradual increase in support for property rights suggest that any claim of landowner rights will have at least some chance of success. The uncertainty of evolving doctrines and shifting votes has replaced the staid certainty of the decades of abdication. If the double standard of landowner rights has not been broken, it at least has been cracked. Despite calls for a return to the era of "benign silence,"[161] the Court will probably continue its halting advance toward property rights.

The Supreme Court has been remarkably silent on the subject of procedural due process for landowners, but this is an area with rich potential, even with the current Court alignment. As the Court examines regulatory takings claims, it may come to see that "normal" delays, which may tie up property owners for years,[162] can deprive basic constitutional rights. Even Norman Williams and his coauthors, in the midst of an outraged attack on compensation for takings, paused to acknowledge that delays in the land regulatory process are "pervasive" and "ubiquitous, vicious, and devoid of any resemblance of procedural due process."[163] As the Court sees more examples of procedural abuses, the justices may be willing at least to reduce the time landowners are left twisting in the regulatory breeze.

Regulatory takings cases will likely produce close votes, which at least holds open the possibility of precedent-setting victories. Much will depend on the application of *First English*. The symbolic importance of this victory is immense as the shock waves settle through a planning community unaccustomed to constitutional restraints. But translating principle into remedies depends on a willingness to find a taking, and *Nollan* is an ambiguous precedent that suggests takings will still be rarely found absent a physical invasion, although regulators will have to be more cautious in their reasoning. If the hope of just compensation slowly fades in light of the Court's creativity in explaining away apparent takings, then *First English* may be consigned to the shelf of hoary precedents next to *Pennsylvania Coal*, receiving reverent nods from the justices but never taken seriously.

The revival of landowner rights by the Supreme Court has been modest and reluctant, more a consequence of the gradual extension of existing doctrine—protection of preferred rights and specific constitutional clauses, prohibitions of physical invasions without compensation—than a dramatic leap in a new direction. While the Court has not become an aggressive defender of the constitutional rights of landowners, its occasional shows of support send a message to the members of the planning community and elected officials that they must indeed know the Constitution, a message they had grown unaccustomed to hearing, and tell the polity that property may be something worth protecting. In the land use area, the Court is no longer just the good little soldier of hierarchy.

PART III: THE FUTURE OF LANDOWNER RIGHTS AND REGULATION

Chapter 7

Feudalism and Liberalism

Within the traditions of property law... there is nothing particularly radical in visualizing land being owned by the sovereign and being channelled out again to persons who would hold it only as long as they performed the requisite duties which went with the land.

—E. F. Roberts[1]

China is a planners' paradise. There is no gap between plan making and plan implementation. Nor is there any private developer to lure or browbeat into conformance.... What the government plans, it simply does.... The institutional framework for plan making is remarkably similar to what most planners say works best.

—David Callies[2]

The liberal vision of the founders that private property would provide the independence and responsibility on which to anchor democracy has been obscured by the growth of the state during the twentieth century. A more hierarchical perspective, that possession of private property is encumbered by obligations to the state, has gained prominence. David Callies wrote that studying the land use planning procedures of foreign nations "provides a glimpse of things to come" and saw similarities between Chinese planning and the visions of American planners.[3] Egalitarianism, although critical of hierarchical norms, has added to the trend toward state control and

owner obligations. In an era of architectural review boards, historical preservation committees, conservation commissions, coastal
commissions, wetlands committees, open-space initiatives, growth
moratoria, and subdivision exactions, to name a few of the tools of
the modern planner, signs of a revival of landowner rights must be
placed in a sobering context. Liberalism justified a freer society built
on the ashes of feudalism, so it is ironic that "feudal" so aptly describes the direction in which property rights have evolved. Landowners are becoming "stewards" who hold their property rights at
the pleasure of the state.

THE NEW FEUDALISM OF REGULATION

Sir Henry Maine captured the essence of the transformation
from feudalism to liberalism when he described the shift from status to contract,[4] which in cultural terms is a movement down the
grid axis, from high to low. Rather than life being prescribed by one's
station, relations became relatively fluid and voluntary with the
contract serving as the legal tool to formalize the new relationships.
Most fundamental were changes affecting land. "As feudalism declined," Robert Nelson has written, rents and taxes replaced "military and other customary feudal obligations," and land became
alienable."To the people of the time such changes seemed very radical in nature, contrary to their basic concept of feudal society—as
in fact they were."[5] The great waves of public regulation of property
signify a turning away from liberal virtues of individual control
back toward feudal notions of status and obligation. As Ellen
Frankel Paul noted, "rather than [seeing landowners] as absolute
owners free to determine how their land should be used, disposed of,
or developed . . . government now sees its function in more inter-
ventionist if not feudal terms."[6] The notion that private property
may be obsolete has grown along with environmentalism. John Mc-
Claughry wrote that

> it is clear that the operational goal of this [environmental]
> movement is the centralization of all power over land. . . . The
> supreme irony of this movement is its determination to move
> forward by moving backward—backward to feudalism. . . .
> That superior is no longer the King, since in a moment of pos-
> sible irrationality our forefathers scuttled the idea of monarchy
> in 1776, but the State, a less personal but more permanent
> institution.[7]

The shift toward a modern feudalism has been propelled by statutes and court decisions requiring that prescribed environmental and social factors play increasingly large roles in determining land use. As McClaughry wrote with typically pungent sarcasm, "This neo-feudal movement has placed a high premium on the services of lawyers. After all, if the goal is to undo a system of rights developed and solidified over five to six centuries, the only choice is between lawyers and Bolsheviks, and the latter have long since fallen out of favor on this side of the water."[8] This retreat from contract to status has been endorsed by justices and commentators. In California, Justice Tobriner led the call for the imposition of enlightened feudalism upon property owners, and the California Supreme Court has been a leader in developing a doctrine of the "public trust" that could eventually bring all land under state control.[9]

In a pair of law review articles (the first written with Joseph Grodin, who would later join the California Supreme Court after Tobriner's departure), Tobriner assessed the changes in modern society and the role of the courts. They remain splendidly provocative articles because Tobriner and Grodin portray hierarchy not simply as an expression of their own preferences but as an unavoidable response to fundamental social changes. The most activist justice on one of the most "liberal" courts in the nation saw himself as a servant of history, following the clear directives of society. Tobriner and Grodin wrote in 1967:

> Ours is a society of organization. It is a complex, interdependent society in which knowledge and function are exceedingly specialized and economic and political power highly centralized. . . . Such tendencies . . . bear enormous significance for the individual in our society. They imply increased regulation of his behavior by both governmental and non-governmental institutions. . . . The common law responds in part to the challenges of organized society by reformulating common law principles to impose duties and obligations on the basis of status or relationship.[10]

From the perspective of Tobriner and Grodin, that man is everywhere in the chains of centralized organization is an empirical fact, a condition that the courts have not created but one which they must accommodate. Economic and political power *are* centralized; behavior *is* increasingly regulated. The role of the courts is only to reduce the suffering, to make the chains fit as comfortably as possible by (as in the feudal tradition) "imposing duties and obligations on the basis of status or relationship." Man cannot be free, so he must be restrained correctly. Again in 1972, Tobriner wrote as if he were a bystander rather than a leader in the legal changes: "The impact of an industrialized, semi-collectivized society, pressing for a status-like responsibility, made itself felt upon the body of the law. The courts responded."[11]

Classical social and economic liberalism was dead from Tobriner's perspective. He argued that legal theory built on an individualist model was obsolete in an era of big business, big government, and big unions. "The great challenge to the legal system today," Tobriner and Grodin wrote, "is accommodation to the new industrial state. Rigid dependence upon legalistic concepts associated with nineteenth century society is as anachronistic for that purpose as is use of classical economic theory to explain the modern economy."[12] Individual contract and property rights and the economic theory of market capitalism were anachronistic. But if these foundations of liberalism were now obsolete, where could they look for guidance? Tobriner and Grodin found a model in an earlier age when "the society of the Middle Ages was relatively static." "The feudal system and its agrarian economy produced a hierarchy of relationships. . . . An individual's "place" in society . . . basically was fixed by the circumstances of his birth."[13]

Tobriner asserted that in the latter part of the twentieth century society had returned to status-bound relationships. The trend in the courts, according to Tobriner, "has been the development of the concept of status obligation" for many industries "by reason of their role, their function, their status, in society."[14] The courts have imposed common law "duties and obligations on the basis of status or relationship," and similar changes have taken place in constitutional and statutory law.[15]

In the new feudal system, the judges would be like kings, prescribing obligations and duties. The emergent New Feudalism is not intended to return the common people to serfdom, Tobriner disclaimed, but to use the power of government to look after their interests for them. How can the courts judge what is best for people? The correct mission, according to Tobriner, is to reduce the inequalities of life by aggressively applying due process and equal protection principles on behalf of deserving groups and to impose special liabilities on business. "Society . . . is becoming more and more integrated and collectivized at the same time that its economic imbalance becomes more acute."[16] The courts must respond to "the plight of the poor."[17] How the courts could eradicate inequality by harkening back to the status-bound world of hierarchy Tobriner did not explain.

E. F. Roberts has advocated that all property be socialized so that it may be laden with restrictive conditions and then resold to private owners.[18] He has predicted the end of personal property rights and argued that such a break with liberalism was really nothing new, given the feudal origins of property rights. Instead of the knighthood obligations of old, Roberts wrote, property holders would be subject to the mandates of a state master plan. He was quite correct that a return to essentially feudal property rights is well within the traditions of property law, which goes back to the common law of the Middle Ages. But the great tradition of America starts with the ideas of John Locke, not the reign of William the Conqueror. Within the liberal tradition, the feudal encumbrance of property is radical indeed.

Arguments for the feudallike encumbrance of private property have been heard throughout this century. Francis S. Philbrick waxed nostalgic for feudalism in 1938, writing that "in case of feudalism it is regrettable that there could not have been preserved the idea that all property was held subject to the performance of duties—not a few of them public."[19] These sentiments were echoed nearly thirty years later by John Cribbet, a legal scholar, who asserted that "the concept behind [feudal duties] was sound. . . . The use of land is of more than private concern."[20] With the rise of liberalism, property was not freely alienable and with far fewer encumbrances. "It may be," he speculated, "that the wrong concepts of feudalism survived—that we threw out the baby and kept the bath."[21]

The shift beginning in the 1970s toward greater neighborhood control in politics and regulation, coinciding with the rise of the environmental movement, empowered communities to impose obligations to protect the status quo. "When zoning is employed to protect community character," wrote Robert Nelson in 1977, "its closest historical antecedents are found in feudal land tenure."[22] In effect, wrote Nelson, communities "owned" rights to private property and could control its use. "As under feudal tenure," he wrote, "ownership rights and governing authority are joined, though in the modern case exercised collectively through local government instead of individually by the feudal lord."[23] The discretionary nature of recent local land use controls, which can be highly responsive to community political pressure, makes them a form of collective community rights, according to Nelson. "We can conclude," he wrote, "that in future social systems personal rights may be increasingly superseded by collective rights . . . exercised by many small groups and organizations, making them private collective rights for all practical purposes."[24] This is a radical change, as group "rights" are not rights in the liberal sense of protecting the individual but licenses for collective control. Modern land use controls have brought feudal mechanisms of control back over the individual while resorting to the language of liberalism, the language of rights.

ENVIRONMENTAL HIERARCHY

Environmentalism, a major engine powering the advance of hierarchical regulation, is a relatively recent phenomenon. "It is very rare in America to encounter any antipathy to new development," wrote John Delafons more than twenty years ago.[25] Any planner, land use attorney, citizen activist, or developer might wonder today what planet he was talking about. Land use controversies dominate local political agendas and headlines, and battles can be long, heated, and bitter. But Delafons was writing from a different perspective, as a British observer accustomed to extensive local control over land use. He also was writing of Texas and the Sunbelt, a region where the libertarian culture traditionally has been stronger and the hierarchical culture weaker. And he was writing in a different age, before the environmental movement burst upon the state of American public policy.

Despite a torrent of criticism of planning as elitist, oppressive, or simply wrongheaded, reliance on planning and control continues to grow. "There is more centralized planning today than there has ever been," according to Frank Popper, "but it is less likely to be comprehensive, more likely to be specialized, oriented to particular purposes: programs for hazardous waste facilities, farmland protection, wetlands and floodplain regulation, groundwater protection, industrial- and energy-facility siting, sensitive-area protection, state parks and forests."[26] The denominator common to all these areas is environmentalism,[27] which, albeit in a rather piecemeal fashion, has reinvigorated the notion that liberal freedom should be constrained by roles prescribed by experts. As Michael Vasu has put it, "At the basis of this . . . consensus . . . is the firm belief that all important human endeavors can and should be planned."[28] He sees the future as one of even greater comprehensive planning and control:

"The social and environmental complexity of the next two decades will generate an even greater demand for planning in the United States. . . . A society socialized to revere credentials will instinctively turn for guidance to those possessing formal education and membership in professional planning organizations."[29]

The revival of liberal concern for property rights is occurring at the same time that people are looking to expertise and control for environmental solutions. In cultural terms, libertarianism and hierarchy are on a collision course. Mainstream environmentalism provides a major challenge to the liberal socioeconomic system. "The decline of feudalism and the rise of . . . market institutions," wrote Robert Nelson, "was not coincidental, [and] the most basic principle of environmentalism is its opposition to the market verdict."[30] The new hierarchy, drawing on an old hierarchical culture of feudalism, is making itself felt through the imposition of obligations on property owners at the local, state, and federal levels, and I will now review developments at these levels before concluding with some comments on the challenges presented by the new hierarchy to personal freedom.

THE NEW FEUDAL COMMUNITY

Land use regulation has been predominantly a local product, and it is here that Robert Nelson sees the shift toward feudal obligations as most striking as neighborhoods use discretionary permit processes to impose duties on those who would use their land. Certainly new controls continue to sprout at the local level. "Especially in big cities," according to Popper, "planning is now more pervasive, sophisticated, and effective than it has ever been."[31] Local regulatory reforms have had three related aspects: greater neighbor control, greater citizen participation, and more discretionary procedures. Gone for the most part is nearly exclusive reliance on anticipatory zoning, which creates a comprehensive order for a community and ensures predictability. The hierarchical model of zoning envisioned by its pioneers never quite became reality, as rezonings and variances blurred the distinctions between zones. The new planning, rather than reject the case-by-case approach that has typified regulatory practice in many communities, has accommodated it by emphasizing the intensive evaluation by specialists of each land use proposal and extensive community participation.

As the local regulatory process has become more discretionary, so have the criteria, with the great growth of aesthetic,[32] design review, and historic preservation controls, which delegate matters of taste to public arbitration.[33] Even when a land use proposal meets all applicable zoning regulations, local boards may scrutinize architectural styles, building colors, sign designs, and the like for their tastefulness. Writing in the 1960s, John Delafons said it was "doubtful whether the new [aesthetic] controls will survive the scrutiny of the courts."[34] But survive they have, viewed by many courts as just another way to promote the public welfare over private property interests.[35] Communities may require architectural conformity,[36] or they may mandate variety, with the proper contribution to variety to be decided on a case-by-case basis.[37]

The new local regulatory regime is hierarchical in its reliance on specialized roles and the imposition of obligations (or grid, in the cultural model) on owners, but it is far more participatory than the original hierarchy of zoning. Robert Nelson sees the "creation of tight public controls of a highly discretionary nature over neighborhood quality" as essentially the same as collective private property rights.[38] Such collective rights are a contradiction in terms, as they entail a rejection of the liberal conception of rights, particularly property rights, as protecting private autonomy from public interference, yet they secure an entity—the community—distinct from the state. Nelson sees this development as evoking aspects of feudalism, including its limitations on personal freedom. The new "local growth controls," he writes, "can be objected to on the grounds that they openly limit personal residential mobility. The feudal quality of local growth controls is thus very explicit."[39]

Even Houston, long the model of libertarian land use control with its reliance on private covenants ("unzoned, unfettered, and mostly unrepentant"),[40] is gradually adopting public regulation.[41] Although zoning continues to be rejected by the voters (despite persistent efforts by city leaders to get it approved), Houston has instituted several regulatory schemes that apply to sex businesses, billboards, mobile homes, scenic districts, and historic landmarks. These incremental measures are seen as responding to specific social or environmental problems and thus as less objectionable than a comprehensive program of regulation.[42]

Advocacy of social hierarchy may be controversial in a liberal polity steeped in the language of liberty and equality yet seem less objectionable and more politically potent when covered with the patina of environmentalism. The homeowner who objects to commercial development or low-income housing in his neighborhood because he doesn't want offensive people or land uses to disturb his suburban idyll may seem selfish or prejudiced yet can capture an aura of respectability by objecting to the potential "environmental degradation" of the neighborhood. The not-in-my-backyard (NIMBY) syndrome can hide self-interest behind purported social interest.

In many municipalities, the explosion of neighborhood interest and participation in the regulatory process has coincided with a shift from at-large elections to district elections.[43] Where this occurs, veterans of neighborhood land use disputes often have the recognition, experience, and organization to mount successful campaigns for office. This is precisely what happened in Houston where a federal judge required district elections for the city council. In the next election, in 1981, several neighborhood activists were elected to the council, and the new mayor, Kathy Whitmire, shifted control of the city planning commission to neighborhood interests.[44] Ironically, while many social and environmental policy specialists have been stressing the regional consequences of land uses, the political process has decentralized local control even more, to the neighborhood level. Cities such as San Francisco became "balkanized," with community activists jealously guarding their turf, hostile to change and outsiders.[45]

STATE ENVIRONMENTAL CONTROLS

With the growth of the environmental movement in the early 1970s, a few states moved toward statewide land use controls, to the applause of many commentators. Fred Bosselman and Davis Callies dubbed the shift to state power the "quiet revolution."[46] Quiet indeed it was, so quiet that the revolution fizzled. Land use regulation remained overwhelmingly a local matter, although a few states such as Vermont,[47] Oregon,[48] and Hawaii[49] have imposed at least partial state control of land use.[50] In Vermont, for example, state-appointed regional commissions control permits for large projects and those at high elevations. The legislation, known as Act 250, was prompted as a supplement, rather than a replacement, for local control by focusing on the impact of large second home and ski resort developments catering to people outside the state. The law provided for a reduction of state control in towns that adopted zoning controls and made some exceptions for agricultural and forestry interests. Nonetheless, its implementation has remained controversial in a state with traditions of local autonomy and individualism. As one Vermont builder said, "The older guys especially can't deal with the state bureaucracy because they don't expect it, they weren't brought up with it."[51]

Generally, state land use control has been limited to states that see themselves as attractive vacation or second-home areas vulnerable to domination by larger outside interests. Yet every state has enacted one more more environmental statutes such as controls on coastal zones,[52] wetlands, mining, and flood plains, that effect use of private property.[53] New Jersey, for example, so far has rejected statewide land use control yet has

> state-required and state-reviewed local planning; regional planning for the rural quarter of the state in the Pinelands near Philadelphia and Atlantic City and the urban 30-square mile, high-growth Hackensack Meadowlands . . . ; state hazardous waste, coastal zone, wetlands, and farmland protection laws that are among the strongest in the country; and the nationally unique Mount Laurel[54] legislation governing the local placement and amount of new low-income housing.[55]

State environmental regulations likely will expand and may in sum be as substantial in their impact as explicit state land use controls but often are seen as less objectionable because of the "environmental" cachet. Some states, including Pennsylvania,[56] also have constitutional provisions protecting resources, which could become potent sources of limits on private property,[57] and sympathetic state judges have stretched statutory and common law doctrines[58] to reach private land use. Many states, for example, have "little NEPAs," modeled after the National Environmental Policy Act that require environmental impact statements for public developments, and the California courts have applied the state version to large private projects as well.[59] At the state level, then, as at the local level, the hierarchical imposition of obligations on owners has grown. State controls are even more likely than local ones to put a premium on the expertise of specialists, and John McClaughry sees these measures as the heart of the New Feudalism.[60]

Although environmental statutes aimed at specific concerns of pollution or resource use may be more palatable politically than a comprehensive scheme of state land use control, they can create a morass of conflicting, overlapping layers of bureaucracy. "By the early 1980s," according to Frank Popper, "California had 41 agencies besides the coastal commissions with overlapping responsibilities for planning land use in the coastal zone—the Energy Commission, the Forestry Board, the State Lands Commission, and the Public Utilities Commission, to name a few."[61] Property owners now must contend with not only local bureaucracy but also overlapping layers of piecemeal state controls, which can add additional substantive restrictions on rights and new procedural labyrinths.

FEDERAL REGULATION OF PRIVATE LAND

Never has there been explicit federal land use regulation. At the height of the environmental movement, planning interests and environmentalists,[62] led in Congress by Senator Henry Jackson and Representative Morris K. Udall promoted the Land Use Planning Act, which would have provided $800 million in 3:1 matching grants to states that developed comprehensive land use planning processes. The measure was defeated in the House in 1974 by seven votes. A successor, the Land Use Resource Conservation Act of 1975, also failed to become law.

But the same Congress that repeatedly said no to national land use regulation nonetheless passed major environmental statutes that restrict the use of land.[63] The National Environmental Policy Act,[64] which took effect in 1970s, requires thorough anticipation and mitigation of environmental effects of federal projects and served as the model for comparable state legislation. Although it did not apply directly to private land, NEPA added credibility to the belief that the full consequences of any project can and should be anticipated, inspiring comprehensive, discretionary local review processes for private projects. To give a few other examples, the Endangered Species Act [65] is renowned for the power it gives courts to stop development dead in its tracks; the Surface Mining Control and Reclamation Act[66] is the major act restricting strip mining; and "Superfund"[67] imposes substantial cleanup obligations and costs on businesses. Congress has also passed legislation to promote protection of farmlands[68] and coastal areas,[69] to require clean air[70] and clean water,[71] and to limit use of pesticides[72] and toxic substances[73]—all of which have significant impact for property use. The extent of federal regulation is remarkable, considering that the federal government, according to the Constitution, is limited to a few enumerated powers and unlike the states has no general police power to regulate for the public welfare.[74]

Direct federal regulation of land use is likely to become more prevalent, even without the enactment of a national land planning scheme, because of the government's power to control the land it owns,[75] which composes a large proportion of the nation, particularly in the West. Environmental specialists increasingly urge the protection of entire ecosystems, which could entail not only federal purchase of additional lands but also direct federal regulation of large tracts of adjoining private property.[76] Since the 1970s, the federal government has been buying easements to protect hiking trails, which in less litigious times depended on the good graces of private owners. Although this has involved only a minor expenditure of federal funds,[77] the exercise of direct federal protection could have great effect on the millions of privately owned acres that lie along the serpentine trail routes if the government asserted power to regulate adjoining private land use.[78]

ENVIRONMENTALISM AND THE PUBLIC TRUST

Many regulatory initiatives reflect a feudal (or hierarchical) perspective that use of land entails specific obligations to the state or community. As such, they present a challenge to the liberal (or low-grid) tradition of individual rights. When landowners present constitutional challenges to regulation, courts must resolve the conflicts between these competing visions. How far the courts are willing to extend constitutional rights is critical to the balance between the individual and the state, and we have seen that in general property rights are getting more attention than they have in some time, although the change is rather modest. The renewal of rights is challenged by new waves of regulation, and the battles in the courts are likely to be frequent and sharp. But there is another trend that may derail the judicial confrontation of rights and regulation—the expansion of the public trust doctrine.

The public trust was intended to ensure that private ownership of property would not obstruct navigable waterways so that commerce and transportation would not be impaired.[79] But in the age of environmentalism, the old doctrine, which facilitated the interaction of private owners and consequently the use of their land, is being wedded to the new gospel of preservation and obligation to prevent the use of property not only in navigable waterways but in any waterways, down to the smallest stream, and by extension to the watersheds from which they flow, which entail all land.

When an owner is deemed by the courts to hold property subject to the public trust, the trust doctrine trumps any rights the property owner may claim. In effect, the owner does not own certain use rights to the property because they are held in perpetuity as a public trust. Joseph Sax argued (and his view has been supported by the courts) that the public trust is not a repudiation of property rights because the rights never entailed what is subject to the trust.[80] What has never been granted to a private owner can never be taken away, as it was not the owner's to begin with. While this may not be a repudiation of a specific constitutional property right in a specific context, it is a repudiation of the entire concept of property rights.[81] Once a court imposes a public trust obligation, questions of constitutional rights are moot. There can be no takings claim if there is no property right that can be taken.

The environmentalist argument that all natural resources[82] and wild creatures[83] are public resources legitimates the extension of the public trust doctrine to all private land. At this point, property rights would cease to function, and the job of the courts when regulatory permits were challenged by opponents would be to decide whether the government may permit the specific use of land in question consistent with the public trust. As we saw in the chapter on California, the high court in that state has led the way in extending the public trust doctrine further and further to private land. The most formidable constitutional obstacle to the complete imposition of the public trust doctrine is, and likely will continue to be, the general acceptance by the courts of the doctrine that the state may not entirely deprive an owner's land of economic value without paying compensation. Courts will be reluctant to apply the public trust to an entire holding if it would so blatantly destroy all value. But that does not mean the courts will not tolerate huge reductions of value stemming from the imposition of a public trust on substantial portions of property.

Wetlands in particular have been given great protection by state and local governments and courts and by the Army Corp of Engineers and the Environmental Protection Agency.[84] In *Just v. Marinette County*,[85] for example, the Wisconsin Supreme Court relied on the public trust doctrine to justify prohibition of any wetland development on the grounds that it would eventually affect public navigable waters. Property owners essentially no longer have rights to develop wetlands, must comply with extensive permitting procedures, and can be obligated to "replace" wetlands that may be affected by their proposed property uses.[86] One property owner was even sentenced to three years in prison (the Supreme Court refused to hear his appeal) for putting clean fill and topsoil on his property without the proper permit, which he had been led to believe was not necessary.[87] And wetlands have been defined generously to include much land that is only occasionally damp and would not be recognized as wetlands but for the identification of certain plants by specialists. Wetlands are basically the drainage bins of fields, forests, and developed land, so the statutory and public trust restrictions on wetlands[88] will likely be pushed by environmentalists to incorporate entire watersheds.

THE CHALLENGE TO PROPERTY RIGHTS

It is a curious irony that as liberalism has been declared triumphant on the world stage of ideology[89] and Eastern Europe moves toward regimes of individual rights, private property, and free enterprise, there should be such enthusiasm in American environmental circles for the eclipse of individual property rights by feudallike obligations. As Sondra Berchin has written, "every parcel of land possesses developmental potential which impinges on a public interest."[90] We may protect a system of private property rights because it is just, because we believe it essential to the autonomy of the liberal individual, or because it may make possible the most efficient distribution and use of resources, but it is foolish to argue that private actions do not have public consequences, or vice versa. Public and private, individual and society, are inescapably intertwined. When it is asserted that the public has or should have control over natural resources and that private owners are trustees or servants obligated to serve the public will, the implications for the loss of individual autonomy are profound.

In the new hierarchical world, individual property rights are anachronisms that serve only to "stir special atavistic memories" of the "pioneering past," in the words of Justice Hans Linde, a nationally regarded member of the Oregon Supreme Court.[91] The full implementation of hierarchical control over land use could require the elimination of private property rights or at least the legal separation of rights to use land from rights of ownership. As long as property remains in private hands, individuals may claim they are entitled to decide the uses of their own land, either alone or through negotiation with the government, and thus state control will be incomplete. Berchin, in a blend of wishful thinking and perceptive analysis, has claimed that "land ownership has been redefined so that it no longer entails a constitutional right to develop. . . . There is every reason to believe that this trend will continue until all developmental rights are under state control."[92] Whereas the courts, even the U.S. Supreme Court, have insisted that governments if they wish to avoid paying compensation leave property owners with at least some "reasonably beneficial" (that is, economically viable) use of their land, Berchin argues that development of natural areas is inherently an unreasonable use of property and thus can be forbidden.[93] Other academics, such as Joseph Sax, share Berchin's belief in the obsolescence of private property. "We are going to have to come to terms," according to Sax, "with the prospect that planning (a word Americans don't like much), rather than property, is going to be a principal engine of social benefit production in the future."[94] Americans may resist his prescription, however, not just because they have an aversion to the term "planning" but also because they sense that the shift from property to planning requires a fundamental removal of power from individuals. The future of property rights in the courts will be contentious and difficult to predict because while courts are paying more attention to property rights and to applications of "personal" rights to private property, many judges and justices also are quite sympathetic to environmentalist arguments for public control. Judges have an increasingly sophisticated understanding of ecology and pollution, according to James Hite, an agricultural economist, and consequently "this heightened scientific understanding allows contemporary judges to see some controls as reasonable today, where the same controls would have seemed unreasonable and arbitrary to scientifically less enlightened judges a generation or two ago."[95]

Hite recognized the threat posed by this environmental "enlightenment" to private property rights, writing, "Strictly construed, [judicial acceptance of environmental restrictions] might be seen as a threat to all private property rights, making the 'taking' clause irrelevant. All developments are likely to have some adverse effect on ecosystems."[96] Yet he dismissed the possibility that public control over development could lead to public prohibition of development and thus to the deprivation without compensation of private rights to use property. "Such an extension of the doctrine would be untenable with the rationale for conservation," he wrote. "Conservation is a legitimate activity of government because the public welfare requires it; if government controls begin to be premised on protection and preservation of natural objects for their own sake to the extent of preventing human economic activity, the public welfare would not be served."[97] Yet once we have accepted that constitutional rights are porous and may be breached at will by a public entity pursuing its claim of the "public welfare," then (unlike the cut and dried distinction seen by Hite) there is no qualitative distinction between conservation that allows limited private use of property and preservationism that does not. If our only criterion of constitutionality is the promotion of the public welfare, not the severity of the deprivation of individual rights, only the personal preferences of judges will keep property "rights" (if permission to use one's property devoid of philosophical or constitutional anchor can be called a right) from vaporizing.

THE NEED FOR PROPERTY RIGHTS

*The instant I enter on my own land, the bright
idea of property, of exclusive right, of independence, exalt my mind. . . . This formerly rude
soil has established all our rights; on it is
founded our rank, our freedom, our power as
citizens.*

—*J. Hector Crevecoeur*[98]

*The Old Feudalism was not without virtue. . . .
It was a strong force for social stability. . . . The
problem of the Old Feudalism was that it stifled individual liberty, productivity, and self-government. And that will also be the problem
of the New Feudalism.*

—*John McClaughry*[99]

Property rights are at the core of liberalism, the political vision of individual freedom and limited government that animated the American Revolution. As John Gray has written, "Private property is the embodiment of individual liberty in its most primordial form."[100] And that liberty is at stake in the feudal challenge to private property rights. "Where an excess of power prevails," warned James Madison nearly two hundred years ago, "property of no sort is duly respected. No man is safer in his opinions, his person, his faculties, or his possessions."[101] As Edward Erler put it, "The right to property serves as the litmus test because it is the right which is derivative from life and liberty. . . . In a sense, the right to property serves as a kind of 'early warning system' to invasion of life and liberty."[102]

In creating the American political experiment, the founders drew on an eclectic mix of political philosophies, homespun wisdom, and practical experience. But the figure whose impact is most pervasive is John Locke, who argued that human freedom is just not simply for social reasons, so that it may create a virtuous citizenry[103] or maximize welfare,[104] but also because it is a natural right of individuals. Government was to further that freedom by protecting those natural rights, which are superior, not instrumental, to the state. From the Declaration of Independence on, the political debate presumed that the rights of man were natural and inalienable. The Federalists objected to a bill of rights for the Constitution not because they did not recognize those rights but because they trusted to their institutional arrangements to curb government interference[105] and saw an enumeration of rights as a dangerous precedent that might prove too restrictive.[106] The most liberal legacy of the Constitution, the Bill of Rights, was added at the insistence of Anti-Federalists as the price of ratification. Despite their considerable differences, the two sides[107] of the founding debate shared assumptions of natural rights, including the rights of property. The founding of the American Republic may have been a "Machiavellian moment,"[108] but the moment created a polity rooted in and dedicated to Lockean liberalism.[109]

In his essay on property, Madison wrote: "That alone is a *just* government, which *impartially* secures to every man, whatever is his *own*" (emphasis in original).[110] This security is provided according to Madison through governmental protection of property rights. In this, Madison followed Locke, who reasoned that governments are formed to provide the security that individuals lack on their own and thus that "the great and chief end" of government is the protection of property rights.[111] Property rights would enable personal freedom. Property in the Lockean sense is expansive, including all products of human creativity, not just land or material possessions. In contrast with New Deal jurisprudence—in which the freedom of the individual is split into parts, only some of which are graced by legal and normative protection while others are left vulnerable to invasion by the state—personal, political, and property rights are seen as inseparable, for without property rights, personal and political freedom would be illusory. "In its larger and juster meaning," Madison wrote in his essay on property, it "embraces every thing to which a man may attach a value and have a right."[112] One has property not only in land, buildings, and merchandise but also in

> his opinions and the free communication of them . . . his religious opinions and the profession and practice dictated by them . . . in the safety and liberty of his person . . . in the free

use of his faculties and free choice of the objects on which to employ them. In a word, as a man is said to have a right to his property, he may equally be said to have a property in his rights.[113]

From the liberal perspective, the concepts of property and of rights become virtually indistinguishable. Social justice is not possible without recognition of the dignity and autonomy of each individual, and it is property rights that provide that protection. It is property that protects one's ideas, one's creations, and one's possessions. By securing what is one's own, property secures individual identity. And it is property that makes economic and consequently political freedom possible, as citizens are not beholden to the largess of the state. As Erler said, Madison "understood the right to property in its full political sense—as a fence to life and liberty. And, in its political meaning, property was understood as the comprehensive right."[114]

Locke rooted the right of property in personal autonomy. "Every man has a property in his own person," he wrote; "this nobody has any right to but himself. The labor of his body and the work of his hands, we may say, are properly his."[115] Because no one has a legitimate claim over us, the fruits of our identity—our ideas, creations, and possessions—are also uniquely ours. The rights of property do not suppress human variety and expression but enable them. "It is precisely the openness of human nature and the indeterminacy of what is available to satisfy our desires which justifies an emphasis on private ownership,"[116] and it is this diversity of aspirations and attainment that suffers when the individualistic institution of private property is supplanted by the feudal obligations of central control. If we had identical abilities and preferences, hierarchical constraints would not mean the triumph of the preferences of the few over the many or even of the many over the unfortunate few. But because each person is unique, the fruits of liberty are tenuous without a constitutional element that creates a sphere of autonomy around the individual. "It is the individual diversity of faculties that makes property itself individual, that is, private," according to Erler.[117] Property, to put it in the language of social science, "operationalizes" liberty; it makes liberty functional and measurable.

Private property is far from the dehumanizing and alienating force portrayed by Marx. Property is the material expression of humanity—or one's humaneness[118]—not the triumph of materialism over humanity. Nearly thirty years ago, Milton Friedman pointed out that the socialist opponents of individualism had distorted the debate on free markets and private property: "The great achievement of capitalism has not been the accumulation of property, it has been the opportunities it has offered to men and women to extend and develop and improve their capacities. Yet the enemies of capitalism are fond of castigating it as materialist, and its friends all too often apologize for capitalism's materialism as a necessary cost of progress."[119]

It is ironic that centralized control has been advocated under the label of the ideology that it undermines—liberalism. "As a supreme, if unintended complement, the enemies of the system of private enterprise have thought it wise to appropriate its label," noted Joseph Schumpeter.[120] I have used the term in its classic sense, as the political philosophy based on individual freedom, not as a synonym for hierarchy. How fitting that the distortion of liberalism has made the label the subject of loathing among the American public, which remains wary of governmental control.[121]

LIBERTY AND SOCIETY

Good fences make good neighbors.
      —Robert Frost[122]

Liberalism is a political doctrine requiring that the state be limited so that individuals may flourish. It does not require that persons retreat, as Tocqueville feared, into lonely shells. But rather than dictate correct social relations, it allows individuals to choose their attachments. "The right to property is the great fence to liberty," Erler wrote, "because it is the fence to consent."[123] When we are free, we are free to be together as well as alone. Liberalism can enrich community because it is freely chosen and valued. As Charles Murray has noted, liberalism is compatible with all sorts of social attachments.[124] Independence enriches social life. Secure in ourselves, we can reach out to others; we need not fear that society will take what is rightfully ours.

The self-responsibility and empathy that freedom based on property rights can engender was for the founders an important element of the liberal polity. The free republic, they believed, depended on the virtue of the citizenry, and "virtue in turn could flourish only in a society of autonomous citizens, rendered independent through the possession of property, particularly landed property," Charles Hobson has written.[125] Virtue did not imply conformity with an imposed public conception of the good but the character to act freely and responsibly. Private property and individual freedom would nurture the moderation that comes from knowing one will be responsible for one's actions. And virtue would enable political independence as individuals will have the character and economic independence to stand up to the state.

"The opposite of virtue," according to Hobson, "was 'corruption,' a state characterized by dependence, either of citizens upon each other or upon the government."[126] Corruption is seen as the debasement of spirit and character bred by dependence. When one is no longer responsible for one's actions, when sustenance is provided by the state and behavior constrained by the state, responsible social action is no longer engendered. The combination of feudal controls and public entitlements saps the personal and political character encouraged by freedom. No wonder, then, that as Alan Ryan has stated, "The historical record is that only those modern societies with some kind of a capitalist economy based on private property and the market have been innovative, politically liberal and intellectually progressive."[127]

Any single regulation will not spell the end of freedom, the end of creativity, the end of the liberal polity. But it is important not to forget, in a zeal to embrace the security of hierarchical controls, the fundamental strengths of a system of private property rights. The consequences of private rights may at times be chaotic, ugly, or rude. But along with those costs come the rewards of freedom. Feudallike controls cannot be placed on individuals without eroding freedom, dignity, and virtue. It is worth taking seriously the challenges to the little freedoms of everyday life posed by the New Feudalism.

LIBERALISM AND THE MODERN STATE

We have always been a nation obsessed with liberty. . . . From the days of Williams and Wise to those of Eisenhower and Kennedy, Americans have talked about practically nothing else but liberty. Not the good man, but the free man has been the measure of all things in this "sweet land of liberty."
                                        —Clinton Rossiter[128]

We were the first to assert that the more complicated the forms assumed by civilization, the

more restricted the freedom of the individual
must become.
                                   —*Benito Mussolini*[129]

Private property may be fundamental to personal freedom, but is freedom still viable? However much Americans may be "obsessed with liberty," is it no more than a futile, anachronistic yearning? It is easy to argue that classical liberalism is like classical art or architecture—interesting to contemplate, admirable for the historical attainment it represents, but irrelevant or remote from the tenor and problems of the day. It can be said that classical liberalism, with its emphasis on the individual, is archaic in the age of the global village. In an era of nuclear weapons and industrial pollution, turning the individual free may be irresponsible; in an era of large complex organizations, it may be unfeasible. Tobriner and Grodin asserted that modern man is organization man, necessarily constrained by social obligation and government regulation to forgo his personal preferences for the greater good. But the eclipse of individualism is not inevitable. The tenets of liberalism—that no one owns or controls another person; that individuals may protect their autonomy through the institution of property rights, may govern themselves through limited, constitutional democracy, and may control their social and economic arrangements through voluntary association and freely bargained contracts—need not be consigned to the history books.

Socialism has provided the major intellectual challenge to liberal capitalism during the twentieth century, and socialism is everywhere in retreat, exposed as a brutal ideology that can be maintained only with the barrel of a gun. When given an opportunity for self-determination, nations in Eastern Europe have moved to embrace liberal government and individual rights. Czechoslovakia, fortunate perhaps in these momentous times to have a writer for a leader, has found its aspirations expressed through Vaclav Havel. Shortly after the Communists were driven from power, he spoke to his fellow citizens of his nation's experiences. What of the social state, which was to be the salvation of man from his own greed, which was, as Tobriner might put it, to impose the correct duties and obligations? "The previous regime, armed with its arrogant and intolerant ideology, denigrated man into a production force," said Havel. "It made talented people who were capable of managing their own affairs and making an enterprising living in their own country into cogs in some kind of monstrous, ramshackle, smelly machine whose purpose no one can understand."[130]

What had been the fate of the workers, who were to reign as collective conquerors over the forces of liberal capitalism? "The state, which calls itself a state of the working people, is humiliating and exploiting the workers," said Havel.[131] What of the natural environment? Have resources fared better under collective, socialist rule? "We have laid waste to our soil and the rivers and the forests that our forefathers bequeathed to us, and we have the worst environment in the whole of Europe."[132] Socialism may be a social and economic failure, but worse has been its destructive effect on personal character. "We have become morally ill. We have learned not to believe in anything, not to have consideration for one another and only to look after ourselves. Notions such as love, friendship, compassion, humility and forgiveness have lost their depth and dimension."[133] Collectivism, promoted as serving the nobler aims of man, has debased his morality.

Czechoslovakia, guided by Havel and its liberal finance minister, Vaclav Klaus, is moving quickly to implement free-market reforms, including privatization of property. It is revealing that Havel did not seek to excuse liberalism as a morally shallow system made necessary by its material advantages. Prosperity is not the point. Human freedom, empathy, and dignity are. Although socialism was materially disastrous, more important, it was a moral failure because it denigrated individuals and drove them into apathetic shells. The future, according to Havel, would depend on citizens taking control of their lives and understanding that social justice and political freedom must come from individual action. To abandon self-initiative for the complacency of dependency would be moral abdication: "All of us are responsible, each to a different degree, for keeping the totalitarian machine running. . . . We cannot lay all the blame on those who ruled before, not only because this would not be true but also because it could detract from the responsibility each of us now faces—the responsibility to act on own our initiative, freely, sensibly and quickly."[134]

What remarkable language in an era when law and policy commentators are quick to absolve individuals from responsibility for their fates and to rationalize deprivations of freedom in the name of liberalism. Perhaps it is too easy for privileged scholars in the West to forget the basic foundations of liberal freedom, and we can benefit from those who know all too well what happens to humanity when private property is eclipsed by centralized conceptions of the public good. As the philosopher John Gray has cautioned, "Socialist and revisionary liberal claims neglect the vital role . . . that the institution of private property and its corollary, the free market, play in constituting and protecting the basic liberties of the individual."[135]

The failures of socialism and the strong natural desire for freedom suggest the desirability of liberalism, but they do not erase doubts about its viability. It may be disconcerting that Tobriner and Grodin rationalized the New Feudalism in language similar to Mussolini's defense of fascism, but perhaps we have no choice on small, complex Spaceship Earth. Man wants to be free, as seen in the jubilation across Eastern Europe, but can he be? Must the rights of the individual bow to social utility?

Modern life need not spell the end of liberalism. Centralized control assumes that those who are doing the planning possess superior knowledge or wisdom that makes them able to predict and accommodate the future. But no one can know what challenges the future will present, what discoveries will most benefit mankind, or what public and private preferences will be. Centralized control commits us to "one guess about the future."[136] This not only suppresses freedom, but also increases error. When people can use their property as they wish, they not only serve their own needs but also provide a greater diversity of uses. If indeed modern problems require coordinated solutions, those solutions are more likely to be found and coordinated effectively through a system of private property and free choice. As Friedrich Hayek has argued, liberal capitalism is effective because competitive markets act as discovery mechanisms, quickly feeding information about preferences and new developments between interested parties.[137] And the "hidden hand" remains effective in the technological postindustrial age because, as Hayek wrote, "Far from being appropriate only to comparatively simple conditions, it is the very complexity of the division of labor under modern conditions which makes competition the only method by which such co-ordination can be adequately brought about."[138]

Liberty may be more, not less, viable today. The global village brings individuals closer together, which may enable people to control their own destinies more effectively. In the language of economics, the transaction costs are lower. With improved education, transportation, and communication, it is easier to exchange the information about preferences that makes voluntary interaction effective. The computer and communications revolutions mean people can work in their homes or anywhere across the country and still be in contact with other workers, customers, friends, and compatriots. There is more, not less, opportunity for workplace freedom now.

There are more, not fewer, chances for individuals to find outlets for their talents. True, the world is smaller, more interdependent; that only creates more opportunities for people to interact freely. Tobriner's (and Grodin's) account of modern history was selective. The surrender of human freedom is not inevitable.

LIBERALISM AND POLITICAL CULTURE

Experience should teach us to be most on our
guard to protect liberty when the Government's
purposes are beneficent. . . . The greatest dan-
gers to liberty lurk in insidious encroachment
by men of zeal, well-meaning but without un-
derstanding.
                                        —Justice Brandeis[139]

The conflicts between rights and regulation are rich with implications for how we will be allowed or required to live, for the balance of what I have called political cultures. Liberalism is at heart a "low-grid" political philosophy relying on private property rights to protect personal freedom. In this respect, liberalism has the most in common with the libertarian political culture, as neither group-based decisions nor external controls are required. But liberalism is a political, not a social, philosophy, and it leaves room for (and encourages, I have argued) freely chosen group attachments and awareness, which are the core of the egalitarian political culture. If the egalitarian ideal (rather than the coercive egalitarianism often promoted in public policy) is to be pursued, it must have an environment of personal freedom. Freedom equally shared and equality freely chosen will be possible only if the feudal consequences of the growing regulatory state are understood and guarded against and if the centrality of property to liberty is understood and protected.

In a liberal democracy, the courts must be the prime protectors of the individual. In cultural terms, legislatures are the elites of the hierarchy, creating rules (or increasing grid) for the polity. It falls to the courts to preserve the individual freedom, to "lower the grid." Fortunately, this is a task for which the courts, accustomed to examining government claims of public need and the nature and extent of private rights and applying nuances of theory and doctrine to the nuts and bolts of everyday life, are well suited. The courts have gradually returned to the field of land use regulation and are looking more critically at new controls. In the concluding chapter, I will summarize developments in constitutional protections of landowner rights; consider their consequences for liberty, order, and equality; and suggest changes in constitutional analysis that would provide protection of landowners while still allowing a substantial role for the regulatory state.

Chapter 8

Land, Culture, and the Constitution

It may well be true that our generation talks and thinks too much of democracy and too little of the values which it serves. It cannot be said of democracy, as Lord Acton truly said of liberty, that it "is not a means to a higher political end. It is itself the highest political end."
—*Friedrich Hayek*

This chapter is both a conclusion and an introduction. My main purpose has been to show that conflicts between cultures are embodied in land use disputes and that the increased skepticism about land use regulation and the increased attention to property rights reflect the influence of the libertarian and egalitarian cultures. Here I will summarize these developments. But I also wish to suggest how property rights might receive greater protection while still leaving room for regulation and the influence of the different political cultures. Where rights and regulation should go, as opposed to where they have come, could easily fill another book. That is a project for another day, but since I have been critical of many restrictions on the rights of landowners, it is fair to ask just what I think should be done about it. I hope this chapter will provide at least a partial answer. What I want to suggest here is that trusting entirely to government to determine land uses does not serve any of the three cultures well and that common ground can be found for the greater protection of property rights.

FREEDOM AND DEMOCRACY

The Supreme Court has implied in many land use cases that somehow the public good is identified with majoritarian rule alone, discarding its role as the guardian of minority rights. The burden in a Supreme Court case typically has been on the property owner to prove that a land use restriction is utterly without rational relation to any imaginable public purpose. Proving this is impossible since a creative judge could imagine a rational basis even for laws passed by a legislature of certified lunatics, and consequently property rights have been effectively abandoned for most of this century. Yet when preferred constitutional rights were at stake, the court at times has been quite bold in confronting legislatures. Were the court to profess such blind faith in the political branches of government in other areas, there would have been no *Brown v. Board of Education*,[1] no *Brandenburg v. Ohio*.[2]

The Court justified its abdication of constitutional property rights in part by asserting that property owners can look out for their own interests quite well in the political realm.[3] If the pressures on legislators somehow resulted in enlightened rule promoting the public good while safeguarding individual rights, perhaps dependence on the political branches for the protection of individual freedoms would not be troubling. But "if, as frequently alleged, individuals are grasping, greedy monsters in the market place," Bruce Johnson has asked skeptically, "by what magic are they transformed into farsighted altruists in the privacy of the polling booth?"[4] According to Johnson, protecting the land use decisions of individuals actually provides more restraint than entrusting them to government, for private individuals must consider the demands of the market, while political majorities can command resources without such a check. Democratic bodies may excel at tapping majority sentiment but for that very reason may be a threat to individual rights. Hayek criticized the "misleading and unfounded belief that, so long as the ultimate source of power is the will of the majority, the power cannot be arbitrary. . . . It is not the source but the limitation of power which prevent it from being arbitrary."[5] The unconcerned attitude of the court flies in the face of everything we know about the

capture of the legislative and regulatory processes by vested interests, large or small.[6] "Such 'guardianship' by state legislatures
alone," David Callies has cautioned, "is not a particularly comforting prospect."[7]

"WRETCHED NURSERIES OF UNCEASING DISCORD"

The smaller the jurisdiction, the more rights to use land may
be endangered. Local governments enact the lion's share of property
regulation, and they may be the political arenas most vulnerable to
capture. In defending the proposed constitution, James Madison
turned the logic of Montesquieu on its head and argued that a large
republic would be less likely than a small one to fall prey to dominance by factions, and thus individual freedom would be more
secure.[8] He rooted his judgment in his observations of Virginia, a
large state that he considered moderate in politics and tempera-
ment, and small Rhode Island, which according to Charles Hobson
was "the scene of the most virulent factional politics of the 1783s."[9]
Said Madison of Rhode Island, "Nothing can exceed the wickedness
and folly which continue to reign there. All sense of Character as
well as of Right is obliterated."[10] Alexander Hamilton also un-
leashed a torrent of denunciation at Montesquieu's ideal small re-
publics, calling them "an infinity of little, jealous, clashing
tumultuous commonwealths, the wretched nurseries of unceasing
discord and the miserable objects of universal pity or contempt."[11]
Hamilton may have been a bit hot under the collar, but anyone
who has witnessed the primordial clashes of local land use regulation will recognize more than a kernel of truth in his invective. Local legislative bodies produce the bulk of land use regulations, and
the pressures to cater to organized neighborhood groups can be
great. Participation in local elections and hearings tends to be low
but intense, dominated by neighborhood activists who can afford
the time to learn about local politics and attend often-drawn-out
proceedings, who have the skills to sift through pages of staff reports
and participate effectively in regulatory review processes, and who
feel strongly enough to make it all seem worthwhile. As Clifford
Weaver and Richard Babcock have put it, "The neighborhoods are
run by the people who, instead of bowling on Monday night, go out
and harass their elected officials and they don't care right from
wrong; they enjoy the conflict."[12] While most people try to get on
with their private lives, participatory local regulation is most vulnerable to domination by self-interested factions.[13]

Given the rapid growth of land use regulations with various schemes to force property owners to provide public benefits without compensation such as rent reductions, open space, accessways, and low-income housing, it strains credibility to argue that property interests dominate state and local politics. The potential builders of apartments, office buildings, and the like and the individuals who might benefit from them are often out-of-towners unrepresented in the politics of the municipality that in response to citizen pressures, may impose special burdens on them or seek to keep them out altogether. "It is a rare municipal legislature," according to Richard Babcock, "that will reject what it believes to be the wishes of the neighbors."[14] It is not hard to count votes, particularly when passing an ordinance may satisfy political pressure groups, burden only some landowners, and provide public benefits without raising taxes. "When an entity tells an individual property owner that he must leave his land vacant for public recreational use (or view, or buffer), or that he may only develop it if he provides some public service or dedicates part of the property to public use," observe Berger and Kanner, "it does not take a computer to calculate which side the greater number of votes is on."[15] Especially at the local level, officials may be under strong pressures from voters and activists seeking benefits without costs or seeking to impose their preferences on others.

PRIVATE PROPERTY AND PERSONAL FREEDOM

In the far distance a helicopter skimmed down
between the roofs, hovered for an instant like a
bluebottle, and darted away again with a curv-
ing flight. It was the Police Patrol, snooping
into people's windows.

> —*George Orwell*[16]

By allowing property rights to be denigrated, courts have tolerated the erosion of personal freedoms. Constantly expanding land use regulations threaten personal privacy, creativity, and entrepreneurship. Regulations may specify the relations of who may live in a house together. They can dictate what colors a house or business may be painted and its architectural style. They may require that an owner, without compensation, avoid using a private field or forest that the public likes to look at and require that a church maintain the appearance of a structure even if it drains finances intended for religious purposes. They may forbid individuals to sell items made in their living rooms or offer services from their homes.

Strengthening the role of the courts in protecting property rights does not require that all rights be treated equally. Ely has argued that free speech is so directly tied to democracy that it merits the highest protection.[17] That may be, but it does not follow that other rights should be abandoned entirely. Egalitarians may believe that equal protection and free expression deserve more protection than property rights, and hierarchists may think that no rights should receive the nearly ironclad protection of the strict scrutiny test, but they may still agree with libertarians that property rights merit significant protection, whether to further personal rights or to provide the individual with a modicum of dignity in the larger polity.

Fortunately, property rights are making a slow comeback in many jurisdictions. Indeed, the growth of regulation has helped stimulate attention to rights as innovative land use controls have created new conundrums of freedom and responsibility. Courts "have increasingly isolated selective land use controls for differential and searching judicial treatment," according to Daniel Mandelker.[18] Critical review of government motivations under substantive due process has survived in state courts and is returning to prominence as state courts regain stature. Even the Supreme Court has heightened its scrutiny of government rationality, judging from equal protection[19] and takings[20] cases in the 1980s. And courts have been increasingly willing to strike down land use regulations that impinge on preferred rights such as privacy, expression, and equal protection. These cases are important steps in raising awareness about the relations between personal freedom and property. The future of property rights will depend in large part on the willingness of liberal judges and justices who may not have high regard for private property but may not fear to venture into the turbulent waters of judicial activism to protect property rights when they coincide with preferred rights.[21]

PRIVATE PROPERTY AND FREE EXPRESSION

It is not likely that land rights will soon be protected with the same zeal as free speech, but at least courts in the 1980s acknowledged that protecting expression may require protecting property.[22] "Government shouldn't be allowed," Stephen Chapman has declared, "to use regulatory tools designed for traffic control to impose thought control."[23] But life is not so simple. An ordinance that controls the location and hours of bookstores to reduce neighborhood congestion or traffic distractions may impair free expression as well as economic rights of the owners. In *Metromedia, Inc. v. San Diego*,[24] for example, the Supreme Court overturned a ban on billboards because of concern that legitimate speech interests would be curtailed.[25] The California court struck down an ordinance forbidding nude entertainment because the bumps and grinds of the dancer in *Morris v. Municipal Court (People)*[26] fell under the rubric of free expression. Even when courts side with the government, the standards the government must meet are higher than in regulatory cases not implicating preferred rights. Expressive elements have enabled owners and users of property to gain a degree of protection unusual for an economic use of property. The Supreme Court has indicated, for example, that "adult" entertainment establishments may be dispersed or concentrated in a municipality but may not be entirely eliminated.[27] In contrast, Mandelker has noted, "no doctrine in zoning law requires ample opportunity for particular commercial uses. The Courts have not adopted an 'adequate number of sites' doctrine for bakeries, for example."[28] Some commentators have suggested that land use regulations restricting adult entertainment should be subject to the highest level of judicial scrutiny, the strict scrutiny test, under which a government restriction is struck down unless shown to be necessary to promote a compelling state interest.[29]

Most state courts have come to accept that aesthetic concerns alone, absent impacts on public health or safety, may justify regulation of property.[30] But imposing public standards restricts expression of individual tastes. Ordinances may prohibit certain architectural styles, or require that the design of a building or a sign be approved by a public commission,[31] for example. Historical preservation regulations can require maintenance of building facades, forbid modifications, and even specify use of certain materials. John Costonis has criticized aesthetic and historic regulation for preserving "emotional stability" at the cost of creative freedom.[32] One town, according to Richard Babcock, "simply stated that in any block no house 'shall be substantially similar or substantially dissimilar from any other house.' " As he said, "Many courts have upheld such nonsense."[33] In a dispute admittedly not involving high art, a New York judge upheld a regulation that banned clotheslines in front yards because, he said, it "simply proscribes conduct which is unnecessarily offensive to the visual sensibilities of the average person."[34] Aesthetic regulations have mushroomed in recent years, and as more courts are forced to consider the ramifications for expressive freedom, it is likely that constitutional limits will grow.

REGULATION AND RELIGION

The religious uses of property are just beginning to get special dispensation, so to speak, from the courts. As land use controls have become more extensive, they have begun to intrude on the functioning of churches.[35] In New York City, for example, a historic preservation ordinance drew a court challenge because of the financial burden it imposed on a church struggling to fund its religious activities while maintaining its old structure.[36] And as churches branch out from religious activities, their endeavors may provoke conflicts with governments accustomed to regulating economic or property interests with little restraint.[37] Gradually, the free exercise clause and its state constitutional counterparts are creating a foundation for uses of private property by religious groups,[38] and the cases point out how land use may be tied to basic personal freedoms. In *Church of Latter Day Saints v. Amos*,[39] the Supreme Court concluded that the free exercise clause permitted a Mormon church to discriminate on the basis of religion when hiring employees for nonreligious, nonprofit activities. An injunction against a church day-care center violated the First Amendment, a Missouri appellate court ruled.[40] Susan Goldberg has argued that ordinances that require special permits for homeless shelters violate freedom of religion because housing the homeless is a "fundamental religious obligation."[41]

The free exercise clause is only half the constitutional story when it comes to activities related to religion. The establishment clause has a quite different effect, keeping the church out of the state rather than the state out of the church. As such, it does not provide a basis for constitutional protection of property uses. But it can limit the purposes a government may serve and the methods it may employ in controlling the use of land. Grendel's Den, a watering hole in Cambridge, Massachusetts, successfully challenged the denial of its liquor license based on the objection of a nearby church. In *Larkin v. Grendel's Den, Inc.*,[42] the Supreme Court ruled that giving local churches a veto over the location of bars was too great an entanglement of church and state. A business serving liquor normally would not have a constitutional leg to stand on, the court made clear. The bar benefited simply because the city picked the wrong reason to deny the permit.

EQUALITY, FREEDOM, AND PROPERTY

Land use regulation can be a tool for perpetuating inequality. When a large housing development is denied, perhaps a wealthy developer will suffer a setback. But so will the families and individuals who were seeking an opportunity to live in that community. When home occupations are forbidden, the livelihoods of many people may be hurt. The courts have given two basic responses to the inegalitarian implications of land use controls. The first is the liberal, low-grid route of limiting the reach of governmental control. Regulations that deny opportunities to individuals or preferred groups may be struck down so that the state does not create or perpetuate inequality. In *Cleburne v. Cleburne Living Center*,[43] the Supreme Court struck down an ordinance that required neighborhood approval of group homes for the mentally retarded, reasoning that such a broad prohibition was not a rational way to deal with concerns about traffic, crowding, and the like. The court professed to be only using the traditional rational basis test, yet is seems clear that a special concern for the retarded guided the decision. Several commentators have urged that the courts apply stricter scrutiny whenever land use regulations affect the retarded.[44]

In Pennsylvania, the state supreme court has struck down bans on multifamily housing[45] and acreage requirements.[46] Although those decisions have been predominantly based on substantive property rights, the court has also reasoned that the opportunities of the less affluent land users who wish to live in the suburbs merit protection. For a brief period during its assault on exclusionary zoning, the New Jersey Supreme Court also supported this liberal strategy of removing government obstacles to equal opportunity in housing.[47] Regulations forbidding mobile homes have been criticized for restoring freedom[48] and limiting housing choices for the poor.[49] The Pennsylvania Court struck down such a ban in *Geiger v. Zoning Hearing Board of North Whitehall*.[50] When regulation is identified with exclusion, private property rights may be appreciated as a common basis with which egalitarians and libertarians can resist the constraints, or grid, of hierarchy.

But the New Jersey court primarily has taken a second, very different tack in combating inequality. Although the state supreme court assailed the inegalitarian evils of land use regulation, the court decided the cure required more regulation. Rather than allow individual owners and consumers to determine housing patterns, the court ordered that each developing community accommodate a correct share of low-income residents.[51] The *Mount Laurel* doctrines do not bode well for the pursuit of equality and liberty through rights, but the difficulties of interpreting[52] and implementing[53] the court's will and questions about the legitimacy of the court's involvement in policy-making[54] have deterred other state courts from following the New Jersey lead. According to a study of the aftermath of *Mount Laurel II*, "Perhaps the worst burden overhanging the *Mount Laurel* process is the manner of its birth. With the judicial involvement came intense controversy, . . . which has discouraged politicians everywhere and judges outside of New Jersey from embracing the approach."[55]

PRIVACY AND PROPERTY

Since property provides an area of autonomy for the individual, it is not surprising that the use of real property (buildings and land) entails issues of privacy. As with freedom of speech, property owners have been able to gain court hearings, and even victories, in dispute that otherwise likely would have been dismissed. Indeed, the case that began the Supreme Court's modern era of attention to property issues was a privacy case, *Belle Terre v. Boraas*,[56] in which it was argued that an ordinance restricting the number of unrelated individuals who could live in a home intruded on a private, personal decision. The Court upheld the regulation under the minimal security it was accustomed to applying to land use regulations. But three years later, in *Moore v. East Cleveland*,[57] the Court rejected a zoning ordinance that regulated the composition of family households and explicitly relied on a substantive due process right of privacy. The tradition of extending constitutional protection to natural rights to use property had returned, although now embedded in the language of privacy.

Of course, that does not ensure that the courts will be quick to enforce landowner rights. In California, for example, the supreme court has been indifferent to many incursions on the privacy of property owners, such as the demands by the California Coastal Commission for public easements. But many state courts, including those of California, have used a right of privacy to strike down restrictions on home occupancy and group homes. Although the courts have tolerated the designation of single-family zones to be composed only of detached houses, state courts often have balked when municipalities sought to limit "families" to traditional concepts of the nuclear family and in some cases have gone beyond the protections provided by the U.S. Supreme Court. In *Santa Barbara v. Adamson,*[58] the California Supreme court found that the state constitution protected the right of unrelated people to live together. The high courts of Michigan[59] and New York[60] have made similar rulings. A California court held that the state constitutional right of privacy protected a group home, which in this case provided custodial care for children.[61] As Tamila Jensen has pointed out, the line between restricting land uses and excluding land users is thin at best: "From its very inception, 'residential character' implied certain values, a certain kind of residential character, and even a certain kind of resident [nuclear family in detached home]. . . . It is a short, logical and often irresistible step from separating and limiting *uses* to separating and limiting *who can use.*"[62]

DUSTING OFF THE TAKINGS CLAUSE

The takings clause gives the clearest constitutional protection to landowners: If the government covets your property, it must pay for it. Takings doctrine is thus less susceptible to the frequent criticism of substantive due process, that it is unmoored to any constitutional standard. The U.S. Constitution does not even include the word *substantive* in the due process clause, let alone specify what it might mean. The Constitution does, however, clearly say that government may not take property without just compensation. Just what constitutes a taking, a public use, and just compensation is not immediately apparent, but the level of specificity is similar to that of the expressive and criminal rights clauses, which the courts regularly interpret and enforce. Protection of landowner rights, then, can be compatible with the *United States v. Carolene Products Co.*[63] dictum that the court should support only specific clauses of the constitution and need not raise the specter of a rogue court.

However, the takings clause gathered judicial dust for decades, ritually acknowledged but rarely enforced, as the Supreme Court was loath to find any regulation of land to require compensation. But the Supreme Court gave the clause renewed luster in two cases in June of 1987. In *First English Evangelical Lutheran Church of*

Glendale v. Los Angeles County,[64] the Court made clear that takings of property, even if temporary and regulatory, required compensation. That modest ruling sent tremors through the regulatory community[65] as it was the most emphatic statement on behalf of landowner rights that the court had made in six decades. *First English* "has been hailed universally by the development community and has driven municipal officials to the nadir of melancholy," according to Victor Delle Donne.[66] It was as if Lassie had clearly pronounced, "Give me a bone, please." The statement was unremarkable, but the context made it dramatic.

First English finally laid to rest the holding of the California Supreme Court that regulatory takings would never require compensation because to do so might constrain land use regulation.[67] Other states had required compensation for confiscatory regulations based on both state and federal constitutions. In *Burrows v. Keene,*[68] for example, the New Hampshire Supreme Court ruled that a regulation that effectively forbade development of a parcel was a taking requiring compensation.[69]

Requiring governments to pay for takings will not secure rights or add any burden to land use planners unless the courts find actual takings. The Supreme Court made a foray into the muddy waters of defining a taking soon after *First English* by ruling in *Nollan v. California Coastal Commission*[70] that demanding a public easement without a clear relationship to the impact of the proposed land use was a taking. The state could take coastal property from private owners, but it must pay for it. The case was atypical in that it involved a state-sanctioned physical invasion by the public. But Justice Scalia's requirement that there be a nexus between the condition imposed and the impact of a property use can be applied to the myriad exactions that commonly are imposed on property owners.[71]

The greatest impact of *Nollan* is in the federal courts and in states such as California that had given the landowner scant constitutional support. But if the Supreme Court proves reluctant ever to find an actual taking, the victory in *Nollan* will be prove to be more exception than rule. One year after *Nollan,* the Court returned to its forgiving stance toward government when it declined to find a rent control ordinance, which put a special burden on landlords with low-income tenants, to be taking.[73] But *First English* and *Nollan* have a significance beyond specific legal victories for landowners. As courts grapple with the regulatory takings problem, they engender a dialogue on the role property serves in protecting individual rights, and this can have a ripple effect of stimulating more consideration in legal and policy circles of the nature of property rights.

MAKING SENSE OF THE TAKINGS CLAUSE

The confusion by courts of takings doctrine with substantive due process has lessened the effectiveness of federal and state takings clauses as shields against government intrusion. The distinction is important because otherwise two independent constitutional protections are reduced to one, so that meeting a single standard absolves government from its obligation to meet both. And when that single standard is watered down to permit virtually anything to pass, as is the case under the rational basis test, the rights become empty shells. As Holmes warned of the prohibition on takings without compensation, "When this seemingly absolute protection is found to be qualified by the police power, the natural tendency of human nature is to extend the qualification more and more until at last private property disappears."[74] Although property has not disappeared, Holmes anticipated the fate that befell *rights* to use property in the decades since the New Deal. Even commentators generally supportive of regulatory measures such as David Callies have bemoaned the collapse of two constitutional protections into one. "The United States Supreme Court," he wrote, "blithely and uncritically continues to equate the power to condemn and the power to forbid."[74]

The takings clause should be considered first by the courts, lest substantive due process be used to excuse takings. But the Supreme Court has typically found that a restriction that advances a legitimate state interest (the substantive due process test) is not a taking.[75] The issues may often overlap, but to coincide is not to be identical. The takings question should be whether the restrictions imposed on a property owner's rights are so extensive as to constitute a taking of some of those rights. Whether the actions by the government are sufficiently related to an appropriate objective is the due process question. In the first instance, the emphasis is on the harm to the owner, in the latter, it is on the legitimacy of the governmental act. The issue of the government's justification, I will suggest below, may be incorporated into the public use question once a taking has been found in order to decide whether the taking will be permitted. To pass constitutional muster, an action by the state should surmount both obstacles.

A governmental action that bears a sufficient relation to a legitimate objective may still impose such a burden on the property owner as to deprive rights and thus require compensation. What can be condemned (with compensation through eminent domain) cannot always be forbidden (through regulations pursuant to the police power). A municipality may have the power to condemn and purchase property for a park, but it does not follow that a private owner may be forbidden without compensation from using his property in any way other than as a park. A regulatory restriction such as a ban on rebuilding in fire-prone areas may be found to have sufficient justification under the police power yet so restrict rights of the owner as to constitute a taking. Substantive due process and takings pertain to two different questions: First, how strong is the relationship of a restriction on property to the demands of the general welfare, and second, how substantial is the interference with the rights of the owner? A particular measure may be essential or frivolous, and its impact on the owner may be severe or trivial.

Legitimate police power regulations have been considered immune from compensation demands. Even in *Nollan,* the sole case during the 1980s in which the Supreme Court found that a regulatory body had taken an owner's property, Justice Scalia indicated that a ban on rebuilding a coastal home instead of the demand for an easement would be a permissible exercise of the police power and would not require payment despite its confiscatory impact.

Because of the virtual blanket exception for police power regulation provided under the lenient due process test of minimal rationality, courts can dismiss takings claims without seriously weighing the impact on the rights of the landowner. This creates a logical absurdity: The Constitution requires that any taking of property serve a public use, which the Court considers synonymous with a public purpose. Thus, the class of regulations promoting a public purpose would overlap with the class of takings for public uses. But if the action serves a public purpose, it is not considered a taking, and thus no compensation need be paid. The classes of public purposed regulation and takings become mutually exclusive, the distinction hinging on whether the government has chosen to offer compensation. Not surprisingly, the Supreme Court has never found in half a century a regulatory act (absent a physical invasion) to require payment.[76]

The power to decide whether compensation is required has been abdicated to the legislatures and regulatory agencies. When they wish to use the eminent domain power to condemn with compensation, the elastic interpretation of the public use clause legitimates whatever action they wish to take. If they wish to avoid paying (and in a democracy, where the taxlevyers may be voted out by the taxpayers, there is great incentive to do so), their actions will be upheld under the equally indulgent standard for police power regulation. Using minimal substantive due process to decide whether there has been any taking in effect exempts government from the just compensation mandate.

The point of protecting rights is to protect the freedom of the individual, not to tell government what to do. The takings clause logically focuses on the detriment to the individual by asking what has been deprived. Substantive due process, in contrast, is preoccupied with the rationality and perhaps even the wisdom of governmental actions. Critics may argue that courts should not protect property rights because it requires butting in and telling legislatures what they should do. There is a much greater risk of judicial policy making under due process analysis than under the takings clause. If we keep the emphasis on the harm to the rights of the individual through takings analysis, courts will limit the legislative power only when it is used to substantially deprive personal freedom.

FREEDOM TO USE PROPERTY

Ability to choose, not the security of profit, marks freedom. Choice is what allows an owner to create what he wishes with his property, to reflect his character, his aspirations, his beliefs. And freedom provides the test of responsibility, that one can decide what to do, make the effort, and live with the consequences. Whether we consider the importance of property for developing character, personal expression, generating political independence, or economic entrepreneurship, it is autonomy in use that makes it possible. Yet it is this freedom that has been most ignored by the courts.

As Elizabeth Patterson[77] has shown, under current doctrine some property rights, such as the rights to hold and transfer title to property, receive greater protection than other property rights. The power to exclude other individuals from one's land has withstood the erosive force of New Deal jurisprudence, as can be seen in *Loretto v. Teleprompter Manhattan CATV Corp.*[78] and *Nollan.* Although the Supreme Court has been cool toward "economic" rights, the economic aspects of property have been given some respect by the court. The denial of "reasonable, investment-backed expectations" has been one ground for finding a taking, although the court has been reluctant to do so.[79]

The court has been least protective of the right to control the use of one's property. Under current takings doctrine, a restriction on land use may not be a taking if it leaves the owner with at least one "reasonably beneficial use," whether or not the owner wishes to pursue that use. This confuses the power to decide use with economic expectations. If a state deposits a ready-made apartment building on an individual's land and orders her to operate it, it has effectively destroyed her rights to use land, even if it guarantees her an adequate profit. In contrast, speech rights are not violated only when no "reasonably beneficial speech" is permitted. Freedom lies in choosing what to say, not in having state permission to express "correct" speech.

TAKING PROPERTY THROUGH BURDENSOME PROCEDURES

Regulatory commissions have learned well that they do not have to give a final, unequivocal no to prevent land uses. Governments may skirt compensation requirements if they avoid making substantive decisions; that is the lesson that emerges from the long series of takings cases[80] culminating in *First English*. For years the Court ducked the compensation issue by claiming that it could not determine whether a taking had occurred because not every possible use of the property had been explicitly forbidden, so it was conceivable that some proposal might someday be approved. Of one such opinion, Michael Berger complained that the court was "out of touch with the real world. Planning commissions do not make it their business to tell property owners specifically how they will be allowed to develop their property."[81]

No matter how many times an owner is shot down before a regulatory panel, there always remains the possibility that someday the owner will discover the golden key, the land use proposal that wins approval. It can be "darned difficult" to allege a taking in court, according to David Callies, unless the owner has been "denied a lot of permits" for "virtually all potentially economic uses."[82] Regulatory procedures become difficult to attack when officials engage in complicated stalling tactics without ever directly saying "absolutely not, ever."[83] "Often the problem is not a discrete regulation," Berger and Gideon Kanner have observed, "but a course of conduct, involving moratoria, delays, broken promises, unreasonable demands for 'dedication' of property or 'donation' of money in lieu thereof, chilling publicity, bad faith, and the like."[84] The regulatory process itself, as well as the outcomes, can deprive owners of the use of their land. The courts should recognize this danger and develop standards for when obstructive procedures effectively deny the use of land. As the use of land is being denied, this becomes a takings issue rather than simply procedural due process.

The potential for procedural denial of land use has increased in recent years. In response to charges that regulation was dominated by an elite few, courts and legislatures moved to open up the administrative process to incorporate more voices.[85] At the same time, major regulatory initiatives such as state and national environmental policy acts, wetlands protection legislation, and statewide open-space plans, have placed unprecedented burdens on local and state regulators to investigate and mitigate a myriad potential environmental effects.[86] Regulatory officials have far more to do and many more voices that must be heard, and the result is a lengthy, complex decision process. This can leave the owner as a lone voice in a very deep wilderness with no clear way out.

The result of weak protections of landowner rights and flexible open procedures is that regulation often becomes a "monumental crap game," according to Berger and Kanner.[87] Accommodating everyone's opinion, doing extensive studies to show that every potential effect of a land use has been anticipated and mitigated, and completing a series of hearings and approvals can render property effectively useless for a seemingly endless period. The process can deprive property rights even when officials are just trying to do their jobs; When there is animosity toward the owner or the land uses she proposes, the potential for abuse is greater. Communities opposed to certain land uses can use preliminary studies to impose "de facto moratoria. . . . The planning process postpones for months or years the development capability of property."[88] Even Norman Williams, a vigorous defender of land use controls, and his coauthors have concluded that intentional delays are "pervasive" and that abuses of the regulatory process are "ubiquitous, vicious and devoid of any resemblance of procedural due process."[89] Not only do these abuses offend notions of fair play; they also can deny the use of property just as surely as a quick, emphatic rejection of a permit.

Courts often have indulged the procedural fiction that conditions imposed on land use are "voluntarily" accepted. It is therefore ostensibly the owner and not the government that has restricted use of property, and thus there has been no taking. Alas, when courts are apathetic, property owners may have little choice but to play along with the manipulative strategies of regulatory officials. If an applicant wishes to have her proposal approved, she often must accept the modifications and conditions recommended by planning staff. She cannot afford to say no if the alterative is to abandon the proposed use. Yet courts cling to the myth that the government and the owner are like independent parties freely contracting in an open market. In *In the Matter of Egg Harbor Associates (Bayshore Center)*,[90] for example, the New Jersey Supreme Court upheld the imposition of socioeconomic quotas on developments under the purview of the state Department of Environmental Protection on the grounds that the owners were free to reject the conditions. But such a choice is hollow. Each governmental unit, be it a town or a state agency, has a monopoly on the regulatory process, and the owner has nowhere else to go for approval.

BRINGING FAIRNESS BACK TO PROCEDURE

Three rules would allow the courts to consider whether procedural delays and denials amount to takings. First, the courts should drop the fiction that the acceptance of conditions is voluntary. Discretionary conditions attached to land use permits or contained in ordinances should be evaluated under the same standards as mandatory regulations. Second, regulatory commissions, when they deny a permit, should be assumed to have denied all use of the property unless they have specified as part of the legal record examples of land uses that would meet with their approval. They would then not be able to deprive an owner of the use of his property while escaping judicial scrutiny by requiring an applicant to reapply endlessly for approvals that would never be granted. The designated alternatives would help the courts determine whether the restrictions on the owner were severe enough to require compensation.[91] If a regulatory commission denied a use proposal without indicating a specific set of alternatives that would be approved, it should be assumed that the government has denied all use of the property and compensation awarded.

These two rules could further discourage governments from making decisions. By never taking final action on applications, neither denying nor approving with conditions, officials could prevent the use of land while delaying indefinitely the day of constitutional reckoning. The third recommendation is that courts allow an owner to show that administrative delays have denied the use of property, contrary to Rehnquist's suggestion in *First English* that "normal" delays and uncertainties could not constitute a taking. The courts could then decide what compensation would be due and how soon a regulatory decision must be rendered to avoid further obligations.

The Supreme Court is likely to remain divided about the extent of substantive rights of landowners, but procedural issues may attract greater consensus. As it cautiously returns to the field of land use regulation, the Court may give more thought to the Byzantine procedures that characterize many of these cases. Giving owners a fair shake can appeal to egalitarian and hierarchical concern for fairness and dignity. While the cultures would clash over the substantive standards of what constitutes a taking, it does not promote the ideal of any culture, except perhaps that of despotism, to perpetuate an unending regulatory maze.

PUBLIC USE

The threat that payment may be required may constrain regulators from excessive demands or abusive procedures. But when a government is willing to compensate and employs the eminent domain power to condemn property, the only constitutional limit is that a "public use" must be served. The Supreme Court has proclaimed that a "public use" is the same as a "public purpose" under the due process test.[92] Whether one prefers this broad view or a more literal interpretation of public use, the state must provide some rational justification for its action. A strict interpretation of public use would greatly narrow the scope for legitimate governmental takings. Property could be taken only if it would be owned and used by the public, as for highways and army bases. Such an interpretation might be most compatible with libertarian landowner rights[93] and with plain-meaning constitutional interpretation, but it would eliminate whole categories of restrictions that persons of a more hierarchical or egalitarian bent might consider important for the public, such as aesthetic regulation or rent controls.

On the other hand, it can be argued that there should be no substantive limit on the power of eminent domain. From a hierarchical perspective, government might properly expect private owners to surrender their property for the greater good of the group. And requiring compensation would in itself discourage governmental excess. There remains, however, room for considerable abuse if the government can forcefully purchase any attribute of property it wishes. The city of Oakland even sought to condemn the Oakland Raiders football team to keep the idols of local fans from fleeing to the sunny South.[94] Another questionable use of eminent domain was upheld in *Poletown Neighborhood Council v Detroit*[95] by the Michigan Supreme Court. General Motors desired property for a proposed new plant, so Detroit simply condemned the land and sold it to the company.[96] In *Hawaii Housing Authority v. Midkiff*,[97] the U.S. Supreme Court upheld a state plan to force large private landowners to sell homeowners the lots on which their houses stood. This transfer of private property through government coercion has been criticized as an abuse of the eminent domain power,[98] and certainly the Court stretched the limit of "public use."[99] If the legitimate ends and means of government are without limit, property may be condemned and purchased at any time for any purpose. This is where the great abuses permitted by the "any conceivable rational basis" test of substantive due process comes home to roost in takings analysis. Even if we grant that the public use limits should be roughly equivalent with considerations of public purpose, we need not go to the extreme of virtual abdication.

A literal interpretation of the public use clause could limit government more than would be acceptable from different cultural perspectives. But a literal view also might be too expansive. Suppose, for example, a city wishes to practice its fire-fighting techniques, so evicts a family from its home, purchases the property, and burns the building to the ground. It might be a valid public use and the loss compensated, but still the government went too far, I would argue, by forcing the sale rather than competing on the open market. The reasons why the city coveted that particular piece of property might not be substantial enough to justify its action. A standard is needed that will guard against compensated abuses of property rights.

PUTTING THE RATIONALITY BACK IN RATIONALITY REVIEW

There are two ways constitutional limits may be placed on compensated condemnations. The first would be to put some bite into substantive due process and equal protection review and require that when an exercise of the eminent domain power has been challenged or a regulatory taking found, the governmental action must pass both of these separate tests. Whether the action passed or not, partial payment for a temporary taking would be required. If it passed, the government could pay for a permanent taking if it wished to proceed.

The alternative approach would be to incorporate a substantive standard of rationality into public use review. An advantage would be that rationality would not be considered until after a taking had been found. The first question would be the extent of the deprivation of the owner's rights, not the rationality of the act, so that takings would be less likely to slip by uncompensated. Incorporating rationality review into the public use question also would take the court out of the business of critically reviewing trivial legislation. The court would consider the legislative motives only when significant deprivations of property rights had occurred. If on the other hand we are concerned that citizens not be henpecked by trivial regulation, we may wish to emphasize a separate due process test for land use regulations, to be passed even when no taking has occurred.

If substantive rationality review is to be an effective limit, it must use a higher standard than the "any conceivable rational basis" test used by the Court since the New Deal to justify challenged governmental regulations of property. In recent years, the Supreme Court has had second thoughts about its leniency and on occasion has struck down a governmental action even under the bargain-basement scrutiny of rational basis. *Cleburne* was a notable example in which the Court concluded that the mentally retarded did not deserve special protection but that the ordinance, a restriction on group homes, failed even under the weakest standard of review. Rationality with teeth, as in *Cleburne*, requires the justices to look at the reasons proffered for a governmental restriction rather than create their own reasons and reject those that are clearly facades for unacceptable intentions. The vast majority of governmental restrictions would likely survive such a test, but particularly egregious abuses would fail. Yet even this modest step was condemned by Justice Marshall in his *Cleburne* concurrence as a "small but regrettable step back toward the days of *Lochner v. New York*."[100]

A rational basis test that is taken seriously would not be adequate to ensure justice for the landowner, for reason is not equivalent to fairness. If rights do not outweigh reason or rationality, rights are reduced to utilitarian conveniences to be tolerated only when government does not find them troublesome. For example, zoning a landowner's property for open space, effectively preventing him from using it, is a quite rational method of preserving space without taxing the public, although it would be unjust. Likewise, suppressing freedom of speech or stripping criminal suspects of their rights may be rational and effective ways to protect community order, but that does not make them constitutional.

A SUBSTANTIAL STANDARD FOR SUBSTANTIVE REVIEW

One way to avoid abuses of rationality would be to extend the highest scrutiny—the "compelling interest" test now used for preferred rights such as free speech—to all rights. No property could be taken unless it was necessary to promote a compelling governmental interest. Bernard Siegan,[101] Douglas Kmiec,[102] and other critics sympathetic to libertarianism have proposed that land use controls be struck down unless necessary to achieve a "vital and pressing" governmental interest, perhaps a slightly less demanding standard. Such a high hurdle is unlikely to win friends except among libertarians. It may be that property is as essential as other rights that receive strict protection such as privacy and protection of favored groups. But it is more important that property rights receive serious protection (a point on which egalitarians and hierarchists might concur with libertarians) than that all remnants of a double standard be obliterated, to which egalitarians would object. Mandelker, for example, would apply the vital and pressing interest test in land use cases only for parties (minorities, the disabled) and rights (expression, privacy) prominent on the egalitarian agenda.[103] Even if a double standard remained, property rights could receive significant protection.

The slippery standard of midlevel constitutional scrutiny, under which legislation is required to bear a substantial relationship to an important governmental objective, would protect liberal property rights while still accommodating considerable regulation.[104] The substantial relationship is the most crucial of the two factors, as it eliminates two possibilities: First, that the rights of the landowner will be limited for naught when there is but a remote relation between the hardship imposed on the owner and the governmental objective being pursued. Second, that reasons might be cavalierly proffered while the actual purposes of the legislation go unspoken. It may be more acceptable for a regulatory board to claim it is only seeking to safeguard the environment, not exclude socially undesirables. Yet large-lot zoning, for example, may have only a remote or

uncertain relation to the stated goal and a direct relation to the il-
licit goal. Requiring a substantial relationship makes it easier to
trace the actual purposes of the legislation and focus on its likely
effects. Requiring an important governmental objective gives the
state the flexibility to pursue goals that may not be "compelling" or
"pressing" while eliminating the restriction of rights in the pursuit
of illegitimate or trivial goals. Since the means-end relation is more
crucial than the goal, the next best alternative would be to require
a substantial relationship to a legitimate purpose.

Of the jurisdictions I have studied, Pennsylvania comes closest
to applying a substantial relationship test in land use disputes. Although the court sometimes speaks the language of rational basis, it
is clear that it is searching for more substantial justifications than,
say, the California court. Constitutional decisions in Pennsylvania
roughly have been split in half, with landowners about as likely to
lose as to win. There is a certain crude justice in that, and the outcome of particular cases hinges closely on the facts involved. The
drawback of the Pennsylvania court's approach in the 1980s was
that it relied on substantive due process rather than takings analysis
when evaluating most regulations. Instead of compensation, an
owner was more likely to secure an injunction against the town and
possibly a builder's remedy authorizing him to go ahead with his development plans.

That approach is inferior to requiring compensation for regulatory takings, I have argued, because it can be both too stringent
and too lenient. It encourages meddling with the means and ends of
government, as when the Pennsylvania court required that a town
meet a high standard of efficiency in services,[105] without first considering whether the harm to the property owner is sufficient to justify interference with the democratic process. And the builder's
remedy may force a local government to accept an owner's plan
when other alternatives might be more acceptable to the town and
still meet constitutional standards. On the other hand, the most
common remedy under due process, an injunction, may not deter a
government from subsequent unconstitutional actions. Encourag-
ingly, the Pennsylvania court recently adopted takings analysis for
land use controls, emphasizing the burden imposed on the owner
rather than the rationality of the governmental action.[106]

The U.S. Supreme Court took a step toward midlevel scrutiny
in *Nollan* when it required that a condition placed on the use of
property bear a substantial relationship to the governmental interest that might justify denying use of the property. Scalia's search for
real, not imaginary, justifications for the easement demanded of the

Nollans drew a rebuke from Brennan that "the Court imposes a standard of precision for the exercise of a State's police power that has been discredited for the better part of this century."[107] Perhaps not for the better part of the century but certainly for the longest part, and *Nollan* is a welcome step toward returning common sense to constitutional adjudication. If the Court considered the government's justification second, after deciding whether the deprivation of the owner's right had been so severe as to constitute a taking, then truly the jurisprudential light at the end of the takings tunnel would be seen.

Midlevel scrutiny generates neither the moral fervor nor the legal certainty of the "any conceivable rational basis" and strict scrutiny tests. No rights or parties can be universally worshiped or condemned. Where strict scrutiny is white and rational basis black, midlevel scrutiny shows only gray. If we yearn for artificial certainty, the simplistic notions of rational basis or strict scrutiny are desirable. If our goal is accommodation of competing political cultures within a liberal framework of rights, a more subtle, particularistic alternative such as the substantial relationship test is required. That test would decide whether government might proceed with a taking once a substantial deprivation of rights had been found. It would not excuse the refusal to pay compensation.

The delineation of landowner rights will never be an easy task. At their best, midlevel takings and due process review not only give each party a fair hearing but also raise the quality of the cultural and legal dialogue on land use controls and rights. Seeking substantial reasons requires that assertions not only be stated but also supported, whereas the "any conceivable rational basis" test encourages vapid doctrine and creates a void easily filled by arbitrary state control.

PROPERTY RIGHTS AND THE THREE CULTURES

The makers of our Constitution undertook to
secure conditions favorable to the pursuit of
happiness. . . . They conferred, as against the
government, the right to be let alone—the
most comprehensive of rights and the right
most valued by civilized man.
                              —Justice Brandeis[108]

Property rights are not just for libertarians. As long as individual dignity and freedom are valued, there will be a role for property rights. Attempting to separate rights of property from personal rights has proved difficult at best and ultimately unsatisfactory. Property is not simply the domain of the developer and the corporation. Young families and retirees have property; minorities and disabled persons have property; property, creative and real, can be treasured by artists, writers and political activists. Even developers are human and merit constitutional protection.[109]

Property interests are universal in a liberal democracy, and property rights can accommodate each of the fundamental cultures. If there is a place for everything in the hierarchy, there is a proper sphere for personal autonomy, however limited. I may answer to king and general yet still be lord of my modest manor. And property rights, by protecting against arbitrary or capricious treatment, can restrain officials from exceeding or abusing their special roles. Freedom is essential if equality is to be freed from the shackles of coercion, and liberty of property may ultimately be inseparable from other individual freedoms such as expression. Egalitarianism and libertarianism, as low-grid cultures, may be united by a mutual regard for equal opportunity and self-government. Hierarchy, however, may exclude both democracy and individual freedom if all is dependent on governance by elites. But rule by philosopher-kings would be a rejection of the liberal tradition. If we assume that the introduction of hierarchical concepts in American public policy, such as the prediction and regulation of land use effects by government specialists, is an attempt to build some order and community within the liberal framework, limits on the reach of government become crucial to the legitimacy of hierarchy in the polity.

Separation of powers provides a basic check on domination by a segment of government.[110] Williams and his coauthors argued that governments should not be required to pay for confiscatory regulations because to do so would "upset . . . the delicate balance between co-equal branches of government that has served well for 200 years."[111] Yet balance requires two active participants, and the U.S. Supreme Court got off the seesaw of landowner justice before the New Deal and has only hesitantly returned to the playground. There is no "balance" when the great weight of legislative and executive government can be pressed upon the property owners while the judicial branch of government sits on the sidelines. When the courts close their eyes to abuses of property rights, they have abandoned their role in republican government.[112] If hierarchy can coexist with liberal freedom, there must be a role for the courts, and the individual.

Feudal-type property restrictions can impede the security of freedom at the core of liberalism. Yet land use regulation cannot go home again to the indulgent days of the New Deal judicial regime. The perception that the government has unlimited power to restrict the "economic" interests of landowners has been seriously shaken by recent court decisions. The regulatory state will continue to be pervasive, but now legislators and administrators will have to include the constitution in their calculations.

The courts are on a journey of discovery, rethinking the limits of governmental power over the landowner. Underlying the judicial debate is the conflict between what I have characterized as the three cultures of the American polity—libertarianism, hierarchy, and egalitarianism. Although government regulation of land is likely to remain ubiquitous, the thoughtful discussion of rights and powers can encourage respect for rights, appreciation of the nuances of limited government, and understanding of the centrality of property to personal liberty and liberty to the American polity. The growing dialogue on property rights can help keep the excesses of democracy from extinguishing the flame of liberalism.

PART IV: APPENDIXES

Appendix A

Pennsylvania Supreme Court Constitutional Land Use Cases and New Jersey Exclusionary Cases

PENNSYLVANIA CASES

Hughes v. Pennsylvania Department of Transportation, 514 Pa. 300, 523 A.2d 747 (1987)

Ridley Arms, Inc. v. Ridley Township, 515 Pa. 542, 531 A.2d 414 (1987)

Western Pennsylvania Socialist Workers 1982 Campaign v. Connecticut General Life Insurance Co., 512 Pa. 23, 515 A.2d 1331 (1986)

Geiger v. Zoning Hearing Board of North Whitehall, 510 Pa. 231, 507 A.2d 361 (1986)

Highland Park Community Club of Pittsburgh v. Zoning Board of Adjustment of Pittsburgh, 509 Pa. 605, 506 A.2d 887 (1986)

Fernley v. Board of Supervisors of Schuylkill Township, 509 Pa. 413, 502 A.2d 585 (1985)

Boundary Drive Associates v. Shrewsbury Board of Supervisors, 507 Pa. 481, 491 A.2d 86 (1985)

In re Appeal of Elocin, Inc., 501 Pa. 348, 461 A.2d 771 (1983)

Layne v. Zoning Board of Adjustment of Pittsburgh, 501 Pa. 224, 460 A.2d 1088 (1983)

In re Appeal of M. A. Kravitz, 501 Pa. 200, 460 A.2d 1075 (1983)

Hopewell Township Board of Supervisors v. Golla, 499 Pa. 246, 452 A.2d 1337 (1982)

Miller & Son Paving, Inc. v. Wrightstown, 499 Pa. 80, 451 A.2d 1002 (1982)

Redevelopment Authority of Oil City v. Woodring, 498 Pa. 180, 445 A.2d 724 (1982)

Hardee's Food Systems, Inc. v. Pennsylvania Department of Transportation, 495 Pa. 514, 434 A.2d 1209 (1981)

Pennsylvania v. Tate, 495 Pa. 158, 432 A.2d 1382 (1981)

National Wood Preservers, Inc. v. Pennsylvania Department of Environmental Resources, 489 Pa. 221, 414 A.2d 37 (1980)

SELECTED PENNSYLVANIA PRECEDENTS

Surrick v. Zoning Hearing Board of Upper Providence, 476 Pa. 182, 382 A.2d 105 (1978)

Willistown v. Chesterdale Farms, Inc., 462 Pa. 445, 341 A.2d 466 (1975)

Appeal of Kit-Mar Builders, 439 Pa. 466, 268 A.2d 765 (1970)

Appeal of Girsh, 437 Pa. 237, 263 A.2d 395 (1970)

National Land and Investment Co. v. Kohn, 419 Pa. 504, 215 A.2d 597 (1965)

NEW JERSEY EXCLUSIONARY CASES

The Hills Development Co. v. Bernards, 103 N.J. 1, 510 A.2d 621 (1986)

In the Matter of Egg Harbor Associates (Bayshore Center), 94 N.J. 358, 464 A.2d 1115 (1983)

Southern Burlington County NAACP v. Mount Laurel (Mount Laurel II), 92 N.J. 158, 456 A.2d 390 (1983)

Pascack Association, Ltd. v. Washington, 74 N.J. 470, 379 A.2d 6 (1977)

Oakwood at Madison, Inc. v. Madison, 72 N.J. 481, 371 A.2d 1192 (1977)

Southern Burlington County NAACP v. Mount Laurel (Mount Laurel I), 67 N.J. 151, 336 A.2d 713 (1975)

Appendix B

California Supreme Court Constitutional Land Use Cases

People v. Superior Court (Lucero), 49 Cal. 3d 14, 774 P.2d 769, 259 Cal. Rptr. 740 (1989)

Russ Building Partnership v. San Francisco, 44 Cal. 3d 839, 750 P.2d 324, 244 Cal. Rptr 682 (1988)

Pennell v. San Jose, 42 Cal. 3d 365, 721 P.2d 1111, 228 Cal. Rptr. 726 (1986)

Halaco Engineering Co. v. South Central Coast Regional Commission, 42 Cal. 3d 52, 720 P.2d 15, 227 Cal. Rptr 667 (1986)

Candid Enterprises, Inc. v. Grossmont Union High School District, 39 Cal. 3d 878, 705 P.2d 876, 218 Cal. Rptr. 303 (1985)

Baker v. Burbank-Glendale-Pasadena Airport Authority, 39 Cal. 3d 862, 705 P.2d 866, 218 Cal. Rptr. 293 (1985)

Griffin Development Co. v. Oxnard, 39 Cal. 3d 256, 703 P.2d 339, 217 Cal. Rptr. 1 (1985)

Redevelopment Agency of Burbank v. Gilmore, 38 Cal. 3d 790, 700 P.2d 794, 214 Cal. Rptr. 904 (1985)

Fisher v. Berkeley, 37 Cal. 3d 644, 693 P.2d 261, 209 Cal. Rptr. 682 (1984)

Pardee Construction Co. v. Camarillo, 37 Cal. 3d 465, 690 P.2d 701, 208 Cal. Rptr. 228 (1984)

Nash v. Santa Monica, 37 Cal. 3d 97, 688 P.2d 894, 207 Cal. Rptr 285 (1984)

Santa Monica Pines, Ltd. v. Rent Control Board of Santa Monica, 35 Cal. 3d 858, 679 P.2d 27, 201 Cal. Rptr. 593 (1984)

Carson Mobilehome Park Owners' Association v. Carson, 33 Cal. 3d 184, 672 P.2d 1297, 197 Cal. Rptr 284 (1983)

Pacific Legal Foundation v. California Coastal Commission, 33 Cal. 3d 158, 655 P.2d 306, 188 Cal. Rptr. 104 (1982)

Los Angeles v. Venice Penisula Properties, 31 Cal. 3d 288, 644 P.2d 782, 182 Cal. Rptr. 599 (1982)

California v. Superior Court (Fogerty), 29 Cal. 3d 240, 625 P.2d 256, 172 Cal. Rptr 713 (1981)

California v. Superior Court (Lyon), 29 Cal. 3d 210, 625 P.2d 239, 172 Cal. Rptr. 696 (1981)

Arnel Development Co. v. Costa Mesa, 28 Cal.3d 511, 620 P.2d 565, 169 Cal. Rptr. 904 (1980)

Perez v. San Bruno, 27 Cal.3d 875, 616 P.2d 1287, 168 Cal. Rptr. 114 (1980)

Santa Barbara v. Adamson, 27 Cal.3d 123, 610 P.2d 436, 164 Cal. Rptr. 539 (1980)

Metromedia, Inc. v. San Diego, 26 Cal.3d 848, 610 P.2d 407, 164 Cal. Rptr. 510 (1980)

White v. County of San Diego, 26 Cal.3d 897, 608 P.2d 728, 163 Cal. Rptr. 640 (1980)

Berkeley v. Superior Court (Santa Fe), 26 Cal.3d 515, 606 P.2d 362, 162 Cal. Rptr. 327 (1980)

270 Appendix B

Los Angeles County v. Berk, 26 Cal.3d 201, 605 P.2d 381, 161 Cal. Rptr. 742 (1980)

RELATED CASES AND SELECTED PRECEDENTS

People v. Mayoff, 42 Cal.3d 1302, 729 P.2d 166, 233 Cal. Rptr. 2 (1986)

Building Industry Association of Southern California, Inc. v. Camarillo, 41 Cal.3d 810, 718 P.2d 68, 226 Cal. Rptr. 81 (1986)

People v. Cook, 41 Cal. 3d 373, 710 P.2d 299, 221 Cal. Rptr. 499 (1985)

National Audobon Society v. Superior Court (Los Angeles Department of Water and Power), 33 Cal.3d 419, 658 P.2d 709, 18 Cal. Rptr. 346 (1983)

Press v. Lucky Stores, 34 Cal.3d, 667 P.2d 704, 193 Cal. Rptr. 900 (1983)

Morris v. Municipal Court (People), 32 Cal.3d 553, 652 P.2d 51, 186 Cal. Rptr. 494 (1982)

Oakland v. Oakland Raiders, 32 Cal.3d 60, 646 P.2d 835, 183 Cal. Rptr. 673 (1982)

Agins v. Tiburon, 24 Cal.3d 266, 598 P.2d 25, 157 Cal. Rptr. 372 (1979)

South Coast Regional Commission v. Gordon, 18 Cal.3d 832, 558 P.2d 867, 135 Cal. Rptr. 781 (1977)

Birkenfeld v. Berkeley, 17 Cal.3d 129, 550 P.2d 1001, 130 Cal. Rptr. 465 (1976)

Associated Home Builders of the Greater Eastbay, Inc., v. Livermore, 18 Cal.3d 582, 557 P.2d 473, 135 Cal. Rptr. 41 (1976)

Marks v. Whitney, 6 Cal.3d 251, 491 P.2d 374, 98 Cal. Rptr. 790 (1971)

Appendix C

United States Supreme Court Constitutional Land Use Cases

Phillips Petroleum Co. v. Mississippi, 484 U.S. 469, 108 S. Ct. 791 (1988)

Pennell v. San Jose, 485 U.S. 1, 108 S. Ct. 849 (1988)

Nollan v. California Coastal Commission, 483 U.S. 825, 107 S. Ct. 3141 (1987)

First English Evangelical Lutheran Church of Glendale v. Los Angeles County, 482 U.S. 304, 107 S. Ct. 2378 (1987)

United States v. Cherokee Nation of Oklahoma, 480 U.S. 700, 107 S. Ct. 1487 (1987)

Keystone Bituminous Coal Association v. Debenedictis, 480 U.S. 470, 107 S. Ct. 1232 (1987)

Arcara v. Cloud Books, 478 U.S. 697, 106 S. Ct. 3172 (1986)

MacDonald, Sommer, & Frates v. Yolo County, 477 U.S. 340, 106 S. Ct. 2561 (1986)

Renton v. Playtime Theatres, 475 U.S. 41, 106 S. Ct. 925 (1986)

United States v. Riverside Bayview Homes, 474 U.S. 121, 106 S. Ct. 455 (1985)

Cleburne v. Cleburne Living Center, 473 U.S. 432, 105 S. Ct. 3249 (1985)

Williamson County Regional Planning Commission v. Hamilton Bank of Johnson City, 473 U.S. 172, 105 S. Ct. 3108 (1985)

Hawaii Housing Authority v. Midkiff, 467 U.S. 229, 104 S. Ct. 2321 (1984)

Kirby Forest Industries, Inc. v. U.S., 467 U.S. 1, 104 S. Ct. 2187 (1984)

Larkin v. Grendel's Den, Inc., 459 U.S. 116, 103 S. Ct. 505 (1982)

Loretto v. Teleprompter Manhattan CATV Corp., 458 U.S. 419, 102 S. Ct. 3164 (1982)

Metromedia, Inc. v. San Diego, 453 U.S. 490, 101 S. Ct. 2882 (1981)

Hodel v. Indiana, 452 U.S. 314, 101 S. Ct. 2376 (1981)

Hodel v. Virginia Surface Mining & Reclamation Association, 452 U.S. 264, 101 S. Ct. 2352 (1981)

Schad v. Mt. Ephraim, 452 U.S. 61, 101 S. Ct. 2176 (1981)

San Diego Gas & Electric Co. v. San Diego, 450 U.S. 621, 101 S. Ct. 1287 (1981)

Agins v. Tiburon, 447 U.S. 255, 100 S. Ct. 2138 (1980)

Pruneyard Shopping Center v. Robins, 447 U.S. 74, 100 S. Ct. 2035 (1980)

RELATED CASES AND SELECTED PRECEDENTS

U.S. v. Dunn, 480 U.S. 294, 107 S. Ct. 1134 (1987)

California v. Ciraulo, 476 U.S. 207, 106 S. Ct. 1809 (1986)

Oliver v. U.S., 466 U.S. 170, 104 S. Ct. 1735 (1984)

Penn Central Transportation. Co. v. New York City, 438 U.S. 104, 98 S. Ct. 2646 (1978)

Moore v. East Cleveland, 431 U.S. 494, 97 S. Ct. 1932 (1977)

Young v. American Mini Theatres, Inc., 427 U.S. 50 (1976)

Belle Terre v. Boraas, 416 U.S. 1, 94 S. Ct. 1536 (1974)

Berman v. Parker, 348 U.S. 26, 75 S. Ct. 98 (1954)

United States v. Causby, 328 U.S. 256 (1946)

United States v. Carolene Products Co., 304 U.S. 144, 58 S. Ct. 778 (1938)

Euclid v. Ambler Realty Co., 272 U.S. 365, 47 S. Ct. 114 (1926)

Pennsylvania Coal Co. v. Mahon, 260 U.S. 393, 43 S. Ct. 158 (1922)

Notes

CHAPTER 1

1. In *United States v. Carolene Products Co.*, 304 U.S. 144 (1938), Justice Stone suggested guidelines by which the Court could distinguish interests that deserved special protection from those that did not, thus creating a rationale for the court's virtual abandonment, in the face of intense political pressure, of property and economic rights. The history of Supreme Court treatment of property rights is reviewed in Chapter 3.

2. All zoning is fundamentally exclusionary. Indeed, that is the idea behind zoning—keeping out uses that some citizens consider undesirable. But when legal scholars and judges refer to exclusionary zoning, it is usually a euphemism for a much narrower category of excluded uses—low- and moderate-income housing. By requiring large lot sizes and minimum floor areas and forbidding multifamily housing, it is argued, communities discriminate against the poor and racial minorities. In *Southern Burlington County NAACP v. Mount Laurel*, 67 N.J. 151, 336 A.2d 713 (1975), the New Jersey Supreme Court found certain restrictive zoning rules to violate the state constitution, and in *Southern Burlington County NAACP v. Mount Laurel*, 92 N.J. 158, 456 A.2d 390 (1983), the court prescribed extensive remedial measures. These cases, known as *Mount Laurel I* and *Mount Laurel II*, and their progeny are discussed in Chapter 4.

3. By "fundamental" I mean the preferred rights that survived the doctrinal purge of the New Deal. Although commonly used, "fundamental rights" is redundant when applied in the constitutional context. By virtue of their inclusion in the constitution, rights are fundamental—prior to and superior to the exercise of governmental power. But the phrase has become popular as a way to distinguish rights that do not offend post–New Deal sensibilities from those that do. Nonfundamental by implication, the latter are placed in a sort of legal limbo, as if they are in the Constitution by accident.

4. *Schad v. Mt. Ephraim*, 452 U.S. 61 (1981).

5. *Larkin v. Grendel's Den,* 459 U.S. 116 (1982).

6. *Cleburne v. Cleburne Living Center,* 473 U.S. 432 (1985).

7. 482 U.S. 304 (1987).

8. 483 U.S. 825 (1987).

9. Dissenting from a decision rejecting a constitutional challenge to a restriction of private land use, Justice Brennan asked, "If a policeman must know the Constitution, then why not a planner?" *San Diego Gas & Electric Co. v. San Diego,* 450 U.S. 621, 662 (1981). Brennan's argument, that governments could be required to pay compensation if their restrictions on the use of private property were too severe, would later be vindicated by the court in *First English.*

10. The initiative process blurs the distinction between statutory advantages and constitutional rights. Some states allow citizens to change their constitutions directly at the polls. But while initiatives may lead to profound changes, the numbers by which they are proposed and passed pale in comparison to legislative statutes and local ordinances. The quantitative difference is so great as to constitute a qualitative distinction. And initiatives, like constitutional provisions, may languish in legal limbo if the courts are reluctant to enforce them.

11. Norman Williams, Jr., *American Planning Law: Land Use and the Police Power* 93 (Princeton: Rutgers, 1974).

12. In Chapter 4, I discuss the different paths Pennsylvania and New Jersey have taken from similar constitutional language.

13. See William J. Brennan, Jr., *State Constitutions and the Protection of Individual Rights,* 90 Harv. L. Rev. 489 (1975). State judges also have been outspoken advocates of reliance on state constitutions. See Hans A. Linde, *First Things First: Rediscovering the States' Bills of Rights,* 9 U. Balt. L. Rev. 379 (1980).

14. See *Developments in State Constitutional Law* (Bradley D. Mc-Graw, ed.) (St. Paul: West Publishing Co., 1985); *State Supreme Courts: Policymakers in the Federal System* (Mary Cornelia Porter and G. Alan Tarr, eds.) (Greenwood Press, 1982).

15. *Supra* note 2.

16. The *Mount Laurel* cases have been the subject of countless books, articles, and conferences. See, for examples, the symposia in 15 Rutgers L.J. 513 (1984) and 14 Seton Hall L. Rev. 832 (1984).

17. James C. Kirby, Jr., *Expansive Judicial Review of Economic Regulation,* in *Developments in State Constitutional Law, supra* note 14, at 146.

18. See Williams, *supra* note 11, and Robert M. Anderson, *American Law of Zoning* (3rd. ed.) (Rochester: Lawyers Co-operative Publishing Co., 1986).

19. Joseph F. DiMento, Michael D. Dozier, Steven L. Emmons, Donald G. Hagman, Christopher Kim, Karen Greenfield-Sanders, Paul F. Waldau and Jay A. Woollacott, *Land Development and Environmental Control in the California Supreme Court: The Deferential, the Preservationist, and the Preservationist-Erratic Eras*, 27 UCLA L. Rev. 859 (1980).

20. *Id.* at 906.

21. Williams, *supra* note 11, at 93.

22. In California, when the state supreme court accepts an appeal, the intermediate appellate court decision is superseded entirely and has no precedental value whatsoever.

23. Richard Cowart, Vermont Public Utilities Commission and Department of City and Regional Planning, University of California, Berkeley; Robert Ellickson, then at Stanford Law School, now at Yale Law School; Douglas Kmiec, who was then with the U.S. Department of Justice and has since returned to Notre Dame Law School; Jan Krasnowiecki, Pepper, Hamilton, and Scheetz, Philadelphia; Andrea Peterson, Boalt Law School; Joseph Sax, now at Boalt Law School, formerly at University of Michigan Law School; Bernard Siegan, University of San Diego Law School; Dan Tarlock, Chicago-Kent Law School.

24. See Williams, *supra* note 11, at 115–16; Richard F. Babcock and Charles L. Siemon, *The Zoning Game Revisited* 293 (Boston: Oelgeschlager, Gunn and Hain, 1985); and Michael M. Berger and Gideon Kanner, *Thoughts on the White River Junction Manifesto: A Reply to the "Gang of Five's" Views on Just Compensation for Regulatory Taking of Property.* 19 Loy. L.A.L. Rev. 685, 738 (1986).

25. Many other state courts, such as those in Arizona, New Hampshire, and Virginia, are known for striking down land use regulations now and again. I briefly surveyed their regulatory cases, but none were as consistently protective of property rights as Pennsylvania.

26. Williams, *supra* note 11, at 78.

27. Robert C. Ellickson and A. Dan Tarlock, *Land Use Controls*, (Boston: Little, Brown and Co., 1981).

28. See tables in Chapter 4.

29. See Russell S. Harrison, *State Court Activism in Exclusionary-Zoning Cases*, in *State Supreme Courts: Policymakers in the Federal System, supra* note 14, at 55.

30. Curiously, the New Jersey Supreme Court, which issued the most prominent exclusionary zoning opinion in *Mt. Laurel,* was recommended both as a protective and an unprotective court. One authority referred to New Jersey doctrine as "completely wild."

31. Martin Shapiro, *The Constitution and Economic Rights,* in *Essays on the Constitution of the United States* 74 (M. Judd Harmon, ed.) (Port Washington, N.Y.: Kennikat Press, 1978).

32. In *Lochner v. New York,* 198 U.S. 45 (1905), the Supreme Court struck down a state statute that limited the number of daily and weekly hours bakers could work. The state argued that the legislation was necessary to eliminate oppressive working conditions, but the court found there was insufficient reason to limit the freedom of employers and employees to establish their own work relationships. *Lochner* became a symbol of an era in which the court sought to enforce some substantive limits on the power of the state in property or economic matters.

33. Government regulations would not be held unconstitutional, the court announced in *Carolene Products,* "unless in the light of the facts made known or generally assumed it is of such a character as to preclude the assumption that it rests upon some rational basis within the knowledge and experience of the legislators." This became known as the "any conceivable rational basis" test, under which virtually all regulation of property has been routinely upheld. In the famous footnote 4, Justice Stone suggested that exceptions from this general rule of accommodation should be made for rights protected by specific provisions in the Bill of Rights, including rights of expression and criminal procedure; rights essential to the political process, such as voting; and the rights of "discrete, insular minorities." This became the rationale of the double standard, which provides strong protection for preferred rights and essentially no protection for most property rights, even though the takings clause, a major constitutional source of property rights, meets the "specific provision" criterion.

34. The New Jersey Supreme Court, in striking down zoning ordinances that effectively excluded the poor, emphasized that government control of private land use was important, but that it should be done in a manner that would ensure a more egalitarian distribution of housing.

35. William O. Douglas, *Law Reviews and Full Disclosures,* 40 Wash. L. Rev. 227, 229 (1965).

36. *Id.* at 228.

37. See Norman Williams, Jr., R. Marlin Smith, Charles Siemon, Daniel R. Mandelker and Richard F. Babcock, *The White River Junction Manifesto,* 9 Vt. L. Rev. 193 (1984).

38. Berger and Kanner, *supra* note 24, at 688.

39. *Id.* at 689.

40. Robert M. Anderson, *Introduction* (to Symposium on Exclusionary Zoning), 22 Syracuse L. Rev. 465, 473 (1971).

41. Norman Williams Jr. and Thomas Norman, *Exclusionary Land Use Controls: The Case of North-Eastern New Jersey,* 22 Syracuse L. Rev. 475, 501 (1971).

42. Ellen Frankel Paul, *A Reflection on Epstein and His Critics,* 41 U. Miami L. Rev. 235, 238 (1986).

43. A clear introduction to the application of constitutional principles to land use regulation is found in *Land Use and the Constitution: Principles for Planning Practice* (Brian W. Blaesser and Alan C. Weinstein, eds.) (Chicago: Planners Press, 1989). Another source with only a modicum of legalese is Robert R. Wright and Susan Webber Wright, *Land Use in a Nutshell* (2nd ed.) (St. Paul: West Publishing Co., 1985).

44. This is a generic discussion of federal and state constitutional law and cannot adequately reflect the variety found at the state level. Citations in this sections are to the relevant clauses in the constitutions of the U.S., California, and Pennsylvania. Constitutional developments in each of those jurisdictions are reviewed in detail in subsequent chapters.

45. Judge-made law governing property, contracts, and the like, based on court precedents, rather than on interpretation of constitutions or statutes.

46. The Fifth Amendment of the U.S. Constitution states in part: "No person shall . . . be deprived of life, liberty, or property, without due process of law." In *Barron v. Baltimore* (1805), the Supreme Court ruled that the original ten amendments applied only to the federal government. Following the Civil War, due process requirements were imposed on state governments by the Fourteenth Amendment, which states in part: "Nor shall any State deprive any person of life, liberty, or property, without due process of law." At the state level, due process protections are rooted in a variety of clauses. Some states have explicit due process clauses; the California Constitution [art. I, §7(a)], states: "A person may not be deprived of life, liberty or property without due process of law." Other constitutions have "law of the land" clauses or general rights clauses as sources of "due process" protections. In Pennsylvania, art I, §9, of the constitution specifies that in regard to criminal defendants, "nor can he be deprived of his life, liberty or property, unless by the judgment of his peers or the law of the land," and art. I, §1, states: "All men are born equally free and independent, and have certain inherent and indefeasible rights, among which are those of enjoying and defending life and liberty, of acquiring, possessing, and protecting property and reputation, and of pursuing their own happiness."

47. Approval of a zoning map and text is a legislative act. Logically, changes in zoning designations (rezonings) are legislative as well. Yet rezonings may affect only a single property of a single owner, making the process vulnerable to either favoritism or hostility toward a particular individual. The Oregon Supreme Court has ruled that such "quasi-judicial" proceedings are subject to due process requirements. See *Fasano v. Board of Commissioners of Washington County,* 264 Or. 574, 507 P.2d 23 (1973).

48. Particularly in the land use field, where local governments play an important role, the terms *law* and *regulation* tend to be used rather loosely. *Law* may refer to an entire corpus of legislative enactments and judicial rulings, as in "land use law," or just to judicial decisions and doctrines, as in "constitutional law." Strictly speaking, laws are statutes enacted by Congress or the state legislatures, pursuant to their constitutional authority. Local governments, or municipalities, are "creatures of the state," that is, creations of state governments, having no inherent sovereignty. Local governments, which include counties, cities, towns or townships, and boroughs, may enact ordinances, which technically are not laws. "Local law," however, usually means ordinances. Regulations are enacted by administrative agencies pursuant to statutory authorization. The distinction at the state and federal levels between regulation and statutory law breaks down at the local level, however, where administrative boards typically dispose of particular cases and recommend "regulatory" changes to the local governing body for approval.

49. "No state shall make or enforce any law which shall . . . deny to any person within its jurisdiction the equal protection of the laws." The clause has been held equally applicable to the federal government through the Fifth Amendment due process clause. *See also* California Constitution, art I, §7(a): "A person may not be . . . denied equal protection of the laws." The Pennsylvania Constitution does not have an explicit, general guarantee of equal protection, although comparable protections have been implied in art. I, §1, which protects "certain inherent and indefeasible rights." Art. I, §28 prohibits discrimination based on gender.

50. Every state constitution contains a clause, some more explicit than others, requiring compensation for property taken. The California Constitution (art. I, §19) states: "Private property may be taken or damaged for public use only when just compensation, ascertained by a jury unless waived, has first been paid to, or into court for, the owner." The Pennsylvania Constitution (art. I, §10) requires "nor shall private property be taken or applied to public use, without authority of law and without just compensation being first made or secured."

51. The First Amendment reads, in part: "Congress shall make no law respecting an establishment of religion, or prohibiting the free exercise thereof; or abridging the freedom of speech." According to the California

Constitution [art. I, §2(a)], "Every person may freely speak, write and publish his or her sentiments on all subjects, being responsible for the abuse of this right. A law may not restrain or abridge liberty of speech or press." Art. I, §4 provides, in part, "Free exercise and enjoyment of religion are guaranteed. . . . The Legislature shall make no law respecting an establishment of religion." According to art. I, §7, of the Pennsylvania Constitution, "The free communication of thoughts and opinions is one of the invaluable rights of man, and every citizen may freely speak, write and print on any subject, being responsible for the abuse of that liberty." Religious freedom is secured by art. I, §3: "All men have a natural and indefeasible right to worship Almighty God according to the dictates of their own consciences. . . . No human authority can, in any case whatever, control or interfere with the rights of conscience, and no preference shall ever be given by law to any religious establishment."

52. Pa. Const., art. I, §1. Nearly identical language is found in art. I, §1, of the California Constitution.

53. Houston for decades was noted for its absence of zoning and reliance on private covenants. See Bernard Siegan, *Other People's Property* 12 (Lexington, Mass.: Lexington Books, 1976). Houston recently has adopted piecemeal land use regulations, although covenants remain predominant. See James Peters, *Houston Gets Religion,* in *The Best of Planning* 323 (American Planning Association) (Chicago: Planners Press, 1989), and J. Brian Phillips, *Progressivism comes to Houston,* 40 Freeman 72 (1990).

54. 276 U.S. 272 (1928).

CHAPTER 2

1. Quoted in *The Profession,* in *The Best of Planning* 1 (American Planning Association) (Chicago: Planners Press, 1989).

2. Aaron Wildavsky, *Choosing Preferences by Constructing Institutions: A Cultural Theory of Preference Formation,* 81 Am. Pol. Sci. Rev. 3 (1987).

3. Cultures provide answers for the two great questions of life: "Who am I?" and "What will I do?" More precisely, to what degree do individuals define themselves as members of a group (and act accordingly) and to what degree are individual actions constrained by rules? The first dimension is "group" and the second is "grid." Together they define the four basic forms of social organization: hierarchy (high group, high grid), egalitarian (high group, low grid), libertarian (low group, low grid), and despotism (low group, high grid).

Despotism, the imposition of rules of behavior when group responsibility and value agreement are lacking, has little to recommend it except to the despot. It is rarely an important category in the analysis of public policy and tends to be used by advocates of other political cultures, who may portray their opponents as indistinguishable advocates of despotic evil.

The group and grid framework was developed by the anthropologist Mary Douglas. See Douglas, Natural Symbols: Explorations in Cosmology (2nd ed.) (London: Barrie and Jenkins, 1973), and Douglas, Cultural Bias in In the Active Voice 183 (London: Routledge & Kegan Paul, 1982). For a version that is closer to the way I apply cultural labels in policy analysis, see Wildavsky, supra note 2.

4. James Metzenbaum, The Law of Zoning 106, 105 (New York: Baker, Voorhis and Company, (1930).

5. Newman Baker, Legal Aspects of Zoning 35 (Chicago: University of Chicago Press, 1927).

6. Melvin R. Levin, Introduction, in The Best of Planning, supra note 1, at xi.

7. Michael Lee Vasu, Politics and Planning: A National Study of American Planners 5 (Chapel Hill: University of North Carolina Press).

8. See, later in this chapter, discussion of egalitarian attacks on exclusionary zoning.

9. Vasu, supra note 7, at 10–11.

10. See Peter P. Witonski, The Historical Roots of American Planning, in The Politics of Planning: A Review and Critique of Centralized Economic Planning 131 (San Francisco: Institute for Contemporary Studies 1976).

11. John Dewey, Liberalism and Social Action 55 (New York: Putnams, 1935).

12. Robert M. Anderson, Introduction (to Symposium on Exclusionary Zoning) 22 Syracuse L. Rev. 465 (1971); see also Ira Michael Heyman, Legal Assaults on Municipal Land Use Regulation, in The Land Use Awakening: Zoning Law in the Seventies 51 (Robert H. Freilich and Eric O. Stuhler, eds.) (Chicago: American Bar Association Press, 1981).

13. James Metzenbaum, supra note 4, at 127.

14. Constance Perin, Everything in Its Place: Social Order and Land Use in America (Princeton: Princeton University Press, 1977).

15. James Metzenbaum, supra note 4, at 128.

16. Bruno Lasker, The Atlanta Zoning Plan, 48 Survey 114 (April 22, 1922).

17. Id. at 115.

18. *See* William M. Randle, *Professors, Reformers, Bureaucrats, and Cronies: The Players in Euclid v. Ambler,* in *Zoning and the American Dream: Promises Still to Keep* 31 (Charles M. Haar and Jerold S. Kayden, eds.) (Chicago: Planners Press, 1989).

19. Although environmentalism relies heavily on hierarchical controls, there is vigorous philosophical dispute in the environmental community between the "resource-management" school rooted in Progressive ideology and the egalitarian "deep ecologists," as I discuss later in this chapter.

20. Robert R. Linowes and Don T. Allensworth, *The Politics of Land Use: Planning, Zoning and the Private Developer* 149 (New York: Praeger, 1973).

21. *See* Richard F. Babcock, *Ecology and Housing: Virtues in Conflict,* in *Billboards, Glass Houses and the Law* 139 (Colorado Springs: Shepard's, 1977); Lawrence A. Chickering, *Land Use Controls and Low Income Groups: Why Are There No Poor People in the Sierra Club,* in *No Land Is an Island* (San Francisco: Institute for Contemporary Studies, 1975), and the discussion of environmentalism and equality later in this chapter.

22. *See,* later in this chapter, the discussion of the libertarian critique of presumptions of knowledge by centralized authorities.

23. Victor John Yannacone, Jr., John Rahenkamp and Angelo I. Cerchione, *Impact Zoning: Alternative to Exclusion in the Suburbs,* in *The Land Use Awakening: Zoning Law in the Seventies* 154 (Robert H. Frielich and Eric O. Stuhler, eds.) (Chicago: American Bar Association Press, 1981).

24. Michael Thompson has integrated the Hollings typology into a cultural analysis similar to the one employed here. *See* Thompson, *The Cultural Construction of Nature and the Natural Destruction of Culture* (International Institute of Applied Systems Analysis, Working Paper 84–92, 1984).

25. C. S. Holling, *Myths of Ecological Stability: Resilience and the Problem of Failure,* in *Studies on Crisis Management* 101 (C. F. Smart and W. T. Stanbury, eds.) (Canada: Institute for Research on Public Policy, 1978).

26. *Id.* at 102–03.

27. T. O'Riordan, *Environmental Ideologies,* 9 Env't & Plan. A 3, 6 (1977).

28. *Id.* at 6–7.

29. Richard F. Babcock, *The Zoning Game: Municipal Practices and Policies* 19 (Madison: University of Wisconsin Press, 1966).

30. Eric H. Steele, *Community Participation and the Function of Rules: The Case of Urban Zoning Boards,* 9 Law & Pol'y 279, 298 (1987).

31. Clifford L. Weaver and Richard F. Babcock, *City Zoning: The Once and Future Frontier* 159 (Chicago: Planners Press, 1979).

32. *See* Perin, *supra* note 14.

33. *See* Orlando E. Delogu, *Local Land Use Controls: An Idea Whose Time Has Passed,* 36 Me. L. Rev. 261 (1984).

34. *See* R. Babcock, *supra,* note 29; Jan Z. Krasnowiecki, *Abolish Zoning,* 31 Syracuse L. Rev. 719 (1980) and John W. Reps, *Requiem for Zoning,* in *Land Use Control: Present Problems and Future Reform* (D. Listokin, ed.) (New Brunswick, N.J.: Rutgers University, 1964) for more disparaging words about variances.

35. Carol M. Rose, *Planning and Dealing: Piecemeal Land Controls as a Problem of Local Legitimacy,* 71 Calif. L. Rev. 837 (1983).

36. Steele, *supra* note 30, at 298.

37. "Fashioning effective coalitions is a task calling for considerable energy, shrewdness, tolerance, patience, and a willingness to compromise," Levin has written. "The most politicized members of the profession, however, are hot-blooded, dogmatic sectarians who are convinced that compromise is tantamount to selling out." Melvin R. Levin, *The Conscience of the Planner,* in *The Best of Planning,* supra note 1, at 7, 10.

38. Alan A. Altshuler, *The City Planning Process* 200 (Ithaca: Cornell University Press 1965).

39. Levin, *supra* note 6, at xii.

40. *Id.* at xi.

41. *Id.* at xii.

42. Ellen Frankel Paul, *Property Rights and Eminent Domain* 7 (New Brunswick: Transaction Books, 1987).

43. Exactions, such as the coastal commission demand for an easement, and zoning are examples of the use of the police power to limit private control of land.

44. Condemnation of property for redevelopment, as in the case of the watch repairer, is an example of eminent domain, as is condemnation of land for a public highway.

45. Paul described another scenario in which a "retired salesperson who, through hard work and thrift," saved up to buy a coastal lot on which to "build a small hideaway where you can spend your declining years close to nature" is frustrated by the California Coastal Commission, which demanded a public easement. The grant would violate the conditions of the

property deed, and thus no house could be built, and the value of the property, and the modest worker's dreams, are destroyed. *"This is the police power,"* Paul concluded. *Supra,* note 42, at 7–8.

46. *Liberty, Democracy and the Founders* 41 Pub. Interest 39, 47 (1975).

47. Bernard H. Siegan, *Other People's Property* 102 (Lexington, Mass: Lexington Books, 1976).

48. Paul, *supra* note 42, at 254–60.

49. Richard A. Epstein, *Takings: Private Property and the Power of Eminent Domain* (Cambridge, Mass.: Harvard University Press, 1985).

50. *Id.* at 314–24.

51. *Id.* at 303–305.

52. *Id.* at 178–81.

53. *Id.* at 176–77, 186–88.

54. *Id.* at 263–73.

55. *Id.* at 279–80.

56. *Id.* at 281.

57. See Friedrich A. Hayek, *The Discipline of Freedom,* in 3 *Law Legislation and Liberty* 163 (Chicago: University of Chicago Press, 1979).

58. Friedrich A. Hayek, *Competition as a Discovery Procedure,* in 3 *Law, Legislation and Liberty, supra* note 57, at 67.

59. *Id.* at 254.

60. William Moshofsky, *The Regulatory Trampling of Landowner Rights,* 35 Bus. & Soc'y Rev. 26, 28 (1980).

61. James L. Huffman and Reuben C. Plantico, *Toward a Theory of Land Use Planning: Lessons from Oregon,* 14 Land & Water L. Rev. 1 (1979).

62. Vincent Ostrom, *Some Paradoxes for Planners: Human Knowledge and Its Limitations,* in *The Politics of Planning: A Review and Critique of Centralized Planning* (A. Lawrence Chickering, ed.) (San Francisco: Institute for Contemporary Studies, 1976).

63. Eamon Butler, *Hayek: His Contribution to the Political and Economic Thought of Our Time* 94 (London: Temple Smith, 1983).

64. Siegan, *supra* note 47, at 3.

65. *Id.* at 122.

66. Moshofsky, *supra* note 60, at 28.

67. *See* James M. Buchanan and Gordon Tullock, *The Calculus of Consent* (Ann Arbor: University of Michigan Press, 1962). For a recent overview of the research on "public choice," *see* James D. Gwartney and Richard E. Wagner, *Public Choice and the Conduct of Representative Government*, in *Public Choice and Constitutional Economics* 3 (Greenwich, Conn.: JAI Press, 1988).

68. M. Bruce Johnson, *Piracy on the Coast*, 55 Calif. Real Est. Mag. 22, 24 (1975).

69. Much of the work on free-market environmentalism has been produced by the Center for Political Economy and Natural Resources and its descendants, the Political Economy Research Center and the Foundation for Research on Economics and the Environment. *See* John Baden, *Earth Day Reconsidered* (Washington, D.C.: Heritage Foundation, 1980); Baden and Richard Stroup, *Bureaucratic Myths and Environmental Management* (San Francisco: Pacific Research Institute, 1983); Baden and Donald Leal, *The Yellowstone Primer* (San Francisco: Pacific Research Institute, 1990); and Terry Anderson and Donald Leal, *Free Market Environmentalism* (San Francisco: Pacific Research Institute, 1990).

70. Coase has pointed out that if private property rights are fully defined, so that no social costs are "external" to market calculations, then the market may produce socially optimal solutions. Ronald H. Coase, *The Problem of Social Cost*, 3 J. L. & Econ. 1, 1960.

71. See John Delafons, *Land Use Controls in the United States* (2nd ed.) (Cambridge, Mass.: MIT Press, 1969); see also Siegan, *supra* note 47.

72. See Murray N. Rothbard, *For a New Liberty: The Libertarian Manifesto* 260–261 (rev. ed.) (New York: Collier Books, 1978).

73. Gordon C. Bjork, *Life, Liberty and Property: The Economics and Politics of Land-Use Planning and Environmental Controls* (Lexington, Mass.: Lexington Books, 1980).

74. Rothbard, *supra* note 72, at 254–62.

75. See William Tucker, *The Excluded Americans* (Washington, D.C.: Regnery Gateway, 1990).

76. Holling, *supra* note 25, at 99.

77. Rothbard, *supra* note 72, at 320, 321.

78. In grid-grid terms, egalitarianism and libertarianism are both low-grid cultures, while hierarchy and egalitarianism are both high group.

79. C. Edwin Baker, *Property and Its Relation to Constitutionally Protected Liberty,* 134 U. Pa. L. Rev. 741, 815 (1986).

80. Jennifer Nedelsky, *Private Property and the Limits of American Constitutionalism: The Madison Framework and It's Legacy* (Chicago: University of Chicago Press, 1990).

81. Jerry L. Mashaw, *Administrative Due Process: The Quest for a Dignitary Theory,* 61 B. U. L. Rev. 885, 930 (1981).

82. *See* Richard Stewart, *The Reformation of American Administrative Law,* 88 Harv. L. Rev. 1667 (1975).

83. Mashaw, *supra* note 81, at 904.

84. Stewart, *supra* note 82, at 1667.

85. Patrick McAuslan, *The Ideologies of Planning Law* 5 (New York: Pergamon Press, 1980).

86. *But see* Christopher D. Stone, *Should Trees Have Standing? Toward Legal Rights for Natural Objects* (Los Angeles: William Kaufman, 1974), for a discussion of how courts might act *as if* nature had a voice.

87. *See* Mary Douglas and Aaron Wildavsky, *Risk and Culture* (Berkeley: University of California Press, 1982) for a discussion of the relation between "sectarianism," essentially what I term egalitarianism, and environmentalism.

88. O'Riordan, *supra* note 27, at 5. Similar contrasts have been drawn by Stephen Cotgrove between a hierarchical "dominant social paradigm" and an egalitarian "alternative environmental paradigm," and by the egalitarian environmentalists Bill Devall and George Sessions between a "dominant position," which they oppose, and a "minority tradition," which they advocate. *See* Stephen Cotgrove, *Risk, value conflict and political legitimacy,* in *Dealing With Risk* 122 (Richard F. Griffiths, ed.) (Manchester: Manchester University Press, 1981), and Bill Devall and George Sessions, *Deep Ecology* 18–19 (Salt Lake City: Peregrine Smith Books, 1985).

89. O'Riordan, *supra* note 27, at 5.

90. See Arne Naess, *Self-realization in Mixed Communities of Humans, Bears, Sheep and Wolves,* 22 Inquiry 231 (1979); and Murray Bookchin, *The Ecology of Freedom: The Emergence and Dissolution of Hierarchy* (Palo Alto, Calif.: Cheshire Books, 1982).

91. *See* Arne Naess, *Identification as a Source of Deep Ecological Attitudes* in *Deep Ecology* 256 (Michael Tobias, ed.) (San Diego: Avant Books, 1985).

92. David Gancher, *When is Ecology Deep/Shallow?* San Francisco Sunday Chron. & Examiner Book Rev., Apr. 28, 1985, at 1.

93. *See* Naess, *The Shallow and the Deep, Long-Range Ecology Movements: A Summary,* 16 Inquiry 95 (1973).

94. Devall and Sessions, *supra* note 88, at 66.

95. O'Riordan, *supra* note 27, at 3.

96. Devall and Sessions, *supra* note 88, at ix.

97. *Id.* at 7.

98. *See* Garrett Hardin, *The Tragedy of the Commons,* 162 Science 1243 (1968).

99. Devall and Sessions, *supra* note 88, at 35.

100. O'Riordan, *supra* note 27, at 4.

101. Wrote George Sessions, "Supporters of deep ecology have consistently called for decentralized, non-hierarchical, fully democratic social structures." Sessions, *1984: A Postscript,* appendix to Devall and Sessions, *supra* note 88, 254 at 255. *See also* Charles Birch and John B. Cobb, *The Liberation of Life: From the Cell to the Community* (Cambridge: Cambridge University Press, 1983).

102. O'Riordan, *supra* note 27, at 4; see also E. F. Schumacher, *Small Is Beautiful: Economics as if People Really Mattered* (New York: Harper and Row, 1973).

103. Although no Greens hold office in the name of their party, as is the case in West Germany, they have been effective in interest-group politics, and in jurisdictions, such as California, that permit legislative ballot initiatives and where environmentalism is an important political force. Witness the "Big Green" initiative on the November 1990 ballot in California. The Greens have also been active in Australia, Great Britain, and Belgium. *See* Devall and Sessions, *supra* note 88, at 9.

104. Harold Gilliam, *What is Deep Ecology?* This World, San Francisco Sunday Chron. & Examiner, July 24, 1988, at 18.

105. Quoted in Devall and Sessions, *supra* note 88, at 37.

106. Amory B. Lovins, *Soft Energy Paths: Toward a Durable Peace* 23 (Cambridge: Bollinger, 1977), quoted in Timothy W. Luke, The Political Economy of Social Ecology and Voluntary Simplicity 21 (presented at the annual meeting of the American Political Science Association, 1984).

107. O'Riordan, *supra* note 27, at 5.

108. A. Lawrence Chickering, *Land Use Controls and Low Income Groups: Why Are There No Poor People in the Sierra Club*, in *No Land Is an Island* (San Francisco: Institute for Contemporary Studies, 1975). *See also* Richard F. Babcock, *Ecology and Housing: Virtues in Conflict*, in Babcock, *Billboards, Glass Houses and the Law: And Other Land Use Fables* 139 (Colorado Springs: Shepard's, 1977.

109. Harold Gilliam, *Shades of Green*, This World, San Francisco Sunday Chron. & Examiner, July 24, 1988, at 18.

110. *Id.* at 18.

111. McAuslan, *supra* note 85, at 266.

112. See *Pennell v. San Jose*, 485 U.S. 1 (1988), discussed in Chapter 6.

113. Linowes and Allensworth, *supra* note 20, at 62.

114. Paul and Linda Davidoff, *Opening Up the Suburbs: Toward Inclusionary Land Use Controls*, 22 Syracuse L. Rev. 590, 519 (1971).

115. Norman Williams, Jr. and Thomas Norman, *Exclusionary Land Use Controls: The Case of North-Eastern New Jersey*, 22 Syracuse L. Rev. 475, 479 (1971).

116. See discussion of the *Mount Laurel* decisions of the New Jersey Supreme Court in Chapter 4.

117. Yannacone, Rahenkamp, and Cerchione, *supra* note 23, at 158.

118. Robert C. Ellickson and A. Dan Tarlock, *Land Use Controls* 812 (Boston: Little, Brown and Co., 1981).

119. Anthony Downs, *Opening Up the Suburbs* (New Haven, Conn: Yale University Press, 1973), quoted in *id.* at 803.

120. Daniel R. Mandelker, *Environment and Equity: A Regulatory Challenge* 81 (New York: McGraw-Hill, 1981).

121. Norman Williams, Jr., *The Background and Significance of Mt. Laurel II*, 26 Wash. U. J. Urb. & Contemp. L. 3, 4 (1984).

122. Note, *Developments in the Law: The Interpretation of State Constitutional Rights*, 95 Harv. L. Rev. 1324, 1498 (1982).

123. Linowes and Allensworth, *supra* note 20, at 62.

124. *Id.* at 64.

125. It could be argued that municipal lines are drawn in such a way as to divide and conquer what would otherwise by a regional majority opposed to zoning. This would seem to contradict arguments that district

elections, as opposed to at-large elections, best secure representation for the poor and minorities. It would be interesting to study land use policies in metropolitan areas where urban and suburban governments have been merged, such as Atlanta and Sacramento, to see whether majorities have demanded reforms in suburban zoning.

126. Baker, *supra* note 79.

127. Reich, *The New Property*, 73 Yale L. J. 733 (1964).

128. Radin, *Property and Person*, 34 Stan. L. Rev. 957 (1982).

129. Radin, *Residential Rent Control*, 15 Phil. & Pub. Aff. 350 (1986).

130. Steele, *supra* note 30, at 281.

131. Rothbard, however, asserts that parents have no obligation to nourish their children to keep them alive, and that children have an "absolute right to run away." Murray N. Rothbard, *The Ethics of Liberty* 100, 102 (Atlantic Highlands, N.J.: Humanities Press, 1982).

132. Peter J. Steinberger, *Ideology and the Urban Crisis* (Albany: State University of New York Press, 1985).

CHAPTER 3

1. Walton Hamilton, *Common Right, Due Process and Antitrust*, 24 Law & Contemp. Probs. 24, 32 (1940). *See also* Frank R. Strong, *The Economic Philosophy of Lochner: Emergence, Embrasure and Emasculation*, 15 Ariz. L. Rev. 419, 428 (1973) (goal of Court was "enshrining of competitive capitalism as *the* one type of economic organization compatible with the Constitution"). On the "conservatism" (if protecting classically liberal property rights is conservative) of the Court before the New Deal, *see* Arnold Paul, *The Conservative Crisis and the Rule of Law* (New York: Harper and Row, 1969); Loren P. Beth, *The Development of the American Constitution 1877–1917*, (New York, Harper and Row, 1971)? and Clinton Lawrence Rossiter, *Conservatism in America: The Thankless Persuasion* 128–162 (New York: Knopf, (1962).

2. The concept that the due process clauses imply limits on the substance, and not just the procedure, of laws and regulations is discussed in Chapter 1.

3. *Lochner v. New York*, 198 U.S. 45 (1905).

4. *Roe v. Wade*, 410 U.S. 113, 174 (1973) (White, J., dissenting); *id.* at 222 (Rehnquist, J., dissenting); *Cleburne v. Cleburne Living Center*, 473 U.S. 432 (1985) (Marshall, J., concurring) (majority opinion [discussed in Chapter 6] "a small and regrettable step back toward the days of *Lochner v.*

New York"). See Mary Cornelia Porter, *Lochner and Company: Revisionism Revisited* in *Liberty, Property, and Government: Constitutional Interpretation Before the New Deal* 11 (Ellen Frankel Paul and Howard Dickman, eds.) (Albany: State University of New York Press, 1989).

5. The "Old Court" lasted from 1897, when economic regulation was first held violative of the due process clause (*Allgeyer v. Louisiana*, 165 U.S. 578), until 1937, when the court abandoned serious review of economic regulation (*West Coast Hotel v. Parrish*, 300 U.S. 379).

6. Between 1890 and 1936, the Supreme Court struck down an average of 8.6 legislative acts each year, compared with an average of 16.2 annual invalidations by the Warren Court between 1960 and 1969. Bernard H. Siegan, *Economic Liberties and the Constitution* 128 (Chicago: University of Chicago Press, 1980).

7. In *Allgeyer v. Lousiana*, Justice Peckham asserted that the due process clause of the Fourteenth Amendment: "embraced the right of the citizen to be free in the enjoyment of all his faculties, to be free to use them in all lawful ways; to live and work where he will, to earn his livelihood by any lawful calling; to pursue any livelihood or avocation; and for that purpose to enter into all contracts which may be proper, necessary, and essential to his carrying out to a successful conclusion the purposes above mentioned."

8. See *Griswold v. Connecticut*, 381 U.S. 479 (1965); *Roe v. Wade.*

9. Porter, *supra* note 4, at 19. See also Wallace Mendelson, *Separation, Politics and Judical Action,* 52 Ind. L. J. 313, 322 (1977); and Siegan, *supra* note 6, at 110.

10. Martin Shapiro, *The Constitution and Economic Rights* in *Essays on the Constitution of the United States* 74, 81 (M. Judd Harmon, ed.) (Port Washington, NY: Kennikat Press, 1978).

11. 165 U.S. at 585.

12. *Euclid v. Ambler Realty Co.,* 272 U.S. 365 (1926).

13. *Euclid v. Ambler Realty Co.,* 297 F. 307, 318.

14. 272 U.S. at 379.

15. *Id.* at 388.

16. Siegan, *supra* note 6, at 128.

17. 277 U.S. 183 (1928).

18. The lot belonging to Nectow was on a block devoted entirely to industrial uses, although there were residences just across the street.

Nectow successfully challenged the designation of a 100-foot strip of the property as residential. A contract to sell the entire property for industrial use fell through because of the zoning designation. A report ordered by the lower court found that no practical use could be made of the residential portion, because planned road widening would reduce its width to the point that it would be economically unfeasible to develop. The Supreme Court found that the zoning restriction lacked a substantial relation to the public health, safety or welfare, the test of substantive due process. The application of the ordinance appears to be a violation of the takings clause, by effectively confiscating the property. Justice Sutherland's (the author of *Euclid* as well) emphasis on the lack of a substantial public justification, while significant for protecting rights pursuant to the due process clause, leaves open the implication that the state might effectively confiscate property, without compensation, if it had a better reason. I discuss this confusion of takings an due process doctrines, which continues to bedevil the Court, in the concluding chapter.

19. *Moore v. East Cleveland*, 431 U.S. 494 (1977).

20. *West Coast Hotel v. Parrish*, 300 U.S. 379.

21. 304 U.S. 144 (1938).

22. *Id.* at 152.

23. *Id.* at 154.

24. Since the mid-1970s, the Court has gradually blurred the distinction between protected and unprotected rights, and between the different levels of scrutiny. In the area of land use regulation, *Moore v. East Cleveland*, 431 U.S. 494 (1977), was a watershed case. The Court struck down a zoning ordinance on due process grounds because it included a very restrictive definition of family. The analysis employed was more searching than that typically applied under the "rational basis" test, and drew sharp rebukes in the dissenting opinions of Justices Stewart and White.

25. *Id.* at 152.

26. An interesting and controversial exception has been in the area of affirmative action. Although the Court applies strict scrutiny to state actions discriminating against any racial group, including Caucasians, it has found that some "compelling interests" legitimate what is often called "reverse" discrimination. See *Regents of the University of California v. Bakke*, 438 U.S. 265 (1978).

27. Norman Williams, Jr., *The Background and Significance of Mount Laurel II*, 26 Wash. U. J. Urb. & Contemp. L. 4 (1984).

28. Shapiro, *supra* note 10, at 78. For less cynical accounts of the New Deal court, see Alpheus T. Mason, *The Supreme Court from Taft to Warren*

(Baton Rouge: Louisiana State University Press, 1958), and Arthur S. Miller, *The Supreme Court and American Capitalism* (New York: Free Press, 1968).

29. Shapiro, *supra* note 10, at 85.

30. *See* Robert B. Mckay, *The Preference for Freedom*, 34 N.Y.U.L. Rev. 1184 (1959); Loren P. Beth, *The Case for Judicial Protection of Civil Liberties*, 17 J. Pol. 112 (1955); Edwin C. Baker, *Property and Its Relation to Constitutionally Protected Liberty*, 134 U. Pa. L. Rev. 741 (1986).

31. Robert G. McCloskey, *Economic Due Process and the Supreme Court: An Exhumation and Reburial*, 1962 Supreme Court Review 34, 62.

32. Most governmental restrictions on land use, particularly before the environmental protection era, have been products of local governments. *But see* Robert Higgs and Charlotte Twight, *National Emergency and the Erosion of Private Property Rights*, 6 Cato J. 747 (1987) on court deference to federal encroachments on property rights.

33. Norman Williams, Jr., *American Planning Law: Land Use and the Police Power* 82 (Princeton.: Rutgers, 1974).

34. *Berman v. Parker*, 348 U.S. 26 (1954).

35. *Goldblatt v. Hempstead*, 369 U.S. 590, 592 (1962).

36. 348 U.S. at 32.

37. *Id.* at 33.

38. 260 U.S. 393 (1922).

39. *Id.* at 415.

40. *Nollan v. California Coastal Commission*, 483 U.S. 825 (1987) (discussed in Chapter 6 and in the conclusion), provided the first instance since *Mahon* of a land use restriction, in this case the attachment of a public beach easement to a permit to build a replacement house, being invalidated as a taking. But the state action legitimated a physical invasion, so the failure of the Court to strike down any regulatory restriction on private use of property, as distinguished from requiring public access, continues to this day.

41. 328 U.S. 256 (1946).

42. 444 U.S. 164 (1979).

43. *Loretto v. Teleprompter Manhattan CATV Corp.*, 458 U.S. 419 (1982) (discussed in Chapter 6).

44. Douglas W. Kmiec, *Protecting Vital and Pressing Governmental Interests—A Proposal for a New Zoning Enabling Act,* 30 Wash. U. J. Urb. & Contemp. L. 19, 22 (1986).

45. Siegan complains that "freedom in the use of property has vanished in most of this country." Bernard H. Siegan, *Other People's Property* 55 (Lexington, Mass.: Lexington Books, 1976). *See also* Roger Pilon, *Property Rights, Takings and a Free Society,* 6 Harv. J. L. & Pub. Pol'y 165 (1983).

47. *Compare* Joseph L. Sax, *Takings and the Police Power,* 74 Yale L.J. 36 (1964), and *Takings, Private Property and Public Rights,* 81 Yale L.J. 149 (1971).

47. Joseph L. Sax, *Some Thoughts on the Decline of Private Property,* 58 Wash. L. Rev. 481 (1983).

48. *See also* Sondra E. Berchin, *Regulation of Land Use: From Magna Carta to a Just Formulation,* 23 UCLA L. Rev. 904 (1976).

49. See David L. Callies, *Regulating Paradise: Is Land Use a Right or a Privilege?,* 7 U. Hawaii L. Rev. 13 (1985).

50. *Seuss Builders Co. v. Beaverton,* 656 P.2d 306,309 (1982).

51. Herman Schwartz, *Property Rights and the Constitution: Will the Ugly Duckling Become a Swan?* 37 Am. U. L. Rev. 9 (1987).

52. A. E. Dick Howard, *State Courts and Constitutional Rights in the Day of the Burger Court,* 62 Va. L. Rev. 873, 891 (1976).

53. Monrad G. Paulsen, *The Persistence of Substantive Due Process in the States,* 34 Minn. L. Rev. 91, 117 (1950).

54. *See* Williams, *supra* note 33, for an account of the evolution of state courts during this period.

55. *Id.* at 106.

56. *Id.* at 91.

57. *See* Donald E. Wilkes, Jr., *The New Federalism in Criminal Procedure,* 62 Ky. L. J. 421 (1974).

58. Thomas Cooley, *A Treatise on the Constitutional Limitations Which Rest Upon the Legislative Power of the States of the American Union* (8th ed.) (Boston: Little, Brown and Company, 1927).

59. Ronald K. L. Collins, *Reliance on State Constitutions: Some Random Thoughts,* in *Developments in State Constitutional Law* 1, 5 (Bradley D. McGraw, ed.) (St. Paul, Minn.: West Publishing Co., 1985).

60. John P. Frank, Review of *Developments in State Constitutional Law*, (Bradley D. McGraw, ed.) and *State Supreme Courts: Policymakers in the Federal System* (Mary Cornelia Porter and G. Alan Tarr, eds.), 63 Tex. L. Rev. 1339, 1340 (1985).

61. Stanley Mosk, *State Constitutionalism After Warren: Avoiding the Potomac's Ebb and Flow*, in *Developments in State Constitutional Law*, *supra* note 59, at 201.

62. Shirley A. Abrahamson, *Homegrown Justice: The State Constitutions*, in *Developments in State Constitutional Law*, *supra* note 59, at 311.

63. A Nixon appointee, Burger led the court from 1969 and 1986.

64. *See* opinion of Justice Powell in *Regents of Univ. of California v. Bakke*, 438 U.S. 265 (1978), permitting consideration of race in college admissions, and the Burger opinion in *Fullilove v. Klutznick*, 448 U.S. 448 (1980), upholding the guarantee of 10 percent of governmental contracts to "minority business enterprises."

65. *See* majority opinion by Burger in *Swann v. Charlotte-Mecklenburg Bd. of Educ.*, 402 U.S. 1 (1971).

66. *See*, for example, *Harris v. New York*, 401 U.S. 222 (1971), limiting rule, established in *Mapp v. Ohio*, 367 U.S. 643 (1961), excluding unconstitutionally obtained evidence; *New York v. Quarles*, 467 U.S. 649 (1984), creating exception to limits on interrogation established in *Miranda v. Arizona*, 384 U.S. 436 (1966); *Ross v. Moffit*, 417 U.S. 600 (1974), refusing to extend right to counsel of *Gideon v. Wainwright*, 372 U.S. 335 (1963), to additional appellate proceedings.

67. Wilkes, *supra* note 58, at 421.

68. Frank, *supra* note 60, at 1339.

69. *Id.*

70. Peter U. Galie and Lawrence P. Galie, *State Constitutional Guarantees and Supreme Court Review*, 82 Dick. L. Rev. 273 (1978).

71. William J. Brennan, Jr., *State Constitutions and the Protection of Individual Rights*, 90 Harv. L. Rev. 489, 491 (1977).

72. Howard, *supra* note 52, at 874.

73. *See* Henry Clay, *Human Freedom and State Constitutional Law: Part One, the Renaissance*, 70 Mass. L. Rev. 161 (1985).

74. Ronald K. Collins and Peter Galie, *Models of Post-Incorporation Judicial Review: 1985 Survey of State Constitutional Individual Rights Decisions*, 16 Publius 111 (1986). *See also* Collins, *supra* note 59.

75. Edward J. Sullivan, *The Rise of State Constitutional Limits on Planning and Zoning Powers*, 1988 Proc. Inst. on Plan., Zoning, & Eminent Domain 8-1, 8–46.

76. *See*, for example, Robert R. Linowes and Don T. Allensworth, *The Politics of Land Use: Planning, Zoning and the Private Developer* 62 (New York: Praeger, 1973) ("We cannot solve a single one of our other domestic problems without launching a direct attack on community zoning."). The egalitarian critique of exclusionary zoning is discussed in Chapter 2, and in the analysis of the *Mount Laurel* cases of New Jersey in Chapter 4. Egalitarian concern for "personal" rights also implicates aspects of property. *See*, for example, Margaret Jane Radin, *Property and Person*, 34 Stan. L. Rev. 957 (1982). Support for property rights perceived as compatible with personhood is discussed in Chapter 2 and in the concluding chapters.

77. Williams, *supra* note 33, at 107.

78. R. Marlin Smith, *The Uncertain State of Zoning Law in Illinois*, 60 Chi.[-]Kent L. Rev. 119 (1984).

79. *See* Norman Williams, Jr. and Thomas Norman, *Exclusionary Land Use Controls: The Case of North-Eastern New Jersey*, 22 Syracuse L. Rev. 475 (1971).

CHAPTER 4

1. *See* Russell S. Harrison, *State Court Activism in Exclusionary-Zoning Cases*, in *State Supreme Courts: Policymakers in the Federal System* 65 (Mary Cornelia Porter and G. Alan Tarr, eds.) (Westport, Conn.: Greenwood Press, 1982); and Robert F. Silkey and Lawrence F. Dickie, *A Survey of the Judicial Responses to Exclusionary Zoning*, 22 Syracuse L. Rev. 537 (1971).

2. *National Land and Investment Co. v. Kohn*, 419 Pa. 504, 215 A.2d 597, 610 (1965).

3. *Id.*

4. Although the Pennsylvania court has not always made clear the constitutional basis for its holdings, its doctrine forbidding exclusionary measures are generally based on art. I, §1, of the state constitution, which reads: "All men are born equally free and independent, and have certain inherent and inalienable rights, among which are those of enjoying and defending life and liberty, of acquiring, possessing and protecting property and reputation, and of pursuing their own happiness."

5. *See The Second Treatise of Government* (orig. pub. 1690) (Indianapolis: Bobbs-Merrill, 1952).

6. For a modern libertarian statement, see Robert Nozick, *Anarchy, State and Utopia* (New York: Basic Books, 1974).

7. *See* Friedrich A. Hayek, "Competition as a Discovery Procedure," in 3 *Law, Legislation and Liberty* 67 (Chicago: University of Chicago Press, 1979).

8. *See* Milton Friedman, *Capitalism and Freedom* (Chicago: University of Chicago Press, 1962).

9. 215 A.2d at 612.

10. *Id.*

11. *Id.* at 608, 611.

12. *Id.* at 612.

13. *See* Bernard H. Seigan, *Land Use Without Zoning* (Lexington, Mass.: Lexington Books, 1972).

14. Roberts is not alone in his cultural ambiguity. In opinion polls, the American public has been found to support both government regulation and strong property rights. *See* Herbert McClosky and John Zaller, *The American Ethos: Public Attitudes Toward Capitalism and Democracy* (Cambridge, Mass.: Harvard University Press, 1984).

15. 215 A.2d at 607.

16. *Id.*

17. 437 Pa. 237, 263 A.2d 395 (1970).

18. 439 Pa. 466, 268 A.2d 765.

19. *Girsh*, 263 A.2d at 397.

20. *Id.* at 399.

21. *See* Roger Pilon, *Property Rights, Takings and a Free Society*, 6 Harvard J.L. & Pub. Pol'y 165 (1983).

22. 263 A.2d at 398.

23. The libertarian, "low grid, low group" rationale in the cultural model.

24. The "high group" rationale in the cultural model.

25. 268 A.2d at 767.

26. *Id.* at 770.

27. *Id.* at 768.

28. *Id.* at 768, 769.

29. The section states: "All men are born equally free and independent, and have certain inherent and inalienable rights, among which are those of enjoying and defending life and liberty, of acquiring, possessing and protecting property and reputation, and of pursuing their own happiness."

30. *Girsh,* 263 A.2d at 399, 400.

31. *See* Norman Williams, Jr., *American Planning Law: Land Use and the Police Power* 136–39 (Princeton: Rutgers University Press, 1974); Leonard S. Rubinowitz, *Exclusionary Zoning: A Wrong in Search of a Remedy,* 6 U. of Mich. J.L. Ref. 625 (1973); and Norman Williams, Jr. and Thomas Norman, *Exclusionary Land Use Controls: The Case of North-Eastern New Jersey,* 22 Syracuse L. Rev. 475 (1971).

32. Rubinowitz, *supra* note 31, at 638.

33. Williams and Norman, *supra* note 31, at 498–99.

34. *Id.* at 502.

35. 67 N.J. 151, 336 A.2d 713 (1975).

36. 92 N.J. 158, 456 A.2d 390 (1983).

37. *See* Ernest Erber, *The Road to Mount Laurel,* in *The Best of Planning* 250, 253 (American Planning Association) (Chicago: Planners Press, 1989); and Jerold S. Kayden and Leonard A. Zax, *Mount Laurel II: Landmark Decision on Zoning and Low Income Housing Holds Lesson for Nation,* 1984 Zoning and Planning Law Handbook 365.

38. Quoted in Howard Kurtz, *New Jersey's Ground-Breaking Supreme Court: Rulings on Social Issues Produce National Reputation for Innovation, as Well as Local Backlash,* Wash. Post, Dec. 28, 1988, at A4, col. 1.

39. Quoted in Bruce S. Rosen, *A Bold Court Forges Ahead,* Nat. L.J., Nov. 5, 1984 at 38.

40. *See,* for example, 14 Seton Hall L. Rev. 829 (1986) and 15 Rutgers L.J. 513 (1984).

41. 103 N.J. 1, 510 A.2d 621 (1986).

42. 72 N.J. 481, 371 A.2d 1192 (1977).

43. 371 A.2d at 1268.

44. Kurtz, *supra* note 38, at A4.

45. *Mount Laurel I,* 336 A.2d at 716.

46. Perin, *Everything in Its Place: Social Order and Land Use in America* (Princeton: Princeton University Press, 1977).

47. This would be the standard procedure under a judicial test, be it rational basis or strict scrutiny, that evaluates the relationship between the end sought to be served by the government and the means employed. The role of the court would be to limit the excesses of government. The power to enact policies to serve political interests remains with the legislature, subject to the judicial check.

48. *The Hills Development Co. v. Township of Bernards,* 103 N.J. 1, 510 A.2d 621 (1986) (upholding legislative creation of state Council on Affordable Housing).

49. 336 A.2d at 724.

50. G. Alan Tarr and Mary Cornelia Aldis Porter, *State Supreme Courts in State and Nation* 223 (New Haven: Yale University Press, 1988).

51. *Id.*

52. *See* his concurring opinion in *Mount Laurel I* and his dissent in *Pascack Association, Ltd. v. Washington,* 74 N.J. 470, 379 A.2d 6 (1977), discussed below.

53. *See* Jesus Rangel, *New Jersey Panel Orders Housing Despite a Suburb's Lack of Space,* N.Y. Times, Oct. 19, 1988, at 1, and Gary T. Hall, *It Can Happen Here: Mount Laurel Litigation and Developed Towns,* N.J.L.J., Mar. 30, 1989, at 58.

54. 336 A.2d at 732.

55. Williams and Norman, *supra* note 31, at 503. The New Jersey court has enjoyed a symbiotic relation with Norman Williams. Williams filed an amicus brief in *Mount Laurel,* and Justice Hall's opinion is laced with references to Williams's writings. For his part, Williams has anointed Justice Hall as "America's leading zoning judge," who "towers above all the others" (Williams, *supra* note 31, at 89, 98). The cheerleading of Professor Williams is reminiscent of the tempest over the columnist George Wills's involvement in the 1980 presidential campaign. Will helped candidate Reagan prepare for the debates and then praised his performance.

56. 336 A.2d at 727.

57. *Id.* at 724.

58. Henry Maine, *Ancient Law* (London: John Murray, 1901).

59. *See* Bernard H. Siegan, *Other People's Property* (Lexington, Mass.: Lexington Books, 1976).

60. Quoted in Anthony DePalma, *Getting Off the Hook: The Ticklish R.C.A. Issue,* N.Y. Times, May 1, 1988, Sec. 8, at 4, col. 4.

61. Alan Mallach, *Blueprint for Delay,* N.J. Rptr., Oct. 1985, at 20, 27.

62. 336 A.2d. at 733, 734.

63. *Id.* at 723.

64. *Id.* at 733–34.

65. *Id.* at 733.

66. *Id.*

67. *See* Sara Rimer, *Black and White in 2 Worlds,* N.Y. Times, Dec. 12, 1987, at 1.

68. *See* Anthony Lukas, *Beyond Yonkers: Cracking Gilded Ghettos,* N.Y. Times, Aug. 8, 1988, at A15.

69. 366 A.2d at 734.

70. *Id.* at 749.

71. *Id.*

72. *Id.* Perhaps the basis for Pashman's sociological conclusions is the satirical song "Little Boxes" about the "rows of ticky-tack" in the San Francisco suburb of Daly City.

73. *Id.*

74. *Id.* at 750.

75. Payne, *Delegation Doctrine in the Reform of Local Government Law: The Case of Exclusionary Zoning,* 29 Rutgers L. Rev. 803, 812–13 (1976).

76. The classic statement of this theory that local government enables citizens to "vote with their feet" is Charles Tiebout, *A Pure Theory of Local Expenditures,* 64 J. Pol. Econ. 416 (1956).

77. Editorial, Wall St. J., Apr. 3, 1975.

78. 72 N.J. 481, 371 A.2d 1192 (1977).

79. 371 A.2d at 1200.

80. Jerome G. Rose, *The Mt. Laurel II Decision: Is It Based on Wishful Thinking?,* 12 Real Est. L.J. 115, 117 (1983).

81. But, consistent with the egalitarian critique, only to the extent needed to meet its "fair share."

82. 371 A.2d at 1200.

83. Although, in the New Jersey tradition, Conford did not express any concern for landowner rights.

84. 371 A.2d at 1208 (emphasis in original).

85. Ernest Erber has argued that the court shifted course in *Oakwood* because the group urging aggressive inclusionary measures "was out-lawyered before the state supreme court." Erber, *supra* note 37, at 253.

86. 371 A.2d at 1263.

87. Rose, *supra* note 80, at 117.

88. The endorsement of variances by Pashman, who also advocated centralized land-use control, is interesting. The variance has been the un-wanted child of land use scholarship, frequently criticized for weakening the preordained order of planning. *See* Carol M. Rose, *Planning and Dealing: Piecemeal Land Controls as a Problem of Local Legitimacy,* 71 Calif. L.R. 837 (1983). Pashman's recommendation indicates that he viewed the hierarchical tool of land use planning as subservient to the egalitarian goal of leveling communities.

89. 336 A.2d at 1229, 1231.

90. *See* Jerome G. Rose, *Waning Judicial Legitimacy: The Price of Judicial Promulgation of Urban Social Policy,* 20 Urb. Law. 801 (1988).

91. *See* G. Alan Tarr and Russell S. Harrison, *Legitimacy and Capacity in State Supreme Court Policymaking: The New Jersey Court and Exclusionary Zoning,* 15 Rutgers L.J. 514 (1984).

92. Quoted in Richard Lehne, *The Quest for Justice* 134 (N.Y.: Longman, 1978).

93. 74 N.J. 470, 379 A.2d 6 (1977).

94. 379 A.2d at 11.

95. *See* Anthony Downs, *Opening Up the Suburbs.* (New Haven: Yale University Press, 1973).

96. 379 A.2d at 13. Note that the New Jersey court is more willing than the Pennsylvania court to accept the preservation of community character as a legitimate governmental purpose, as long as it fits the court's preferences.

97. *Id.* at 11.

98. *Id.* at 13.

99. *Id.* at 19.

100. *Id.*

101. *Id.* at 24.

102. *Id.* at 31.

103. Concurring in *Surrick v. Zoning Hearing Board of Upper Providence*, 476 Pa. 182, 382 A.2d 105, 115 (1978).

104. 462 Pa. 445, 341 A.2d 466 (1975). *Willistown* was the first exclusionary case decided by the Pennsylvania Supreme Court after *Mount Laurel.*

105. 341 A.2d at 468.

106. *Id.*

107. *Id.*

108. On belief in the compatibility of liberty and equality in the Jacksonian era, *see* Aaron Wildavsky, *Choosing Preferences by Constructing Institutions: A Cultural Theory of Preference Formation*, 81 Am. Pol. Sci. Rev. 3, 13 (1987).

109. Stephen G. Kopelman, *Regional General Welfare: The End of a Trend*, 1985 Inst. Plan., Zoning & Eminent Domain 2–1, 2–21.

110. 476 Pa. 182, 382 A.2d 105 (1978).

111. In *Girsh*, the court found that the failure of a township to accommodate multifamily housing constituted a total prohibition, and was unconstitutional.

112. Nix noted that intent must be proven under an equal protection claim, but not under a due process claim. Under equal protection, a plaintiff asserts that a land use restriction unconstitutionally discriminates against a class of people, while a due process claimant asserts only that the town has excluded all individuals from pursuing a particular land use. Forbidding the land use explicitly listed in an ordinance is quite clearly both intentional and effective, and thus intent is not necessary to a due process argument. But the connection between excluding a particular land use and excluding a different class of persons is more arguable, so the court requires that the discrimination be intentional. Indeed, if banning a use effectively excludes people, than allowing the use should remedy the exclusion, and thus the equal protection argument and the need to show intent can be avoided. The Pennsylvania court, Nix emphasized, is directly concerned with the exclusion of uses, of classes of people (382 A.2d at 110, note 10).

Another way to analyze the Pennsylvania distinction between due process and equal protection is to argue that intent must be shown to prove unconstitutional offenses to equality, but not for offenses to individual liberty. Certainly that is compatible with the Pennsylvania court's libertarian leanings. Interestingly, the New Jersey court does not require that intent be shown in exclusionary attacks (the court seems to assume that limiting equality is the driving motivation for local land ordinances) and reads equal protection language into its due process or "law of the land" clause. As the New Jersey court wishes to require positive actions by local governments to promote housing for the poor, it cannot expect that intentional discrimination be proven, as this would make it more difficult for plaintiffs to win. But the New Jersey court cannot be satisfied with the Pennsylvania emphasis on due process, as this would justify only the removal of barriers to individual actions, not the eqalitarian remedies the court prefers.

113. 382 A.2d at 110.

114. *Id.* at 115.

115. *Id.* at 114.

116. *Mount Laurel II*, 92 N.J. 158, 456 A.2d 390, 415 (1983).

117. By 1983, Judge Conford, the temporary justice who had written the majority opinions in *Pascack* and *Oakwood*, and Justice Mountain, a voice of caution in his *Oakwood* and *Mount Laurel I* concurrences, were no longer on the court. The new chief justice, Robert Wilentz, wrote the *Mount Laurel II* opinion for a unanimous court. Justice Pashman joined the opinion, which came shortly before his retirement.

118. 456 A.2d at 410.

119. *Id.* at 417.

120. *Id.* at 447.

121. *Id.* at 451.

122. *Id.* at 416.

123. Justice Wilentz did not explain why his "lessons" are so clear and if they are, why they are so difficult for other mortals to learn.

124. 456 A.2d at 429.

125. 37 N.J. 232, 181 A.2d 129. Justice Hall, author of *Mount Laurel I*, had dissented in *Vickers*.

126. On changes in mobile homes and barriers to their use, see also Douglas W. Kmiec, *Manufactured Home Siting: Overview, Regulatory Challenges and a Proposal for Federal Deregulation*, 1984 Zoning & Plan. L. Handbook 397.

127. 456 A.2d at 418.

128. *Id.* at 441.

129. The state source of substantive due process doctrine.

130. 456 A.2d at 415.

131. *Id.*

132. 456 A.2d at 449.

133. *See* Dennis J. Coyle, *A Critical Theory of Community* (Institute of Governmental Studies Working Paper 87–5, 1987).

134. 456 A.2d at 449.

135. *Id.*

136. *See* Bernard H. Siegan, *The President's Commission on Housing: Zoning Recommendations,* Urb. Land, Nov. 1982, at 24.

137. Douglas W. Kmiec, *Protecting Vital and Pressing Governmental Interests—A Proposal for a New Zoning Enabling Act,* 30 Wash. U.J. Urb. & Contemp. L. 19, 26 (1986).

138. *Id.*

139. Wilentz avoids mentioning the constitutional term, *takings,* which limits state confiscation.

140. 456 A.2d at 446, note 12.

141. By repeatedly referring to owners as builders, developers, or speculators, Wilentz is able to portray owners as "mere economic actors" and more easily avoid questions of property rights.

142. 456 A.2d at 415.

143. Rose, *supra* note 90, at 837 (emphasis in original).

144. Quoted in Kurtz, *supra* note 38, at A4.

145. Norman Williams, Jr., *The Background and Significance of Mount Laurel II,* 26 Wash. U.J. Urb. & Contemp. L. 3, 4 (1984).

146. Kurtz, *supra* note 38.

147. *See* Steve Dobkin, Geoffrey Smith, and Earle Tockman, *Zoning for the General Welfare: A Constitutional Weapon for Lower-Income Tenants,* 13 N.Y.U. Rev. L. & Soc. Change 911 (1985).

148. Erber, *supra* note 37, at 254.

149. Tarr and Porter, *supra* note 50, at 185.

150. *See* Rose, *supra* note 90.

151. Williams, *supra* note 144, at 23.

152. Jerold S. Kayden and Leonard A. Zax, *Mt. Laurel II: Landmark Decision on Zoning and Low Income Housing Holds Lesson for Nation,* 1984 Zoning & Plan. L. Handbook 365, 381.

153. 94 N.J. 358, 464 A.2d 1115 (1983).

154. 103 N.J. 1, 510 A.2d 621 (1986).

155. On his reputation as one of the more conservative justices on the New Jersey court, Schreiber has said, "I was considered one of the most conservative members of the court, but that's in New Jersey. Put me in Indiana, and I'd be a wild man." Quoted in Kurtz, *supra* note 38.

156. 464 A.2d at 1119.

157. *Id.*

158. *Id.* at 1128.

159. The low-income housing requirement may well violate the takings clause of the U.S. Constitution. In *Nollan v. California Coastal Commission,* 483 U.S. 825 (1987), the U.S. Supreme Court ruled that a condition imposed on coastal development that was unrelated to the impact of the development was a taking requiring compensation.

160. *Mount Laurel: Slow, Painful Progress,* N.Y. Times, May 1, 1988, Sec. 8, at 1, 4.

161. Tarr and Porter, *supra* note 50, at 273.

162. N.J.S.A. 52:27D-301–329 (West, 1986).

163. *See* Paula A. Franzese, *Mount Laurel III: The New Jersey Supreme Court's Judicious Retreat,* 18 Seton Hall L. Rev. 30 (1988).

164. 510 A.2d at 621.

165. 510 A.2d at 621.

166. *Id.* at 642.

167. *Id.* at 650.

168. 499 Pa. 246, 452 A.2d 1337 (1982).

169. *See* Christopher P. Markley, *Agricultural Land Preservation: Can Pennsylvania Save the Family Farm?* 87 Dickenson L. Rev. 595 (1983).

170. Andrew Kinzler and George A. Ritter, *Twilight Zoning in New Jersey: The Exclusionary Effect of Agricultural Zoning,* Urb. Land. Dec. 1983, at 7, 9.

171. *See* Jacqueline P. Hand, *Right to Farm Laws: Breaking New Ground in the Preservation of Farmland,* 45 U. Pittsburgh L. Rev. 289 (1984).

172. *See* Anthony R. Arcaro, *Avoiding Constitutional Challenges to Farmland Preservation Legislation,* 24 Gonzaga L. Rev. 475 (1989).

173. 452 A.2d at 1343.

174. *Surrick v. Zoning Hearing Board of Upper Providence,* 476 Pa. 182, 382 A.2d 105 (1978).

175. 452 A.2d at 1343.

176. *Id.*

177. *Id.* at 1345.

178. *Id.*

179. 507 Pa. 481, 491 A.2d 86 (1985).

180. Thomas Buchanan, *Innovative Zoning for the Preservation of Agricultural Land—Boundary Drive Associates v. Shrewsbury Township Board of Supervisors,* 59 Temp. L.Q. 861, 875 (1986).

181. *Id.*

182. 501 Pa. 200, 460 A.2d 1075 (1983).

183. 501 Pa. 348, 461 A.2d 771 (1983).

184. 437 Pa. 237, 263 A.2d 395 (1970).

185. 460 A.2d at 1080 (1983).

186. *Id.* at 1081.

187. Victor R. Delle Donne, *Land Use,* 54 Pa. B.A.Q. 35 (1983).

188. *See* Note, *The Pennsylvania Supreme Court, Applying the Surrick Test, Has Held That a Municipality Can Meet Its Fair Share Obligation by Providing for Some Form or Forms of Multi-Family Dwellings, but a Municipality Need Not Provide for Every Conceivable Subcategory of Such Dwellings,* 23 Duquesne L. Rev. 263 (1984).

189. 461 A.2d at 773 (1983).

190. Delle Donne, *supra* note 187, at 35.

191. *Elocin,* 461 A.2d at 775.

192. *Kravitz,* 460 at 1084.

193. *Kravitz,* 460 A.2d at 1087.

194. *Id.* at 1084.

195. 509 Pa. 413, 502 A.2d 585 (1985).

196. *Fernley v. Board of Supervisors of Schuykill,* 76 Pa. Cmwlth. 409, 464 A.2d 587 (1982).

197. 502 A.2d at 588.

198. *Id.,* at 592.

199. *See Williamson County Regional Planning Commission v. Hamilton Bank of Johnson City,* 473 U.S. 172, 105 S. Ct. 3108 (1985).

200. *See Agins v. Tiburon,* 24 Cal. 3d 266, 598 P.2d 25, 157 Cal. Rptr. 372 (1979).

201. *San Diego Gas & Electric Co. v. San Diego,* 450 U.S. 621, 101 S. Ct. 1287 (1981).

202. 483 U.S. 825, 107 S. Ct. 3141 (1987).

203. Victor R. Delle Donne, *Land Use,* 56 Pa. B.A.Q. 172, 174 (1985). But in the post-*Nollan* era, the Pennsylvania court has begun to see regulations as takings. *See* United Artists Theater Circuit, Inc. v. Philadelphia, 595 A.2d 6 (1991).

204. 502 A.2d at 596.

205. *Id.,* at 595.

206. *Compare* the New Jersey Supreme Court's willingness to abandon the builder's remedy in *Hills Development,* discussed earlier.

207. 510 Pa. 231, 507 A.2d 361 (1986).

208. *Geiger v. Zoning Hearing Board of North Whitehall,* 85 Pa. Cmwlth. 362, 481 A.2d 1249.

209. *See* Wendy Schermer, *Mobile Homes: An Increasingly Important Housing Resource That Challenges Traditional Land Use Regulation— Geiger v. Zoning Hearing Board of North Whitehall,* 60 Temp. L.Q. 583 (1987).

210. McDermott did not ask if there had been a total ban of a legitimate use or if North Whitehall was a logical area for growth. Cases with

exclusionary implications in which both questions were ignored by a plurality of the court can be found in box 4 of Table 4.

211. 507 A.2d at 362.

212. 507 A.2d at 365.

213. *Id.* at 367.

214. The current state constitution was adopted in 1874.

215. "All men are born equally free and independent, and have certain inherent and indefeasible rights, among which are those of enjoying and defending life and liberty, of acquiring, possessing and protecting property and reputation, and of pursuing their own happiness." Pa. Const., art. I, §1.

216. Although a similar constitutional basis in New Jersey has not stopped its court from weakening landowner rights.

217. 495 Pa. 158, 432 A.2d 1382 (1981).

218. Williams, *supra* note 31, at 79.

219. *Id.* at 139. Williams was referring to a particular justice, but his judgment is an apt description of the court as well. Property rights advocates might phrase it somewhat differently. For them, the bite of the Pennsylvania court can be quite painful, while the bark of rhetoric is music to their ears.

220. This may in part be because landowner rights and state regulatory powers keep each other in check. Given the threat of constitutional rejection, regulators may be less willing to restrict property rights in novel ways, and thus landowners have less cause to sue. In California, where property owners have found little court protection, the burden of landowner suits remains high, perhaps because court indulgence has emboldened regulators to experiment with new schemes, pushing property owners to sue in the hope that at some point the courts will intervene. I have not found any evidence that protecting landowner rights significantly increases the workload of the courts.

221. In *Appeal of Miller*, 511 Pa. 631, 515 A.2d 904 (1986), the court was asked to strike down an ordinance that restricted occupancy of single-family homes to persons related by blood, marriage, or adoption and no more than one unrelated person. The court declined to consider the constitutional issue but ruled that a household that included a woman; her foster daughter; seven unrelated boarders who were retarded, handicapped or aged; and an assistant qualified as a family under an earlier ordinance that defined a family as a "housekeeping unit." Since Miller had started taking in boarders before the more restrictive ordinance was enacted, her house-

hold was deemed a legal nonconforming use. *See* Victor R. Delle Donne, *Land Use*, 58 Pa. B.A.Q. 173 (1987).

222. *See People v. Superior Court (Lucero)*, 49 Cal. 3d 14, 774 P.2d 769, 259 Cal. Rptr. 740 (1989); and *Metromedia, Inc. v. San Diego*, 26 Cal. 3d 848, 610 P.2d 407, 164 Cal. Rptr. 510 (1980); discussed in Chapter 5.

223. 512 Pa. 23, 515 A.2d 1331 (1986).

224. 495 Pa. 158, 432 A.2d 1382 (1981).

225. 447 U.S. 74, 100 S. Ct. 2035 (1980).

226. *Robins v. Pruneyard Shopping Center*, 23 Cal. 3d 899, 592 P.2d 341, 153 Cal. Rptr. 854 (1979).

227. For reviews of state constitutional protection of speech rights on private property, see John A. Ragosta, *Free Speech Access to Shopping Malls Under State Constitutions*, 37 Syracuse L. Rev. 1 (1986), and Sanford Levinson, *Freedom of Speech and the Right of Access to Private Property Under State Constitutional Law*, in *Developments in State Constitutional Law* 51 (Bradley D. McGraw, ed.) (St. Paul, Minn.: West Publishing Co., 1985).

228. 432 A.2d at 1391.

229. 515 A.2d at 1338.

230. Justice Nix dissented, disparaging the "mere fact" that the property was privately owned. *Id.* at 1342.

231. The Declaration of Rights is the first part of the Pennsylvania Constitution and is very similar to the Bill of Rights added to the U.S. Constitution.

232. 515 A.2d at 1335.

233. *Id.*

234. *Id.* at 1339.

235. In his dissenting opinion in *Western Pennsylvania Socialist Workers*, Justice McDermott caustically referred to Hutchinson's sermon on the natural law origins of the Pennsylvania constitution as "the poristic thickets in the plurality's disquisition." 515 A.2d at 1341.

236. Curiously, Justice Hutchinson played an important role in decisions against the interests of landowners. He wrote as many opinions (three) in support of local governments as any justice in the 1980s, and all three were majority opinions. But only one of these opinions, *Boundary Drive*, was in a particularly important case.

237. 461 A.2d at 775.

238. *Fernley,* 502 A.2d at 591 (1985).

239. *Id.* at 1342.

240. *See,* for example, *Conroy-Prugh Glass Co. V. Comm.,* 456 Pa. 384, 322 A.2d 598. As I noted earlier in this chapter, by 1991 the court had begun to adopt the U.S. Supreme Court's doctrine than regulations may be takings requiring compensation.

241. *See Miller v. Beaver Falls,* 368 Pa. 189, 82 A.2d 34.

242. On Pennsylvania takings standards, see Thomas J. Dempsey, *Eminent Domain,* 55 Pa. B.A.Q. 64 (1984).

243. 498 Pa. 180, 445 A.2d 724, 726–27 (1982).

244. 445 A.2d at 727.

245. Many other states, such as Oregon and New York, allow aesthetic regulation without compensation. *See Oregon City v. Hartke,* 240 Or. 35, 400 P.2d 255 (1965), and *Cromwell v. Ferrier,* 19 N.Y.2d 263, 225 N.E.2d 749, 279 N.Y.S.2d 22 (1967).

246. 523 A.2d 747 (1987).

247. *Id.* at 752.

248. *Id.*

249. The restaurant would still have a driveway on a side street.

250. 495 Pa. 514, 434 A.2d 1209 (1981).

251. 434 A.2d at 1211.

252. 515 Pa. 542, 531 A.2d 414 (1987).

253. 522 A.2d at 1074.

254. *Id.*

255. *Id.* at 1075.

256. 489 Pa. 221, 414 A.2d 37 (1980).

257. 414 A.2d at 48.

258. *See* Grayson P. Hanes and J. Randall Minchew, *On Vested Rights to Land Use and Development,* 46 Wash. & Lee L. Rev. 373 (1989).

259. 509 Pa. 605, 506 A.2d 887 (1986).

260. Boardinghouses include meals.

261. 501 Pa. 224, 460 A.2d 1088 (1983).

262. The court suggested that the ban on boardinghouses was intended to exclude commercial establishments, but as Nix noted in dissent, one or two meals does not a restaurant make, and that renting rooms may well be more commercial, appealing to travelers. 460 A.2d at 1090.

263. Or by reading due process rationality review into a statute, as in *Ridley Arms.*

264. The weight given to opinions increases with the frequency of opinion writing. That way, a justice who wrote few opinions does not have his overall score distorted by them.

CHAPTER 5

1. Although California has the nation's leading agricultural economy, the population is overwhelmingly urban and suburban.

2. *See* Gus Bauman and William H. Ethier, *Development Exactions and Impact Fees: A Survey of American Practices,* 50 L. & Contemp. Probs. 51 (1987), and Richard W. Stevenson, *Debate Grows on Development Fees,* N.Y. *Times,* Feb. 16, 1989.

3. Edmund L. Andrews, *The Curse of California's Proposition 13,* N.Y. Times, June 17, 1988, at A35.

4. On California, see Robert Reinhold, *The New California Dream: Closing the Door,* N.Y. Times, June 12, 1988.

5. *See* Bernard J. Frieden, *The Environmental Protection Hustle* (Cambridge, Mass.: The MIT Press, 1979), on the effect of regulation on housing costs.

6. Norman Williams, Jr., *American Planning Law: Land Use and the Police Power* 76 (Princeton: Rutgers, 1974).

7. Richard F. Babcock and Charles L. Siemon, *The Zoning Game Revisited* 293 (Boston: Oelgeschlager, Gunn and Hain, 1985).

8. 477 U.S. 340 (1986).

9. 485 U.S. 1 (1988).

10. 483 U.S. 825 (1987).

11. In his considerable writings on land use law, Williams makes it clear that he is very supportive of regulatory limits on property rights. Perhaps to ease the pangs of his conscience, he consistently refers to property owners as "developers," as if to assure us that only greedy, environmentally

insensitive money grubbers, and not average Joes and grandmothers, are the victims of regulatory might.

12. Williams, *supra* note 6, at 115–16.

13. Michael M. Berger and Gideon Kanner, *Thoughts on the White River Junction Manifesto: A Reply to the "Gang of Five's" Views on Just Compensation for Regulatory Taking of Property,* 19 Loy. L.A.L. Rev. 685, 738 (1986).

14. California justices are appointed but must face reconfirmation votes by the public. Justices Bird, Grodin, and Reynoso were thrown out by the electorate, and their replacements, John A. Arguelles, David N. Eagleson, and Marcus M. Kauffman, all resigned after brief terms. Nearly half of the members of the court, then, are new since 1989. And Justice Broussard has announced he will retire during 1991.

15. 24 Cal. 3d at 275, 276.

16. *Id.* at 273.

17. The fallacy of Richardson's argument is that he has confused two different questions: Has there been a taking? Did the municipality exceed its police power? If a taking of property has occurred, property rights have been deprived to precisely the same degree, whether or not the government action was lawful. A taking is a taking, and compensation should be required in either case. Once the taking issue has been decided, the court should consider whether the government has exceeded its police power. If so, then the taking is unlawful and should be abandoned, and the property owner should be compensated for the temporary taking. If the restriction is within the power of the government, it may choose to discontinue the restriction and pay compensation for the temporary taking or may retain the restriction and pay proportionately greater compensation, in addition to which the owner should be compensated for the period during which the property was effectively taken. I think this analysis follows logically from the takings clause, and it is compatible with the U.S. Supreme Court's opinion in *First English Evangelical Lutheran Church of Glendale v. Los Angeles County,* 482 U.S. 304 (1987), in which it chastised the errant California court. I discuss takings analysis in greater detail in the final chapter.

18. 24 Cal. 3d at 282.

19. An advisory booklet for local administrators in California even urged municipalities, confident that the owner will eventually surrender, simply to keep reenacting ordinances and permit denials, with minor variations, that have been struck down in the courts. See Justice Brennan's dissent in *San Diego Gas & Electric Co. v. San Diego,* 450 U.S. 621 (1981), discussed in Chapter 6.

20. 24 Cal. 3d at 282.

21. See the epigraph to this chapter.

22. The public trust is a specific doctrine, discussed later in this chapter, that may eliminate private rights to property. Here I use the term more generally, as it typifies the court's attitude toward regulation of land.

23. 39 Cal. 3d 862, 705 P.2d 866, 218 Cal. Rptr. 293 (1985).

24. I discuss former justice Tobriner's appreciation of feudalism in the conclusion of this chapter and in the penultimate chapter.

25. The court is sometimes vague about which constitutional clause is the basis for the rights claim. As the court invariably rejects the property owner's plea, perhaps precision is pointless. But most regulatory cases are litigated under the takings clause of the California Constitution (art. I, §19), usually with a substantive due process claim attached (art. I, §7a).

26. *Pennell v. San Jose*, 42 Cal. 3d 365, 721 P.2d 1111, 228 Cal. Rptr. 726 (1986).

27. In *Birkenfeld*, 17 Cal. 3d 129, 550 P.2d 1001, 130 Cal. Rptr. 465, the court struck down an ordinance that required owners of 16,000 rental units in Berkeley to file separate applications for every unit anytime a rent increase was sought and that set no deadlines on how long the rent board could take to review each of the 16,000 applications. The clear intent of the ordinance was to prevent rent increases by drowning landlords in a bottomless sea of paperwork. The court objected to these procedural abuses, not to the principle of rent control.

28. 130 Cal. Rptr. at 465.

29. 304 U.S. 144.

30. But as we shall see in a later section, the California court does show some concern for procedural abuses, even when the victims are property owners. In vested rights and eminent domain cases, the votes tended to be closer, and property owners won occasional victories.

31. Some egalitarians have denigrated property rights while seeking to protect aspects of property deemed personal. For Radin, this means imposing rent control to further "personhood" of tenants. *See* Margaret Jane Radin, Residential Rent Control, 15 Phil. & Pub. Affs. 350 (1986), and a critique, Dan Greenberg, *Radin on Personhood and Rent Control*, 73 Monist 642 (1990) (rent control may not promote personhood).

32. *See* Werner Z. Hirsch, *Law and Economics: An Introductory Analysis* 182–88 (2nd ed.) (San Diego: Academic Press, 1988); Thomas Hazlett, *Rent Controls and the Housing Crisis*, in *Resolving the Housing*

Crisis: Government Policy, Decontrol and the Public Interest 277 (M. Bruce Johnson, ed.) (Cambridge, Mass.: Ballinger, 1982), and Anthony Downs, *Residential Rent Controls: An Evaluation* (Washington: Urban Land Institute, 1988).

33. 33 Cal. 3d 184, 672 P.2d 1297, 197 Cal. Rptr. 284 (1983).

34. If being more reasonable than Berkeley is the standard of constitutionality, protection is weak indeed.

35. 197 Cal. Rptr. at 286.

36. 37 Cal. 3d 644, 693 P.2d 261, 209 Cal. Rptr. 682 (1984).

37. 209 Cal. Rptr. at 685.

38. In the final chapter, I discuss this distinction more fully.

39. 209 Cal. Rptr. at 690.

40. The potential numbers of hardship tenants were not trivial. Families earning less than 80 percent of median family income could qualify for hardship consideration.

41. 228 Cal. Rptr. at 734.

42. *Id.* at 735.

43. *Id.* at 730.

44. *Id.* at 734.

45. *Id.* at 736.

46. *Id.*

47. The ordinance specified that economic hardship "must be weighed" by the hearing officer, and even Justice Grodin acknowledged this could give hardship "potentially overriding weight."

48. "The alleviation of undue hardship" is listed as one of the basic goals, followed by "assurance to landlords of a fair and reasonable return."

49. On the rather bizarre extremes to which Berkeley, an exceptionally zealous city, has gone in forcing landlords to endure the whims and cruelties of their tenants and the city government, *see* William Tucker, The Excluded Americans 214–224 (Washington: Regnery Gateway, 1990). For a more general commentary on Berkeley politics, see Peter Collier & David Horowitz, *Slouching Towards Berkeley: Socialism in One City*, 94 Pub. Interest 47 (1989).

50. On the saga on rent control in Santa Monica, *see* Mark E. Kann, *Middle Class Radicalism in Santa Monica* (Philadelphia: Temple Univer-

sity Press, 1986), and Tracy Wilkinson, *Santa Monica: A House Divided by Rent Control*, L.A. Times, April 29, 1989. Even in California, Santa Monica has been exceptional in its affluence and its pursuit of "progressive" politics. In cultural terms, the city has strengthened hierarchy while using egalitarian rhetoric.

51. 37 Cal. 3d 97, 688 P.2d 894, 207 Cal. Rptr. 285 (1984).

52. 688 P.2d at 896.

53. It is indicative of the weak protections of property rights in California that landowners might plausibly resort to a constitutional amendment intended to forbid slavery. Ironically, Radin, *supra* note 31 at 367, compares landlords to slaveholders. Santa Monica landlords apparently disagree about who is the slave and who is the master.

54. 207 Cal. Rptr. at 289.

55. *Id.* at 290.

56. *Id.* at 293.

57. *Id.* at 292.

58. On the fiscal pressures for exactions, see Ana Arana, *Doing Deals*, in *The Best of Planning* 457 (American Planning Association) (Chicago: Planners Press, 1989).

59. Cal. Pub. Res. Code sec. 27100.

60. Mitchell F. Disney, *Fear and Loathing on the California Coastline: Are Coastal Commission Property Exactions Constitutional?* 14 Pepperdine L. Rev. 357 (1987). *See also* Ward Tabor, *The California Coastal Commission and Regulatory Takings*, 17 Pacific L.J. 863 (1986).

61. 33 Cal. 3d 158, 655 P.2d 306, 188 Cal. Rptr. 104 (1982).

62. Justices Bird and Reynoso agreed with the decision but did not join the court's opinion.

63. Mitchell Disney, *supra* note 60 at 357, told of an acquaintance who was required to grant an easement when he sought to rebuild his fire-gutted home near the coast, despite an explicit statutory exemption. Rather than comply or face an exhaustive series of administrative and court appeals to force the commission to comply, the owner sold the property.

64. 188 Cal. Rptr. at 115.

65. *Id.* at 114.

66. 34 Cal. 3d, 667 P.2d 704, 193 Cal. Rptr. 900 (1983).

67. 193 Cal. Rptr. at 904.

68. 39 Cal. 3d 878, 705 P.2d 876, 218 Cal. Rptr. 303 (1985).

69. In 1980 alone, the district received $4.7 million through twenty-four agreements it had previously negotiated.

70. 218 Cal. Rptr. at 305.

71. Consider the implications if the class for comparison was defined so narrowly in a sex discrimination case, such as *Craig v. Boren*, 429 U.S. 190 (1976), in which a state set a minimum drinking age of 21 for men and 18 for women. If a young man sued, and the court reasoned that the appropriate class for comparison purposes included all men between the ages of 18 and 21, then there would be no discrimination because all men in that age bracket had been treated the same. By narrowly defining the class, the court would have eliminated the central issue of the case—discriminatory treatment based on gender.

72. *See* discussion of exclusionary zoning later in this chapter and in Chapter 4.

73. Sarah E. Wilson, *Private Property and the Public Trust: A Theory for Preserving the Coastal Zone,* 4 UCLA J. Envtl. L. & Pol'y 57 at 58, 59 (1984).

74. See Jan S. Stevens, *The Public Trust,* 14 U.C. Davis L. Rev. 195 (1980), for a historical review of the public trust.

75. 6 Cal. 3d 251, 491 P.2d 374, 98 Cal. Rptr. 790.

76. 6 Cal. 3d at 259–60.

77. *See* Note, *The Public Trust Doctrine in California, Florida and New Jersey: A Critique of Its Role in Modern Land Use Law,* 41 Rutgers L. Rev. 1349 (1989).

78. Joseph F. DiMento, Michael D. Dozier, Steven L. Emmons, Donald G. Hagman, Christopher Kim, Karen Greenfield-Sanders, Paul F. Waldau, and Jay A. Woollacott, *Land Development and Environmental Control in the California Supreme Court: The Deferential, the Preservationist, and the Preservationist-Erratic Eras,* 27 UCLA L. Rev. 859 (1980) [hereinafter *Land Development*].

79. 26 Cal. 3d 515, 606 P.2d 362, 162 Cal. Rptr. 327 (1980).

80. 31 Cal. 3d 288, 644 P.2d 782, 182 Cal. Rptr. 599 (1982).

81. 29 Cal. 3d 240, 625 P.2d 239, 172 Cal. Rptr. 696 (1981).

82. 29 Cal. 3d 210, 625 P.2d 256, 172 Cal. Rptr. 713 (1981).

83. 172 Cal. Rptr. at 718.

84. On environmental uses of the public trust, especially as applied to wetlands, see Mary Kyle McCurdy, *Public Trust Protection for Wetlands*, 19 Envtl. L. 683 (1989).

85. Between them, Clark and Richardson accounted for seven of the nine dissenting votes in the four trust cases. Clark would undoubtedly have joined in the *Venice Peninsula* dissent as well, but by 1982 he had left the court. Justice Manuel joined Clark's dissent in *Santa Fe,* and Otto Kaus dissented in *Venice Peninsula.*

86. 182 Cal. Rptr. at 616.

87. 33 Cal. 3d 419, 658 P.2d 709, 18 Cal. Rptr. 346 (1983).

88. On the Mono Lake controversy and the application of the public trust to streams, see Jan S. Stevens, *The Public Trust and In-Stream Uses,* 19 Envtl. L. 605 (1989).

89. *Land Development, supra* note 78.

90. In cultural terms, the court was promoting its own hierarchical value of environmental protection rather than its usual deference to the hierarchy of local government. The relation between hierarchy and environmentalism is discussed in Chapter 2.

91. Wilson, *supra* note 73, at 90, 91.

92. 35 Cal. 3d 858, 679 P.2d 27, 201 Cal. Rptr. 593 (1984).

93. 44 Cal. 3d 839, 750 P.2d 324, 244 Cal. Rptr. 682 (1988).

94. 42 Cal. 3d 52, 720 P.2d 15, 227 Cal. Rptr. 667 (1986).

95. *See* Grayson P. Hanes and J. Randall Minchew, *On Vested Rights to Land Use and Development,* 46 Wash. & Lee L. Rev. 373 (1989).

96. *See* Donald G. Hagman, *The Vesting Issue: The Rights of Fetal Development Vis-a-Vis the Abortions of Public Whimsy,* 7 Envtl. L. 519 (1977).

97. *Pardee Construction Co. v. Camarillo,* 37 Cal. 3d 465, 690 P.2d 701, 208 Cal. Rptr. 228 (1984).

98. 208 Cal. Rptr. at 235.

99. 18 Cal. 3d 832, 558 P.2d 867, 135 Cal. Rptr. 781 (1977).

100. 720 P.2d at 35.

101. 28 Cal. 3d 511, 620 P.2d 565, 169 Cal. Rptr. 904 (1980).

102. 620 P.2d at 572.

103. 169 Cal. Rptr. at 914.

104. Costa Mesa had rezoned the Arnel property to a planned development district prior to approving subdivision plans. Planned development zones (often called PUDs or PDRs) may not significantly affect the overall density of development but do allow more flexibility than traditional zoning when designing large developments and thus are often favored by both developers and city officials.

105. *See,* for example, the leading Oregon case, *Fasano v. Board of County Commissioners of Washington County,* 264 Or. 574, 507 P.2d 23 (1973).

106. 169 Cal. Rptr. at 909.

107. The effect on the region is another matter. Tobriner is correct that prospective tenants will be affected, most likely adversely, by any down zoning. But if they do not yet live in Costa Mesa, they cannot even vote. The only assurance offered by Tobriner that local initiatives would not be contrary to the regional welfare is that the court could require a "reasonable relationship" to regional welfare. But the court has traditionally been quite liberal in its interpretation of "reasonable."

108. *Zoning by Initiative in California: A Critical Analysis,* 12 Loy. L.A.L. R. 903, 923 (1979).

109. In a regulatory proceeding removed from the public eye, the danger may be just the reverse. The concentrated interests who have the most to lose may "capture" the agency.

110. 169 Cal. Rptr. at 913.

111. 26 Cal. 3d 897, 608 P.2d 728, 163 Cal. Rptr. 640 (1980).

112. 163 Cal. Rptr. at 648.

113. 38 Cal. 3d 790, 700 P.2d 794, 214 Cal. Rptr. 904 (1985).

114. The leading federal case on this issue is *Berman v. Parker,* 348 U.S. 26 (1954).

115. *Oakland v. Oakland Raiders,* 32 Cal. 3d 60, 646 P.2d 835, 183 Cal. Rptr. 673 (1982).

116. 183 Cal. Rptr. at 681.

117. *Id.* at 684.

118. See *Property* (orig. pub. 1792), in 14 *The Papers of James Madison* 267 (Robert A. Rutland, Thomas A. Mason, Robert J. Brugger, Jeane K. Sis-

son, and Fredrika J. Teute, ed.) (Charlottesville, Va.; University Press of Virginia, 1981). See also John Locke, *The Second Treatise of Government* (orig. pub. 1690) (Indianapolis: Bobbs-Merrill, 1952) (property as "lives, liberties and estates").

119. A federal highway beautification law required compensation for owners of billboards near highways.

120. 26 Cal. 3d 848, 610 P.2d 407, 164 Cal. Rptr. 510 (1980).

121. 610 P.2d at 431.

122. Including labor picket signs and political messages in a resident's yard.

123. State courts are split on whether aesthetics alone justify police power regulation. *Compare Oregon v. Hartke,* 240 Or. 35, 400 P.2d 255 (1965), upholding aesthetic regulation, with *Mayor and City Council of Baltimore v. Mano Swartz, Inc.,* 268 Md. 79, 299 A.2d 828 (1973), and *see* Samuel Bufford, *Beyond the Eye of the Beholder: A New Majority of Jurisdictions Authorize Aesthetic Regulation,* 48 UMKC L. Rev. 125 (1980).

124. As aesthetic concerns involve no physical invasion (in contrast to, say, pollution and noise), the libertarian argument would be that they are a matter of personal taste, not public nuisance, and thus cannot be imposed on landowners, especially without compensation.

125. This is a classic takings issue, but Tobriner considers it as one of several due process arguments. Doing so eliminates the need to consider that while the city may have acted in accordance with due process, it might still be required to compensate owners for destroying the value of their property. The blurring of due process and takings questions pervades many California cases.

126. 164 Cal. Rptr. at 528.

127. 164 Cal. Rptr. at 517. Compare this statement with the query by Justice Brennan in *San Diego Gas* that if "a policeman must know the Constitution, then why not a planner?" 450 U.S. 621, 662 (1981).

128. See *Schad v. Mt. Ephraim,* 452 U.S. 61 (1981).

129. 32 Cal. 3d 553, 652 P.2d 51, 186 Cal. Rptr. 494 (1982).

130. 186 Cal. Rptr. at 503.

131. 652 P.2d at 53.

132. *Griswold v. Connecticut,* 381 U.S. 479 (1965).

133. The section states: "All people are by nature free and independent and have inalienable rights. Among these are enjoying and defending

life and liberty, acquiring, possessing, and protecting property, and pursuing and obtaining safety, happiness, and privacy."

134. Lest the city create undue hardship for the rich, the city exempted servants from the limit.

135. 27 Cal. 3d 123, 610 P.2d 436, 164 Cal. Rptr. 539 (1980).

136. 164 Cal. Rptr. at 545.

137. Even though both rights are mentioned in the same constitutional clause, art. I, § 1, *supra*, note 133.

138. 164 Cal. Rptr. at 542–43.

139. *Baker v. Burbank-Glendale-Pasadena Airport Authority*, 39 Cal. 3d 862, 705 P.2d 866, 218 Cal. Rptr. 293 (1985).

140. Baker also filed a nuisance suit.

141. The flights could be seen as physical invasions of the airspace above Baker's home, for which the U.S. Supreme court has required payment. See *United States v. Causby*, 328 U.S. 256 (1946), in which military flights disturbed the Causbys and drove 150 of their chickens to suicide. The Court ruled that the government in effect had appropriated an easement and must compensate the owners. See also *Loretto v. Teleprompter Manhattan CATV Corp.*, 458 U.S. 419, 102 S. Ct. 3164 (1982), discussed in the next chapter, in which television cables were deemed a physical invasion.

142. 218 Cal. Rptr. at 297.

143. 705 P.2d at 869.

144. It would be interesting to see how the court would decide if government efforts to preserve the natural or built environment conflicted with individual guarantees of privacy or expression. Suppose a city historic preservation ordinance forbade owners of designated buildings, including homes, from altering the original interiors of the buildings. Would the regulation be an unconstitutional invasion of personal rights or a reasonable land use regulation? A related conflict recently arose in New York where church officials argued that historic preservation demands imposed such great cost burdens on the church that freedom to practice religion, usually a preferred right, was infringed. *See* discussion of impact of free exercise clause on land use regulation in *Principles of Planning Practice* 130–39 (Brian W. Blaesser and Alan C. Weinstein, eds.) (Chicago: Planners Press, 1989).

145. 41 Cal. 3d 373, 710 P.2d 299, 221 Cal. Rptr. 499 (1985).

146. 42 Cal. 3d 1302, 729 P.2d 166, 233 Cal. Rptr. 2 (1986).

147. 221 Cal. Rptr. at 503, quoting *Katz v. United States*, 389 U.S. 347 (1967).

148. *Id.* at 504.

149. *Id.*

150. See *Oliver v. U.S.*, 466 U.S. 170 (1984), and *California v. Ciraulo*, 476 U.S. 207 (1986), discussed in Chapter 6.

151. *Id.* at 505.

152. 710 P.2d at 306.

153. 233 Cal. Rptr. at 7.

154. Much to the benefit of local farm and garden suppliers.

155. *Associated Homes Builders of the Greater Eastbay, Inc. v. Livermore*, 135 Cal. Rptr. 41, 44 (1976).

156. *Id.*

157. 18 Cal. 3d at 603.

158. *Southern Burlington County NAACP v. Mount Laurel* (Mount Laurel I), 67 N.J. 151, 336 A.2d 713 (1975), discussed in Chapter 4.

159. Most notably, *National Land and Investment Co. v. Kohn*, 419 Pa. 504, 215 A.2d 597 (1965), also discussed in Chapter 4.

160. Donald G. Hagmon, *The American Dream as Public Nightmare, or, Sam, You Made the Front Yard Too Long*, 3 UCLA J. Envtl. L. & Pol'y 219 (1983).

161. *Id.*

162. 18 Cal. 3d at 602.

163. 135 Cal. Rptr. at 44.

164. 18 Cal. 3d at 616.

165. *Id.*

166. 41 Cal. 3d 810, 718 P.2d 68, 226 Cal. Rptr. 81 (1986).

167. But even the legislature had not seriously challenged exclusionary regimes, as the statute specifically exempted the most common exclusionary tools, including large-lot zoning, agricultural preservation districts, and "temporary" moratoria on new construction.

168. 226 Cal. Rptr. at 90.

169. California opinions are often mercifully brief, say fifteen pages, compared with the eighty-page epic works that sometimes emanate from New Jersey.

170. Matthew O. Tobriner and Joseph R. Grodin, *The Individual and the Public Service Enterprise in the New Industrial State*, 55 Calif. L. Rev. 1247, 1249 (1967).

171. *Id.* at 1249.

172. In the penultimate chapter, I discuss the feudal character of regulatory controls and their challenge to liberalism.

173. In their study of California environmental cases in the 1970s, DiMento and his coauthors described a court that has been overwhelmingly deferential yet increasingly taking an activist, preservationist role. *Land Development, supra* note 78.

174. Despotism is the fourth type of political culture in which constraints are imposed without concern for the welfare of others. It is "grid" without "group." *See* the discussion of the grid-group model early in Chapter 2.

175. Lucas was appointed associate justice in 1984, and chief justice in 1987.

176. *Baker,* in which Grodin concurred in an opinion by Reynoso.

177. Grodin also wrote the majority opinion in the *Cook* aerial search case, which is not included in the tabulations.

178. In *Cook,* Grodin sounded downright libertarian, emphasizing the vital role served by private property in protecting personal privacy, and declared that the court must be true to the "precious liberties derived from the Framers." 221 Cal. Rptr. at 504. But he came back to his progovernment senses in *Mayoff.*

179. 24 Cal. 3d at 282.

180. Only Bird came even close, voting in twenty-one land use cases.

181. *Land Development, supra* note 78, at 806.

182. Stephen R. Barnett, *The Emerging Court,* 71 Calif. L. Rev. 1134, 1139 (1983).

183. *See* Philip Tarrizosa, *The Elusive Stanley Mosk,* Calif. Law, March 1989, at 63.

184. 18 Cal. 3d at 618.

185. See discussion of the *Mount Laurel* cases in Chapter 4.

186. 207 Cal. Rptr. at 292.

187. 163 Cal. Rptr. at 648.

188. Lucas rejected the privacy claims in both marijuana aerial search cases, which may indicate a predisposition to side with the state in criminal litigation. "No one has a reasonable expectation of privacy in the conduct of his criminal affairs," Lucas declared in *Cook*.

189. 209 Cal. Rptr. at 690.

190. Barnett, *supra* note 182, at 1188.

191. *See* Marcus M. Kauffman, Crisis in the Courts, Calif. Law., Aug. 1990, at 28. Kauffman was briefly a justice on the state supreme court.

192. See Robert Egelko, *The Duke Puts a New Face on the Supreme Court*, 19 Calif. J. 236 (1988).

193. None of these three justices voted in more than two constitutional land use cases.

194. *See* Bill Blum, *Toward a Radical Middle*, Calif. Law., Jan. 1991, at 48.

CHAPTER 6

1. 482 U.S. 304.

2. 483 U.S. 825.

3. The Court had not found a regulation to be a taking since *Pennsylvania Coal Co. v. Mahon*, 260 U.S. 393 (1922).

4. *See* Comment, *First English Evangelical Lutheran Church of Glendale v. County of Los Angeles and Nollan v. California Coastal Commission: The Big Chill*, 52 Albany L. Rev. 325 (1987).

5. *See* Lee P. Symons, *Property Rights and Local Land-Use Regulation: The Implications of First English and Nollan*, 18 Publius (No. 3) 81 (1988).

6. Justice Stewart, in *Lynch v. Household Finance Corp.*, 405 U.S. 538, 552 (1972).

7. William J. Brennan, Jr., *The Equality Principle: A Foundation of American Law*, 20 U.C. Davis L. Rev. 673 (1987).

8. 304 U.S. 144 (1938). The Court suggested that "commercial" regulation should be given only minimal review, unlike legislation that affected

specific constitutional rights, political rights, or the rights of "discrete and insular" minorities. In practice, constitutional specificity came to mean less than the type of rights involved: The expressive, equality, and privacy rights preferred by the justices were strongly protected, and property rights received little attention. See Chapter 3 for more discussion of *Carolene Products* and its consequences.

9. Charles Reich, *The New Property*, 73 Yale L. J. 733 (1964).

10. *Goldberg v. Kelley*, 397 U.S. 254 (1970).

11. *Cleveland Board of Education v. Lafleur*, 414 U.S. 632 (1974).

12. *Goss v. Lopez*, 419 U.S. 565 (1975).

13. *See* William J. Brennan, Jr., *State Constitutions and the Protection of Individual Rights*, 90 Harv. L. Rev. 489, 492 (1977), and James L. Oakes, *"Property Rights" in Constitutional Analysis Today*, 56 Wash. L. Rev. 583 (1981).

14. *Griswold v. Connecticut*, 381 U.S. 479 (1965).

15. *Roe v. Wade* (1973).

16. Wrote Douglas: "Some arguments suggest that *Lochner* should be our guide. But we decline that invitation. . . . We do not sit as a super-legislature." 381 U.S. at 481–82. Rather, Douglas argued, the right of privacy is protected by the "penumbras" that emanate from specific amendments. *Id.* at 483, 484. *Lochner v. New York*, 198 U.S. 45 (1905), is the most famous "liberty of contract" case.

17. *See* concurrences by justices Goldberg, Harlan, and White in *Griswold* and the majority opinion of Justice Blackmun in *Roe*.

18. *See Shapiro v. Thompson*, 394 U.S. 618 (1969).

19. *United States Trust Co. v. New Jersey*, 431 U.S. 1 (1977).

20. *Allied Structural Steel v. Spannaus*, 438 U.S. 234 (1978).

21. Richard F. Babcock, *The Zoning Game: Municipal Practices and Policies* 110 (Madison: University of Wisconsin Press, 1966).

22. 416 U.S. 1, 94 S. Ct. 1536 (1974).

23. 416 U.S. at 3.

24. The *Belle Terre* case was in this sense the reverse of *Nectow v. Cambridge*, 277 U.S. 183 (1928), which, although a victory for one landowner, ushered in the era of abdication.

25. *See Warth v. Seldin*, 422 U.S. 490 (1975) (plaintiffs lacked standing to challenge alleged exclusionary zoning); *Arlington Heights v. Metropolitan Housing Development Corp.*, 429 U.S. 252 (1977) (rejection of housing development did not violate Equal Protection Clause), and *Penn Central Transportation Co. v. New York City*; 438 U.S. 104 (1978) (forbidding construction of a highrise above historic station not a taking).

26. *Moore v. East Cleveland*, 431 U.S. 949 (1977).

27. The grandchild came to live with his grandmother after his mother had died. Under the East Cleveland ordinance, people could live with both their parents and their children, so a grandparent could live with a grandchild if the intervening generation of parents was in the same household.

28. The Court opinion by Justice Powell was criticized by a defender of the double standard of constitutional rights for its reliance on "naked substantive due process" grounds. Lupu, *Untangling the Strands of the Fourteenth Amendment*, 77 Mich. L. Rev. 981, 1017 (1979).

29. *Agins v. Tiburon*, 24 Cal. 3d 266, 598 P.2d 25, 157 Cal. Rptr. 372 (1979), discussed in Chapter 5.

30. *Robins v. Pruneyard Shopping Center*, 23 Cal. 3d 899, 592 P.2d 341, 153 Cal. Rptr. 854 (1979).

31. William W. Van Astyne, *The Recrudescence of Property Rights as the Foremost Principle of Civil Liberties: The First Decade of the Burger Court*, 43 Law & Contemp. Probs. 66, 73 (1980).

32. Although there was a free speech claim in *Pruneyard*, it was in opposition to the owner's claim of a property right to exclude.

33. *Pruneyard Shopping Center v. Robins*, 447 U.S. 74 (1980).

34. *Id.* at 93.

35. *Id.* at 98.

36. *Id.* at 82.

37. *Id.* at 84.

38. 458 U.S. 419 (1982).

39. See also the Court's hierarchy of personal property in the discussion of search cases later in this chapter.

40. *Agins v. Tiburon*, 447 U.S. 255 (1980).

41. In land use litigation, that is.

42. In *Pennsylvania Coal Co. v. Mahon*, 260 U.S. 393, 415 (1922), the Court held that severe regulations could be takings, but it never clearly defined what it meant by "too far."

43. 447 U.S. at 261.

44. See *MacDonald, Sommer, & Frates v. Yolo County*, 477 U.S. 340 (1986).

45. *Agins* (1980); *San Diego Gas & Electric Co. v. San Diego*, 450 U.S. 621 (1981); *Williamson County Regional Planning Commission v. Hamilton Bank of Johnson City*, 473 U.S. 172 (1985), and *MacDonald* (1986).

46. 447 U.S. at 260.

47. See discussion of *Southern Burlington County NAACP v. Mount Laurel* (Mount Laurel I), 67 N.J: 151, 336, A.2d 713 (1975); *Southern Burlington County NAACP v. Mount Laurel* (Mount Laurel II), 92 N.J. 158, 456 A.2d 390 (1983); and related cases in Chapter 4.

48. See *First English*, discussed later in this chapter.

49. See discussion of *First English* and governmental avoidance of takings claims later in this chapter and in the concluding chapter.

50. Only court decisions with full opinions are included. Since the Court schedules arguments for only a fraction of the appeals that are filed, the Court refuses to hear most landowner claims each year. As a consequence, many more lower court rulings upholding governmental regulation become final judgments.

51. 473 U.S. 432 (1985).

52. See C. Edwin Baker, *Property and Its Relation to Constitutionally Protected Liberty*, 134 U. Penn. L. Rev. 741 (1986); Stephen J. Massey, *Justice Rehnquist's Theory of Property*, 93 Yale L. J. 541 (1984); and Van Astyne, *supra* note 31.

53. Van Astyne, *supra* note 31, at 82.

54. 453 U.S. 490 (1981).

55. 452 U.S. 61 (1981).

56. 459 U.S. 116 (1982).

57. See Scott David Godshall, *Land Use Regulation and the Free Exercise Clause*, 84 Colum. L. Rev. 1562 (1984); and Susan L. Goldberg, *Gimme Shelter: Religious Provision of Shelter to the Homeless as a Protected Use Under Zoning Laws*, 30 Wash. U.J. of Urb. & Contemp. L. 75 (1986).

58. John J. Costonis, *Making Sense of the Taking Issue*, 1984 Zoning & Plan. L. Handbook 109, 116.

59. *Agins, San Diego Gas, Hamilton Bank, MacDonald,* and *First English.*

60. *Pennell v. San Jose,* 485 U.S. 1 (1988).

61. 242 U.S. 526.

62. 453 U.S. at 490.

63. *Id.*

64. 249 U.S. 269 (1919).

65. 285 U.S. 105 (1932).

66. *See Virginia State Board of Pharmacy v. Virginia Citizens Consumer Council,* 425 U.S. 748 (1976), and *Central Hudson Gas & Electric Corp. v. Public Service Commission,* 447 U.S. 557 (1980).

67. As was the case in *Young v. American Mini-Theatres,* 427 U.S. 50 (1976).

68. Daniel R. Mandelker, *The Free Speech Revolution in Land Use Control,* 60 Chi.[-]Kent L. Rev. 51, 54 (1984).

69. 452 U.S. at 67.

70. The city might specify what colors the store could be painted or what dimensions the structure must conform to, for example, without concerning the court. Uses might similarly be restricted as long as they were not perceived as expressive. If Schad preferred to run a video-game parlor at his shop, it is not likely the court would interfere with a ban, deferring to local government in areas of "economic" regulation.

71. 452 U.S. at 78.

72. Commentators have different favorite examples of the search for "any conceivable rational basis." One of the classics is *Williamson v. Lee Optical,* 348 U.S. 483 (1955), in which a regulation forbade opticians from putting old lenses in new frames without a prescription. Rather than consider that the legislation may have simply been intended to enrich optometrists, the court hypothesized that the prescription requirement might be related to a general concern for public health. *See also Ferguson v. Skrupa,* 372 U.S. 726 (1963), in which the court excused a special-interest law making the debt-adjusting business the exclusive domain of lawyers.

73. 452 U.S. at 81.

74. *Id.* at 89.

75. 459 U.S. at 131.

76. *Id.* at 129.

77. Daniel R. Mandelker, *Group Homes: The Supreme Court Revives the Equal Protection Clause in Land Use Cases,* 1986 Inst. on Plan. Zoning & Eminent Domain 3–1, 3–13.

78. 473. U.S. at 441–45.

79. *Id.* at 442–43.

80. *Id.* at 450.

81. *Id.* at 458. *Williamson,* is discussed *supra,* note 71.

82. *Id.,* quoting *Williamson,* 348 U.S. at 489.

83. The court reports are rich with examples of the high court making excuses for blatantly discriminatory legislation. For a discussion of the role of hot dogs in community preservation, see *New Orleans v. Dukes,* 427 U.S. 297 (1976).

84. 473 U.S. at 460.

85. Although from the perspective of the land use specialist, making all constitutional law a category of land use law might be entirely reasonable!

86. 466 U.S. 170 (1984).

87. *Id.* at 179.

88. *Id.* at 178.

89. *Id.* at 195.

90. *Id.* at 192.

91. *Id.* at 180, quoting *Boyd v. United States,* 116 U.S. 616, 630 (1886).

92. See *California v. Ciraulo,* 476 U.S. 207 (1986).

93. 480 U.S. 294 (1987).

94. 480 U.S. at 312.

95. 304 U.S. at 152.

96. *Chicago B. and Q. Railroad v. Chicago,* 166 U.S. 226 (1897). As the Bill of Rights does not apply directly to the states, this indirect application to the states is itself a form of substantive due process. The "specifics" doctrine, then, cannot avoid substantive due process, which the *Carolene* opinion purported to reject.

97. *Nectow,* 277 U.S. 183 (1928), was the last zoning considered by the court for many decades. On physical invasions, *see* for example *U.S. v. Causby,* 328 U.S. 256 (1946) (air space), and *Kaiser Aetna v. U.S.,* 444 U.S. 164 (1979) (private lagoon).

98. 458 U.S. at 448.

99. *See* Eugene A. Boyle, *The Status of the Public Use Requiem: Post-Midkiff,* 30 Wash. U.J. Urb. & Contemp. L. 115 (1986); David L. Callies, *A Requiem for Public Purpose: Hawaii Housing Authority v. Midkiff,* 1985 Inst. on Plan. Zoning & Eminent Domain 8–1; and Robert H. Freilich and Eugene R. Pal, Jr., *New Developments in Land Use and Environmental Regulation,* 1985 Inst. on Plan. Zoning & Eminent Domain 1–1.

100. 348 U.S. 26.

101. *Id.* at 32.

102. *Id.*

103. 467 U.S. 229 (1984).

104. Justice Marshall did not participate in the decision.

105. *See* Thomas J. Coyne, *A Final Requiem for the Public Use Limitation on Eminent Domain,* 60 Notre Dame L. Rev. 388 (1985); Julie Sullwold Hernandez, *Can They Do That? Taking from Peter and Giving to Paul: The Public Use Limitation after Hawaii Housing Authority v. Midkiff,* 15 Sw. U.L. Rev. 817 (1985); James Janda, *The Supreme Court's Assault on Private Ownership of Property,* 90 Dickenson L. Rev. 1990 (1984); and Susan Lourne, *A New Slant on Social Legislation: Taking from the Rich to Give to the Well-to-Do,* 25 Nat. Resources J. 773 (1984).

106. For a sampling, *see* Ross A. Macfarlane, *Testing the Constitutional Validity of Land Use Regulations: Substantive Due Process as a Superior Alternative to Takings Analysis,* 57 Wash. L. Rev. (1982) (court confuses takings and due process precedents); Richard A. Epstein, *Not Deference, but Doctrine: The Eminent Domain Clause,* 1982 Sup. Ct. Rev. 351 ("sorry performance of the Supreme Court"); Carol M. Rose, *Mahon Reconstructed: Why the Taking Issue Is Still a Muddle,* 57 So. Calif. L. Rev. 561 (1984); and Gus Bauman, *The Supreme Court, Inverse Condemnation, and the Fifth Amendment: Justice Brennan Confronts the Inevitable,* 15 Rutgers L. J. 15 (1983) ("most vexing issue of American land use law").

107. For a pungent contrast, *compare* Norman Williams, Jr., R. Marlin Smith, Charles Siemon, Daniel R. Mandelker, and Richard F. Babcock, *The White River Junction Manifesto,* 9 Vt. L. Rev. 193 (1984) [hereinafter *The Manifesto*], and Michael M. Berger and Gideon Kanner, *Thoughts on the White River Junction Manifesto: A Reply to the "Gang of Five's"*

Views on Just Compensation for Regulatory Taking of Property, 19 Loyola L. A. L. Rev. 685 (1986).

108. Williams and his coauthors have suggested that even this pretense is unnecessary, arguing that Holmes was being careless and didn't mean what he said. Even though the court was considering the constitutional rights of the property owner, Holmes meant "taking" to refer generally to invalid regulation, according to the authors, and it is merely coincidental that the takings clause is a major source of landowner rights.

109. *Pennsylvania Coal,* 260 U.S. at 415.

110. Joseph Sax expressed puzzlement that what he perceived as the withering away of property rights, including the trend toward noncompensation, "should be occurring simultaneously with the blossoming of the 'me' generation." *Some Thoughts on the Decline of Private Property,* 58 Wash L. Rev. 481, 493 (1983). Assuming for the sake of argument that there is or was a "me" generation, this coincidence does not seem at all surprising; getting something for nothing from a private landowner is a very rational expression of private greed through public means.

111. 450 U.S. at 653.

112. *Id.* at 652.

113. *Id.* at 656 (emphasis in original).

114. *Id.* at 657.

115. *Id.* at 662.

116. *Id.*

117. 473 U.S. 172 (1985).

118. 477 U.S. 340 (1986).

119. Gus Bauman, *Dejà Vu, or Et Tu Supreme Court?* 37 Land Use L. & Zoning Dig. 3 (July 1985).

120. 482 U.S. at 340.

121. 483 U.S. at 842.

122. *First English Evangelical Church of Glendale v. County of Los Angeles,* 210 Cal. App. 3d 1353, Cal. Rptr. (1989), *cert. denied,* 110 S. Ct. 107, L. Ed. 2d 950 (1990).

123. *See Penn Central,* 438 U.S. 104 (1978), for a discussion of takings standards.

124. *See Hadacheck v. Sebastian,* 299 U.S. 394 (1915) (prohibition of brickyard), and *Goldblatt v. Hempstead,* 369 U.S. 590 (1962) (excavation restriction that destroyed sand and gravel business).

125. Gus Bauman, *The Longest Running Show in Town,* 38 Land Use L. & Zoning Dig. 3 (Sept. 1986).

126. 482 U.S. at 321.

127. *Id.* at 334.

128. The sequence of these cases is reminiscent of the one-two reapportion punch (stretched out over two years) of *Baker v. Carr,* 369 U.S. 186 (1962), and *Reynolds v. Sims,* 377 U.S. 533 (1964), which heralded the court's entry into a major new area of activism.

129. William Fulton, *Exactions Put to the Test,* in *The Best of Planning* 126, 128 (American Planning Association) (Chicago: Planners Press, 1989).

130. On impact fees, *See Candid Enterprises, Inc. v. Grossmont Union High School District,* 39 Cal. 3d 878, 705 P.2d 876, 218 Cal. Rptr. 303 (1985), and *Russ Building Partnership v. San Francisco,* 44 Cal. 3d 839, 750 P.2d 324, 244 Cal. Rptr 682 (1988), discussed in Chapter 5.

131. For reviews of the variety of exactions imposed on developers, *see* Gus Bauman and William H. Ethier, *Development Exactions and Impact Fees: A Survey of American Practices,* 50 L. & Contemp. Probs. 51 (1987), and R. Marlin Smith, *From Subdivision Improvement Requirements to Community Benefit Assessments and Linkage Payments: A Brief History of Land Development Exactions,* 50 L. & Contemp. Probs. 5 (1987),.

132. As Scalia implies, the Nollans could be required to give an easement for beach access if the coastal commission's reasoning had been stronger.

133. Bauman and Ethier, *supra* note 131, at 55–56.

134. 458 U.S. 419, 433.

135. 444 U.S. 164, 176 (1979) (in *Kaiser-Aetna,* compensation was required for public access to private marina).

136. 483 U.S. at 831.

137. *Id.* at 857.

138. Sax, *supra* note 110, at 494.

139. 483 U.S. at 833.

140. *Id.* at 845.

141. 482 U.S. at 315.

142. 480 U.S. 470 (1987).

143. James S Burling, Takings and Wetlands: A Swamp Half Full Is Still a Swamp 5 (presented to CLE Int'l, Seattle, Wash., May 18, 1990).

144. 480 U.S. at 509.

145. *See Gardner v. New Jersey Pinelands Commission,* 125 N.J. 193, 593 A.2d 251 (1991).

146. 484 U.S. 469 (1988).

147. 485 U.S. 1 (1988).

148. On the feeling of relief that the Supreme Court had not lost its senses, *See* Charles H. Clarke, *Rent Control and the Constitutional Ghosts and Goblins of Laissez-Faire Past: Pennell v. San Jose,* 14 U. Dayton L. Rev. 115 (1988).

149. 484 U.S. at 492.

150. *Id.* at 493.

151. *Id.,* quoting from Alfred A. Porro, Jr. and Lorraine S. Teleky, *Marshland Title Dilemma: A Tidal Phenomenon,* 3 Seton Hall L. Rev. 323, 325–26 (1972).

152. 485 U.S. at 13.

153. *Id.*

154. On argument that rent control requires compensation, *see Making Room at the Inn: Rent Control as a Regulatory Taking,* 38 Wash. U.J. Urb. & Contemp. L. 305 (1986).

155. *See Block v. Hirsh,* 256 U.S. 135 (1921) (upheld wartime rent control), and *Fischer v. Berkeley,* 475 U.S. 260 (1986) (rejected antitrust challenge to rent control).

156. Takings cases are counted twice in weighted calculations. This is a nod to those who argue that only these cases, and not the fundamental rights cases, should be considered land use cases. I disagree, as the protection of property rights through transcending personal rights is an important practical and theoretical component in the Court's protection of landowners. But it is fair to consider a justice who sides with property owners in takings cases a stronger supporter of property rights. How much stronger is a qualitative judgment. Rather than ignore this point, I have doubled the

takings cases scores, which is admittedly arbitrary. Nonetheless, I think it makes possible useful comparisons of justices.

157. See Antonin Scalia, *Economic Affairs as Human Affairs*, in *Economic Liberties and the Judiciary* 31 (James A. Dorn and Henry G. Manne, eds.) (Fairfax, Va.: George Mason University Press, 1987).

158. Justice Marshall did not participate in the case.

159. *San Diego Gas*, 450 U.S. at 662.

160. 473 U.S. at 460.

161. Gerald Bowden and Lewis G. Feldman, *Take It or Leave It: Uncertain Regulatory Taking Standards and Remedies Threaten California's Open Space Planning*, 15 U. Calif. Davis L. Rev. 371 (1981).

162. *See* Joseph F. DiMento, *"But It's Only Planning": Planning and the Taking Issue in Land Development and Environmental Control Law*, 1984 Zoning & Plan. L. Handbook 91.

163. *The Manifesto, supra* note 107, at 242.

CHAPTER 7

1. E.F. Roberts, *The Demise of Property Law*, 57 Cornell L. Rev. 1, 43 (1971).

2. David L. Callies, *Land Use Controls: Of Enterprise Zones, Takings, Plans and Growth Controls* 14 Urb. Law. 781, 845 (1982).

3. *Id.* at 782, 845.

4. Maine, *Ancient Law* (London: John Murray, 1901).

5. Robert H. Nelson, *Zoning and Property Rights* 118 (Cambridge, Mass: MIT Press, 1977).

6. Ellen Frankel Paul, *Property Rights and Eminent Domain* 8 (New Brunswick, N.J.: Transaction Books, 1987).

7. McClaughry, *The New Feudalism—State Land Use Controls*, in *No Land Is an Island* 38 (San Francisco: Institute for Contemporary Studies, 1975).

8. *Id.* The irony is that variants of bolshevism seem to be in greater vogue on *this* side of the water, at least among university faculty, than in the Eastern nations long under its yoke.

9. See discussion of public trust cases in Chapter 5.

10. Matthew O. Tobriner and Joseph R. Grodin, *The Individual and the Public Service Enterprise in the New Industrial State*, 55 Calif. L. Rev. 1247, 1249 (1967).

11. Matthew O. Tobriner, *Retrospective: Ten Years on the California Supreme Court*, 20 UCLA L. Rev. 5, 12 (1972).

12. Tobriner and Grodin, *supra* note 10, at 1283.

13. *Id.* at 1249.

14. Tobriner, *supra* note 11, at 6.

15. Tobriner and Grodin, *supra* note 10, at 1249.

16. Tobriner, *supra* note 11, at 5.

17. *Id.* at 12.

18. Roberts, *supra* note 1.

19. *Changing Conceptions of Property in Law*, 86 U. Pa. L. Rev. 691, 710 (1938).

20. John E. Cribbet, *Changing Concepts in the Law of Land Use*, 50 Iowa L. Rev. 245, 247 (1965).

21. *Id.*

22. Nelson, *supra* note 5, at 116.

23. *Id.*

24. *Id.* at 119.

25. Delafons, *Land Use Controls in the United States* 3 (2nd ed.) (Cambridge, Mass.: MIT Press, 1969) [first published 1962].

26. Frank J. Popper, *Land Use and the Environment* (Introduction), in *The Best of Planning* 188, 193 (American Planning Association) (Chicago: Planners Press, 1989).

27. For an authoritative review of environmental statutes that regulate use of property, *see* Linda A. Malone, *Environmental Regulation of Land Use* (New York: Clark Boardman, 1990).

28. Michael Lee Vasu, *Politics and Planning: A National Study of American Planners* 4 (Chapel Hill: University of North Carolina Press, 1979).

29. *Id.* at 5.

30. Nelson, *supra* note 5, at 145.

31. Popper, *supra* note 26.

32. *See* James P. Karp, *The Evolving Meaning of Aesthetics in Land-Use Regulations*, 15 Colum. J. Envtl. L. 307 (1990).

33. *See* Note, *You Can't Build That Here: The Constitutionality of Aesthetic Zoning and Architectural Review*, 58 Fordham L. Rev. 1013 (1990).

34. Delafons, *supra* note 25, at 60.

35. *See* Samuel Bufford, *Beyond the Eye of the Beholder: A New Majority of Jurisdictions Authorize Aesthetic Regulation*, 48 UMKC L. Rev. 125 (1980).

36. *See State ex. rel. Stoyanoff v. Berkeley*, 458 S.W. 2d 305 (Mo. 1970).

37. *See Novi v. Pacifica*, 169 Cal. App. 3d 678, 215 Cal. Rptr. 239 (1985) (requirement of architectural "variety" serves general welfare). On the First Amendment issues raised by architectural review, *see* Note, *Architecture, Aesthetic Zoning, and the First Amendment*, 28 Stan. L. Rev. 179 (1975).

38. Nelson, *supra* note 5, at 21.

39. *Id.* at 164.

40. James Peters, *Houston Gets Religion*, in *The Best of Planning* 323 (American Planning Association) (Chicago: Planners Press, 1989).

41. Despite the lack of zoning, public planning has nonetheless played a significant role, as through infrastructure development and subdivision controls. *See* Roscoe H. Jones, *Houston—City Planning Without Zoning* in *Zoning: Its Costs and Relevance for the 1980s* 45 (Vancouver, B.C.: Fraser Institute, 1980).

42. *See* J. Brian Phillips, *Progressivism Comes to Houston*, 40 Freeman 72 (1990).

43. Two trends in the 1970s pushed political power to the neighborhoods. Courts began to strike down at-large elections as discriminatory toward racial and ethnic minorities, which might dominate in a district but not in an entire municipality, and scholars and commentators argued that neighborhood control better captured the ideal of "government by the people." *See* David Morris and Karl Hess, *Neighborhood Power: The New Localism* (Boston: Beacon Press, 1975).

44. Peters, *supra* note 40, at 324.

45. *See* Dennis J. Coyle, *The Balkans by the Bay*, Pub. Interest, Spring 1988, at 67.

46. Bosselman and Callies, *The Quiet Revolution in Land Use Control* (Washington, D.C.: Council on Environmental Quality, 1971).

47. Vermont Act 250, Vt. Stat. Ann. tit. 10, ch. 151 (1970).

48. 1969 Or. Laws, ch. 324; 1973 Or. Laws, ch. 80. *See* Or. Rev. Stat., sections 197.005–.850 (1983).

49. Hawaii Land Use Law 1961, Hawaii Rev. Stat. ch. 205 (1968).

50. *See also* Maine Site Location Law 1970, Me. Rev. Stat. Ann. tit. 38, secs. 48–488 (Supp. 1970), and Florida Environmental Land and Water Control Act 1970, Fla. Stat. Ann. ch. 380 (1972).

51. Quoted in Frank J. Popper, *The Politics of Land Use Reform* 188 (Madison, Wisc.: University of Wisconsin Press, 1981).

52. See Chapter 5 for a discussion of recent legal battles over coastal regulation in California.

53. *See* R. Robert Linowes and Don T. Allensworth, *The States and Land-Use Control* (New York: Praeger, 1975); Daniel P. Selmi and Kenneth A. Manaster, *State Environmental Law* (New York: Clark Boardman, 1990).

54. *See* the discussion of The *Mount Laurel* cases are discussed in Chapter 4.

55. Popper, *supra* note 26, at 193.

56. *See* Franklin L. King, *The Pennsylvania Environmental Protection Amendment*, 57 Pa. B.A.Q. 85 (1986).

57. *See* Oliver A. Pollard III, *A Promise Unfulfilled: Environmental Provisions in State Constitutions and the Self-Execution Question*, 5 Va. J. Nat. Resources L. 351 (1986).

58. *See* discussion of the expansion of the public trust doctrine in Chapter 5.

59. *See* Daniel P. Selmi, *The Judicial Development of the California Environmental Quality Act*, 18 U.C. Davis L. Rev. 197 (1984).

60. McClaughry, *supra* note 7, at 37.

61. Popper, *supra* note 26, at 192.

62. Most commentators in legal and environmental journals supported the initiative, although there were a few dissenting voices concerned about adding yet another level of bureaucracy to land use control. *Compare* Martin R. Healy, *National Land Use Proposal: Land Use Legislation of Landmark Environmental Significance*, 3 Env'l Aff. 355 (1974), and John

McClaughry, *The National Land Use Planning Act: An Idea We Can Do Without*, 3 Env'l Aff. 595 (1974).

63. For a thorough compilation, see *U.S. Environmental Laws* (Washington, D.C.: Bureau of National Affairs, 1986).

64. 42 U.S.C 4321; amended 1975.

65. 16 U.S.C. 1531, approved 1973; amended 1984.

66. Enacted in 1977 and expanded in 1987.

67. The Comprehensive Environmental Response, Compensation, and Liability Act of 1980, 42 U.S.C. 9601, approved 1980, amended 1984.

68. The Farmland Protection Policy Act of 1981.

69. The Coastal Barrier Resources Act of 1982.

70. The Clean Air Act, 42 U.S.C. 7401, approved 1955, amended 1983.

71. The Federal Water Pollution Control Act, as amended by the Clean Water Act of 1977 (commonly referred to as the Clean Water Act), 33 U.S.C. 136, approved 1972, amended 1984.

72. Federal Insecticide, Fungicide, and Rodenticide Act, 7 U.S.C. 136, approved 1972, amended 1984.

73. The Toxic Substances Control Act, 15 U.S.C. 2601, approved 1976, amended 1984.

74. A sympathetic Supreme Court has expanded the commerce clause to make regulation of interstate trade a pretext for virtually any controls the government might wish to place on private individuals. One of the more egregious examples is *Wickard v. Filburn*, 317 U.S. 111 (1942), in which the Court held that a farmer could be penalized for growing wheat to be consumed on his own farm, reasoning that if the farmer did not grow his own wheat, he would have to buy more, and some of that might come from out of state and thus involve interstate commerce. By that logic, Congress could forbid the growing of gardens for home consumption, although it has not yet chosen to make criminals of green thumbs.

75. *See* George Cameron Coggins, *The Developing Law of Land Use Planning on the Federal Lands*, 61 U. Colo. L. Rev. 307 (1990).

76. *See* Comment, *Protecting National Parks from Developments Beyond Their Borders*, 132 U. Pa. L. Rev. 1189 (1984).

77. At least minor in the context of trillion-dollar budgets.

78. *See* John S. Davis, *The National Trail System Act and the Use of Protective Federal Zoning*, 10 Harv. Envtl. L. Rev. 189 (1985).

79. *See* Charles F. Wilkinson, *The Headwaters of the Public Trust: Some Thoughts on the Source and Scope,* 19 Envtl. L. 425 (1989), on the ancient roots of the public trust and its historical context.

80. Joseph L. Sax, *The Limits of Private Rights in Public Waters,* 19 Envtl. L. 473 (1989).

81. *See* Note, *The Public Trust Doctrine in California, Florida and New Jersey: A Critique of Its Role in Modern Land Use Law,* 41 Rutgers L. Rev. 1349 (1989).

82. *See* Richard J. Lazarus, *Changing Conceptions of Property and Sovereignty in Natural Resources: Questioning the Public Trust Doctrine,* 71 Iowa L. Rev. 631 (1986).

83. *See* Gary D. Meyers, *Variation on a Theme: Expanding the Public Trust Doctrine to Include Protection of Wildlife,* 19 Envtl. L. 723 (1989), and Holmes Rolston III, *Property Rights and Endangered Species,* 61 U. Colo. L. Rev. 283 (1990).

84. For a detailed review of the laws affecting use of private wetlands, see William L. Want, *The Law of Wetlands Regulation* (New York: Clark Boardman, 1990).

85. 56 Wisc.2d 7, 201 N.W.2d 761 (1972).

86. *See This Wetland Is Your Land, This Wetland Is My Land: Sec. 404 of the Clean Water Act and Its Impact on the Private Development of Wetlands,* 4 Admin. L.J. 197 (1990).

87. *See* Paul D. Kamenar, *Private Property Rights: An Endangered Species,* 40 Freeman 164 (1990).

88. *See* Mary Kyle McCurdy, *Public Trust Protection for Wetlands,* 19 Envtl. L. 683 (1989), on application of the public trust doctrine to wetlands in California.

89. *See* Francis Fukuyama, *The End of History?* Nat'l Int., No. 16, 1989, at 3.

90. Sondra E. Berchin, *Regulation of Land Use: From Magna Carta to a Just Formulation,* 23 UCLA L. Rev. 904, 934 (1976).

91. *Seuss Builders Co. v. Beaverton,* 656 P.2d 306, 309 (1982).

92. Berchin, *supra* note 90, at 934.

93. *Id.* at 905.

94. Joseph L. Sax, *Some Thoughts on the Decline of Private Property,* 58 Wash. L. Rev. 481, 495 (1983).

95. James C. Hite, *Room and Situation: The Political Economy of Land-Use Regulation* 102 (Chicago: Nelson-Hall, 1979).

96. *Id.* at 102–03.

97. *Id.* at 103.

98. J. Hector St. John de Crevecoeur, *Letters from an American Farmer* 54 (orig. pub. 1782) (New York: Penguin Books, 1981).

99. McClaughry, *supra* note 7, at 56.

100. Gray, *Liberalism* 62 (Minneapolis: University of Minnesota Press, 1986). Or as Alan Ryan put it, "A society dedicated to liberty achieves it by respecting individual property." *Property* 36 (Minneapolis: University of Minnesota Press, 1987).

101. Madison, *Property* (orig. pub. 1792) in 14 *The Papers of James Madison* 266 (Robert A. Rutland and Charles F. Hobson eds.) (Charlottesville,: University Press of Virginia, 1983).

102. Edward J. Erler, *The Great Fence to Liberty: The Right to Property in the American Founding* in *Liberty, Property and the Foundations of the American Constitution* 56 (Ellen Frankel Paul and Howard Dickman, eds.) (Albany: State University of New York Press, 1989).

103. Political thinkers from Aristotle to the Anti-Federalists have seen social benefit in the self-responsibility entailed in land ownership. *See* Aristotle, *Politics* (E. Barker, ed.) (Oxford: Clarendon Press, 1947); Niccolo Machiavelli, *Discourses on Livy* and *The Prince*; and Herbert J. Storing, *What the Anti-Federalists Were For* (Chicago: University of Chicago Press, 1981).

104. Utilitarian defenders of liberal capitalism are indebted to David Hume, *Essays Moral Political and Literary* (London: Oxford University Press, 1963). The modern school of "law and economics" posits wealth maximization as the criterion for economic systems. *See* Richard Posner, *The Economic Analysis of Law* (2nd ed.) (Boston: Little Brown, 1977). For these political economists, "the proposition that no man will sow where another will reap founds the general case for recognizing property rights." Ryan, *supra* note 100, at 104.

105. *The Federalist*, especially No. 10 and No. 51 (James Madison).

106. *The Federalist* No. 78 (Alexander Hamilton).

107. "Various sides" would be more precise, given the substantial differences among the Federalists and especially the Anti-Federalists.

108. The most influential work emphasizing the debt owed by the founders to classical republican theory is J.G.A. Pocock, *The Machiavellian*

Moment: Florentine Political Thought and the Atlantic Republican Tradition. (Princeton: Princeton University Press, 1975).

109. Louis Hartz most forcefully stated the dominance of Lockean liberalism in American political thought. Hartz, *The Liberal Tradition in America* (New York: Harcourt Brace Jovanovich, 1955).

110. Madison, *supra* note 101, at 266 (emphasis in original).

111. John Locke, *The Second Treatise of Government* 71 (orig. pub. 1690) (Indianapolis: Bobbs-Merrill, 1952).

112. Madison, *supra* note 101, at 266.

113. *Id.*

114. Erler, *supra* note 102, at 58.

115. Locke, *supra* note 111, at 17.

116. Ryan, *supra* note 100, at 86.

117. Erler, *supra* note 102, at 57.

118. Wrote Erler: "It is not so much one's equal participation in the species—or one's 'species beingness' as it has been called—but one's individuation within the species that is uniquely human." *Id.* at 57.

119. Milton Friedman, *Capitalism and Freedom* 169 (Chicago: University of Chicago Press, 1962).

120. Schumpeter, *History of Economic Analysis* 394 (New York: Oxford University Press, 1954). *See also* Friedman, *supra* note 119, at 6 and Friedrich A. Hayek, *The Road to Serfdom* ix (Chicago: University of Chicago Press, 1944).

121. Witness Michael Dukakis's tepid embrace of the label in the waning days of his unsuccessful presidential campaign in 1988.

122. Frost, *The Poems of Robert Frost* 35 (New York: The Modern Library, 1939).

123. Erler, *supra* note 102, at 58.

124. Murray, *In Pursuit of Happiness and Good Government* (New York: Simon and Schuster, 1988).

125. Charles F. Hobson, *Republicanism, Commerce, and Private Rights: James Madison's Path to the Constitutional Convention of 1787* in *Liberty, Property and the Foundations of the American Constitution* 86 (Ellen Frankel Paul and Howard Dickman, eds.) (Albany: State University of New York Press, 1989).

126. *Id.*

127. Ryan, *supra* note 100, at 88.

128. *Conservatism in America* 72 (New York: Vintage Press, 1962).

129. Quoted in Hayek, *supra* note 120, at 43.

130. Vaclav Havel, *Our Freedom*, Wash. Post, Jan. 3, 1990, at A15.

131. *Id.*

132. *Id.*

133. *Id.*

134. *Id.*

135. Gray, *supra* note 100, at 62.

136. Eamon Butler, *Hayek: His Contribution to the Political and Economic Thought of Our Time* 94 (London: Temple Smith, 1983).

137. Friedrich A. Hayek, *Competition as a Discovery Procedure*, in 3 *Law, Legislation and Liberty* 67 (Chicago: University of Chicago Press, 1979).

138. Hayek, *supra* note 120, at 48.

139. Dissenting in *Olmstead v. United States*, 277 U.S. 438, 479 (1928).

CHAPTER 8

1. 347 U.S. 483 (1954).

2. 395 U.S. 44 (1969).

3. *See* William H. Riker and Barry R. Weingast, *Constitutional Regulation of Legislative Choice: The Political Consequences of Judicial Deference to Legislatures*, 74 Va. L. Rev. 373 (1988) (court wrong to assume that legislatures can or will protect property rights).

4. Bruce M. Johnson, *Piracy on the Coast*, 55 Calif. Real Est. Mag. 22, 25 (Feb. 1975).

5. Friedrich A. Hayek, *The Road to Serfdom* 71 (Chicago: University of Chicago Press, 1944).

6. *See* James M. Buchanan and Gordon Tullock, *The Calculus of Consent* (Ann Arbor: University of Michigan Press, 1962); Anthony Downs, *An Economic Theory of Democracy* (New York: Harper & Row, 1957); James D.

Gwartney and Richard E. Wagner, *Public Choice and the Conduct of Representative Government,* in *Public Choice and Constitutional Economics* 3 (Gwartney and Wagner, eds.) (Greenwich, Conn.: JAI Press, 1988); and Mancur Olson, *The Logic of Collective Action: Public Goods and the Theory of Groups* (Cambridge: Harvard University Press, 1971).

7. David L. Callies, *A Requiem for Public Purpose: Hawaii Housing Authority v. Midkiff,* 1985 Inst. on Plan. Zoning & Eminent Domain 8-1, 8-30.

8. *The Federalist* Nos. 10 and 51.

9. Charles F. Hobson, *Republicanism, Commerce, and Private Rights: James Madison's Path to the Constitutional Convention of 1787* in *Liberty, Property and the Foundations of the American Constitution* 85, 96 (Ellen Frankel Paul and Howard Dickman, eds.) (Albany: State University of New York Press, 1989).

10. *Id.*

11. *The Federalist* No. 9.

12. Clifford L. Weaver and Richard F. Babcock, *City Zoning: The Once and Future Frontier* 187 (Chicago: Planners Press, 1979).

13. *See* Dennis J. Coyle, *The Balkans by the Bay,* Pub. Interest, Spring 1988, at 67.

14. Richard F. Babcock, *The Zoning Game: Municipal Practices and Policies* 141 (Madison: University of Wisconsin Press, 1966).

15. Michael M. Berger and Gideon Kanner, *Thoughts on the White River Junction Manifesto: A Reply to the "Gang of Five's" Views on Just Compensation for Regulatory Taking of Property,* 19 Loyola L.A.L. Rev. 685, 741 (1986).

16. *1984* 6 (New York: Harcourt Brace Jovanovich, 1949).

17. John Hart Ely, *Democracy and Distrust* (Cambridge, Mass.: Harvard University Press, 1980).

18. Daniel R. Mandelker, *The Free Speech Revolution in Land Use Control,* 60 Chi.-Kent L. Rev. 51 (1984).

19. *See Cleburne v. Cleburne Living Center,* 473 U.S. 432 (1985), in which minimal scrutiny was far more searching that usual.

20. *See Nollan v. California Coastal Commission,* 483 U.S. 825 (1987), in which the commission's rationale for demanding a property easement was rejected.

21. Land use attorney and scholar Mandelker, for example, has argued that rights related to real property (buildings and land) should be vigilantly protected only for minorities or when serving preferred rights. Daniel R. Mandelker, *Reversing the Presumption of Constitutionality in Land Use Litigation: Is Legislative Action Necessary?* 30 Wash. U.J. Urb. Contemp. L. 5 (1986).

22. On judicial application of expressive rights to private property, *see* Dwight H. Merriam and Brian R. Smith, *The First Amendment in Land Use Law*, 14 ALI-ABA Course Materials J. 43 (Feb. 1990).

23. *Using Zoning Ordinances as a Backdoor Route to Censorship*, Oakland Tribune, Nov. 6, 1985, at B7.

24. 453 U.S. 490 (1981).

25. On sign restrictions and the legal issues they raise, *see* Daniel R. Mandelker and William R. Ewald, *Street Graphics and the Law* (Washington, D.C.: Planners Press, 1988).

26. 32 Cal. 3d 553, 652 P.2d 51, 186 Cal. Rptr. 494 (1982).

27. *See Renton v. Playtime Theatres*, 475 U.S. 41 (1986), and *Young v. American Mini Theatres, Inc.*, 427 U.S. 50 (1976).

28. Mandelker, *supra* note 18, at 54.

29. *See* Alfred C. Yen, *Judicial Review of the Zoning of Adult Entertainment*, 12 Pepperdine L. Rev. 651, 653 (1985) (courts should invalidate any regulation intended to restrict protected speech, or that effectively bans adult uses, unless a compelling justification can be shown), and David J. Christiansen, *Zoning and the First Amendment Rights of Adult Entertainment*, 22 Val. U. L. Rev. 695 (1988) (time, place and manner regulations of adult business should be subjected to strict judicial scrutiny).

30. *See* Samuel Bufford, *Beyond the Eye of the Beholder: A New Majority of Jurisdictions Authorize Aesthetic Regulation*, 48 UMKC L. Rev. 125 (1980).

31. *See* Annette B. Kolis, *Architectural Expression: Police Power and the First Amendment*, 16 Urb. L. Ann. 273 (1979).

32. John J. Costonis, *Icons and Aliens* 1 (Urbana: University of Illinois Press, 1989).

33. Richard F. Babcock, Review of *Icons and Aliens*, 42 *Vanderbilt L. Rev.* 1535, 1537 (1989).

34. As Babcock said, "What a dreadful criterion!" *Id.* at 1536.

35. *See* Comment, *Zoning Ordinances Affecting Churches: A Proposal for Expanded Free Exercise Protection,* 132 U. Pa. L. Rev. 1131 (1984).

36. *See St. Bart's Embattled,* Economist, Feb. 6, 1982.

37. *See* Laurie Reynolds, *Zoning the Church: The Police Power Versus the First Amendment,* 64 B.U.L. Rev. 767 (1984).

38. *See* Scott David Godshall, *Land Use Regulation and the Free Exercise Clause,* 84 Colum. L. Rev. 1562 (1984).

39. 483 U.S. 327 (1987).

40. The state supreme court agreed with the decision on appeal but ducked the constitutional issue, holding instead that the day-care center was a permitted accessory use under the zoning ordinance. *Richmond Heights v. Richmond Heights Presbyterian Church,* 764 S.W.2d 647 (Mo. 1989).

41. Susan L. Goldberg, *Gimme Shelter: Religious Provision of Shelter to the Homeless as a Protected Use Under Zoning Laws,* 30 Wash. U.J. Urb. & Contemp. L. 75, 76 (1986).

42. 459 U.S. 116 (1982).

43. 473 U.S. 432 (1985).

44. See Mandelker, *supra* note 21; Ronald K. L. Collins, *Reliance on State Law: Protecting the Rights of People With Mental Disabilities,* 13 Vt. L. Rev. 305 (1988); and Comment, *Exclusion of Community Facilities for Offenders and Mentally Disabled Persons: Questions of Zoning, Home Rule, Nuisance, and Constitutional Law,* 25 DePaul L. Rev. 918 (1976).

45. *See Fernley v. Board of Supervisors of Schuylkill Township,* 509 Pa. 413, 502 A.2d 585 (1985).

46. *See National Land and Investment Co. v. Kohn,* 419 Pa. 504, 215 A.2d 597 (1965).

47. *See Oakwood at Madison, Inc. v. Madison,* 72 N.J. 481, 371 A.2d 1192 (1977).

48. *See* Douglas Kmiec, *Manufactured Home Siting: Overview, Regulatory Challenges and a Proposal for Federal Deregulation,* 1984 Zoning & Plan. L. Handbook 397.

49. *See* Wendy Schermer, *Mobile Homes: An Increasingly Important Housing Resource That Challenges Traditional Land Use Regulation— Geiger v. Zoning Hearing Board of North Whitehall,* 60 Temp. L.Q. 583 (1987).

50. 510 Pa. 231, 507 A.2d 361 (1986).

51. *See Southern Burlington County NAACP v. Mount Laurel* (Mount Laurel I), 67 N.J. 151, 336 A.2d 713 (1975), and *Southern Burlington County NAACP v. Mount Laurel* (Mount Laurel II), 92 N.J. 158, 456 A.2d 390 (1983).

52. The *Mount Laurel* doctrine has been "New Jersey's Full Employment Act for lawyers and Planners." Jerome G. Rose, *Waning Judicial Legitimacy: The Price of Judicial Promulgation of Urban Social Policy*, 20 Urb. Law. 801, 820 (1988).

53. By 1988, thirteen years after *Mount Laurel I*, fewer than 2,000 "*Mount Laurel*" units of low-and moderate-income housing had been built in just fourteen communities. The court had estimated the need at 277,000 units. Anthony DePalma, *Mount Laurel: Slow, Painful Progress*, N.Y. Times, May 1, 1988, Sec. 8, at 1, Col. 2.

54. *See* Rose, *supra* note 52, and G. Alan Tarr and Mary Cornelia Aldis Porter, *State Supreme Courts in State and Nation* (New Haven: Yale University Press, 1988).

55. Martha Lamar, Alan Mallach and John M. Payne, *Mount Laurel at Work: Affordable Housing in New Jersey, 1983–1988*, 41 Rutgers L. Rev. 1197, 1277 (1989).

56. 416 U.S. 1 (1974).

57. 431 U.S. 494 (1977).

58. 610 P.2d 436 (1980).

59. *Charter Township of Delta v. Dinolfo*, 351 N.W.2d 831 (1984).

60. *McMinn v. Town of Oyster Bay*, 66 N.Y.2d 544 (1981), and *Baer v. Town of Brookhaven*, 73 N.Y.2d 942 (1989).

61. *Ahwahnee Hills School v. City of Madera*, 204 Cal. Rptr 628 (1984).

62. Tamila C. Jensen, *From Belle Terre to East Cleveland: Zoning, the Family, and the Right to Privacy*, 13 Fam. L.Q. 1, 19 (1979) (emphasis in original).

63. 304 U.S. 144 (1938).

64. 482 U.S. 304 (1987).

65. *See* Lee P. Symons, *Property Rights and Local Land-Use Regulation: The Implications of First English and Nollan*, 18 Publius (No. 3) 81 (1988), and Comment, *First English Evangelical Lutheran Church of*

Glendale v. County of Los Angeles and Nolan v. California Coastal Commission: The Big Chill, 52 Albany L. Rev. 325 (1987).

66. Victor R. Delle Donne, *Land Use,* 58 Pa. B.A.Q. 173, 180 (1987).

67. *Agins v. Tiburon,* 24 Cal. 3d 266, 598 P.2d 25, 157 Cal. Rptr. 372 (1979).

68. 432 A.2d 15 (1981).

69. *See also Rippley v. City of Lincoln,* 330 N.W.2d 505 (N.D. 1983); *Corrigan v. City of Scottsdale,* 720 P.2d 513 (Ariz. 1986); and *Zinn v. Wisconsin,* 334 N.W.2d 67 (Wis. 1983).

70. 483 U.S. 825 (1987).

71. For an application of *Nollan* away from the shore, see *Seawall Associates v. City of New York,* 542 N.E.2d 1059 (N.Y. 1989), and Dennis J. Coyle, *Private Property and Public Takings: Regulating the Regulators in New York,* 1 St. Const. Commentary & Notes 15 (1990).

72. *Pennell v. San Jose,* 485 U.S. 1 (1988).

73. *Pennsylvania Coal v. Mahon,* 260 U.S. 393 (1922).

74. Callies, *supra* note 7, at 8–30.

75. *See Penn Central Transportation Co. v. New York City,* 438 U.S. 104 (1978).

76. Even *Nollan* involved physical access to the beach.

77. Elizabeth Patterson, *Property Rights in the Balance— The Burger Court and Constitutional Property,* 43 Md. L. Rev. 518 (1984).

78. 458 U.S. 419 (1982).

79. See *Penn Central,* 438 U.S. 104 (1978).

80. *See* especially *Agins v. Tiburon,* 447 U.S. 255 (1980); *Williamson County Regional Planning Commission v. Hamilton Bank of Johnson City,* 473 U.S. 172 (1985); and *MacDonald, Sommer, & Frates v. Yolo County,* 477 U.S. 340 (1986).

81. Michael M. Berger, *Anarchy Reigns Supreme,* 29 Wash. U.J. Urb. & Contemp. L. 39, 55 (1985).

82. David L. Callies, *The "Full Bore" Application of Hamilton Bank,* 38 Land Use L. & Zoning Dig. 4, 5 (Sept. 1986).

83. After one Court decision, *Hamilton Bank,* held that development permit denials were not comprehensive and final enough to be considered a taking, "the collective municipal sigh of relief upon the announcement of

the Supreme Court's decision was audible throughout the land." Victor R. Delle Donne, *Land Use*, 56 Pa. B.A.Q. 172, 174 (1985).

84. Berger and Kanner, *supra* note 15, at 737.

85. *See* Richard F. Babcock, *Citizen Participation: A Suburban Suggestion for the Central City*, in *Billboards, Glass Houses and the Law* 25 (Colorado Springs: Shepard's, 1977); Richard Stewart, *The Reformation of American Administrative Law*, 88 Harv. L. Rev. 1667 (1975); and Clayton P. Gillette, *Plebiscites, Participation, and Collective Action in Local Government Law*, 86 Mich. L. Rev. 930 (1988).

86. See chapter 7.

87. Berger and Kanner, *supra* note 15, at 700.

88. Joseph F. DiMento, *"But It's Only Planning": Planning and the Taking Issue in Land Development and Environmental Control Law*, 1984 Zoning & Plan. L. Handbook 91.

89. Norman Williams, Jr., R. Marlin Smith, Charles Siemon, Daniel R. Mandelker, and Richard F. Babcock, *The White River Junction Manifesto*, 9 Vt. L. Rev. 193, 242 (1984) (hereinafter *The Manifesto*).

90. 94 N.J. 358, 464 A.2d 1115 (1983).

91. If a zoning ordinance specified the land uses available to an owner as a matter of right, for example, and the owner had unsuccessfully sought an exception, the court could then decide whether the zoning restrictions required compensation. Under a more discretionary zoning category, such as a planned-use development, the rejection of a permit should be accompanied by a statement of what alternative plan would be accepted. If the owner challenged the decision, the court could consider whether the alternative plan sufficed to avoid a taking.

92. *See Berman v. Parker*, 348 U.S. 26 (1954) and *Hawaii Housing Authority v. Midkiff*, 467 U.S. 229 (1984).

93. Ellen Frankel Paul has argued that "the power of eminent domain, whether or not accompanied by the payment of compensation, is wholly unjustified," *Moral Constraints and Eminent Domain: A Review Essay of Richard Epstein's Takings: Private Property and the Power of Eminent Domain*, 55 George Wash. L. Rev. 152, 174 (1986).

94. *Oakland v. Oakland Raiders*, 32 Cal. 3d 60, 646 P.2d 835, 183 Cal. Rptr. 673 (1982). The California Supreme Court could find no legal reason why such an attempt could not be made, although Rose Bird, no slouch when it came to supporting governmental control of property, was troubled by the broader implications of the decision. Is there no limit to what can be

condemned? Can any business be taken in order to preserve jobs in the community? Can any employment contracts be taken?

95. 410 Mich. 616, 304 N.W.2d 455 (1981).

96. The owners forced to sell were private individuals, and the beneficiary was a private company. Yet the court upheld the taking as for a public use. In dissent, Justice Ryan recommended a test for limiting takings that bears consideration: Any taking would have to be justified as being a public necessity; continuing public accountability would be required; and the site would need to be selected by a public agency, not a private individual or company. These requirements would help prevent the use of the eminent domain power to reallocate private resources. But public necessity must be construed with modest generosity, or the discretion of government would be sharply limited. For example, are public parks truly necessary? Just what a public necessity is, is a bit of a mystery.

97. 467 U.S. 229 (1984).

98. *See* Note, *The Supreme Court's Assault on Private Ownership of Property*, 90 Dickenson L. Rev. 1990 (1984), and Note, *A New Slant on Social Legislation: Taking from the Rich to Give to the Well-to-Do*, 25 Nat. Resources J. 773 (1984).

99. *See* Note, *Can They Do That? Taking from Peter and Giving to Paul: The Public Use Limitation after Hawaii Housing Authority v. Midkiff*, 15 Sw. U.L. Rev. 817 (1985), and Thomas J. Coyne, *A Final Requiem for the Public Use Limitation on Eminent Domain*, 60 Notre Dame L. Rev. 388 (1985).

100. 473 U.S. 460. In *Lochner*, 198 U.S. 45 (1905), the court overturned a limit on bakers' hours as a violation of the substantive due process right of "liberty of contract," and the case has ever since been a symbol of the supposedly illegitimate judicial protection of "economic" rights.

101. Bernard H. Siegan, *The President's Commission on Housing: Zoning Recommendations*, 41 Urb. Land 24 (Nov. 1982).

102. Douglas W. Kmiec, *Protecting Vital and Pressing Governmental Interests—A Proposal for a New Zoning Enabling Act*, 30 Wash. U.J. Urb. & Contemp. L. 19 (1986).

103. Mandelker, *supra* note 21.

104. The Supreme Court's jurisprudence of gender discrimination under the equal protection clause is probably the most well-known area in which a midlevel test is commonly applied. *See Craig v. Boren*, 429 U.S. 190 (1976).

105. *See Ridley Arms, Inc. v. Ridley Township*, 522 A.2d 1069 (1987).

106. *See United Artists Theater Circuit, Inc. v. Philadelphia,* 595 A.2d 6 (1991), in which the court struck down a historic preservation ordinance.

107. 483 U.S. at 842.

108. *Olmstead v. United States,* 277 U.S. 438, 478 (1928).

109. "We challenge *The Manifesto's* implicit notion," wrote Berger and Kanner in their reply to a diatribe against property rights, "that litigants have to be pure of heart before they can assert their constitutional rights in an effective fashion. The notion that building homes is somehow inherently wicked, or even suspect, is preposterous." Berger and Kanner, *supra* note 15, at 688 (replying to *The Manifesto, supra* note 89).

110. *See Federalist* Nos. 10 and 51 (James Madison).

111. *The Manifesto, supra* note 89, at 233.

112. *See Federalist* No. 78 (Alexander Hamilton), and Dennis J. Coyle, *A Wallflower Court at the Legislative Dance,* Baltimore Sun, July 5, 1991, at 11A, Col. 1.

Bibliography

Abrahamson, Shirley A. *Reincarnation of State Courts*. 36 Sw. L.J. 951 (1982).

Abrahamson, Shirley A. *Homegrown Justice: The State Constitutions*, in *Developments in State Constitutional Law* (Bradley D. McGraw ed.). St. Paul, Minn.: West Publishing Co., 1985.

Ackerman, Bruce A. *Private Property and the Constitution*. New Haven, Conn.: Yale University Press, 1977.

Aladjem, David R. E. *Public Use and Treatment as an Equal: An Essay on Poletown Neighborhood Council v. City of Detroit and Hawaii Housing Authority v. Midkiff*. 15 Ecology L.Q. 671 (1988).

Alperovitz, Gar. *Notes Toward a Pluralistic Commonwealth*. 4 Rev. Radical Pol. Econ. 22 (1972).

Altshuler, Alan A. *The City Planning Process*. Ithaca, N.Y.: Cornell University Press, 1965.

Anderson, Robert M. *American Law of Zoning* (3d ed.). Rochester, N.Y.: Lawyers Co-operative Publishing Co, 1986.

Andrews, Edmund L. *The Curse of California's Proposition 13*. N.Y. Times, June 17, 1988, at A35.

Arana, Ana. *Doing Deals*, in *The Best of Planning* 457. Chicago: Planners Press, 1989.

Arcaro, Anthony R. *Avoiding Constitutional Challenges to Farmland Preservation Legislation*. 24 Gonzaga L. Rev. 475 (1989).

Babcock, Richard F. *The Zoning Game: Municipal Practices and Policies*. Madison: University of Wisconsin Press, 1966.

Babcock, Richard F. *Citizen Participation: A Suburban Suggestion for the Central City*, in *Billboards, Glass Houses and the Law* 25. Colorado Springs: Shepard's, 1977.

Babcock, Richard F. *The Zoning Game—Revisited.* 1986 Zoning & Plan. L. Handbook 333.

Babcock, Richard F. Book Review, 42 Vanderbilt L. Rev. 1535 (1989) (reviewing John J. Costonis, *Icons and Aliens*).

Babcock, Richard F., & Charles L. Siemon. *The Zoning Game Revisited.* Boston: Oelgeschlager, Gunn & Hain, & the Lincoln Institute of Land Policy, 1985.

Baker, C. Edwin. *Property and Its Relation to Constitutionally Protected Liberty.* 134 U. Pa. L. Rev. 741 (1986).

Baker, Newman. *Legal Aspects of Zoning.* Chicago: University of Chicago Press, 1927.

Bauman, Gus. *The Supreme Court, Inverse Condemnation, and the Fifth Amendment: Justice Brennan Confronts the Inevitable.* 15 Rutgers L.J. 15 (1983).

Bauman, Gus. *Dejà Vu, or Et Tu Supreme Court?* Land Use L. & Zoning Dig., July 1985, at 3.

Bauman, Gus. *The Longest Running Show in Town.* Land Use L. & Zoning Dig., Sept. 1986, at 3.

Bauman, Gus, & William H. Ethier. *Development Exactions and Impact Fees: A Survey of American Practices.* 50 Law & Contemp. Probs.51 (1987).

Benn, Ted M. *Individual Rights and State Constitutional Interpretations: Putting First Things First.* 37 Baylor L. Rev. 495 (1985).

Benner, Laurence A. *Diminishing Expectations of Privacy in the Rehnquist Court.* 22 John Marshall L. Rev. 825 (1989).

Berchin, Sondra E. *Regulation of Land Use: From Magna Carta to a Just Formulation.* 23 UCLA L. Rev. 904 (1976).

Berdon, Robert I. *Protecting Liberty and Property Under the Connecticut and Federal Constitutions: The Due Process Clauses.* 15 Conn. L. Rev. 41 (1982).

Berger, Michael M. *Anarchy Reigns Supreme.* 29 Wash. U.J. Urb. & Contemp. L. 39 (1985).

Berger, Michael M., & Gideon Kanner. *Thoughts on the White River Junction Manifesto: A Reply to the "Gang of Five's" Views on Just Compensation for Regulatory Taking of Property.* 19 Loy. L.A.L. Rev. 685 (1986).

The Best of Planning. Chicago: Planners Press, 1989.

Birch, Charles, & John B. Cobb. *The Liberation of Life: From the Cell to the Community.* Cambridge: Cambridge University Press, 1983.

Bjork, Gordon C. *Life, Liberty and Property: The Economics and Politics of Land-Use Planning and Environmental Controls.* Lexington, Mass.: Lexington Books, 1986.

Bloom, Joshua. *The Use of Local Ordinances to Combat Private Club Discrimination.* 23 U.S.F. L. Rev. 473 (1989).

Blume, Lawrence, & Daniel Rubinfeld. *Compensation for Takings: An Economic Analysis.* 72 Calif. L. Rev. 569 (1984).

Bonham, Louis Karl. *Unenumerated Rights Clauses in State Constitutions.* 63 Tex. L. Rev. 1321 (1985).

Bookchin, Murray. *The Ecology of Freedom: The Emergence and Dissolution of Hierarchy.* Palo Alto, Calif.: Cheshire Books, 1982.

Bosselman, Fred, & David Callies. *The Quiet Revolution in Land Use Control.* Washington, D.C.: Council on Environmental Quality, 1971.

Bosselman, Fred, David Callies, & John Banta. *The Takings Issue: An Analysis of the Constitutional Limits of Land Use Control.* Washington, D.C.: Council on Environmental Quality, 1973.

Bowden, Gerald, & Lewis G. Feldman. *Take It or Leave It: Uncertain Regulatory Taking Standards and Remedies Threaten California's Open Space Planning.* 15 U.C. Davis L. Rev. 371 (1981).

Boyle, Eugene A. *The Status of the Public Use Requiem: Post-Midkiff.* 30 Wash. U.J. Urb. & Contemp. L. 115 (1986).

Brennan, William J., Jr. *State Constitutions and the Protection of Individual Rights.* 90 Harv. L. Rev. 489 (1977).

Brennan, William J., Jr. *The Equality Principle: A Foundation of American Law.* 20 U.C. Davis L. Rev. 673 (1987).

Broughton, Robert. *The Proposed Pennsylvania Declaration of Environmental Rights.* 41 Pa. B.A.Q. 421 (1970).

Bruce-Briggs, B. *Land Use and the Environment,* in *No Land Is an Island.* San Francisco: Institute for Contemporary Studies, 1975.

Buchanan, Thomas. *Innovative Zoning for the Preservation of Agricultural Land—Boundary Drive Associates v. Shrewsbury Township Board of Supervisors.* 59 Temp. L.Q. 861 (1986).

Bufford, Samuel. *Beyond the Eye of the Beholder: A New Majority of Juris-dictions Authorize Aesthetic Regulation.* 48 UMKC L. Rev. 125 (1980).

Burling, James S. Takings and Wetlands: A Swamp Half Full Is Still a Swamp. Presented to CLE Int'l, Seattle, Wash., May 18, 1990.

Butler, Eamonn. *Hayek: His Contribution to the Political and Economic Thought of Our Time.* London: Temple Smith, 1983.

Callicott, J. Baird. *Animal Liberation: A Triangular Affair.* 2 Envtl. Ethics 311 (1980).

Callies, David L. *Land Use Controls: Of Enterprise Zones, Takings, Plans and Growth Controls.* 14 Urb. Law. 781 (1982).

Callies, David L. *Regulating Paradise: Is Land Use a Right or a Privilege?* 7 U. Haw. L. Rev. 13 (1985).

Callies, David L. *A Requiem for Public Purpose: Hawaii Housing Author-ity v. Midkiff.* 1985 Inst. on Plan., Zoning & Eminent Domain 8–1.

Callies, David L. *The Takings Issue Revisited.* Land Use L. & Zoning Dig., July 1985, at 6.

Callies, David L. *The "Full Bore" Application of Hamilton Bank.* Land Use L. & Zoning Dig., Sept. 1986, at 4.

Chapman, Stephen. *Using Zoning Ordinances as a Backdoor Route to Cen-sorship.* Oakland Tribune, Nov. 6, 1985, at B7.

Chickering, A. Lawrence. *Land Use Controls and Low Income Groups: Why Are There No Poor People in the Sierra Club,* in *No Land Is an Island.* San Francisco: Institute for Contemporary Studies, 1975.

Christiansen, David J. *Zoning and the First Amendment Rights of Adult Entertainment.* 22 Val. U. L. Rev. 695 (1988).

Clarke, Charles H. *Rent Control and the Constitutional Ghosts and Gob-lins of Laissez-Faire Past: Pennell v. San Jose.* 14 U. Dayton L. Rev. 115 (1988).

Clay, Henry. *Human Freedom and State Constitutional Law: Part One, the Renaissance.* 70 Mass. L. Rev. 161 (1985).

Coase, Ronald H. *The Problem of Social Cost.* 3 J.L. & Econ. 1 (1960).

Collier, Peter, & David Horowitz. *Slouching Towards Berkeley: Socialism in One City.* Pub. Interest, No. 94, 1989, at 47.

Collins, Ronald K. L. *Reliance on State Constitutions: Some Random Thoughts,* in *Developments in State Constitutional Law* (Bradley D. McGraw ed.). St. Paul, Minn.: West Publishing Co., 1985.

Collins, Ronald K., & Peter Galie. *Models of Post-Incorporation Judicial Review: 1985 Survey of State Constitutional Individual Rights Decisions.* 16 Publius 111 (1986).

Collins, Ronald K. L. *Reliance on State Law: Protecting the Rights of People With Mental Disabilities.* 13 Vt. L. Rev. 305 (1988).

Comment, *Exclusion of Community Facilities for Offenders and Mentally Disabled Persons: Questions of Zoning, Home Rule, Nuisance, and Constitutional Law.* 25 De Paul L. Rev. 918 (1976).

Comment, *Protecting National Parks from Developments Beyond Their Borders.* 132 U. Pa. L. Rev. 1189 (1984).

Comment, *Zoning Ordinances Affecting Churches: A Proposal for Expanded Free Exercise Protection.* 132 U. Pa. L. Rev. 1131 (1984).

Constitutional Issues in Land Use Regulation. 8 Hastings Const. L.Q. 449 (1981).

Cooley, Thomas. *A Treatise on the Constitutional Limitations Which Rest Upon the Legislative Power of the States of the American Union* (8th ed.). Boston: Little, Brown & Company, 1927.

Costonis, John J. *Making Sense of the Taking Issue.* 1984 Zoning & Plan. L. Handbook 109.

Costonis, John J. *Icons and Aliens.* Urbana: University of Illinois Press, 1989.

Cotgrove, Stephen. *Risk, Value Conflict and Political Legitimacy,* in *Dealing With Risk* (Richard F. Griffiths ed.). Manchester: Manchester University Press, 1981.

Counts, Thomas S. *May Churches Be Excluded from Suburban Residential Areas?* 45 Ohio St. L.J. 1017 (1984).

Coyle, Dennis J. *A Critical Theory of Community.* Institute of Governmental Studies Working Paper 87–5, 1987.

Coyle, Dennis J. *The Reluctant Revival of Landowner Rights.* Presented at the annual meeting of the American Political Science Association, Sept. 1987, *reprinted as* Institute of Governmental Studies Working Paper 87–4.

Coyle, Dennis J. *The Balkans by the Bay.* Pub. Interest, Spring 1988, at 67.

Coyle, Dennis J. *Private Property and Public Takings: Regulating the Regulators in New York.* St. Const. Commentary & Notes, Spring 1990, at 15.

Coyne, Thomas J. *A Final Requiem for the Public Use Limitation on Eminent Domain.* 60 Notre Dame L. Rev. 388 (1985).

Crevecoeur, J. Hector St. John de. *Letters from an American Farmer.* New York: Penguin Books, 1981.

Cribbet, John E. *Changing Concepts in the Law of Land Use.* 50 Iowa L. Rev. 245 (1965).

Davidoff, Paul, & Linda Davidoff. *Opening Up the Suburbs: Toward Inclusionary Land Use Controls.* 22 Syracuse L. Rev. 509 (1971).

Davis, John S. *The National Trail System Act and the Use of Protective Federal Zoning.* 10 Harv. Envtl. L. Rev. 189 (1985).

Delafons, John. *Land Use Controls in the United States* (2d ed.). Cambridge, Mass.: MIT Press, 1969.

Delogu, Orlando E. *Local Land Use Controls: An Idea Whose Time Has Passed.* 36 Me. L. Rev. 261 (1984).

Dempsey, Thomas J. *Eminent Domain.* 55 Pa. B.A.Q. 64 (1984).

Demsetz, Harold. *Toward a Theory of Property Rights.* 57 Am. Econ. Rev. Proc. 347 (1967).

DePalma, Anthony. *Jersey Copes with Planning Mandate.* N.Y. Times, June 12, 1989, at B3.

DePalma, Anthony. *Mount Laurel: Slow, Painful Progress.* N.Y. Times, May 1, 1988, sec. 8, at 1.

Devall, Bill, & George Sessions. *Deep Ecology.* Salt Lake City: Peregrine Smith Books, 1985.

Dewey, John. *Liberalism and Social Action.* New York: Putnam's, 1935.

Diamond, Martin. *Liberty, Democracy and the Founders.* Pub. Interest, No. 41, 1975, at 39.

DiMento, Joseph F., Michael D. Dozier, Steven L. Emmons, Donald G. Hagman, Christopher Kim, Karen Greenfield-Sanders, Paul F. Waldau, & Jay A. Woollacott. *Land Development and Environmental Control in the California Supreme Court: The Deferential, the Preservationist, and the Preservationist-Erratic Eras.* 27 UCLA L. Rev. 859 (1980).

DiMento, Joseph F. *"But It's Only Planning": Planning and the Taking Issue in Land Development and Environmental Control Law.* 1984 Zoning & Plan. L. Handbook 91.

Disney, Mitchell F. *Fear and Loathing on the California Coastline: Are Coastal Commission Property Exactions Constitutional?* 14 Pepperdine L. Rev. 357 (1987).

Dobkin, Steve, Geoffrey Smith, & Earle Tockman. *Zoning for the General Welfare: A Constitutional Weapon for Lower-Income Tenants.* 13 N.Y.U. Rev. L. & Soc. Change 911 (1985).

Donne, Victor R. Delle. *Land Use.* 55 Pa. B.A.Q. 90, 91 (1984).

Donne, Victor R. Delle. *Land Use.* 54 Pa. B.A.Q. 35 (1983).

Dorn, James A. *Introduction: Economic Liberties and the Judiciary.* 4 Cato J. 661 (1985).

Douglas, Mary. *Natural Symbols: Explorations in Cosmology* (2d ed.). London: Barrie and Jenkins, 1973.

Douglas, Mary. *Cultural Bias,* in *In the Active Voice* 183. London: Routledge & Kegan Paul, 1982.

Douglas, Mary, & Aaron Wildavsky. *Risk and Culture: An Essay on the Selection of Technical and Environmental Dangers.* Berkeley: University of California Press, 1982.

Douglas, William O. *Law Reviews and Full Disclosure.* 40 Wash. L. Rev. 227 (1965).

Downs, Anthony. *Opening Up the Suburbs.* New Haven, Conn.: Yale University Press, 1973.

Downs, Anthony. *Residential Rent Controls: An Evaluation.* Washington, D.C.: Urban Land Institute, 1988.

Dunn, John. *Justice and the Interpretation of Locke's Political Theory.* 16 Pol. Stud. 68 (1968).

Dworkin, Ronald. *Takings Rights Seriously.* Cambridge, Mass.: Harvard University Press, 1977.

Economic Foundations of Property Law (Bruce A. Ackerman ed.). Boston: Little, Brown & Co., 1975.

Ellickson, Robert C. *Alternatives to Zoning: Covenants, Nuisance Rules and Fines as Land Use Controls.* 40 U. Chi. L. Rev. 681 (1973).

Ellickson, Robert C., & A. Dan Tarlock. *Land Use Controls.* Boston: Little, Brown & Co., 1981.

Ely, John Hart. *Democracy and Distrust.* Cambridge, Mass.: Harvard University Press, 1980.

The Emergence of State Constitutional Law. 63 Tex. L. Rev. 959 (1985).

Epstein, Richard A. *Not Deference, but Doctrine: The Eminent Domain Clause.* 1982 Sup. Ct. Rev. 351.

Epstein, Richard A. *Toward Revitalization of the Contract Clause.* 51 U. Chi. L. Rev. 703 (1984).

Epstein, Richard A. *Takings: Private Property and the Power of Eminent Domain.* Cambridge, Mass.: Harvard University Press, 1985.

Epstein, Richard A. *An Outline of Takings.* 41 U. Miami L. Rev. 1 (1986).

Epstein, Richard A. *The Last Word on Takings.* 41 U. Miami L. Rev. 253 (1986).

Epstein, Richard A. *Past and Future: The Temporal Dimension in the Law of Property.* 64 Wash. U.L.Q. 667 (1986).

Epstein, Richard A. *Takings: Descent and Resurrection.* 1987 Sup. Ct. Rev. 1.

Erber, Ernest. *The Road to Mount Laurel,* in *The Best of Planning* 250. Chicago: Planners Press, 1989.

Erler, Edward J. *The Great Fence to Liberty: The Right to Property in the American Founding,* in *Liberty, Property and the Foundations of the American Constitution* 43 (Ellen Frankel Paul & Howard Dickman eds.). Albany: State University of New York Press, 1989.

Ewing, Pamina. *Impact Fees in Pennsylvania: Requiring Land Developers to Bear Development-Related Costs.* 50 U. Pitt. L. Rev. 1101 (1989).

Fein, David B. *Historic Districts: Preserving City Neighborhoods for the Privileged.* 60 N.Y.U.L. Rev. 64 (1985).

Fischel, William A. *The Economics of Zoning Laws: A Property Rights Approach to American Land Use Controls.* Baltimore: Johns Hopkins University Press, 1985.

Flaherty, John P. *A Long and Prominent Tradition.* 60 Temple L.Q. 311 (1987).

Frank, John P. Book Review, 63 Tex. L. Rev. 1339 (1985) (reviewing *Developments in State Constitutional Law* (Bradley D. McGraw ed.) & *State Supreme Courts in State and Nation* (G. Alan Tarr & Mary Cornelia Aldis Porter eds.)).

Franzese, Paula A. *Mount Laurel III: The New Jersey Supreme Court's Judicious Retreat.* 18 Seton Hall L. Rev. 30 (1988).

Freyfogle, Eric T. *Land Use and the Study of Early American History* (Book Review). 94 Yale L.J. 717 (1985).

Freilich, Robert H., & Eugene R. Pal, Jr. *New Developments in Land Use and Environmental Regulation.* 1985 Inst. on Plan., Zoning & Eminent Domain 1–1.

Frieden, Bernard J. *The Environmental Protection Hustle.* Cambridge, Mass.: The MIT Press, 1979.

Friedman, Milton. *Capitalism and Freedom.* Chicago: University of Chicago Press, 1962.

Fulton, William. *Exactions Put to the Test,* in *The Best of Planning* 126. Chicago: Planners Press, 1989.

Fulton, William. *On the Beach With the Progressives,* in *The Best of Planning* 318. Chicago: Planners Press, 1989.

Galie, Peter J., & Lawrence P. Galie. *State Constitutional Guarantees and Supreme Court Review.* 82 Dick. L. Rev. 273 (1978).

Gancher, David. *When is Ecology Deep/Shallow?* San Francisco Sunday Chron. & Examiner Book Rev., Apr. 28, 1985, at 1.

Gilliam, Harold. *Shades of Green.* This World, San Francisco Sunday Chron. & Examiner, July 24, 1988, at 18.

Gilliam, Harold. *What Is Deep Ecology?* This World, San Francisco Sunday Chron. & Examiner, July 24, 1988, at 18.

Gilmour, John. *Land Use and the Public Interest.* 56 U. Va. Newsletter 33 (1980).

Godshall, Scott David. *Land Use Regulation and the Free Exercise Clause.* 84 Colum. L. Rev. 1562 (1984).

Goldberg, Susan L. *Gimme Shelter: Religious Provision of Shelter to the Homeless as a Protected Use Under Zoning Laws.* 30 Wash. U.J. Urb. & Contemp. L. 75 (1986).

Greenberg, Dan. *Radin on Personhood and Rent Control.* 73 Monist 642 (1990).

Hagman, Donald G. *The Vesting Issue: The Rights of Fetal Development Vis-à-Vis the Abortions of Public Whimsy.* 7 Envtl. L. 519 (1977).

Hagman, Donald G. *The American Dream as Public Nightmare, or, Sam, You Made the Front Yard Too Long.* 3 UCLA J. Envtl. L. & Pol'y 219 (1983).

Hanes, Grayson P., & J. Randall Minchew. *On Vested Rights to Land Use and Development.* 46 Wash. & Lee L. Rev. 373 (1989).

Hargrove, Eugene C. *Anglo-American Land Use Attitudes.* 2 Envtl. Ethics 121 (1980).

Hardin, Garrett. *The Tragedy of the Commons.* 162 Science 1243 (1968).

Harris, Ralph. *Great Britain: The Lessons of Socialist Planning*, in *The Politics of Planning: A Review and Critique of Centralized Economic Planning* (A. Lawrence Chickering ed.). San Francisco: Institute for Contemporary Studies. 1976.

Harrison, Russell S. *State Court Activism in Exclusionary-Zoning Cases*, in *State Supreme Courts: Policymakers in the Federal System* (Mary Cornelia Porter & G. Alan Tarr eds.). Westport, Conn.: Greenwood Press, 1982.

Hartz, Louis. *The Liberal Tradition in America*. New York: Harcourt Brace Jovanovich, 1955.

Hayek, Friedrich A. *The Road to Serfdom*. Chicago: University of Chicago Press, 1944.

Hayek, Friedrich A. *Competition as a Discovery Procedure*, in *New Studies in Philosophy, Politics, Economics and the History of Ideas*. London: Routledge & Kegan Paul, 1978, & 3 *Law, Legislation and Liberty* 67, Chicago: University of Chicago Press, 1979.

Hayek, Friedrich A. *The Discipline of Freedom*, in 3 *Law Legislation and Liberty* 163. Chicago: University of Chicago Press, 1979.

Hays, S. P. *Conservation and the Gospel of Efficiency*. Cambridge, Mass.: Harvard University Press, 1959.

Hazlett, Thomas. *Rent Controls and the Housing Crisis*, in *Resolving the Housing Crisis: Government Policy, Decontrol and the Public Interest* 277 (M. Bruce Johnson ed.). Cambridge, Mass.: Ballinger, 1982.

Healy, Martin R. *National Land Use Proposal: Land Use Legislation of Landmark Environmental Significance*. 3 Env'l. Aff. 355 (1974).

Heaney, Michael K. *Playing Chess in Wonderland: One Official's View of Mt. Laurel II*. 114 N.J.L.J. 9 (Dec. 6, 1984).

Hernandez, Julie Sullwold. *Can They Do That! Taking from Peter and Giving to Paul: The Public Use Limitation after Hawaii Housing Authority v. Midkiff*. 15 Sw. U.L. Rev. 817 (1985).

Hetherington, John A. C. *State Economic Regulation and Substantive Due Process of Law*. 53 Nw. U.L. Rev. 226 (1958).

Heyman, Ira Michael. *Legal Assaults on Municipal Land Use Regulation*, in *The Land Use Awakening: Zoning Law in the Seventies* (Robert H. Freilich & Eric O. Stuhler eds.). Chicago: American Bar Association Press, 1981.

Higgs, Robert, & Charlotte Twight. *National Emergency and the Erosion of Private Property Rights*. 6 Cato J. 747 (1987).

Hile, Gregory A. *Zoning by Initiative in California: A Critical Analysis.* 12 Loy. L.A.L. Rev. 903 (1979).

Hite, James C. *Room and Situation: The Political Economy of Land-Use Regulation.* Chicago: Nelson-Hall, 1979.

Hobson, Charles F. *Repbulicanism, Commerce, and Private Rights: James Madison's Path to the Constitutional Convention of 1787,* in *Liberty, Property and the Foundations of the American Constitution* 85 (Ellen Frankel Paul & Howard Dickman eds.). Albany: State University of New York Press, 1989.

Holling, C. S. *Myths of Ecological Stability: Resilience and the Problem of Failure,* in *Studies on Crisis Management* (C. F. Smart & W. T. Stanbury eds.). Canada: Institute for Research on Public Policy, 1978.

Howard, A. E. Dick. *State Courts and Constitutional Rights in the Day of the Burger Court.* 62 Va. L. Rev. 873 (1976).

Huffman, James L., & Reuben C. Plantico. *Toward a Theory of Land Use Planning: Lessons from Oregon.* 14 Land & Water L. Review 1 (1979).

Janda, James. *The Supreme Court's Assault on Private Ownership of Property.* 90 Dickenson L. Rev. 1990 (1984).

Jensen, Tamila C. *From Belle Terre to East Cleveland: Zoning, the Family, and the Right to Privacy.* 13 Fam. L.Q. 1 (1979).

Judd, Dennis R., & Robert E. Mendelson. *The Politics Urban Planning: The East St. Louis Experience.* Urbana: University of Illinois Press, 1973.

Kamenar, Paul D. *Private Property Rights: An Endangered Species.* 40 Freeman 164 (1990).

Karlin, Norman. *Zoning and Other Land Use Controls: From the Supply Side.* 12 Sw. U.L. Rev. 561 (1981).

Karp, James P. *The Evolving Meaning of Aesthetics in Land-Use Regulation.* 15 Colum. J. Envtl. L. 307 (1990).

Katz, Stanley N. *Thomas Jefferson and the Right to Property in Revolutionary America.* 19 J.L. & Econ. 467 (1976).

Kayden, Jerold S., & Leonard A. Zax. *Mt. Laurel II: Landmark Decision on Zoning and Low Income Housing Holds Lesson for Nation.* 1984 Zoning & Plan. L. Handbook 365.

Kent-Smith, Henry. *The Council on Affordable Housing and the Mount Laurel Doctrine: Will the Council Succeed?* 18 Rutgers L.J. 929 (1987).

Kinzler, Andrew, & George A. Ritter. *Twilight Zoning in New Jersey: The Exclusionary Effect of Agricultural Zoning.* Urb. Land, Dec. 1983, at 7.

Kirby, James C., Jr. *Expansive Judicial Review of Economic Regulation*, in *Developments in State Constitutional Law* (Bradley D. McGraw ed.). St. Paul, Minn.: West Publishing Co., 1985.

Kmiec, Douglas W. *Deregulating Land Use: An Alternative Free Enterprise Development System.* 130 U. Pa. L. Rev. 28 (1981).

Kmiec, Douglas W. *Manufactured Home Siting: Overview, Regulatory Challenges and a Proposal for Federal Deregulation.* 1984 Zoning & Plan. L. Handbook 397.

Kmiec, Douglas W. *Protecting Vital and Pressing Governmental Interests— A Proposal for a New Zoning Enabling Act.* 30 Wash. U.J. Urb. & Contemp. L. 19 (1986).

Kolis, Annette B. *Citadels of Privilege: Exclusionary Land Use Regulations and the Presumption of Constitutional Validity.* 8 Hastings L.J. 585 (1981).

Kolis, Annette B. *Architectual Expression; Police Power and the First Amendment.* 16 Urb. L. Ann. 273 (1979).

Kopelman, Stephen G. *Regional General Welfare: The End of a Trend.* 1985 Inst. Plan., Zoning & Eminent Domain 2–1.

Kramer, Daniel C. *When Does a Regulation Become a Taking? The United States Supreme Court's Most Recent Pronouncements.* 26 Am. Bus. L.J. 4 (1989).

Krasnowiecki, Jan Z. *Zoning Litigation and the New Pennsylvania Procedures.* 120 Pa. L. Rev. 1029 (1973).

Krasnowiecki, Jan Z. *Abolish Zoning.* 31 Syracuse L. Rev. 719 (1980).

Kurtz, Howard. *New Jersey's Ground-breaking Supreme Court: Rulings on Social Issues Produce National Reputation for Innovation, as Well as Local Backlash.* Wash. Post., Dec. 28, 1988, at A4.

Kury, Franklin L. *The Pennsylvania Environmental Protection Amendment.* 57 Pa. B.A.Q. 85 (1986).

Lamar, Martha, Alan Mallach, & John M. Payne. *Mount Laurel at Work: Affordable Housing in New Jersey, 1983–1988.* 41 Rutgers L. Rev. 1197 (1989).

The Land Use Awakening: Zoning Law in the Seventies (Robert H. Freilich & Eric O. Stuhler eds.). Chicago: American Bar Association Press, 1981.

Lazarus, Richard J. *Changing Conceptions of Property and Sovereignty in Natural Resources: Questioning the Public Trust Doctrine.* 71 Iowa L. Rev. 631 (1986).

Levinson, Sanford. *Freedom of Speech and the Right of Access to Private Property Under State Constitutional Law*, in *Developments in State Constitutional Law*. (Bradley D. McGraw ed.). St. Paul, Minn.: West Publishing Co., 1985.

Levy, Leonard. *Property as a Human Right*. 5 Const. Commentary 169 (1988).

Licata, Charles A., & Jane Massey Licata. *The Environmental Implications of Mount Laurel II*. 15 Rutgers L.J. 627 (1984).

Liebeler, Wesley J. *A Property Rights Approach to Judicial Decisionmaking*. 4 Cato J. 783 (1985).

Linde, Hans A. *First Things First: Rediscovering the States' Bills of Rights*. 9 U. Balt. L. Rev. 379 (1980).

Linde, Hans A. *E Pluribus—Constitutional Theory and State Courts*, in *Developments in State Constitutional Law* (Bradley D. McGraw ed.). St. Paul, Minn.: West Publishing Co., 1985.

Linder, Douglas. *Freedom of Association After Roberts v. United States Jaycees*. 82 Mich. L. Rev. 1878 (1984).

Linowes, R. Robert, & Don T. Allensworth. *The Politics of Land Use: Planning, Zoning and the Private Developer.* New York: Praeger, 1973.

Locke, John. *The Second Treatise of Government*. Indianapolis: Bobbs-Merrill, 1952.

Lourne, Susan. *A New Slant on Social Legislation: Taking from the Rich to Give to the Well-to-Do*. 25 Nat. Resources J, 773 (1984).

Luke, Timothy W. The Political Economy of Social Ecology and Voluntary Simplicity. presented at the annual meeting of the American Political Science Association, 1984.

MacIntyre, Alasdair. *After Virtue: a Study in Moral Theory*. Notre Dame, Ind.: University of Notre Dame Press, 1981.

MacPherson, C. B. *The Political Theory of Possessive Individualism*. New York: Oxford University Press, 1963.

Madison, James. *Property*, in 14 *The Papers of James Madison* 267 (Robert A. Rutland and Charles F. Hobson eds.). Charlottesville, Va.: University Press of Virginia, 1983.

Maine, Henry. *Ancient Law*. London: John Murray, 1901.

Malone, Linda A. *Environmental Regulation of Land Use*. New York: Clark Boardman, 1990.

Maltz, Earl M. *The Dark Side of State Court Activism.* 63 Tex. L. Rev. 995 (1985).

Mandelker, Daniel R. *Environment and Equity: A Regulatory Challenge.* New York: McGraw-Hill, 1981.

Mandelker, Daniel R. *The Free Speech Revolution in Land Use Control.* 60 Chi.-Kent L. Rev. 51 (1984).

Mandelker, Daniel R. *Group Homes: The Supreme Court Revives the Equal Protection Clause in Land Use Cases.* 1986 Inst. on Plan., Zoning & Eminent Domain 3–1.

Mandelker, Daniel R. *Reversing the Presumption of Constitutionality in Land Use Litigation; Is Legislative Action Necessary?* 30 Wash. U.J. Urb. & Contemp. L. 5 (1986).

Marshall, William P. *Discrimination and the Right of Association.* 81 Nw. U.L. Rev. 68 (1986).

Mashaw, Jerry L. *Administrative Due Process: The Quest for a Dignitary Theory.* 61 B.U.L. Rev. 885 (1981).

Massey, Stephen J. *Justice Rehnquist's Theory of Property.* 93 Yale L.J. 541 (1984).

McAuslan, Patrick. *The Ideologies of Planning Law.* New York: Pergamon Press, 1980.

McClaughry, John. *The New Feudalism.* 5 Envtl. L. 675 (1975).

McClaughry, John. *The New Feudalism—State Land Use Controls* in *No Land Is an Island* 37. San Francisco: Institute for Contemporary Studies, 1975.

McClaughry, John. *The National Land Use Planning Act: An Idea We Can Do Without.* 3 Env'l. Aff. 595 (1974).

McCloskey, Robert G. *Economic Due Process and the Supreme Court: An Exhumation and Reburial.* 1962 Sup. Ct. Rev. 34.

McClosky, Herbert, & John Zaller. *The American Ethos: Public Attitudes Toward Capitalism and Democracy.* Cambridge, Mass.: Harvard University Press, 1984.

McCurdy, Mary Kyle. *Public Trust Protection for Wetlands.* 19 Envtl. L. 683 (1989).

McDonald, Forrest. *Novus Ordo Seclorum: The Intellectual Origins of the Constitution.* Lawrence: University of Kansas Press, 1985.

McDougall, Harold A. *The Judicial Struggle Against Exclusionary Zoning: The New Jersey Paradigm.* 14 Harv. C.R.-C.L. L. Rev. 625 (1979).

McDougall, Harold A. *From Litigation to Legislation in Exclusionary Zoning Law.* 22 Harv. C.R.-C.L. L. Rev. 623 (1987).

McDougall, Harold A. *Regional Contribution Agreements: Compensation for Exclusionary Zoning.* 60 Temp. L.Q. 665 (1987).

Mensch, Elizabeth V. *The Colonial Origins of Liberal Property Rights.* 31 Buffalo L. Rev. 635 (1982).

Merriam, Dwight H., & Brian R. Smith. *The First Amendment in Land Use Law.* ALI-ABA Course Materials J., Feb. 1990, at 43.

Metzenbaum, James. *The Law of Zoning.* New York: Baker, Voorhis & Company, 1930.

Meyers, Gary D. *Variation on a Theme: Expanding the Public Trust Doctrine to Include Protection of Wildlife.* 19 Envtl. L. 723 (1989).

Michelman, Frank I. *Property, Utility and Fairness: Comments on the Ethical Foundations of "Just Compensation" Law.* 80 Harv. L. Rev. 1165 (1967).

Monaghan, Justin M., & William Penkethman, Jr. *The Fair Housing Act: Meeting the Mount Laurel Obligation With a Statewide Plan.* 9 Seton Hall Legis. J. 585 (1986).

Moshofsky, William. *The Regulatory Trampling of Landowner Rights.* 35 Bus. & Soc'y Rev. 26 (1980).

Mosk, Stanley. *Contemporary Federalism.* 9 Pac. L.J. 711 (1978).

Mosk, Stanley. *State Constitutionalism After Warren: Avoiding the Potomac's Ebb and Flow,* in *Developments in State Constitutional Law* (Bradley D. McGraw ed.). St. Paul, Minn.: West Publishing Co., 1985.

Naess, Arne. *The Shallow and the Deep, Long-Range Ecology Movements: A Summary.* 16 Inquiry 95 (1973).

Naess, Arne. *Self-realization in Mixed Communities of Humans, Bears, Sheep and Wolves.* 22 Inquiry 231 (1979).

Nedelsky, Jennifer. *Private Property and the Limits of American Constitutionalism: The Madisonian Framework and Its Legacy.* Chicago: University of Chicago Press, 1990.

Nelson, Robert H. *Zoning and Property Rights.* Cambridge, Mass.: MIT Press, 1977.

Nelson, Robert H. *Rethinking Zoning.* Urb. Land, July, 1983, at 36.

Note, *Architecture, Aesthetic Zoning, and the First Amendment.* 28 Stan. L. Rev. 179 (1975).

Note, *Developments in the Law: The Interpretation of State Constitutional Rights.* 95 Harv. L. Rev. 1324 (1982).

Note, *Testing the Constitutional Validity of Land Use Regulations: Substantive Due Process as a Superior Alternative to Takings Analysis.* 57 Wash. L. Rev. 715 (1982) (authored by Ross A. Macfarlane).

Note, *Private Club Discrimination Can Be Outlawed: Roberts v. United States Jaycees.* 19 U.S.F. L. Rev. 413 (1985).

Note, *Richard Epstein on the Foundations of Taking Jurisprudence.* 99 Harv. L. Rev. 791 (1986).

Note, *Private Club Membership—Where Does Privacy End and Discrimination Begin?* 61 St. John's L. Rev. 474 (1987).

Note, *Heightened Scrutiny for Land-Use Regulation Involving Physical Invasion of Private Property—Nollan v. California Coastal Commission.* 8 Miss. Coll. L. Rev. 217 (1988).

Note, *The Public Trust Doctrine in California, Florida and New Jersey: A Critique of Its Role in Modern Land Use Law.* 41 Rutgers L. Rev. 1349 (1989).

Note, *A Blow for Land-Use Planning?—The Takings Issue Re-examined.* 49 Ohio St. L.J. 1107 (1989).

Note, *You Can't Build That Here: The Constitutionality of Aesthetic Zoning and Architectual Review.* 58 Fordham L. Rev. 1013 (1990).

Nozick, Robert. *Anarchy, State and Utopia.* New York: Basic Books, 1974.

Oakes, James L. *"Property Rights" in Constitutional Analysis Today.* 56 Wash. L. Rev. 583 (1981).

Olds, David McNeil. *Taking the Mystery Out of Inverse Condemnation in Pennsylvania.* 54 Pa. B.A.Q. 105 (1983).

O'Riordan, T. *Environmental Ideologies.* 9 Env't. & Plan. A 3 (1977).

Ostrom, Vincent. *Some Paradoxes for Planners: Human Knowledge and Its Limitations, in The Politics of Planning: A Review and Critique of Centralized Economic Planning* 243 (A. Lawrence Chickering ed.). San Francisco: Institute for Contemporary Studies, 1976.

Patterson, Elizabeth. *Property Rights in the Balance—The Burger Court and Constitutional Property.* 43 Md. L. Rev. 518 (1984).

Paul, Ellen Frankel. *A Reflection on Epstein and His Critics.* 41 U. Miami L. Rev. 235 (1986).

Paul, Ellen Frankel. *Moral Constraints and Eminent Domain: A Review Essay of Richard Epstein's Takings: Private Property and the Power of Eminent Domain.* 55 Geo. Wash. L. Rev. 152 (1986).

Paul, Ellen Frankel. *Property Rights and Eminent Domain.* New Brunswick, N.J.: Transaction Books, 1987.

Paulsen, Monrad G. *The Persistence of Substantive Due Process in the States.* 34 Minn. L. Rev. 91 (1950).

Paulsen, Monrad G. *"Natural Rights": A Constitutional Doctrine in Indiana.* 25 Ind. L.J. 123 (1950).

Pavalko, Thomas M. *Subdivision Exactions: A Review of Judicial Standards.* 25 Wash. U.J. Urb. & Contemp. L. 269 (1983).

Payne, John M. *Delegation Doctrine in the Reform of Local Government Law: The Case of Exclusionary Zoning.* 29 Rutgers L. Rev. 803 (1976).

Payne, John M. *From the Courts: A New Constitutional Look in Zoning Ordinances.* 14 Real Est. L.J. 260 (1986).

Payne, John M. *Rethinking Fair Share: The Judicial Enforcement of Affordable Housing Policies.* 16 Real Est. L.J. 20 (1987).

Payne, John M. *Beyond Mount Laurel.* 16 Real Est. L.J. 349 (1988).

Pearlman, Kenneth. *Zoning Religious Uses: Emerging Judicial Patterns.* Land Use L. & Zoning Dig., June, 1985, at 3.

Property (J. Roland Pennock & John W. Chapman eds.). New York: New York University Press, 1980.

Perin, Constance. *Everything in Its Place: Social Order and Land Use in America.* Princeton: Princeton University Press, 1977.

Peters, James. *Houston Gets Religion,* in *The Best of Planning* 323. Chicago: Planners Press, 1989.

Philbrick, Francis S. *Changing Conceptions of Property in Law.* 86 U. Pa. L. Rev. 691, 710 (1938).

Pilon, Roger. *Property Rights, Takings and a Free Society.* 6 Harv. L. & Pub. Pol'y 165 (1983).

Planning Without Prices: The Takings Clause As It Relates to Land Use Regulation without Compensation (Bernard H. Siegan ed.). Lexington, Mass.: Lexington Books, 1977.

Pocock, J. G. A. *The Machiavellian Moment: Florentine Political Thought and the Atlantic Republican Tradition.* Princeton: Princeton University Press, 1975.

The Politics of Planning: A Review and Critique of Centralized Economic Planning (A. Lawrence Chickering ed.). San Francisco: Institute for Contemporary Studies, 1976.

Pollard, Oliver A., III. *A Promise Unfulfilled: Environmental Provisions in State Constitutions and the Self-Execution Question.* 5 Va. J. Nat. Resources L. 351 (1986).

Pollock, Stewart G. *State Constitutions, Land Use, and Public Resources: The Gift Outright,* in *Developments in State Constitutional Law* (Bradley D. McGraw ed.). St. Paul, Minn.: West Publishing Co., 1985.

Porta, David Della. *Procedural Due Process Under the District of Columbia Historic Protection Act.* 33 Cath. U.L. Rev. 1107 (1984).

Porter, Mary Cornelia, & G. Alan Tarr. *The New Judicial Federalism and the Ohio Supreme Court: Anatomy of a Failure.* 45 Ohio St. L.J. 143 (1984).

Posner, Richard. *The Economic Analysis of Law* (2d ed.). Boston: Little Brown, 1977.

Principles of Planning Practice (Brian W. Blaesser & Alan C. Weinstein eds.). Chicago: Planners Press, 1989.

Property: Mainstream and Critical Positions (C. B. MacPherson ed.). Toronto: University of Toronto Press, 1978.

Pulliam, Mark S. *Brandeis Brief for Decontrol of Land Use: A Plea for Constitutional Reform.* 13 Sw. U.L. Rev. 435 (1982).

Radin, Margaret Jane. *Residential Rent Control.* 15 Phil. & Pub. Affs. 350 (1986).

Ragosta, John A. *Free Speech Access to Shopping Malls Under State Constitutions.* 37 Syracuse L. Rev. 1 (1986).

Rangel, Jesus. *New Jersey Panel Orders Housing Despite a Suburb's Lack of Space.* N.Y. Times, Oct. 19, 1988, at 1.

Rawls, John. *A Theory of Justice.* Cambridge, Mass.: Harvard University Press, 1971.

Reich, Charles. *The New Property.* 73 Yale L.J. 733 (1964).

Reps, John W. *Requiem for Zoning,* in *Land Use Control: Present Problems and Future Reform* (D. Listokin ed.). New Brunswick, N.J.: Rutgers University Press, 1964.

Resolving the Housing Crisis: Government Policy, Decontrol and the Public Interest (M. Bruce Johnson ed.). Cambridge, Mass.: Ballinger, 1982.

Reynolds, Laurie. *Zoning the Church: The Police Power Versus the First Amendment.* 64 B.U.L. Rev. 767 (1984).

The Rights Retained by the People: The History and Meaning of the Ninth Amendment (Randy E. Barnett ed.). Fairfax, Va.: George Mason University Press, 1989.

Riker, William H., & Barry Weingast. *Constitutional Regulation of Legislative Choice: The Political Consequences of Judicial Deference to Legislatures.* 74 Va. L. Rev. 373 (1988).

Roberts, E. F. *The Demise of Property Law.* 57 Cornell L. Rev. 1 (1971).

Roberts, Thomas E. *The Regulation of Home Occupations Under Zoning Ordinances—Some Constitutional Considerations.* 56 Temple L.Q. 49 (1983).

Rolston, Holmes, III. *Property Rights and Endangered Species.* 61 U. Colo. L. Rev. 283 (1990).

Rose, Carol M. *Planning and Dealing: Piecemeal Land Controls as a Problem of Local Legitimacy.* 71 Calif. L. Rev. 837 (1983).

Rose, Carol M. *Mahon Reconstructed: Why the Taking Issue Is Still a Muddle.* 57 S. Cal. L. Rev. 561 (1984).

Rose, Carol M. *Possession as the Origin of Property.* 52 U. Chi. L. Rev. 85 (1985).

Rose, Jerome G., & Robert E. Rothman. *After Mt. Laurel: The New Suburban Zoning.* New Brunswick, N.J.: Center for Urban Policy Research, 1977.

Rose, Jerome G. *The Mt. Laurel II Decision: Is It Based on Wishful Thinking?* 12 Real Est. L.J. 115 (1983).

Rose, Jerome G. *New Jersey Enacts a Fair Housing Law.* 14 Real Est. L.J. 195 (1986).

Rose, Jerome G. *Waning Judicial Legitimacy: The Price of Judicial Promulgation of Urban Social Policy.* 20 Urb. Law. 801 (1988).

Rossiter, Clinton. *Conservatism in America.* New York: Vintage Press, 1962.

Rothbard, Murray N., *For a New Liberty: The Libertarian Manifesto* (rev. ed.). New York: Collier Books, 1978.

Rothbard, Murray N. *The Ethics of Liberty.* Atlantic Highlands, N.J.: Humanities Press, 1982.

Rubinowitz, Leonard S. *Exclusionary Zoning: A Wrong in Search of a Remedy.* 6 U. Mich. J.L. Ref. 625 (1973).

Sax, Joseph L. *Takings and the Police Power.* 74 Yale L.J. 36 (1964).

Sax, Joseph L. *Takings, Private Property and Public Rights.* 81 Yale L.J. 149 (1971).

Sax, Joseph L. *Some Thoughts on the Decline of Private Property.* 58 Wash. L. Rev. 481 (1983).

Sax, Joseph L. Book Review, 53 U. Chi. L. Rev. 279 (1986) (reviewing Richard A. Epstein, *Takings: Private Property and the Power of Eminent Domain.*) .

Sax, Joseph L. *The Limits of Private Rights in Public Waters.* 19 Envtl. L. 473 (1989).

Scalia, Antonin. *Economic Affairs as Human Affairs,* in *Economic Liberties and the Judiciary* 31 (James A. Dorn & Henry G. Manne eds.). Fairfax, Va.: George Mason University Press, 1987.

Schermer, Wendy. *Mobile Homes: An Increasingly Important Housing Resource That Challenges Traditional Land Use Regulation—Geiger v. Zoning Hearing Board of North Whitehall.* 60 Temp. L.Q. 583 (1987).

Schwartz, Herman. *Property Rights and the Constitution: Will the Ugly Duckling Become a Swan?* 37 Am. U.L. Rev. 9 (1987).

Schumacher, E. F. *Small is Beautiful: Economics As If People Really Mattered.* New York: Harper & Row, 1973.

Selmi, Daniel P. *The Judicial Development of the California Environmental Quality Act.* 18 U.C. Davis L. Rev. 197 (1984).

Selmi, Daniel P., & Kenneth A. Manaster. *State Environmental Law.* New York: Clark Boardman, 1990.

Shapiro, Martin. *The Constitution and Economic Rights,* in *Essays on the Constitution of the United States* 74 (M. Judd Harmon ed.). Port Washington, N.Y.: Kennikat Press, 1978.

Siegan, Bernard H. *Land Use Without Zoning.* Lexington, Mass.: Lexington Books, 1972.

Siegan, Bernard H. *Other People's Property.* Lexington, Mass.: Lexington Books, 1976.

Siegan, Bernard H. *Economic Liberties and the Constitution.* Chicago: University of Chicago Press, 1980.

Siegan, Bernard H. *The President's Commission on Housing: Zoning Recommendations.* Urb. Land, Nov. 1982, at 24.

Silkey, Robert F., & Lawrence F. Dickie. *A Survey of the Judicial Responses to Exclusionary Zoning.* 22 Syracuse L. Rev. 537 (1971).

Singer, Peter. *Not for Humans Only: The Place of Nonhumans in Ethics,* in *Ethics and Problems of the 21st Century* (K. E. Goodpaster & K. M. Sayre eds.). Notre Dame, Ind.: University of Notre Dame Press, 1979.

Smith, R. Marlin. *From Subdivision Improvement Requirements to Community Benefit Assessments and Linkage Payments: A Brief History of Land Development Exactions.* 50 Law & Contemp. Probs. 5 (1987).

State Supreme Courts in State and Nation (G. Alan Tarr & Mary Cornelia Aldis Porter eds.). New Haven: Yale University Press, 1988.

Steele, Eric H. *Community Participation and the Function of Rules: The Case of Urban Zoning Boards.* 9 Law & Pol'y 279 (1987).

Steinberger, Peter J. *Ideology and the Urban Crisis.* Albany: State University of New York Press, 1985.

Stevens, Jan S. *The Public Trust.* 14 U.C. Davis L. Rev. 195 (1980).

Stevens, Jan S. *The Public Trust and In-Stream Uses.* 19 Envtl. L. 605 (1989).

Stewart, Richard. *The Reformation of American Administrative Law.* 88 Harv. L. Rev. 1667 (1975).

Stone, Christopher D. *Should Trees Have Standing? Toward Legal Rights for Natural Objects.* Los Angeles: William Kaufman, 1974.

Storing, Herbert J. *What the Anti-Federalists Were* **For.** Chicago: University of Chicago Press, 1981.

Sullivan, Edward J. *The Rise of State Constitutional Limits on Planning and Zoning Powers.* 1988 Inst. on Plan., Zoning & Eminent Domain 8–1.

Symons, Lee P. *Property Rights and Local Land-Use Regulation: The Implications of First English and Nollan.* 18 Publius 81 (1988).

Tabor, Ward. *The California Coastal Commission and Regulatory Takings.* 17 Pacific L.J. 863 (1986).

Tarr, G. Alan, & Russell S. Harrison. *Legitimacy and Capacity in State Supreme Court Policymaking: The New Jersey Court and Exclusionary Zoning.* 15 Rutgers L.J. 514 (1984).

Thompson, Michael. *The Cultural Construction of Nature and the Natural Destruction of Culture.* International Institute of Applied Systems Analysis Working Paper 84–92, 1984.

Thompson, Michael, Richard Ellis, & Aaron Wildavsky. *Cultural Theory.* Boulder, Colo.: Westview Press, 1990.

Tiebout, Charles. *A Pure Theory of Local Expenditures.* 64 J. Pol. Econ. 416 (1956).

Tobriner, Matthew O., & Joseph R. Grodin. *The Individual and the Public Service Enterprise in the New Industrial State.* 55 Calif. L. Rev. 1247 (1967).

Tobriner, Matthew O. *Retrospective: Ten Years on the California Supreme Court.* 20 UCLA L. Rev. 5 (1972).

Tucker, William. *The Excluded Americans.* Washington, D.C.: Regnery Gateway, 1990.

U.S. Environmental Laws. Washington, D.C.: Bureau of National Affairs, 1986.

Van Astyne, William W. *The Recrudescence of Property Rights as the Foremost Principle of Civil Liberties: The First Decade of the Burger Court.* 43 Law & Contemp. Probs. 66 (1980).

van den Haag, Ernest. *Notes on the Ideology and Psychology of Planning,* in *The Politics of Planning: A Review and Critique of Centralized Economic Planning* (A. Lawrence Chickering ed.). San Francisco: Institute for Contemporary Studies, 1976.

Vasu, Michael Lee. *Politics and Planning: A National Study of American Planners.* Chapel Hill: University of North Carolina Press, 1979.

Vogel, Ursula. *When the Earth Belonged to All: The Land Question in Eighteenth-Century Justifications of Private Property.* 36 Pol. Stud. 102 (1988).

Waldron, Jeremy. *The Right to Private Property.* New York: Oxford University Press, 1988.

Walling, Richard S. *Mount Laurel Decision Threatens Historic Preservation.* 115 N.J.L.J. 5 (May 2, 1985).

Wax, Steven T. *The Fourth Amendment, Administrative Searches, and the Loss of Liberty.* 18 Envtl. L. 911 (1988).

Weaver, Clifford L., & Richard F. Babcock. *City Zoning: The Once and Future Frontier.* Chicago: Planners Press, 1979.

Wildavsky, Aaron. *Choosing Preferences by Constructing Institutions: A Cultural Theory of Preference Formation.* 81 Am. Pol. Sci. Rev. 3 (1987).

Wilkes, Donald E., Jr. *The New Federalism in Criminal Procedure.* 62 Ky. L.J. 421 (1974).

Wilkinson, Charles F. *The Headwaters of the Public Trust: Some Thoughts on the Source and Scope.* 19 Envtl. L. 425 (1989).

Williams, Norman, Jr. *American Planning Law: Land Use and the Police Power.* Princeton: Rutgers University Press, 1974.

Williams, Norman, Jr. *The Background and Significance of Mount Laurel II.* 26 Wash. U.J. Urb. & Contemp. L. 3 (1984).

Williams, Norman, Jr. *A Look at Implementation.* 14 Envtl. L. 831 (1984).

Williams, Norman, Jr., & Thomas Norman. *Exclusionary Land Use Controls: The Case of North-Eastern New Jersey.* 22 Syracuse L. Rev. 475 (1971).

Williams, Norman, Jr., R. Marlin Smith, Charles Siemon, Daniel R. Mandelker, & Richard F. Babcock. *The White River Junction Manifesto.* 9 Vt. L. Rev. 193 (1984).

Williamson, Oliver E. *Transaction-Cost Economics: The Governance of Contractual Relations.* 22 J.L. & Econ. 233 (1979).

Wilson, Sarah E. *Private Property and the Public Trust: A Theory for Preserving the Coastal Zone.* 4 UCLA J. Envtl. L. & Pol'y 57 (1984).

Witonski, Peter P. *The Historical Roots of American Planning,* in *The Politics of Planning: A Review and Critique of Centralized Economic Planning* (A. Lawrence Chickering ed.). San Francisco: Institute for Contemporary Studies, 1976.

Yannacone, Victor John, Jr., John Rahenkamp, & Angelo I. Cerchione. *Impact Zoning: Alternative to Exclusion in the Suburbs,* in *The Land Use Awakening: Zoning Law in the Seventies* (Robert H. Freilich & Eric O. Stuhler eds.). Chicago: American Bar Association Press, 1981.

Yarborough, Jean. *Jefferson and Property Rights,* in *Liberty, Property and the Foundations of the American Constitution* 65 (Ellen Frankel Paul & Howard Dickman eds.). Albany: State University of New York Press, 1989.

Yen, Alfred C. *Judicial Review of the Zoning of Adult Entertainment.* 12 Pepperdine L. Rev. 651 (1985).

Ziegler, Edward H., Jr. *The Twilight of Single-Family Zoning.* 3 UCLA J. Envtl. L. & Pol'y 301 (1983).

Ziegler, Edward H., Jr. *Single Family Zoning and the New Neighborhoods: Emerging Due Process and Equal Protection Issues.* 1985 Zoning & Plan. L. Handbook 317.

Zoning and the American Dream: Promises Still to Keep (Charles M. Haar & Jerold S. Kayden eds.). Chicago: Planners Press, 1989.

Zumbrum, Ronald A., & Thomas E. Hookano. *No-Growth and Related Land-Use Legal Problems: An Overview,* in *The Land Use Awakening: Zoning Law in the Seventies* (Robert H. Freilich & Eric O. Stuhler eds.). Chicago: American Bar Association Press, 1981.

Index

A

Administrative procedure, 15, 31
Aesthetic regulation, 18, 44, 105,
144–146, 219–220, 243–244
Aerial flights and surveillance, 45,
148–151
Affordable Housing, New Jersey
Council on, 83
Agins v. Tiburon (Calif.), 112,
115–116, 170
Agins v. Tiburon (U.S.), 172–
173, 189
Agricultural preservation,
85–89, 223n
Allgeyer v. Louisiana, 41
*Arnel Development Co. v. Costa
Mesa*, 139–141
*Associated Home Builders of the
Greater Eastbay, Inc., v. Liver-
more*, 151–155, 157

B

*Baker v. Burbank-Glendale-
Pasadena Airport Authority*, 116,
119, 148–149, 157
Bell, John C., 59–60
Belle Terre v. Boraas, 169–
170, 246
Berkeley v. Superior Court (Santa
Fe), 131–132
Berman v. Parker, 44, 187–188

Billboard regulation, 144–146,
176–178
Bird, Elizabeth Rose, 115, 119, 125,
128–129, 143, 158, 160
Birkenfeld v. Berkeley, 119–120
Blackmun, Harry A., 179, 187, 189,
203, 206–207
Bookchin, Murray, 34–35
*Boundary Drive Associates v.
Shrewsbury Board of Supervi-
sors*, 88
Brennan, William A., 94, 185, 189–
191, 196, 203, 207–208, 260
Broussard, Allen E., 139, 158
*Building Industry Association of
Southern California, Inc. v. Ca-
marillo*, 155
Builder's remedy, 73, 77, 83, 94–95,
259
Burger, Warren E., 180, 205, 208
Burrows v. Keene, 248

C

*Candid Enterprises, Inc. v. Gross-
mont Union High School District*, 129–130, 136, 138–139
California Coastal Commission,
126–128, 194, 196
California, regulatory climate in,
112–114
California Supreme Court, 10–11,
112–165; changing membership